THE PROP BUILDING GUIDEBOOK

FOR THEATRE, FILM, AND TV

THE PROP BUILDING GUIDEBOOK

FOR THEATRE, FILM, AND TV

ERIC HART

Focal Press
Taylor & Francis Group

NEW YORK AND LONDON

First published 2013
by Focal Press
70 Blanchard Road, Suite 402, Burlington, MA 01803

Simultaneously published in the UK
by Focal Press
2 Park Square, Milton Park, Abingdon, Oxon OX14 4RN

Focal Press is an imprint of the Taylor & Francis Group, an informa business

Library of Congress Cataloging in Publication Data
Hart, Eric.
The prop building guidebook: for theatre, film, and tv / by Eric Hart.
p. cm.
Includes bibliographical references and index.
1. Stage props–Design and construction. 2. Theaters–Stage-setting and scenery. 3. Motion pictures–Setting and scenery. 4. Television–Stage-setting and scenery. I. Title.
PN2091.S8H255 2012
792.02'5–dc23
2012033584

ISBN: 978-0-240-82138-2 (hbk)
ISBN: 978-0-240-82358-4 (ebk)

Typeset in Univers
by Cenveo publisher service

Printed and bound in India by Replika Press Pvt. Ltd.

Dedication

To Natalie

contents

Preface

This book is meant to arm you with the basic knowledge you may need to build all sorts of props. Making props is a lot about experience and hands-on training combined with personal guidance and critique, but a fair amount of information is still needed, which is what this book aims to provide. A prop maker's knowledge comes from thousands of sources, co-workers, and experiences, and all these little snippets of information form a foundation to help discover new techniques and more efficient processes. What I have attempted to do is collect and collate all these snippets in one place so that you can quickly learn what has already been learned and not waste time reinventing the wheel for what should be basic techniques. Instead, you can spend your time building cool props and perhaps inventing new techniques and uses for materials that you can pass on to others.

Prop makers have supplied theatre with its necessary objects and facsimiles of objects for thousands of years. The film and television worlds have taken advantage of the creativity of talented props artisans. In recent decades, prop making has even become quite a burgeoning hobby, with talented amateurs recreating noteworthy props from cinema down to exacting detail. Likewise, Halloween displays, props for costumed characters at comic book conventions, and even home displays are opportunities for a props artisan to show off his or her skills.

The path to a career in prop making is extremely individual. You can take classes, undergo internships, find a mentor, or just jump straight in, but you will not find another prop maker who has followed the same trajectory. No matter how many objects you learn how to build, you will always come across an item you've never built before. Is there a way to distill the idea of prop building into a unified theory? Can we find a scientific method to approaching the construction of any prop?

I think so, though there's no such thing as the perfect method. Any method you come up with is sure to have exceptions and caveats. And the method I prescribe in this book is only for static three-dimensional props. This is not the book to turn to for trick props, whether mechanical, electrical, or otherwise. This book will show you how to look at an object you wish to create, break it apart into its component parts, and put it all together. Whether you wish to create the deer half from *Lie of the Mind*, a phaser from *Star Trek,* or the Medal of Courage from *The Wizard of Oz*, the thinking process I describe in the following pages will help you.

No book about props can be comprehensive. It is impossible to compress the collective knowledge of all prop makers into a single volume. I have tried to limit this book to the basics of what most prop makers know and the techniques that are generally agreed upon to be standard in our industry. I have done my best to question my own assumptions as I went along and research materials and methods to make sure what I have written is accurate. Nonetheless, my approach will be colored by my own experiences and preferences; this would be true for anyone who attempts a book of this kind. My hope is that even if you disagree with my opinions, at least the facts will all be undisputed, and that if you want to delve deeper into any material or technique I describe here, this book will arm you with enough information that you will know what questions to ask.

Knowing what questions to ask or what information to look up puts you leaps and bounds ahead in your process. Otherwise, you will be grasping around for information, unsure of the terminology to use or what words to search for online, looking at information about sawmills when you really want to learn about cabinetry.

I could not fit everything I wanted into this book, and text and images can only convey so much. You can visit the companion website for this book at www.propbuildingguidebook. com. You will find additional information as well as videos detailing many of the techniques described in this book.

Acknowledgments

This book would not have happened without the endless support and encouragement from my wife, Natalie Taylor Hart. I cannot thank her enough.

Sandra Strawn, my technical editor on this book, helped clarify a number of points and offered many helpful comments and technical tidbits about a number of subjects in this book. Her advice also played a large part in restructuring portions of this book to make it more useful and straightforward.

I would like to thank Stacey Walker, who brought the proposal for this book to her coworkers at Focal Press. She was excited about this project from the get-go and has answered my questions every step of the way. I extend my thanks to all of Focal Press, for taking a chance on me and sharing my belief that a new book on building props is long overdue.

Many thanks go to Jay Duckworth for his tireless cheerleading of my work and all he's taught me in the world of props. All my bosses through the years, especially Randy Lutz, Mark Walston, and Tim Daly, have given me a chance to explore the craft I describe in this book. I would like to thank my teachers as well, especially Tom Fiocchi, Drew Drake, and Elaine Williams. My best wishes go out to all the people I have worked with over the years; you have helped immensely with this book, whether intentionally or not.

Some people have been especially helpful in allowing me to pick their brains and photograph their spaces: Brian Wolfe at Costume Armour, Inc.; Wesley Cannon at Wicked Props; and Paul Pearson, president of Studio Manufacturing. I thank David Silvernail and all the members at ControlBooth for allowing me to ask questions and bounce off some ideas.

Debi Jolly, Anna Warren (who also runs a props-related blog called Fake 'n Bake at http://www.fake-n-bake.blogspot.com/), Harrison Krix (who runs another impressive props site called Volpin Props at http://volpinprops.blogspot.com/), Ryan Trupp, and Andreea Mincic have helped flesh out this book with photographs of their own work, and I am indebted to them.

Finally, I thank my parents, not just for being parents, but for teaching me art, craft, and work through their own lives. Thanks to my brother, who listened to me talk about this book for about two years before I started writing it, and for all his editing and proofreading advice. I also thank my sister, who promises to get this book into libraries across the land.

one

what is a prop?

A prop is a physical object that an actor uses during a performance.

Scholars love to play with all the gray areas of what a prop is or isn't, or speculate about when a real object turns into a prop, but we don't have to deal with these theoretical questions. Even so, that simple statement raises a whole bunch of complex questions. Who is an actor? What is a performance? By a prop, do you mean any kind of object?

Our society understands a performance as something that happens in front of an audience (or in front of a camera for later viewing by an audience). An actor is a person enacting a role in the performance. The actor may be playing him or herself, but he or she is still an actor. Whatever the actor wears is a costume, and whatever is inherent to the place of the performance is the scenery. Any physical "thing" other than the actor, costume, and scenery is a prop (I am not counting "front of house" physical things, such as the audience or the playbills, or supporting infrastructure meant to be ignored by the audience, such as the lighting instruments or the seats. Let's keep things simple here).

The difficulty in distinguishing what exactly a prop is stems from the fact that the scenery, meant to be inherent to the place, is frequently constructed specifically for the performance, so the question of which elements are provided by the scenery department and which are provided by the props department can sometimes be ambiguous. The same is true of costumes, as people may wear items that are not technically clothes, such as eyeglasses and pocket watches.

In any production, matters become less theoretical and more specific; every object and item is discussed by the members of the production team, and responsibility for every element is assigned to the department for whom it makes the most sense. If you are the props master as well as the prop maker, you will want to make sure this happens, especially if you notice something in the script or in the design that can theoretically belong to more than one department but that has not been discussed yet. If you are simply a prop maker working for a props master or in a shop, your job is even easier; you build what you are told to build, regardless of whether you think it is technically a prop or not.

Film and theatre technicians have developed some widely accepted categories of props to help distinguish who is responsible for what. Props are often divided into two major categories: hand props and set props.

Hand Props

A **hand prop** is a prop handled by an actor. These are frequently mentioned in the script and help tell the story. In some Broadway theatres and films, hand props are called **action props** to emphasize the fact that hand props are not necessarily held or manipulated by a hand. Film and television also differentiate hand props into hero props, background props, and stunt props. **Hero props** are meant to be filmed up-close. **Background props** are props that will only be seen in the background. There does not need to be any inherent difference between hero and background props, but to save money, background props are often made with less detail than hero props. **Stunt props** are props used in stunt and action scenes, and thus require special safety considerations. Because film and television prop makers frequently make multiple versions of a prop, one prop may have a hero version in full detail, a quick cast with painted details made for background versions, and casts done in soft foam or rubber for the stunt version.

A **practical** is a prop that behaves as one would expect it to. Lamps that actually light up and alarm clocks that actually ring are considered practical props. The opposite of a practical prop is a **dummy prop**. A box that does not actually open and a cell phone carved from a single chunk of material are dummy props. Practical and dummy props are also called **working props** and **static props**.

You may come across the distinction between **rehearsal props** and **actual props** (or just "actuals"). There does not need to be any inherent difference between the two; rehearsal props are frequently cheaper or simpler versions of the actual props (though hopefully matching the size and weight of the actual prop). They may also be versions of the same item; one is used exclusively for rehearsals, where it gets beat up and worn down, and a new one is switched out for performances.

Figure 1-1: This stunt prop for the film *Jumanji* looks like the hero version that could be opened to reveal a game board, but it is actually just a solid casting with no moving parts. It was used for the scenes where the actors ran around with it.

Figure 1-2: Eyeglasses are typically supplied by the costume department, but these glasses were more of a scientific instrument than a costume piece. Additionally, the stone rings are hand props and can be carried around separately, but they can also be fitted into this pair of glasses. Props like these require careful and early communication with the different departments to determine exactly who is responsible for what. *The Spiderwick Chronicles*, 2008.

A **costume prop** is an item or accessory other than a piece of clothing that is part of a costume. Pocket watches, sword belts, gun holsters, masks, crowns, pipes, glasses, and even jewelry can all be considered costume props. The distinction between a costume prop (or **propstume**) and a hand prop can be murky; typically, a costume prop is used to create a sense of character and appears in the costume designer's rendering, while a hand prop appears in the script and is used to drive the plot forward. Obviously there is a lot of crossover between the costume department and props department on these items; the lead soldier may use his sword in a sword fight while the background soldiers keep their swords sheathed, but everyones sword matches, so the costume and props departments have to be in communication with each other. The costume shop may have a separate "costume crafts" technician or a whole team, while in other situations, it may be tasked to a completely different shop.

A **personal prop** is one that the actor keeps with himself or herself at all times, and is not handled by the props crew. This often includes certain costume props, but it can also refer to items such as a letter that is kept in the pocket and never shared with another actor during the performance.

In theatre, we also designate **consumable props**, sometimes called **perishables**. These are props that are "consumed" during every performance: food (obviously), cigarettes, fake blood, or a piece of paper that gets torn up. These may also be called **running props**, which are props and related items (such as batteries for electrical props) that are replaced or replenished at regular intervals. Some consumables are not replaced after every show; a newspaper, for example, can last for several performances, but it accumulates enough creases and wrinkles that it eventually needs to be swapped out with a fresh copy.

A **breakaway** is a prop that is meant to break or be destroyed during the performance (and hopefully not before).

Over the years, I have seen various attempts to categorize who is responsible for what; some truly bizarre notions occur, such as saying an umbrella is a prop, while a parasol is a costume. The fact is, that it can be different in every production, and each item should be clearly assigned to a department during production meetings so that no false assumptions are made. For some productions, they may just be divided up by capability; the costume department may provide a purse because they have a better purse collection, while the props department builds the masks because they have the tools and people who know how to use the materials.

It may be rigged to break in a predictable manner but can be quickly and easily reassembled (chairs and swords are popular breakaway items), or it can refer to a single-use item that can be broken easily without causing injury, either when struck, or from the shards that are created (bottles cast in sugar glass, for example, can be hit over an actor's head safely and the shards do not cut nearly as easily as glass shards would). The second type of breakaway would also be considered a consumable in theatre. The use of breakaway props often requires coordination with either the stunt department in film and television or the fight director or fight choreographer in theatre.

Set Props

A **set prop** is an object located on the set; the large majority of set props are **furniture**. Set props can also include the rugs and any other distinct items on the floor, walls, or ceilings. **Trim props** are items that hang on the walls, such as curtains, blinds, or pictures. Set props also include "furniture-like" objects, such as a rock used as a seat. More abstract or metaphorical production designs may introduce some ambiguity into this category as the actors use nontraditional or imaginary items as furniture. This category can overlap with the scenery department as some sets may have "built-in" furniture, and some elements may look like furniture but act like scenery.

Set dressings are objects and items placed on the set that are *not* manipulated by actors. Rather, they help create a sense of place and time, or evoke an atmosphere. Imagine a store with no clothes on the rack, or a bar with no liquor on the shelves. In theatre, the props department is in charge of handling the set dressing. In theatre and film, it is the set decoration department rather than the props department that is tasked with dressing the set and providing the set props. If a director is filming a scene and, in a flash of inspiration, has the actor pick up and interact with a piece of set dressing, the props master and set decorator need to get together to transfer the responsibility of tracking and maintaining that object.

Of course, if you have the skills to build the items, you may be hired by the props department for one production, the costume crafts department for another, and the set dressing department for a third. Some independent shops may even be approached by both the set decorator and the props master from the same production to build items. Your skills may even get you work with a practical effects company on a film or doing puppets on a play. While this book is focused on teaching you how to build a "prop," the materials and methods I describe can easily be used to build objects for any number of other purposes.

In Japanese Kabuki theatre, props are divided between real articles used in daily life (*hommono*) and items created specifically for the stage (*koshiraemono*). *Hommono* are typically bought, borrowed, or rented by a props master from thrift shops, secondhand stores, flea markets, auction houses, prop rental houses, and regular stores, both brick-and-mortar and online. What this book is concerned with are the *koshiraemono*, the items created specifically for the stage.

Why Make Rather Than Buy?

A lot of props you may need can simply be bought. This is often cheaper and easier than building a prop. Mass production in countries with lax labor laws and environmental conditions can give you items cheaper than the materials you will need to buy to make them, even though the items have to be shipped around the world. If you keep common items in a prop storage room, or are able to borrow or rent items, acquiring real goods becomes even cheaper.

So why would you need to make your object? The main reason to build a prop is because it is not available. Imaginary objects or pieces designed to specifically fit into the world of the play fall into this category. For example, during a production of *Merchant of Venice*, my wife made a skull upholstered in black velvet and set with shiny jewels. This is not the type of item you can pick up at the local department store.

This category includes existing objects that need to be specific in appearance or size. You can find oil paintings and oil painting reproductions, but if you need an oil painting of your

Figure 1-3: This dragon, the bookcase, and the items in the shelves are items that cannot be bought, rented, or borrowed from anywhere. They all needed to be custom-built. Dragon built by Eric J. Novak.

lead actor in his costume, you must make it. Likewise, a comically oversized coffee mug or furniture built in forced perspective will not be found in stores.

In certain cases, you can simply adapt an object you bought at a store. Keep in mind though, that you may spend more money and labor adapting a piece than you would have if you had simply built it from scratch. An object from a store will already be finished, and if you cut into it, or add parts to it, you will need to match the color and texture of the original, which may be more challenging than just mixing a paint color from scratch. Some store-bought items are not made of the material they appear to be made of, which could create unforeseen problems. Modern furniture is particularly bad in this respect; when you cut into what looks like wood, you discover it is actually stress skin filled with honeycomb paper, and you have no structure inside to attach things too. If you believe your prop is going to undergo many changes during the rehearsal period, it may be wiser to build a prop designed to be adapted, rather than using a store-bought item that undergoes degradation with every change made to it.

The second major reason for building your props is if they need to perform some kind of function different from what they were built for. Most furniture you buy was never designed to be danced on, carried around, leaned on its side, or otherwise mistreated in any number of creative ways an actor or director comes up with. Large props are faked out of papier-mâché and fiberglass because the real deal would be far too heavy to lift and carry in a quick scene change.

A final reason to build a prop is because the actual item is too expensive to buy or rent. Shakespearean plays and grand operas frequently rely on gold objects littered about the stage, but it would be prohibitively costly to buy real gold. Real furniture, especially antiques, is built with expensive hardwoods and labor-intensive finishes that can be indistinguishable from cheaper materials under stage lights and viewed from a distance. Likewise, fake food is often built because the cost of buying and preparing real food every night for every show for

Figure 1-4: Fake body parts also fall in this category. Legal and moral issues aside, we don't use real body parts because they rot and smell and attract vermin. You need to build fake ones that will not degrade over time or make a mess on stage every time they are used.

several weeks (or months or years) is so much more expensive and wasteful than constructing a facsimile.

Who Does What

In theatre, the **props master** is responsible for the hand props, set props (including furniture), practical effects, and set dressing. In theatres with a permanent props shop, the props department may be headed up by a **properties director**, who may act as props master on the shows, or hire separate props masters for some or all of the productions. In Broadway houses, the person responsible for the props may be billed as the **props coordinator**. This is especially true when the props coordinator is not in a union, as the title of "props master" is reserved for union members.

The props are commonly designed by the **set designer** (or scenic designer). Some set designers will draft more unique props in the same that they draft scenery, though many will

Productions with particularly complex or involved effects may hire a separate *effects designer* or coordinator. This person may deal with any and all effects, whether they are part of the scenery or the props. For shows with fire or explosive effects, a *pyrotechnic designer* may be needed, as most locales require a license to design and execute effects dealing with open flame or explosive materials.

leave some or all of the props open for interpretation; it is up to the props master to improvise and make choices, with the set designer approving them. On some occasions, a production may have a **props designer**, either in addition to the set designer, or in lieu of one where no scenic elements are constructed.

For props that need to be built, the props master will rely on **props artisans**. Larger shops will have a small staff of full-time or seasonal artisans; others may hire freelancers on a project-by-project basis. In very small theatres, the props master may need to build some or all of the props, or commission outside contractors to build specialty items. Some theatres distinguish between **props carpenters**, who construct items out of wood, metal, and plastic, such as furniture and semistructural items, and **props craftspeople**, who do sculpting, upholstery, casting, paper props, and the like. They may also have a separate **soft goods artisan**, who handles all fabric-related props, from upholstery to draperies to table coverings.

In film, the props are designed by the **production designer** or **art director**. "Production designer" is essentially a fancier title for art director, who was traditionally the head of the art department. In productions with a production designer, the art director is responsible more for the practical considerations and day-to-day operations of the art department. The title of "set designer" in film is used to describe employees who draft all the scenery and props. The props master is in

charge of supplying the hand props and vehicles such as cars and bicycles. Although not officially a part of the art department, the props master certainly works very closely with the art director and the set decorator. With location filming being the norm, props departments may construct a temporary props shop for the duration of the shoot. This props shop will have a number of **prop makers** to construct and repair the props needed. Often, a props master will have an independent props shop or individual **outside contractors** build the more specialized or tricky props; sometimes, all the props will be subcontracted to save the costs of setting up and running a whole props shop. An outside contractor can be anything from a single prop maker building stuff in his or her basement to an entire company that employs dozens of artisans. Union regulations often prohibit the props master from actually handling any props on set, so all construction and maintenance is fulfilled by separate prop makers. On non-union films, the props master may do some actual construction, particular when the budget is too low to hire additional labor.

On larger films, the set department will have what is known as a mill shop. The **mill shop** is responsible for all the custom wood moldings, turnings, doors, and windows, as well as custom cabinetry and furniture. Some of the carpenters who work in the mill shop are also called "prop makers" even though they work for the set department.

Films use real firearms that have been modified to only fire blanks; these weapons still require the same license as a standard firearm, so a licensed *armorer* is needed whenever guns are called for. While the props master is still ultimately responsible for all weapons, all the practical details and the actual transportation and storage of the guns is mostly handed off to the armorer.

The set dressing and set props are handled by the **set decoration department**. Though much set decoration is bought, rented, and borrowed, many set decoration departments do employ a number of upholsterers and soft goods artisans for window treatments and floor coverings. The set decorator may also contract out custom items to props shops or outside contractors. A props shop may find itself building hand props for the property master and set dressing for the set decorator simultaneously for the same film or show. In fact, this is sometimes coordinated so that the props and set dressing will share the same "look" and feel, like they are part of the same world.

In the heyday of the studio system, each studio had its own in-house props shop that could build anything needed for every movie made. These have all basically disappeared. The few studio shops that still exist in Hollywood act more as independent entities, offering their services to any studio or independent company that wishes to hire them. Some studios even provide an entire shop for rental. All the film needs is an empty warehouse; all the tools and machines are on wheels, and the studio simply loads them onto a truck, drives them to location, and sets them up in the warehouse.

In television, the production designer supervises the procurement of new props, which includes any props that need to be constructed. This can mean supervising a props master who handles all props, or working with vendors directly for smaller productions. Television is very similar to film; the props master has an **inside crew** working at the studio to maintain and rig all the props, while a separate **outside crew** will work with vendors, rental houses, and artisans outside of the television studio. **Outside packagers** basically have their own mini-production staffs, and their property chiefs will work with the inside, or studio, crew. An established show may have an ongoing contract with an outside shop to build all the props needed on a weekly basis. As with film, union regulations prohibit props masters from handling any of the props while in the studio or during shooting.

On commercials and music videos, the props master is much more likely to be "hands on" and build some or all the props needed. This is particularly true on non-union shoots.

A skilled prop maker can work in departments outside of props, such as effects, models, puppetry, and animatronics. They are also not limited to working in theatre, television, or film; one can work in opera, dance, fashion shows, photo shoots, magic shows, or commercials. Prop makers are also needed in the display and exhibition world, creating props for window displays, trade show booths, marketing and PR events, weddings and other social occasions, retail spaces, museums, and other events. Likewise, one can find work at theme parks or haunted houses that are open to the public. Finally, private clients may request props either for their personal use or display.

Getting Started

If you want to be a prop maker, it is important to start working with your hands. All materials and tools possess individual quirks and characteristics that can never be properly conveyed in a book or even in a video. You need to dive in and discover them yourself. You may be afraid to make mistakes. Don't worry; you will. Your first prop will not be perfect. If you start

Figure 1-5: Eric Hart runs a lathe at the Ohio University props shop. Photograph by Andreea Mincic.

off with less expensive and more forgiving materials, your mistakes will at least not put you in debt or frustrate you into giving up. Even experienced prop makers have to go through a learning curve when using unfamiliar materials or machines the first few times. Good prop makers are simply those who have made a lot of props and paid attention to their own processes so they can continually improve their skills with each new project. Every time you do something, you get a little better at doing it.

Project-Based Learning is often more helpful than just rote repetition of certain techniques. If you want to learn welding, for instance, rather than simply running welding beads up and down a piece of scrap steel, you build a small item out of steel using welding. This teaches you "all the things you don't know you don't know." That is, when learning something new, you are not aware of all the information that you need to learn. Want to learn woodworking? Build a birdhouse. Birdhouses remain a popular woodworking project because they are almost as simple to make as a box, but they have just enough angles and shaped holes to make it interesting. Plus, you can build one in an afternoon, and you have a keepsake when you are finished. Want to learn sculpting? Grab a bar of soap and a pocket knife and carve a polar bear. Sewing? Make a pillowcase. Upholstery? Find a drop seat and recover it in new fabric. Casting? Grab a slab of clay, press some objects into it, and pour plaster on top. You don't need fancy equipment or expensive materials if you are just trying to grasp the basics. You can build shapes and structures quickly with cardboard and a hot glue gun, and almost everyone has the ingredients for papier-mâché sitting around their house (newspaper or tissue paper, flour, and water). If you can't figure papier-mâché out, then how will you be able to figure out fiberglass, which involves much more complicated chemistry and setup, as well as a complete understanding of how to minimize the various health risks it entails?

What's Not in This Book

I can't possibly fit all the information about props in a single book. The field is simply too diverse. You have the job of the props master, which includes organizing information about the props from a script, shopping and sourcing items, dealing with directors, designers, stage managers and actors, research, and budgeting. The job of a props director includes a lot of the same responsibilities as the props master, but with the addition of running a props shop. Hiring and managing artisans, storage and organization of a props storage room, keeping tools and supplies in good order, and archiving props bibles are just some of the aspects of a props director's job. Even a props artisan deals with much more than will be presented in a single book: trick props such as breakaways and transforming items, rigging and set dressing, the adaptation and repair of furniture and other bought items, edible props, and far more. This book is concerned with the building of a single, discrete prop. This book describes the process an artisan uses to construct an item to meet all the criteria for it to be used on stage, or whatever its arena of play is.

Props is a large and comprehensive field, and to present all the information pertaining to it in one book would be overwhelming. An encyclopedic set would be more appropriate. I've explained in this introductory portion what I intend to cover in this volume, but just to clarify, I will describe what is *not* in this book just in case any of my readers feel I am being neglectful.

This is a book for a props artisan or prop maker. Props master and properties director are different job titles. While a props master or director occasionally starts out as an artisan or fulfills some prop-making duties as part of their job, their own duties are distinct. (In many smaller theatres, the props master *is* the props artisan, as the entire props department is filled with a single person.) This book will not necessarily focus on reading a script and developing a props list, buying, renting or borrowing props, maintaining and organizing a props stock, or the like.

This book is focused on the single props artisan. Some artisans move up and become managers of shops, and are responsible for an entire crew of artisans. This book will not describe the numerous skills and personality traits needed for keeping a team of talented people working within budget, on schedule, and without conflict, nor will it get into the intricacies of scheduling multiple overlapping projects with staggered due dates.

Even though this book is geared solely toward the props artisan, I feel even that field is too wide to cover in a single volume. I have restricted coverage to constructing objects, and the materials and methods needed to do so. As such, I have avoided discussion of all the numerous tricks and movements that props occasionally need to do. I do not discuss electrical, pneumatic, or mechanical props, nor do I touch on radio-controlled props. I also keep out any sort of trick props, such as breakaways, magic props, edible props, props that are moved or manipulated backstage, and any of the complicated rigging that goes into special effects.

Though the materials and methods of prop making are very similar from props shop to props shop, it is true that props can be made out of nearly anything. I have avoided crafts and techniques that are highly specialized or rarely pop up. Skills like throwing pottery, casting bronze, or electroplating chrome may occasionally be needed in the props shop, but most shops are not set up to do these things. Sometimes, one of the artisans possesses the skills and tools to accomplish these specialized tasks, but if that is not the case, these jobs are outsourced. A props shop will not hire someone who can throw pottery but cannot build a wooden box or carve Styrofoam. This book describes 90% of the skills utilized in prop making, with the rest left up to you.

This book will not focus on using any specific computer software. These skills are becoming more necessary every day in props, from graphics programs to CAD programs for 3D printing and CNC machining. The programs themselves are too numerous, specific, and fast-changing to pay them their due here. I can describe what these programs are capable of, what processes and techniques you can use them for, and what materials they can be used on, but learning the ins and outs of how to operate the programs themselves is up to you to learn. This is how I treat every tool and machine in this book; for instance, I will tell you what a bandsaw is used for and what materials it can cut, but I will not describe how to change the blade on a Powermatic 1791216K 14-inch bandsaw.

You will also notice I only briefly touch on things like CNC routing and 3D printing. While I certainly feel the industry is headed more in that direction, and the skills needed to operate these machines will come more and more in handy as time goes on, they do not fit into my book. The skill sets needed for these are completely different from almost all the skill sets described in this book. Working on a computer and then sending commands to a machine is almost like shopping on the Internet, and this is how I view computer-aided fabrication. Rather than going to a website, finding the part you need, and waiting for it to arrive in the mail, you go to a CAD program, design the part you need, then wait for it to be made on the machine. Same thing, really. What this book does is give you a process to decide what materials to use and what methods to practice to put them together into a prop. You still need to know this method when utilizing a CNC router or 3D printer as part of your prop-making process. For example, most 3D printers print in ABS plastic, and are limited in the size and shape of what they can produce. Only by following a logical process can you arrive at the conclusion that your prop (or a portion of your prop) should be made out of ABS plastic on a 3D printer. Otherwise, you might be using a 3D printer to make things that should have been made out of wood or metal, or spending more time to prepare the drawings for a 3D printer than it would have taken to construct it by hand. So rather than explaining the process of CNC routing and 3D printing, this book treats them as it does raw materials, hardware, and found objects. Just as you would buy a nut and bolt rather than constructing them out of raw metal, so too can you integrate computer fabrication into your overall process.

This book does not deal with set decoration or dressing of the set. In film and television, this is a different department from props, so it does not make sense to include it here. In theatre, though, set decoration falls under the props master's purview. In many smaller departments, the props artisans will be called to work on stage during load-in to assist with hanging window treatments, filling shelves, installing door hardware, and the like.

two

needs and means

Is there a way to describe how to build any prop without specifying what it is? In other words, can a single approach be used both to build a chair and to make a curtain? I find myself using the same mental processes for any prop I need to build, and working alongside other prop makers has shown me that they share a similar thought pattern.

The first part we will look at is figuring out the needs of a prop. By articulating these, we gain a clearer picture of how it should be built. More complex props can first be broken down into simpler parts. Any object can be divided and subdivided until each part has its own distinct set of needs.

These needs can be met with any number of materials, methods, tools, and techniques. The second part of building a prop is looking at what resources you have available. Time and money are your most important resources, but other resources include the size and layout of your shop space, what tools and machines you have available to use, and your skills in working with certain materials. Your resources will limit and inform the choice of materials and techniques for your prop. In other words, what are the means available to you to build your prop? All props will follow this same process: determine all the needs, and then meet them with the means you have available.

What a Prop Needs to Do

What does your prop need to do? It seems like a simple question, but on closer observation it becomes more complex. For starters, your prop needs to have a certain look. Maybe it needs to mimic certain materials. Take into account the physical surroundings where your prop is appearing; there is a difference between a prop that needs to look like solid gold and a prop that needs to look like solid gold under specific stage lights from twenty feet away to an audience. Similarly, the prop may need to match other elements of the production rather than simply having a realistic appearance. If the scenery department has painted large pieces of plywood to imitate mahogany, and you need to build a chair out of mahogany, it may be more visually cohesive for you to use a similar paint treatment rather than building the chair out of actual mahogany.

The visual appearance is not the only quality a prop may need to mimic. Other tactile and perceptive properties may need to be replicated as well. Gold coins being dropped into a metal plate have a distinctive sound which cannot be faked by dropping gold-painted poker chips into a metal-painted wooden plate. A silk flag carried across the stage moves differently from a muslin flag.

If the visual appearance was the only need, then we would simply make every prop out of the material it was meant to be made out of. Gold statues would be made of gold, and a fancy desk would be made of mahogany with ivory inlay and bronze hardware. When we look at the further needs of the prop—strength and weight, time and money, the skills we have, and the machines we have access to—we will see that props cannot always be made out of their intended material. Other times, props are meant to be made out of more stylized or imaginary materials that have no real-world counterpart. This is where theatre magic happens. We must determine what exactly the visual needs of the prop are so we can match it with a material that is best able to mimic our intended material within all our other constraints. It is helpful to remember an old saying used by art directors: "All the camera sees is the last coat of paint." Many materials can have their color and even texture manipulated.

Which material we ultimately choose depends on the overall shape and form of the object; if it is a complicated three-dimensional form, we may wish to use a material that is easily sculpted or carved. If the form is more geometrical, we may wish to construct it out of something that comes in a variety of geometric shapes. Wood, for example, can come in boards, sheets, and dowels. If we need a wooden rod, it is easier to use a dowel than a rectangular piece of wood that we need to shape into a rod.

Besides the physical appearance, you need to ask questions about what else your prop needs to do. Maybe the actors need to dance on it without it falling apart. It may need to fit into a pocket. Sometimes, what a prop needs to do is defined by what it *shouldn't* do. For example, when a prop is dropped during a scene, it shouldn't break.

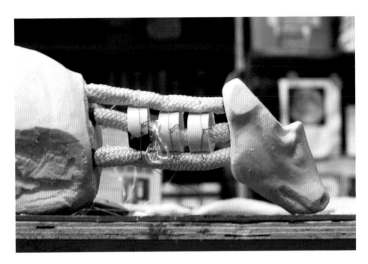

Figure 2-1: This dead lamb prop was built with a flexible neck so when it was carried around, it would flop like a real dead lamb rather than remain stiff like a piece of taxidermy.

scene, and it's too big for that. Building rehearsal props is a topic worthy of its own chapter. Whenever you are unsure of how a prop will be used, or the production team wants to "discover" things during rehearsal, providing them with a rehearsal prop as soon as possible will quickly allow them to hone in on how they wish to use the prop, which gives you a better idea of how to build it.

In theatre and television, the normal wear and tear needs to be kept in mind for props that need to have a long life. Every time a prop is moved, picked up, or even just touched, it places stress on certain areas. A prop that does not hold up to its usage in a scene is a prop that is not properly made. Even in the most carefully choreographed sequences, the actors will still veer from their blocking or treat the props more violently during a performance than they did in rehearsals, so you cannot rely solely on the specifications given by the director or designer. You need to anticipate the worst-case scenario based on your knowledge of the script and the context of the show.

When I am looking at what a static or simple prop needs to do, most of my thought processes focus on how it will be used. Props will be stood on, stepped on, sat on, thrown, dropped, ran into, and generally abused in ways even the director might not foresee. Generally, we find out what the actor is supposed to do with the prop, and extrapolate that to the worst possible scenario. If you are told the actor will stand on a table, assume they will jump on it. If you hear that a vase is supposed to be dropped, you can bet they will be throwing it to the ground with all their might. It is better to overbuild a prop once than to have to rebuild it three times.

Discovering all these things is where collaboration comes in. Initially, the director, stage manager, designer, and props master will develop the props list, with notes on the functions of every prop. This will change as the production progresses, and even more so once rehearsals begin. Even actors will start to chime in about what a prop needs to do. Maybe it's too heavy for the actor to lift every single night. Maybe the actor decides she wants to hide the prop behind her back during a

Figure 2-2: A chair that is tossed to the ground every night will have different structural needs than a chair that is simply sat on. Photograph by Natalie Taylor Hart.

Size and weight are two more needs of a prop. Size is related to the visual appearance and will typically be determined by the designer or art director, but practical considerations will also clarify the limitations on size. An end table may need to be large enough to hold a certain vase, while a dagger may need to be small enough to fit in the pocket of an actor's costume. It is important to bring up questions during production meetings whenever a prop needs to interact with another department's elements.

While it is generally a good idea to keep a prop as light as possible, you can find situations where more weight is desired. In outdoor locations, you may need to add weight to props to keep them from blowing away. It may also aid in realism; if a large suitcase is meant to be fully packed, it would look silly if the actor was able to lift it with one finger. We can snidely remark from the sidelines "why not try *acting* like it is heavy," but it is helpful to aid the actors as much as possible with the props so they can focus on their emotions and intentions rather

Figure 2.3: This "bear trap" worn by Anna Faris in *Scary Movie 4* uses a number of materials to fulfill its various needs. The majority of the body is cast in a rigid polyurethane plastic, as real metal would be too heavy to be worn comfortably. The straps are made from leather, which is a strong, but thin and flexible material that can wrap around the body, as well as being comfortable and providing cushioning on the shoulders. The nails are cast in a soft foam so they appear sharp and pointed, but will not cause injury if they come into contact with skin.

than having to concentrate on simulating an imaginary amount of weight in a suitcase.

In some cases, the balance of the weight is more important than the overall amount. Swords and other stage combat weapons are helped by having most of the weight located near the hands so they can be moved and stopped more quickly and precisely. A tall item can be kept from toppling over by shifting the weight as close to the bottom as possible.

You also have to consider the backstage and off-screen needs of a prop in terms of size and weight. You rarely build a prop in the same place as it is used; it may need to be transported to another room in the building, to another building across town, or even to a film location miles away. The prop must be able to fit through the smallest opening in whatever path it takes. That is often a door or elevator, though it may also be a car trunk or a particularly narrow hallway. If you can find out ahead of time where the prop will need to go, you can build it so it fits, or construct it in such a way that it can be disassembled in the shop and reassembled on location.

In theatres and television studios, you may also need to anticipate fitting the prop backstage when it is not in use. Often it is the designer or house crew who is responsible for this, and what is needed for proper storage may not be determined until the prop is in the space, but occasionally you can anticipate the needs. The weight may be important to consider for backstage purposes as well, particularly in theatre if stagehands or running crew need to move the prop around every night.

Special Needs in Theatre

Theatre and live action props have their own special needs. Because productions have multiple performances over a period of time, theatrical props need to be able to stand up to the repeated demands of each show and not break or fall apart in the middle of a run.

Theatre also has its own needs because of its unique playing spaces. The audience may be located quite a distance from the actual prop. This often means that subtle details will be lost and that the visual appearance may need to be exaggerated in some respects (it may also mean, thankfully, that intricate details seen only up-close can be faked to some extent). In many cases, some audience members will be close while others are far away, so the props artisan needs to find the right balance between how subtle or exaggerated the prop is. Of course, "theatre props in a movie world" have increased the audience's demand for realism, so even a prop seen far away may need more detail than is strictly necessary. Furthermore, playwrights, designers, and directors today may be more familiar with TV and film and thus expect a prop to have all the intricate detail it would have in real life, even if parts of it are facing away from the audience. Actors, too, may expect details that are invisible to the audience. Indeed, a poorly made prop may inhibit an actor from fully inhabiting the world of the play, so while the prop itself may be unseen by the audience, the actor's superficial performance will be experienced by everyone in the theatre.

Theatre has **sightlines**, which are the unobstructed views of each audience member. In thrust stages or theatre-in-the-round, tall props may block part of the action for certain seats. Props, particularly furniture, are frequently shortened or otherwise altered to allow good visibility no matter where you sit. To improve sightlines on proscenium stages, the playing floor may be raked, or sloped so it is taller in the back than in the front. Props that sit on a raked floor need to be counter-raked, or built on an opposite slope, so that when they are placed on the rake, they will sit flat and not tip over. Other props may need to be altered to prevent them from rolling or sliding down the slope.

Props in the theatre need to be made with the safety of the performers, technicians, and audience in mind. Unlike in film, scenes cannot be shot behind protective glass, stunt doubles cannot be switched in, and shots cannot be edited to create the illusion that actors are involved in dangerous events. Everything on stage happens right then and there, and a piece of a prop that comes loose can hit an old lady sitting in the front row.

A theatre production is an organic process; although you receive drawings and models at the beginning, changes happen throughout rehearsal, and can continue even through technical rehearsals and previews. That means an audience may watch the show one night, but you may have to change or alter the prop before another audience sees the show the following night.

Finally, for props used in front of any type of live audience, there may need to be a certain amount of flame proofing involved. This differs depending on the area of the world you are performing in and even the type of venue the production takes place in. You may need to limit your prop's construction to certain types of materials that are flame retardant, or treat/coat the surfaces with a chemical or substance that will make it more flame resistant. The appearance and properties of some materials are altered when thus treated, and some materials resist such treatments, so the level of flame resistance your prop needs should always be considered at the start of the process before you start down a path that will give you trouble later on.

Needs in Film

Making props for film can be different from making them for theatre. In film, props may need to be built quickly and then used for only one day. Theatre needs much sturdier props, or at least props that are more easily repaired. Still, during a film shoot, you do not want your props to break while on set. Every minute wasted costs money, and if filming has to be put on hold for a few minutes to make a repair, it is logged by the assistant director. You do not want the producers to read "waited seven minutes while the prop was glued back together" in the daily logs.

Film shows the prop much closer than one can ever get in a theatre. Subtle details become much more important. An item that fits in the palm of your hand can be filmed so that it appears to be thirty feet tall when projected on a movie screen. Even with film sent straight to video, people can pause the film and examine the props with excruciating clarity.

A props artisan for film needs to understand how the use of lighting and camera lenses can affect the look of the prop.

Shooting a scene with different focal lengths can change the distance from background to foreground and distort how a prop shows up (as you will see in Chapter 6).

Film has no "backstage"; the camera can point in any direction, so film props, more so than theatre props, need to be finished on all sides. In theatre, if the director decides to restage a scene so an unfinished side of a prop will now be visible, you can alter it in between rehearsals (and if they are using rehearsal props, you have until technical rehearsals begin to make the changes). In film, the director may make that decision on the spot, with the expectation that filming can continue immediately. This is not a hard and fast rule; some directors plan and storyboard every shot, and stick with that. In any event, the more you know how the individual filmed sequences will add up to the visual concept, the better. A film shoot feels like a nonstop tech week; props that can be altered quickly or easily are preferable.

Needs in Television

While major props can be planned ahead and prop makers given a few weeks or even months to construct them, when a television show is filming, they may be making a new episode every week, giving the props team only three or four days from the time the script appears to the day filming begins to construct a prop.

Like props in film, props for television may need to look really good when the camera is close. High-definition televisions mean that props can be seen in greater clarity than ever before, so every detail must be perfect. Like props in theatre, television props may need to be able to survive week after week during filming, as well as being stored during the off-season safely enough so they could be brought back out for the next season's shooting.

A successful prop is one that is built to do exactly what it needs to do. The appearance and other physical properties serve the production. It is built to withstand the stresses of its use in a scene as well as not being overly inconvenient when backstage or off-screen. If a prop fulfills all its needs, then it was built correctly. You may find more elegant ways to build the prop, either using better-quality materials or methods that show expertise in more advanced skills. These are not the most important considerations though; as long as a prop fulfills the needs of the production, then it is a properly made prop.

Complex Shapes into Simple Parts

At first glance, a prop may look difficult. Break it down into simple geometric shapes, and its construction becomes more self-evident. When we look at specific materials, we will learn more about what kinds of shapes to break the prop into, but for now it is important to note that very few props are constructed from a single piece of material. Almost every prop is the assemblage of a variety of pieces and parts. When planning the construction of a prop, it is helpful to break down its most characteristic features into basic components, and determine the needs of each of those components.

Reference and Research

The needs of your prop may have initially been given by the designer and director. You may have drawings, photographs, and other reference material. Further research may be required to flesh out the needs of your prop. You may need to gather or generate your own research drawings and photos to get approval for the desired process and final finish. In some cases, you may need to experiment and generate some actual samples that show different paint treatments, textural effects, or other physical information that the designer, director, and the

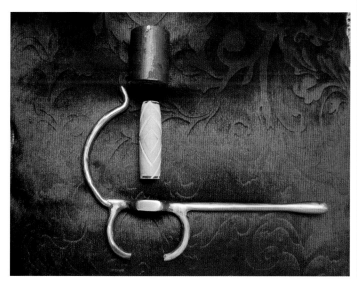

Figures 2-4 and 2-5: This complex looking sword hilt is just a series of simple parts.

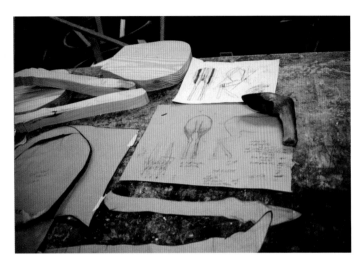

Figure 2-6: To construct this deer carcass for a production of *A Lie of the Mind*, Natalie Taylor Hart not only generated drawings and patterns based off of a real deer, she also had a real deer foot to reference for the color and texture of the fur. Photograph by Natalie Taylor Hart.

rest of the production team may need to be aware of or that they may wish to weigh in on.

Even the most fantastical and imaginary prop will have some basis in reality. One of the biggest shortcomings of a prop maker is the assumption that they know what something looks like; we all know what a dog's head looks like until the time comes to sculpt one. As a prop maker, it is impossible to err on the side of too many reference pictures. The reality of an object is conveyed by the shapes and textures of the parts, how the components fit together, how they respond when handled and manipulated, how light dances off their surfaces, how the pieces sound when moved, and other subtle properties that you have never needed to think of before.

Your Means

If you think about all the questions we need to ask and all the considerations that must be taken into account, you will find that each prop still has a range of materials and methods that

you can use. In order to decide which among these are the best for your prop, we need to look at the second half of our method. What resources are available to us? This provides a way to balance our equation.

Figuring out the cost of a prop, either to fit it in a budget or to make an estimate, is one of the trickiest skills a props artisan must master. Estimating the cost and time for a prop will be covered in detail in Chapter 19. Of course, if you do not know what materials you will be working with or what techniques you will be using, you can't very well estimate the cost and time.

You also need to figure out what materials can conceivably meet your needs. Obviously, if you need a transparent panel, you cannot build it out of wood. You should have a rough grasp of the properties of the different materials; what they are capable of, how they can be shaped and formed, how strong you can make them, how they will affect the weight, and what they will look like. You should also know the amount of time it takes to do comparable tasks with different materials. For example, cutting through a 1″ bar of steel will take far longer than cutting through a 1″ piece of wood. That may make a big difference if you have to cut through a hundred pieces.

The wealth of materials available to you comes in an infinite variety of shapes and sizes. After you break your prop down into smaller components, it makes sense to build them out of materials that are already close in size and shape, or which can easily be manipulated into the correct size and shape. As a simple illustration, let us say you need a tabletop, and it has to be ½ inch thick. You have decided it is best to make the tabletop out of plywood. Plywood comes in a variety of thicknesses, such as ¼ inch, ½ inch, and ¾ inch. Choosing a thickness other than ½ inch would just be silly.

Of course, these choices are not always that obvious. But if you narrow down your range of materials to a few possibilities, it will help you find out what forms those materials come in. For example, part of your prop is a hemisphere. You have determined you can build it out of foam or wood. If you do some research, you will find that you can buy foam hemispheres in a number of sizes. You can buy the right size, and your job is done. If you go with wood, you need to glue together pieces of wood until you have a large enough block, and then figure out how to shape it down into a hemisphere. Think of how much longer that would take.

Some materials are stronger than others. Strength can be looked at in different ways. One parameter is compression strength, or how strong it is when it is pushed together, or crushed. Another parameter is tensile strength, or how strong it is when pulled apart, or stretched. A third parameter is shear strength, which comes into play when a material is pushed or moved from the side. For example, a drywall screw snaps in half when pushed from the side, whereas a nail will bend.

Materials may be strong in one way while being weak in another, and the strength also needs to be considered when determining how materials connect to each other and with what type of fastener.

It is also important to look at what happens to a material when its strength is pushed past the limit. A material may break, such as when Styrofoam is crushed or sheared. A material may bend or buckle, such as when a lot of shear strength is applied to a metal rod. The material may bend and become deformed, or it may return to its original state when the weight is removed. An upholstery pad will be crushed under a small amount of compressive strength, but it will reform to its original state when the weight is removed.

What materials do you know how to work with? Do you have time or money to experiment with new materials for this project? What tools and machines do you have to work with? Will you have to buy, borrow, or rent tools or machines to work with some materials? How readily available are your materials? Can you just go out and buy them? Can you order them from a supplier and have them delivered? If you order them online and they need to be shipped, do you have that much time? How much more expensive will the shipping costs make the material?

What is your space like? Do you have room to work with certain materials and techniques? Do you have the proper safety equipment and setup to use certain materials? You have to know the risks involved with any material or technique you wish to use, because it may turn out that your shop does not have the proper safety infrastructure.

Figure 2-7: All materials can be used safely if you know and use the correct safety procedures. If you cannot use a certain material safely in your shop, you should not consider it as a possibility for your prop.

If you do not have the right kinds of gloves to protect your hands from a certain material or adequate ventilation to work with another, then you cannot consider using it for your prop. This can be hard; as props people, we always want to experiment with new materials and techniques. Our deadlines are often very tight and our budgets slim. It is tempting to let health and safety, especially when dealing with chemicals that have no immediate side effects, take a back seat. This is a mistake. You always need to consider your health and safety. It is never too late to pay attention to your health. Even if you have spent a lifetime paying little attention to your health, you can still make improvements; your body will thank you. Do not despair if you lapse every now and then in watching out for your health. It happens to even the best of us; forgetting to wear your goggles one day is no excuse to leave them off in the future. You just have to keep trying and watching yourself, and trying to make your shop a little safer every day. There is always room for improvement. Maybe one day we can live in a world where safety and health is not an expense that our bosses pressure us to minimize, or a hassle and hurdle to having fun; until then we need to take care of ourselves and remain vigilant for situations that are unsafe or unhealthy, even when working for a company that should, theoretically, be following the laws that safeguard our health.

Sustainability is also a need that is growing in importance these days. Sustainability is the idea that what we do today can be done by future generations. It means we do not use raw materials in a way that will ultimately deplete their source here on earth, or create such a mess of the world that our descendants have to sacrifice just to survive. In many ways, props is already a fairly sustainable field. We save items that otherwise would be thrown away. We store all sorts of objects and goods for future use. We recycle, reuse, repurpose, and upcycle materials, particularly those of us working in low-budget productions or educational settings. Only a props person can take a $100 budget and fill a stage with what looks like thousands of dollars worth of stuff. Of course, you can always make improvements. In our world it is extraordinarily difficult to be fully sustainable, but it is always possible to be more sustainable. As with our health and safety, every day and every production is an opportunity to be a little more sustainable in our choices.

Look at the products and materials you buy. Research and test those that are better for the environment. Consider all aspects of your carbon footprint; often, using a local product is more environmentally beneficial than shipping in a "greener" alternative.

As you plan out the props for a production or event, think of what will happen to them afterward. Do you have room to store them? Is it even worth it to store them? Can you reuse the materials in them? Would other people be interested in taking them once you're done with them? If you think you can repurpose the materials afterward, plan to build your prop in a way that makes it easier to disassemble.

You need to consider the time it will take to work with your choice of materials. The materials and techniques you settle on for your prop will also be determined by your skill level in dealing with them. For instance, you may wish to braze copper and tin together for a prop, but if you have never used a torch before, you may not know the correct material to use, how to set up your tools, how to maneuver the torch, or even how to determine if you were successful when finished.

Experimentation with new materials and techniques is an important part of furthering your skills as a props artisan, but you should either research the methods first, test it out on a sample, or at least have a backup plan at the ready.

Cost and time need to be balanced, as one will affect the other. For example, plywood comes in a number of different styles and grades. If you are using plywood for hidden structural pieces, then the cheapest type will usually suffice. If it is being used as a visual surface, especially a smooth and flat surface, then the cost is only part of the component. A cheaper grade will require filling and sanding to make it as smooth as a finish-grade plywood. You need to figure in the cost of your labor as well as the cost of the material. You also need to take into consideration the fact that the time you spend on sanding and filing cheap materials is time taken away from other projects. When it comes down to it, the cheaper plywood may save you some material costs, but it will end up with a larger overall cost.

If you think the variety of materials used in props shops is vast, you should see what materials you can buy when cost is not an issue. Especially in the world of synthetic, plastic, and composite materials, you can find materials with almost any combination of properties you can imagine.

Of course, no production has infinite money in its budget, and choosing the materials for every prop in a show is one giant compromise. Since the cost of materials is intrinsically linked with the cost of all materials for a show, or even an entire season, the decision cannot always be made in a vacuum. For instance, you may be absolutely convinced that a more expensive material is needed for a prop than was budgeted; you can still use the more expensive material if a cheaper material can be found for another, unrelated prop.

There is no "wrong" way to build a prop; rather, the vocabulary of tips and tricks we have discovered over the years becomes a language of best practices that fulfill our needs in the majority of prop projects. Foam, wood, papier-mâché, plaster, resin, steel, and leather are used time and time again because we already know they will fulfill our needs and the needs of the prop. Yes, the situation occasionally arises for something different; in the *Lord of the Rings* films, the One Ring was an important enough prop to warrant hiring a jeweler to actually forge several copies out of gold, but that is the exception rather than the rule.

The Ways Materials Can be Manipulated

To determine which means will fulfill your needs, it can be helpful to have a general overview of how different materials can be manipulated. I have distilled all techniques into five basic classes: cutting, assembling, bending, modeling, and hardening.

Cutting means the removal of material. If you slice or shear a material, then you separate it into two pieces. If you use a saw or similar blade, you are actually carving a tiny path through the entirety of the material, which separates it into two pieces. You can also cut into a material to create grooves and holes, or carve into it to make three-dimensional designs and shapes. A special type of cutting is known as **machining**, which is the precise removal of material from a solid piece, and is usually done by machines.

Assembling means attaching two or more materials together. In some cases, the two materials become one material, and in other cases, the materials remain distinct but inseparable. Assembly can also be temporary, such as when you bolt two things together.

Bending means deforming a piece of material so that it takes on a new shape without the addition or loss of any material. A bend can be a simple change in direction, such as a coat hanger made from a bent rod. It can also be a much more complex series of deformations over a surface, such as when you mold a sheet of leather into a mask.

Modeling is the shaping of amorphous plastic materials. These materials do not have a specific size or shape, but are more like a lump. Clay is the best example of this type of material. You can carve it to make shapes or add more clay to build up shapes, but you can also push, pull, and smear the clay to alter the surface.

Figure 2-8: Hardening includes materials that "harden" (or, more appropriately, "solidify") into soft and flexible rubbers and elastomers.

Shapes can be created through the **hardening** of liquids, semi-liquids, or pastes into a solid. This can be through drying, such as joint compound, Sculpt or Coat®, clay, etc.; through a chemical reaction, such as resin or other mold-making and casting compounds; or by heating and cooling, such as metal, wax, or Friendly Plastic®. Besides creating shapes, this is also how a lot of coatings, textures, and paints are added to the surface of a material. A liquid or paste is applied, and when it hardens, your prop has a different surface.

You can look at many familiar processes as just a combination of one or more of these basic shaping methods.

Fabrication refers to the construction of items from rigid materials. It is a combination of cutting, bending, and assembling. Metal and plastic are classes of materials that can be fabricated. Wood is also fabricated, though we refer to it as "carpentry," or more specifically as "furniture making" or "cabinet making."

Sculpting can be cutting, modeling, or a combination of both. Some materials can be modeled and then hardened, either through heat, or over time as the result of drying or a chemical reaction.

Making a mold of your sculpture is usually done by hardening a material around it. This gives you a shape with an empty cavity in the shape of your sculpture. When you fill that cavity with another liquid that hardens, you have a copy of your sculpture.

Surface fillers and texturing compounds such as spackle and joint compound are a mix of modeling and hardening.

You may also form shapes by laminating together many smaller sheets to form a continuous skin, such as with papier-mâché and fiberglass. The paper or fiberglass cloth is cut, while the resin or glue saturates the pieces and hardens everything into a continuous skin.

When you come across new or unfamiliar materials, it may be helpful to think back to these five classes of manipulation to determine the best way to shape this new substance.

Workflow

No two prop makers will have the same workflow. We can, however, look at several examples of how to organize your process, and you can decide what works best for you. Some artisans like to jump right in and start cutting and assembling materials, figuring it out as they go along. Others like to plan everything out on paper to the point where building the prop is just a matter of following the steps they've laid out. Depending on the project, I like to work somewhere in the middle. I plan out as much as I can, and then I build what I know needs to be built. At a certain point, I then reevaluate my steps and make a revised plan for the next steps. You can expend a lot of brain power trying to visualize a three-dimensional prop from beginning to end in your head; it becomes far easier to complete the picture once you have started building it, as you now have something real to hold and measure. When planning in the beginning, you want to at least step through all the processes and techniques you will be using, even if you aren't coming up with exact steps.

As an example, suppose you are building an animatronic animal. You cover the whole thing with fake fur. Suddenly, you realize you need to put a motor inside, so you have to cut apart the fur and the skin and the whole thing turns into a big mess. If you plan ahead, you will see that you have to put a motor inside,

so you can build the whole thing with a secret access panel and wrap the fur so as to hide that panel. You don't necessarily need to know what kind of motor you are using, or how you will wire it, or any number of other specifics at this point.

Putting It All Together

Now that you are armed with all the information you need from the other members of the production team, and have a clear idea of what the prop needs to do, and what it needs to look like, you can begin determining how you are going to build it. When faced with a prop of any complexity, the easiest way to start is by breaking it down into its simplest components.

Let's start with a chair. A chair works for our example because thousands of years of development have given us a fairly standardized way to break it down into simple parts. Basically, a chair has four legs, a seat, and a back. Usually, the back

Figure 2-9: A prop chair. Photograph by Natalie Taylor Hart.

legs are attached to the back piece for strength. Otherwise, the back may break off from the stress of leaning back. The legs are also usually attached to each other with stiles, or bars, to keep them from splaying apart. Knowing how a chair is broken down into components lets you build almost anything that needs to look or act vaguely like a chair. If your chair has a decorative back, you simply alter how the back is made, while making the rest of it in the usual way. In the example of the Yoruban throne, we have a chair with many carvings over it. Rather than inventing some difficult method of construction, or attempting the traditional, but excessively time-consuming method of carving it from a solid piece, we simply broke it down into simpler parts.

It's essentially a regular chair that happens to have extra sculptural bits added to it. In talking with the paint department, we discovered that the entire piece will be painted, which gave us the freedom to construct it with any mix of materials we wanted. Thus, the chair could be built from wood as it usually is, while the figures could be sculpted from whatever material the artisan feels most proficient in, and glued on at the end. It even allowed the less experienced students to each sculpt their own figure while another artisan was busy building the chair, saving time and giving the students valuable experience.

Remember how I said this process can also be used on a curtain? For very simple props, we do not think through the steps because they are so obvious, but they are still present. The needs of a curtain are that it has to look and act like a curtain, and it needs to be the size, shape, and color that the designer picked. We choose to make it out of fabric, because it would be silly to try to force a different kind of material to fit all those needs when fabric will fulfill them; it is readily available, and every shop is already well equipped to work with it. We choose a few fabrics to show our designer so that we can make sure the cost of the fabric fits our budget (that is, we avoid giving the designer a fabric swatch for a fabric that costs too much). You might find some compromise here; the absolute perfect fabric may be too expensive, so you have to get the designer to choose a cheaper fabric that may be made from a less exquisite material or have a simpler pattern. To shape the curtain requires cutting it to size, sewing a pocket at the top, and finishing the

Figures 2-10: Yoruban throne. *The Gods Are Not to Blame,* Ohio University, 2004. Scenic design by Natalie Taylor Hart. Photograph by Natalie Taylor Hart.

Figures 2-11: Yoruban throne. *The Gods Are Not to Blame,* Ohio University, 2004. Scenic design by Natalie Taylor Hart. Photograph by Ryan Trupp

hems. These processes should all be within the capabilities of your shop. If not, I suppose one could glue the pocket and hems, though we are starting to get into the realm of ultra-low budget theatre here. Really, if simple sewing is beyond the capabilities of your theatre, you should have made the choice to just purchase existing curtains rather than trying to make them.

So we see that even a curtain follows the same process. Determine the needs, determine your means, and choose the materials and methods that satisfy both. It is nice to know this process is universal, though for props as straightforward as curtains, wooden crates, or paper notes, one usually skips most of the process because the answer is already fairly obvious.

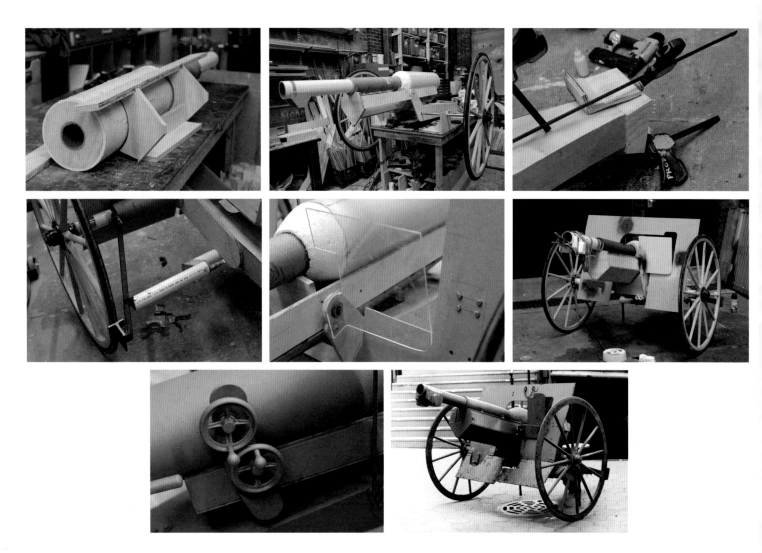

Figures 2-12 to 2-19: The evolution of this cannon shows how different materials are shaped and attached together to form a unified whole. *All's Well That Ends Well*, the Public Theater, 2011. Scenic design by Scott Pask.

three

safety

Prop making is a dangerous occupation. Tools can cut, and machines can maim. Chemicals can irritate your skin, affect your breathing, damage your brain and other organs, and even cause cancer.

If you are self-taught and work on your own, or if you are new to prop making, you may simply be unaware of what harms you are causing your body, as the products we buy and the stores we shop from do not adequately convey how to create a healthy working environment. A person's occupation affects his or her health the most, and if you wish to continue to work throughout your life, you need to understand, avoid and minimize the health hazards inherent in your occupation.

An employee should participate in and practice all the safety and health procedures and policies set out by his or her employer. He or she should correctly use all safety and protective equipment provided. The employee should report all injuries and accidents, as well as notify the supervisor or management of unsafe equipment, practices, or procedures seen in the shop.

One thing about safety is you cannot let the lack of a perfect plan keep you from doing little things. You may think that since you have already done so many unsafe things or inhaled so many toxic fumes in the past, there is no point in starting now. You can never be 100% safe and free from health hazards, but you can always make an effort to be *more* safe and use *less* toxic products.

While I will attempt to give an introduction to proper safety practices in this chapter and reiterate important safety precautions in chapters that delve into specific practices, I simply cannot convey all the necessary safety information in this book. We use far too many specific chemicals and tools, and each has its own specific precautions one must take. It would be careless of me to make general safety recommendations for one class of materials since it may not hold true for your specific situation.

Just because I describe how to use a tool or material in this book does not mean you are ready to use it. Likewise, if you read instructions or a guide to tools or materials, you may still not be ready to use it. Do not assume something is safe just because you read about someone else doing it, or see a video online of someone doing it, or even if you watch a manufacturer of a product demonstrate something. Knowing *how* to use tools and materials does not mean it is safe to do so. You should only use them with the proper **safety infrastructure** in place. By safety infrastructure, I mean any of the following, which may be necessary depending on the situation: ventilation; dust or fume collection; personal protective equipment such as gloves, respirators, goggles, etc; fire protection; training and certification; disposal and cleanup procedures. Certain substances or machines may require even more considerations.

It is vital to think of safety as an infrastructure rather than in terms of what is "good" or "bad." Anything can be "bad" without the proper safeguards, while even "bad" chemicals can be worked with safely in a correctly-equipped shop. A professional shop that builds props out of fiberglass that follows all regulations and suggestions for minimizing the risks of fiberglass work is actually safer than a hobbyist who sands MDF by hand at home but follows no safety guidelines.

Hobbyists and freelancers may feel blessed that they do not need to follow the stringent regulations of industry. However, the laws that govern safety in our workplaces, particularly when it comes to working with toxic and hazardous materials, are woefully inadequate, and our knowledge of how chemicals affect our bodies trail considerably from the sheer amount and variety that are on the market. If anything, safety laws should be the bare minimum you follow, even if you are not legally obligated to. The home hobbyist can, in some cases, be exposed to more hazards than the commercial prop maker, particularly if he or she builds props in or near the same place as he or she lives. A commercial prop maker is only exposed to fumes and vapors while at work, about 8 hours per day. A home hobbyist is exposed to those same chemicals 24 hours a day. Where a commercial prop maker can pour liquid urethane into a mold and go home to fresh air for sixteen hours, a home hobbyist who does the same in his or her living room will be breathing those fumes all night. For physical dangers, a worker is often covered under worker's compensation laws; if you hurt yourself in your own home or shop, you have to pay your own hospital bills.

Throughout this chapter, I frequently make reference to OSHA and other regulations. This book is not a definitive or up-to-date guide to all the regulations out there. I mention them because it is helpful to the prop maker to have at least some idea about what their employer should be doing in terms of health and safety in the workplace; if one has never encountered all these rules and regulations before, it may be a shock to find out what is and is not allowed in a props shop, and this chapter will hopefully make you curious to seek out more information or training classes.

If you are an actual employer responsible for the health and safety of your employees, this chapter is nowhere near comprehensive enough to make that happen. If any of what I write is "news to you," I urge you to find further information, consult an expert, or otherwise acquaint and reacquaint yourself with your responsibilities in this matter.

All too often, companies do not have trained safety people to supervise prop makers. If you work with hazardous substances, the company is required to test common working conditions to check whether you need a respirator or not; if respirators are needed, the company needs a written respirator program, which requires employees getting annual medical checkups, fit-testing for respirators, and many other considerations. I've heard of companies who have tried to get around this requirement by stating that employees are not allowed to work with materials that require respirators. The punch line is that even wood dust is considered a hazardous material that requires the use of a disposable dust mask, which is technically a respirator. A company cannot assume it is safe; chances are, any materials used will have some hazard that needs to be controlled. When props shops without trained safety officers deal with materials such as two-part polyurethanes, fiberglass, industrial paints and adhesives, and plastics, they are certainly placing their employees in danger.

The Well-Dressed Prop Maker

Figure 3-1: The well-dressed prop maker.

The well-dressed prop maker wears clothes and accessories that help protect against accidents and injuries, and avoids wearing things that can lead to harm.

Working with any kind of machine or power tool requires special considerations for dress because of the danger that loose or dangling pieces might get caught; with the high speeds the machines operate at, these bits can quickly pull your person into the danger zone. Neckties, wristwatches, jewelry, and even certain rings should be removed during this kind of work. Long hair should be tied back and up so it will remain out of the way. When wearing an apron, the strings should be tied around the back. Woolen sweaters are a particular danger, as the strands of wool are long and unbroken, so one strand that gets caught can pull a person into a machine before the strand is broken. Long sleeves of any kind are safer when rolled up securely.

Work Gloves

Work gloves make it safer when you are moving or manipulating rough, splintery, or sharp materials. Metal mesh or Kevlar gloves can protect your hands from cuts and sharp knives. Leather gloves are a necessity when welding, and helpful when handling anything hot or rough. Thinner fabric or cotton gloves give less protection but allow more dexterity, and are useful for dirty, splintery, or slippery objects. You will also find chemical-resistant gloves in a props shop, which I will discuss in the section on chemicals.

When working on many power tools and machines, though, work gloves often make it *more* dangerous. Like loose-fitting clothing, gloves can get caught in spinning machinery and pull your whole hand (or even your arm) into the machine. It may sound morbid, but if your bare hand gets caught in a machine, the skin or your finger will tear off before it can pull your whole arm in. Though a missing finger is not an ideal situation, it is preferable to a missing arm.

Safety Glasses

Impact-resistant safety glasses are a must in shops where power tools are used, even if you are not the one using the tool. Note that these are not the same as chemical splash goggles, though you can find glasses that offer both impact and chemical splash protection. Make sure your glasses have side and top protection and fit snugly against your face; you do not want to go through the trouble of wearing glasses only to have a shard of metal fly in from the side and slash your eye. If you wear regular glasses, you can buy safety glasses that fit over your glasses. You can even buy prescription lenses that are rated to be impact-resistant. Many shops require you to wear safety glasses from the moment you enter the shop until you leave it at the end of the day, so it is worth finding a comfortable pair to wear all day. You may also find impact-resistant face shields, which can be worn with or without safety glasses and goggles; they provide protection from impact and splashes to the entire face.

Footwear

Never wear open-toed or open heel shoes to a props shop, theatre, film, or television set. Any place where you are using power tools or chemicals or dealing with heavy materials is no place to have your toes exposed. Many an intern or student has been sent home on his or her first day of work or class for wearing sandals or other inappropriate footwear. Even experienced professionals will be sent home for trying to wear sandals to the shop; it is far too dangerous.

In some shops, you may wish to (or be required to) wear steel-toed boots. If you do a lot of sewing and small craft work, steel-toed shoes are perhaps overkill, particularly if you spend the bulk of your day in a shop separate from the larger power tools. If you are like me and work in all sorts of situations, you may have a pair of regular work shoes and a pair of steel-toed shoes and decide what to wear on a day-to-day basis. Many shops will give you access to a locker or other storage area where you can keep different shoes, as well as changes in clothes or overalls and aprons. This is helpful to keep especially dirty clothes at work all the time so you never track dust and contaminants home with you.

Steel-toed boots that are unsafe and uncomfortable should be avoided. Wear only the ones that meet the appropriate standards in your country. Comfort is also vital. A boot that pinches or rubs your foot can cause more damage in the long term than what it protects you from in the short term. Unlike regular shoes that will "break in," that is, they will stretch and loosen around your foot over time, a steel-toed boot will not. If it feels uncomfortable when you try it on in the store, if it pinches or constrains your toes or feet, it will always feel uncomfortable. It is vital you find a pair that fits you well; you do not want to give yourself an excuse not to wear them. This is true of all footwear.

Even prop makers who avoid heavy machinery need the right kind of shoes. Soft goods artisans and craftspeople may have to stand for long periods of time, so comfortable sneakers with good interior support will prevent fatigue and strain. Wear shoes that tie so that you can adjust them throughout the day. A slightly uncomfortable situation can result in an injury when prolonged all day, every day.

Boots and work shoes should also have a thick sole. You may find yourself stepping on sharp objects. Strong traction and treads are vital for preventing slips and falls, especially on wet surfaces.

Hearing Protection

The loud noise of most power tools will eventually lead to hearing loss. It is not a matter of "if" but rather "when." Hearing loss is gradual and cumulative. The more often you can wear properly rated earmuffs or earplugs when creating noise, the longer you will be able to listen to actors complaining about their props.

Hearing loss can began with exposure to sounds at 85 decibels; the louder the sound, the less time it takes for hearing damage to occur. Even the sound of a hair dryer is loud enough

to cause hearing loss after four hours; once you add up the sounds of all the tools and machines running in a props shop at any one time, you may be surprised at how loud it actually is.

A Clean Shop and a Clean Body

It is not only good practice in general to keep your work area clean, but vital to your safety as well. When you leave tools or supplies on the floor, you will surely forget about them and step on them when backing up while carrying a heavy prop. You can slip or trip on some objects, while heavy or sharp objects can injure your foot. Cords and hoses are a trip hazard and should be kept out of paths where people walk. If you absolutely must run a cord or hose over a walkway, make sure it is running flat and smooth along the ground, and not draped in the air or twisted in spaghetti shapes.

Dusts and liquids on the floor are also slip hazards. Dust left unswept is a double hazard, because every time you drop or

Figure 3-2: This is an actual shop where work was expected to be done.

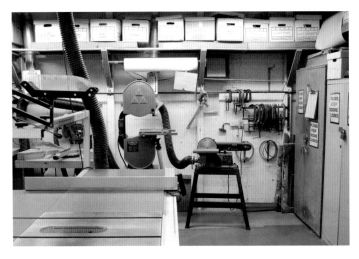

Figure 3-3: The props shop at Berkeley Rep Theatre, on the other hand, has clean floors, well-organized storage, properly labeled flammables cabinets, and adequate dust collection and ventilation.

Figure 3-4: Retractable power cords on the ceiling (such as these at Childsplay Theatre in Arizona) allow you to run electricity to the middle of a room without running a cord along the floor which you can trip over.

push something, or something creates a breeze or gust of wind, you raise the dust back into the air where it can be inhaled.

You should avoid working in a shop alone as much as possible, particularly if you are running power tools or dealing with toxic substances. If you are knocked unconscious, or sustain an injury that prevents you from calling for help, then you can potentially lie on the ground and bleed to death. An opened container or spill of a toxic substance may also go unnoticed and affect your brain to the point where you do not have the mental capacity to realize something is wrong.

As a hobbyist or sole proprietor working out of a home or studio space, this may be more challenging. If possible, having your spouse, roommate, or neighbor check in throughout the day is helpful. Make sure you have a working phone easily accessible; if it is a mobile phone, make sure you get a signal in your shop. It is also vital that you pay particular attention to making sure your safety infrastructure is in solid working order. It is not terribly expensive or challenging to install items such as "kill switches," which are large buttons that when hit will cut all the power to the tools in your shop. With these placed strategically around your shop, you can always hit one with a hand, foot, or other part of your body when a power tool gets out of control or traps you.

Before starting any potentially dangerous, loud, or otherwise hazardous tasks, check to make sure your fellow workers are out of harm's way and prepared for what is coming.

Do not eat or drink in your workplace. If you eat where you work, the dust can settle on your food. Also, you can get trace amounts of toxic materials on your hands and fingers, which will transfer onto your food as you pick it up and put it in your mouth.

Pay attention to your body; it will tell you when you are pushing yourself too hard. If you feel a headache developing, or you start getting dizzy, it can mean any number of things. If you have been working with or around any kinds of chemicals, it is likely that your body has gotten tired of being exposed to toxic substances. In other cases, it may mean you are physically exhausted or haven't been eating well (or enough) lately. This can happen a lot in theatre, television, and film, where heavy workloads and short deadlines leave prop makers sacrificing their own rest and nourishment to prove themselves. Working when exhausted or hungry can leave you slower to react in emergencies, and you may end up making stupid mistakes because you are not thinking clearly. Take a short break to look at what everyone else is working on. Move to a different project for a bit so you can refocus your brain or exercise different parts of your body. Grab a quick snack or even a quick nap if you are allowed; even a brief fifteen or twenty minute nap over a lunch break can sometimes do wonders. If you find you are completely exhausted or ill from chemical exposure, you may even need to go home. If you think you cannot miss even one day of work, imagine what would happen if you had to miss work for the rest of your life.

Drugs and alcohol affect your body and its ability to use tools and machines safely in the shop. Most shops expressly prohibit illegal drugs and alcohol use while at work, or arriving while under the influence. Some legal medications, such as cold medicine, sleeping aids, and painkillers, should also be avoided. Check the labels; if it warns you not to drive or operate heavy machinery, or that it my cause drowsiness, you should avoid power tools as well. Certain drugs, such as daily medications, vitamins, aspirin, and coffee, may be okay to use while at work. Cigarettes and other tobacco products are usually prohibited while indoors, and in some locales they may even be prohibited outdoors within a certain distance of building entrances. Most workplaces retain designated smoking areas where tobacco products can be used during breaks. Remember, in addition to being a health hazard, they can also be a fire and burn hazard, so take care not to smoke around flammable or combustible materials, and to fully extinguish lit cigarettes when finished.

All props artisans should keep up on their tetanus shots. You will most certainly be cut, stabbed, or pierced by metal objects while working, whatever your specific discipline is. Unlike other bacteria, you cannot build an immunity to tetanus through repeated mild exposure, only through vaccination. You only need a tetanus shot every ten years, and they are affordable even if you are an American without health insurance.

Many companies will have you fill out an accident report if you have an injury or accident while working. You should fill these out even if your injury does not require medical attention and you can continue working. If the injury should worsen after several days or weeks, such as when you get a cut that later gets infected and swells, that original accident report would prove to the company and its insurance agents that you received the injury while on the job, and it will remain covered under worker's compensation laws.

Ventilation

Do not breathe anything but air. While a workplace has codes and regulations for ventilation depending on the number of employees and the type of work being done there, it is still incumbent on the employee to watch out for his or her own health. Very few substances other than air are helpful or neutral when they enter the lungs. It is especially bad when you are working with airborne substances all day for several days in a row. If you smell something, then you are breathing chemicals. If you can see dust or fumes in the air, or distortion waves from heat or fumes, then you are breathing chemicals. Of course, some hazardous chemicals cannot be smelled or seen while you are breathing them.

You want to keep as little dust or fumes from getting into the air as possible. If you have a wood shop, a dust collection system hooked up to each of your power tools is ideal. Even if you are wearing a disposable respirator, the other people in your shop might not be, so sucking the dust up before it gets into the air will keep their lungs happy. You can even hook portable power tools up to a vacuum cleaner so they have their own mini-dust collection system. If you are generating dust by hand, or you cannot hook a dust collector up to your tool, you can work on a downdraft table, which is essentially a table with lots of holes that suck the dust into a vacuum cleaner. If even that is unavailable to you, you can just turn a vacuum cleaner on and work right in front of the hose. Dust collectors need to be emptied regularly; be sure when you empty it, you do not breathe the dust or release it back into the shop's air.

The extraction of fumes works on the same principle as dust collection. You can get little fume collectors for soldering, bigger ones for welding, and spray booths for spray painting. You can even use fume hoods for more toxic processes, like you find in a high school chemistry classroom. A fume hood completely surrounds the materials and tools you are using other than a space in the front where your hands can reach in. Fresh air is sucked into the hood through that space, and everything is exhausted away from the workspace. In theory, none of the airborne chemicals can make it back into the room. A glove box works in a similar manner, but the air is completely separated from the air you breathe; you manipulate everything inside with gloves attached to the box itself. Fume hoods or glove boxes are particularly helpful for processes such as casting urethane, which off-gasses hazardous fumes for several hours; you would not want to wear a respirator that whole time.

Spray booths, fume hoods, dust collectors, and similar systems all rely on filters to keep the air clean. Some use particulate filters, which manually prevent dust and other large particles from passing through. Others use chemical filters, which attract and trap certain kinds of airborne chemicals while

Figure 3-6: A properly maintained spray booth will contain fumes, vapors, and gasses and exhaust them out away from the shop.

letting regular air continue through. All of these filters need to be checked and changed regularly or after heavy use. A clogged particulate filter makes the system run less efficiently and can even present a fire hazard in some cases. A chemical filter can only trap so many chemicals before it is "used up" and lets just any old thing flow through it.

You always want to be "upwind" of whatever you are working on. Fresh air should move from your nose toward the dust or hazardous chemicals and into the extraction or collection system. Fresh air can be brought in from open windows or via the room's ventilation system. Fans can be placed in your shop to help move the air around in the proper direction.

Proper Training

Unfortunately, in the world of prop making, we can't always have the ideal training situations. There are a lot of jobs, especially with summer stock and smaller theatres, where an inexperienced person is given the keys to a shop and left to figure everything out on their own. If you are an outside contractor on a film or television show, you are left up to your own devices to deliver a completed prop by a certain day.

Figure 3-5: A sand blasting chamber is a type of glove box. The gloves allow you to manipulate the item inside the chamber, which is completely closed to prevent the airborne particles from entering the general atmosphere of the shop.

Never use a tool or a machine that you have not been trained on. A good vocational or college program will teach you the safe practice on all the machines you will be expected to use. If you find yourself in the workplace having to use equipment that you have never used before, it is okay to ask a supervisor or coworker how. Do not try to figure it out on your own just because you feel you "ought" to know how to use it. None of us are born knowing how to use tools, and every one of us has had to learn how at some point.

Many injuries happen when a prop maker thinks, "I've never done it this way, but just this once ..." Even an accomplished artisan knows when to grab a buddy to help maneuver something through a table saw, or spend the time constructing a jig to hold everything in place while running a router. It is the inexperienced person who thinks good prop making means jumping in as quickly as possible with blades spinning to prove they can do it without assistance.

For experienced prop makers, some accidents come from habit. Your work becomes second nature, and you stop paying attention to it. You are thinking about something else and in that instant, an accident happens.

may even lose your balance and exacerbate your injuries. If you slip with a sharp blade, you only have the weight of the tool to stop; it is much easier to control.

Always be aware of where your fingers (and other body parts) are in relation to the blade or other cutting surface. In graduate school, many of the injuries we suffered while building scenic models happened while holding a straight edge as a guide for a razor blade; the fingers holding the straight edge would stick out into the path of the razor blade, which would cut right through them before we realized it. In high school, I nearly cut my thumb off when it drifted over the top of a spinning table saw blade; I wasn't paying attention to where my hands were in relation to the blade. Likewise, injuries can happen when you can't see where your hands are in relation to the blade. Before making any cut, stop and take a half a second to visually check all your appendages and whether they are in the path of the blade.

Before beginning any action with a tool or machine, double-check that you have good footing and balance. If a tool should slip or otherwise do something unexpected and you are in an unbalanced position, you are likely to fall. While falling itself can be harmful, you might also fall or slip into a sharp blade or a rapidly moving part.

Using Tools

Make sure your tools have sharp bits and blades and are well maintained. Power tools bring up additional safety concerns. Always use the right tool for the job. If something feels dangerous when you are doing it, figure out a better way to do it.

Sharper blades are safer than dull ones. It may seem counterintuitive; after all, running a sharp tool over your skin will certainly cut you deeper than a dull blade. But we are usually not running blades over our skin; we are cutting a material with them. If you have a sharp tool, you do not have to put much effort into it, and the tool will do most of the work for you. If your blade is dull, you have to push and pull with more force in your cuts. If, while struggling and straining, your blade slips, it may hit a part of your body with all of that force; you

Figure 3-7: I cut through this table saw rail with a circular saw because I did not check to see that it was clear of the path of the blade. This could easily have been my hand.

Well-maintained tools are safer. An older but well-built tool that is properly maintained can be safer than a brand new but poorly built one. Spending a few minutes every week or a few hours every month on maintenance will save you from losing a whole weekend or even a few weeks when your tool breaks down. A couple of bucks here and there on replacement parts may save you from having to make a larger purchase down the road. If the tool *feels* unsafe when you are using it, it probably *is* unsafe (assuming you are familiar with the tool and have used others like it).

Some tools require regular oiling, and some need regular cleaning. If you work with wood, the sawdust that accumulates and remains on the metal parts of tools can absorb moisture from the air and promote the formation of rust. Dust can also accumulate inside of tools and machines and gum up the works. If it accumulates on top of a motor, it can actually trap the heat generated by the motor and cause it to overheat or, in rare cases, catch fire.

If you go to use a tool or machine and find that it is broken, do not just leave it for the next guy to discover it is broken. Tag it or put a note on it and let your supervisor or foreman know it needs to be repaired or replaced. Unless you own the tool, do not attempt any repairs without first checking with your supervisor or boss. If you do own the tool, or are responsible for repairs and maintenance, be sure to turn off and unplug the tool before working on it or adjusting it. (Note that for some tools, some adjustments specifically need to be made while the machine is running. These tools will usually have a plate or label prominently displayed telling you if this is the case.)

Once you begin removing or disabling the blade and belt guards or other safety features, you begin risking your own safety or the safety of others who will use the tool after you. If you have not used a tool or machine in awhile, or if you are in a new shop and using a tool or machine for the first time, always double-check it first to make sure all the guards are in place, everything is appropriately adjusted, and parts are aligned correctly. This may require running the machine for a second before placing your material inside.

Always use the right tool for the job. Screwdrivers should not be used as chisels, because the metal is tempered differently, and the tip of a screwdriver can chip or shatter when struck like a chisel. Likewise, a chisel should not be used as a pry bar, because it was not made to withstand forces in that direction and pieces can snap off. These are just two examples of how tools used incorrectly can either damage them or cause you personal harm.

You should never carry a power tool by its cord, or pull it by its cord to unplug it. If you notice the cord breaking or peeling away to reveal the wires inside, you should repair or replace the cord before using it again.

Machines should be unplugged when you are servicing them and when you are changing bits or blades or otherwise setting them up. It is also a good idea to keep them unplugged when you are not using them, so you cannot accidentally turn them on by hitting the power switch.

As with firearms, do not carry portable power tools with your finger on the trigger. Keep it away from the power switch until you are ready to turn on the tool.

For many tools, even hand tools, where the material remains stationary, it is safer to secure the material with clamps, a vise, or to a table. For some tasks, such as cross-cutting a board with a handsaw, you can safely secure the board with just your body. For tasks with more aggressive tools, your hands are not strong enough; if the tool or machine grabs a hold of the material and starts rapidly moving or spinning it, your hand will go along for the ride.

Chemicals and Hazardous Substances

A hazardous substance is any substance that is a physical or health hazard. Physical hazards include chemicals that are explosive, flammable, combustible, compressed, or otherwise unstable or potentially reactive. Health hazards are chemicals in which a study has shown significant evidence of

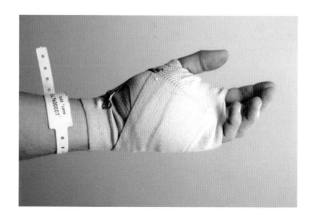

Figure 3-8: Even a tool as innocuous as a cordless drill can send you to the emergency room. This happened because I was in a hurry and became momentarily careless. The drill slipped off the screw, and since I was pushing on it pretty hard, I pushed the bit directly into my other hand, which was holding the two pieces of wood together.

acute or chronic health effects in people exposed to that chemical. These chemicals can be carcinogens, toxins, irritants, corrosives, reproductive hazards, and more. While nearly every product and material we use in a props shop contains at least one hazardous chemical, the important thing to know is how these chemicals can enter our body, how much exposure our bodies can handle, and how to prevent or limit our exposure while using them (*note*: carcinogens have **no** known safe exposure limit). A props shop that follows the correct safety procedures for working with something like fiberglass and resin is less dangerous than a hobbyist who follows none while doing something as innocuous as sanding wood.

Chemicals can affect us in a number of ways. They can have both acute and chronic affects. They can be poisonous on the spot, or they can build up in our body over time. They can have mutagenic effects, causing either cancer or reproductive problems. They can be sensitizers, leading to allergic reactions after enough exposure; in some cases, you can work with a

One of the sensitizers we come into a lot of contact with in the props shop is found in many of the "two-part" resins and foams we use. Materials such as epoxy putty, epoxy glue, auto body filler, fiberglass resin, urethane foam, and casting resin are all sensitizers (the sensitizer is actually in the hardening or curing agent, which is why it is present in so many seemingly unrelated materials). For most people, they will not be affected the first time they use these products; it is after subsequent uses that one can develop a reaction. Some artisans have even used these products for decades without ill effects before suddenly becoming allergic. The reactions can be pretty disturbing: hives all over the skin, open and oozing sores, and even anaphylactic shock in some cases. Once developed, it is irreversible. I have heard of artisans who make their living with their sculpting, molding, and casting skills, but when they become sensitized, they can no longer work with any urethanes, epoxies, polyester resins, fiberglass, spray foam, etc. without a full chemical suit and supplied air respirator. That puts quite a damper on earning a paycheck.

On a personal note, my technical editor, Sandra Strawn, had this happen. After thirty years of working in props, she developed severe allergies to products used in the shop. She had to go on medication, wear a supplied air respirator while teaching and have extensive cleanup of all toxins and allergens in her shop. These tales are not imaginary horror stories, but real consequences of ignoring the inherent hazards of many of the materials we work with in the props shop.

specific chemical for decades without any ill effects, and then overnight develop severe and life-threatening allergies to it with every new exposure. Finally, a chemical may be an irritant, which means it causes temporary discomfort, such as redness or itchiness, upon exposure but disappears once the chemical is removed (though it can be a few hours after the last exposure for the symptoms to fully dissipate). Most irritants will lead to sensitization or more permanent harm with repeated exposure though.

The Chemical Abstracts Service (CAS) maintains a database of every chemical used commercially. As I write this sentence, they have over 67,509,000 chemicals registered. By the time you read this, who knows what that number may be, as they add about 15 every minute. California Proposition 65 is a regulation for the State of California that requires products sold in California to list whether they contain any chemicals known to cause either cancer or developmental problems which is currently around 860 chemicals (this number is certainly higher as some of the chemicals listed are actually categories consisting of multiple CAS numbers). Only about 900 chemicals are believed to have been tested for cancer worldwide.

Perhaps the easiest and most effective step you can take is to always use the **least toxic alternative**. Sure, methyl ethyl ketone will clean paint off of a surface in record time, but it will also clean the brain out of your skull while doing it. Scrubbing the paint with soap and water may take some more elbow grease, but you will not lose the ability to reproduce while doing it. If you do your research, you can almost always find a safer material or substance to work with.

Remember though, safe is not enough; it must also do the job. It is worthless to switch to a "safer" alternative if you have to compromise too many of your prop's needs. It is worth it to invest in the necessary safety infrastructure if a more hazardous product is the only option to get the job done. The key is to (1) know what the harms are and (2) how to minimize them.

It is practically useless to determine what safety infrastructure you need or how toxic different products are in comparison to each other until you know exactly what substances you are working with. For that, you need to know about Material Safety Data Sheets and how to read them.

MSDS

Reading and understanding Material Safety Data Sheet (MSDS) can take a whole book to explain. The most basic definition is that an MSDS will list the manufacturer of a particular product and what chemicals are contained in it. They are also required to list necessary information about the chemicals, such as their toxicity, how much exposure is considered "safe," how they affect you, how you can safely use the product, and what to do in an emergency. You can find much more comprehensive information from your local department of labor, the American Lung Association, or from Arts, Crafts, and Theater Safety (ACTS). Good technical theatre training programs will also educate young artisans in using an MSDS, as will many of the entertainment unions.

Shops are required to maintain a binder accessible to any employee with an MSDS for *every* product they use. A manufacturer is required to send you an MSDS for their product when contacted. Many will put the MSDS on their websites, while a few even package them with the product itself.

Disposing of chemicals depends on your local regulations and what kind of sewage system you are on, as well as what chemicals you are disposing and what the label or MSDS suggests to do. Generally, you should never dump oils, solvents, or toxic chemicals down a drain. You should also avoid dumping liquid materials that will harden, such as plaster or uncured epoxy, as these can solidify inside the pipes and block the plumbing.

Other countries have similar sheets identifying the chemicals in a product and their potential hazards. The United States, Canada, and Australia all refer to these data sheets as an MSDS. In the United Kingdom, they are known as a Control of Substances Hazardous to Health (COSHH) data sheet. The European Union calls them safety data sheets (SDS).

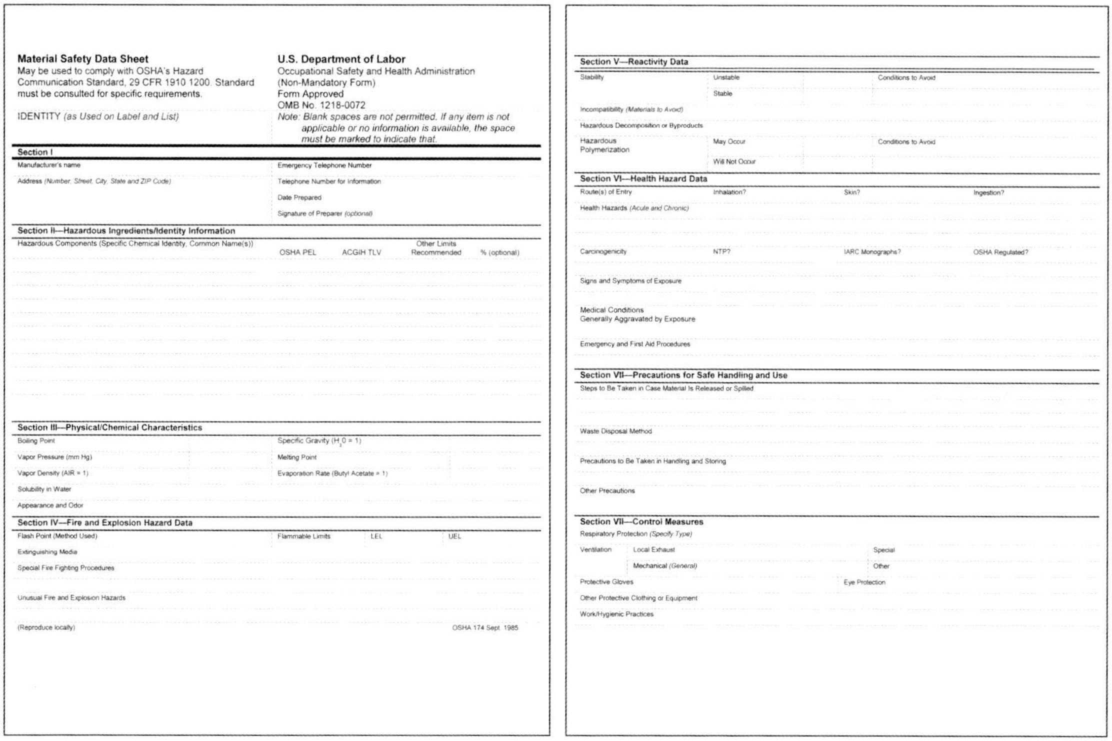

Material Safety Data Sheet
May be used to comply with OSHA's Hazard
Communication Standard, 29 CFR 1910.1200. Standard
must be consulted for specific requirements.

IDENTITY (as Used on Label and List)

U.S. Department of Labor
Occupational Safety and Health Administration
(Non-Mandatory Form)
Form Approved
OMB No. 1218-0072
Note: Blank spaces are not permitted. If any item is not
applicable or no information is available, the space
must be marked to indicate that.

Section I
Manufacturer's name
Emergency Telephone Number
Address (Number, Street, City, State and ZIP Code)
Telephone Number for Information
Date Prepared
Signature of Preparer (optional)

Section II—Hazardous Ingredients/Identity Information
Hazardous Components (Specific Chemical Identity, Common Name(s))   OSHA PEL   ACGIH TLV   Other Limits Recommended   % (optional)

Section III—Physical/Chemical Characteristics
Boiling Point   Specific Gravity (H₂O = 1)
Vapor Pressure (mm Hg)   Melting Point
Vapor Density (AIR = 1)   Evaporation Rate (Butyl Acetate = 1)
Solubility in Water
Appearance and Odor

Section IV—Fire and Explosion Hazard Data
Flash Point (Method Used)   Flammable Limits   LEL   UEL
Extinguishing Media
Special Fire Fighting Procedures
Unusual Fire and Explosion Hazards

(Reproduce locally)   OSHA 174 Sept. 1985

Section V—Reactivity Data
Stability   Unstable   Conditions to Avoid
Stable
Incompatibility (Materials to Avoid)
Hazardous Decomposition or Byproducts
Hazardous Polymerization   May Occur   Conditions to Avoid
Will Not Occur

Section VI—Health Hazard Data
Route(s) of Entry   Inhalation?   Skin?   Ingestion?
Health Hazards (Acute and Chronic)
Carcinogenicity   NTP?   IARC Monographs?   OSHA Regulated?
Signs and Symptoms of Exposure
Medical Conditions Generally Aggravated by Exposure
Emergency and First Aid Procedures

Section VII—Precautions for Safe Handling and Use
Steps to Be Taken in Case Material Is Released or Spilled
Waste Disposal Method
Precautions to Be Taken in Handling and Storing
Other Precautions

Section VII—Control Measures
Respiratory Protection (Specify Type)
Ventilation   Local Exhaust   Special
Mechanical (General)   Other
Protective Gloves   Eye Protection
Other Protective Clothing or Equipment
Work/Hygienic Practices

Figure 3-9: Though an MSDS does not have to follow any specific format, many will be based on the blank sheet provided by OSHA. Adapted from OSHA Form 174.

Labeling

All products you use must be correctly labeled in their containers to identify the name, brand, and manufacturer of the product, along with relevant health and safety information. The label may also tell you exactly what the product does and what it is intended for. Instructions for how to use it may also be listed, including how long it takes to dry or cure, how soon it can be painted or sanded, and what other products it may be compatible or incompatible with. Always read the label before using a product.

OSHA regulations have specific requirements for what needs to be on the labels of products used in a professional shop; the labels that are already on the products' containers are usually sufficient, as long as they do not become obscured with paint or other goop, or wear off and peel away. Unless you fully understand these OSHA regulations, you should not be transferring products to another container with a homemade label. The regulations do allow you to transfer materials to a temporary, unlabeled container for use while you are at work, but if you keep it in there once you are done with the day (or however long your shift is), it becomes a violation.

Even if you work on your own, this is a good practice to follow. You may think you can keep track of everything, but you quickly amass a collection of "mystery containers." The label is there to give you accurate information about what is inside, and to guide you to the correct MSDS for the product for further information. If you do not know what is in a container, you cannot dispose of it properly, because your local regulations have special requirements for disposal of many chemicals. If you get sick while working and need to call your poison control center, you will not be able to tell them what you have ingested if the container has no label. Finally, if there is an emergency spill or fire, the fire department or HazMat team will not know what chemicals they are potentially dealing with.

Reading and deciphering what is actually on a label can be tricky, especially when you consider how companies use marketing to make their products seem safer and more attractive than they probably are. A label that says "for industrial or professional use only" implies that one should know how to find the correct MSDS and refer to it for more information. Some consumer products may also have an MSDS available, but others will only list pertinent information on the label itself. While a label must be explicit about whether it contains harmful or hazardous chemicals, if you remember from our discussion about chemicals a few pages back, we have only tested around 900 of the 65,000,000 chemicals in commercial use for cancerous properties. Keep in mind too that testing for cancerous or developmental problems is a highly flawed process; it is difficult and expensive to test for problems resulting from really long-term exposure, like after decades of use. It can also be difficult to prove that a specific substance actually causes cancer; even if scientists have a lot of correlative evidence of cancer after exposure, until they can prove that it actually *causes* it, a label will not have to list that.

The word *natural* on a label is essentially meaningless. Lead, mercury, snake venom, and cyanide are all "natural" substances, but they are harmful to your health, and can be harmful to the environment if you concentrate them and dump them all down the drain at once.

The term *nontoxic* on a label covers only acute toxins. Any chemicals with chronic effects, such as carcinogens, birth defects, sensitizers, or other cumulative effects can be labeled nontoxic. In addition, chemicals whose hazards are unknown or untested can also be labeled nontoxic.

Figure 3-10: Found while cleaning out an old props shop. Clearly not a helpful label.

Chemical-Resistant Gloves

Some chemicals can affect and irritate your skin, while others can be absorbed through your skin straight into your body. Your hands are one of the primary points of contact as they are on the front lines of touching things. You can buy disposable gloves in a vast assortment of materials, thicknesses, and styles. Different kinds of gloves keep out different kinds of chemicals, so choose one based on what you are working with.

The most common chemicals that absorb through the skin are solvents, and many products we use in props contain solvents: paint (even water-based paint), adhesives, cleaners, etc. Resins, such as epoxy, urethane, or polyester, can also absorb through the skin, as well as lead to sensitization on the skin itself.

Common glove materials for props shops include nitrile (a synthetic rubber), neoprene, and vinyl. Some glove manufacturers make gloves out of propriety materials, while others make gloves with multiple layers of different materials. Latex gloves do not stop any chemicals, and even help some chemicals absorb into your skin faster. Many people develop a latex allergy over time with their use, so you really should keep them out of your shop entirely (except for the few emergency pairs kept in your first aid kit).

Glove manufacturers publish **permeation data charts** showing how long (in minutes) the glove will hold up to being exposed to certain chemicals. Some chemicals will pass right through gloves made of some materials, some chemicals will be stalled for a few minutes, and some will be stopped for a full 8 hours without getting through. Choose the glove that will hold up the longest. It is important to get the permeation chart from the glove manufacturer for the specific gloves you buy as they can differ slightly from similar gloves from another company. There is no single glove you can buy for all chemicals; a nitrile glove may do a great job stopping a chemical in Product A but not in Product B, while a neoprene glove may stop the chemical in Product B but not in Product A. If you hang your permeation data charts near where you keep your gloves, it will make it that much easier to choose the correct kind for the project at hand.

Do not reuse disposable gloves. A glove can work for, at the most, eight hours of use. For many chemicals, you cannot visually see when the glove breaks down and no longer prohibits

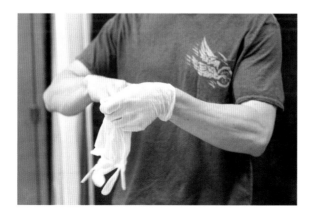

Figure 3-11: Putting on a pair of chemical-resistant disposable gloves.

that chemical from passing through to your skin, so even gloves that still "look good" may no longer provide a suitable barrier.

Check your gloves before putting them on for tears or holes. Do not share gloves with others. You should still wash your hands after you take your gloves off.

Sleeves and Clothes

Your hands are not the only area where you can absorb chemicals. It would be silly to wear gloves while mixing epoxy only to splash it all over your bare arms. If you are using a substance that splashes or spills on your bare arms past your gloves, then your gloves are fairly useless. You can use longer gloves or buy "sleeves" that offer the same kinds of protection against chemicals as gloves do. In certain situations, you may even need an entire protective suit. Sleeves, jackets, and suits that offer chemical protection also provide permeation data charts on how long they can resist various chemicals.

A face shield will keep substances off your face if that is a concern. Chemical splash goggles can be worn to protect your eyes as well.

Even if you are sanding something that has supposedly dried, the dust can still damage or at least irritate your skin if it comes into contact with it.

Respirators

To keep your lungs clean, you must be aware of what chemicals you are dealing with. No single type of respirator will protect against all chemicals or other airborne hazards. A "dust mask" is considered a type of respirator, albeit a disposable one, and is used for keeping particulates, not chemicals, out of your lungs. A true dust mask will list the NIOSH rating for the particulates it stops. Unrated masks, such as so-called "pollen" or "paint" masks, are *completely useless*. If you are dealing with chemicals that give off vapors, you will need a chemical respirator. It is possible to buy cartridges that will filter both particulates and certain chemicals. Again, check the specific ingredients in the MSDS for what you are using to be sure you are using the correct respirator; never take a guess on which one to use.

Not everyone can wear a respirator. Masks do not fit everyone, and some respiratory or heart problems can be made worse because wearing a mask causes extra breathing stress. If your eardrums have been punctured, toxins can enter your lungs through your ears even while wearing a mask. In US workplaces that fall under OSHA guidelines, respirators cannot be worn until the employee is medically certified (usually by an occupational physician), fit-tested, and trained in the use of a respirator. This includes disposable "dust mask" type respirators.

OSHA will also not permit the use of respirators when facial hair or stubble crosses the seal. Employers can actually require employees to shave their beards, or they must keep them from working on tasks that require respirators (which include disposable dust masks).

Different Types of Respirators

Particulate masks (dust masks) are also known as mechanical filter respirators because they work by physically preventing particles from passing while allowing air and gasses through. NIOSH ratings of such masks consist of a letter followed by a number. The letter indicates "oil resistance." The number indicates how many airborne particles are filtered.

Oil Resistance	
N	Not oil-resistant
R	oil-resistant
P	oil-proof

Percentage of particles filtered	
95	Filters at least 95% of airborne particles
99	Filters at least 99% of airborne particles
100	Filters at least 99.97% of airborne particles

N95 is the cheapest and most common type of respirator and sufficient for protection when sanding wood and lumber products, handling powders, and similar dusty tasks with particulates that do not contain oils. N95 masks are usually sufficient for welding as well, as the fumes are actually particulates, but some specialty N95 masks exist for welding that include a carbon filter to catch nuisance vapors from ozone and stray contaminants that burn off. R or P respirators are needed when the particulates contain oil, such as when you are machining metal with cutting oils or spraying WD40. A P100 respirator is also known as a "HEPA" filter and traps the most particulates. There is no harm in using a higher-class respirator than what you need; just be aware that a P100 can be almost 15 times as expensive as an N95 mask, which can add up when you have to use a new one every day.

Some disposable respirators come with valves on the front that are designed to keep you cooler when wearing a mask for long periods of time in hot and dusty environments.

If you are dealing with anything that produces harmful gasses or vapors, you will need a mask with a chemical cartridge (gas is the same size as the air you breathe, so you cannot just physically block it). The most common type of chemical respirator is a half-face mask. The mask itself is reusable, while the cartridges are replaceable. Many types of cartridges exist, and it is important to refer to your MSDS and labels to see exactly what kinds of chemicals you are working with, as no single cartridge blocks all types of chemicals. The most common cartridge used in props is an organic vapors cartridge, which offers respiratory protection against many solvents. Working with formaldehyde requires a different type of cartridge, as does working with ammonia. A chemical cartridge does *not* protect against particulates. If you are dealing with both chemicals and dust, you will need to get a combination particulate/chemical cartridge, or attach a particulate "pre-filter" over the chemical cartridge.

A particulate respirator gets filled up and clogged with particulates over time, and should be replaced when it gets hard to breathe. A chemical respirator gets "saturated" over time until it no longer stops the chemicals it was meant to stop; you will not notice any change in your ability to breathe when it becomes ineffective. It is imperative to keep track of how long you use your chemical respirator—most are only good for 8 continuous hours—and to store it in an airtight container or bag when not in use. A heavy-duty Ziploc bag works well.

A full mask respirator is necessary if the fumes can irritate your skin or eyes, or if there is the risk of splashing. For some tasks, you may need a powered respirator, which uses a motorized fan to force air from a clean source to your face. Air-supplied respirators bring fresh air in from a tank or compressor. These are normally used in props shops when dealing with chemicals no cartridge or filter can stop, such as isocyanates from foaming or casting polyurethanes (urethane resin), or methyl ethyl ketone peroxide used as a hardener in many resins, especially polyester.

A respirator is your last line of defense against chemicals in the air. Through extraction at the source and ventilation, it can sometimes be possible to keep exposure below toxic limits. For especially toxic tasks, like casting urethanes or other resins, you can use a chemical hood or fume box that completely separates you and your air from the chemicals. Remember to always use the least toxic material that will do the job satisfactorily; you may find you are using harmful substances that offer no advantages over less harmful solutions.

Lifting and Carrying

When you lift, carry, or otherwise manipulate heavy items and materials, you put yourself at risk of injury if you do not move your body correctly. Once you injure a muscle, you will only exacerbate the injury if you continue lifting and carrying things incorrectly. It is important to lift and carry things correctly and to know your physical limitations so you do not exceed them.

Lift with your legs, not your back. Carry items as close to your center of gravity as possible. This is not a contest; if something is heavy or awkward to lift and carry, wait for someone to help you. It is the eager amateur who strains his muscles trying

to impress the boss by carrying things heavier than he can handle and moving faster than he should. The pro knows that today is only one day out of many where she will need to lift and carry things; if she wears herself out today, she won't be able to carry things tomorrow, or the next day, and eventually, she will destroy her body to the point where carrying anything will be limited.

Prop makers should understand they have chosen a career that involves lifting and carrying heavy or awkward materials and objects. Many workplaces specifically require employees who can carry a certain amount of weight (anywhere from 50 to 75 pounds is typical). It is a good idea to develop your upper body strength and a strong core and to work on your physical stamina if you intend to do this for a living. Stretching and doing warm ups before the day begins can be beneficial as well.

You will also want to pay attention to how you build your props so they are easy to lift and carry by the people bringing the prop to the theatre or film set, the stage hands and crew who have to move it around, and the actors who may have to manipulate it. This may mean putting handholds or handles on particularly heavy props, or even providing a cart or case to carry it around in. If you have trouble lifting and moving it in the shop, then everyone else who moves it will have trouble as well, so do everyone a favor and create a solution before anyone asks.

Another potential hazard to check for before handing your props off is whether they have any sharp edges, corners, or other protrusions that may cut or injure an actor or crew member. Run your hands and fingers all over the prop, particularly where it will most likely be handled.

Repetitive Posture and Strain

Over 1.8 million US workers a year report musculoskeletal disorders such as carpal tunnel syndrome and back injuries, with 600,000 of these resulting in time off from work. Prop makers are not immune to these. Even though we switch tasks frequently, we can still end up in stooping postures or other unnatural positions for several hours at a time.

If you are setting up to do a task for a few hours, pay attention to the ergonomics of your setup. Standing all day on hard concrete can be especially tiring; soft mats placed underneath your feet help immensely. Sitting all day can be exhausting as well; really, it is the amount of time spent in a position rather than the position itself that can lead to exhaustion. Be sure to switch positions frequently, or at least take breaks where you can stretch your muscles in opposition to how they have been situated. You should have a seat or stool that allows your feet to rest on the floor; your table should also be at a height that allows you to work comfortably. Seats and chairs with adjustable heights are extremely useful in allowing you to adapt your position to the task at hand.

The floors of many props shops are either concrete or something similarly hard and unforgiving. It is worth it to lay down a cushion or mat to stand on if you stand for long periods of time.

Many companies and workplaces have settled on a ten or fifteen minute break every two hours, with an hour meal break every four hours; even if you set your own hours, this is a good schedule to stick with to keep from tiring your muscles out.

Fire Safety

Make sure your shop has an appropriate number of working fire extinguishers in easily accessible areas. Again, a professional shop will have actual regulations as to the number, type, and location of fire extinguishers. Though different countries have slightly different classifications for fires, most separate them into categories such as ordinary combustibles, flammable liquid and gas, electrical, and combustible metals. Fire extinguishers use different extinguishing mediums. Common ones include water, dry chemical, and carbon dioxide (CO_2). Some of these mediums are preferred for certain

In the United States, types of fires are classified according to the following letters:

- A—Ordinary combustibles, such as wood, paper, cardboard, and many plastics
- B—Flammable or combustible liquids, like solvents, kerosene, and alcohol.
- C—Fires involving electrical equipment.
- D—Combustible metals, such as magnesium, titanium, potassium, and sodium.
- K—Found in restaurants and food preparation, these are fires that involve cooking oils, trans-fats, or fats in cooking appliances.

Common types of fire extinguishers include

- Water. This can only put out class A fires. It will only serve to spread class B and K fires to a larger area, and it can excite a class D fire and make it worse. Using it on a class C fire can electrocute you or anything in the vicinity.
- Dry chemical. These may be used to put out different kinds of fires, with common combinations including BC and ABC types of extinguishers.
- Dry powder. The most common type used for extinguishing class D fires. Class D fires cannot be put out with multipurpose fire extinguishers, and fire extinguishers for class D fires often cannot be used for other classes.
- CO_2. Useful for class B and C fires. They do not really work well on class A fires, which could reignite even after this extinguisher is used. Their advantage is that they do not leave any residue like dry chemical extinguishers, so they are useful for extinguishing electrical fires on or near expensive and sensitive electronic equipment.

classifications of fire, while some can actually make certain kinds of fires worse. For instance, you do not want to use a water fire extinguisher to put out an electrical fire, as you will electrocute yourself. Choosing the right type (or types) of fire extinguisher involves consideration of what kinds of fires you can potentially cause in your shop. A combustible metal fire is probably rare to find in a props shop; perhaps you may be building something from magnesium, but even that is an exceedingly specialized material. More likely, a props shop will see fires started by ordinary combustibles (wood, paper, fabric, etc), flammable liquids (alcohol, solvents), flammable gas (propane, butane, oxy-acetylene), and electrical. You can find certain types of fire extinguishers that can deal with all three of these fire classifications.

Welding can be a particularly potent source of potential fires in a shop. Grinding metal and other processes that create hot sparks are other potential sources. Welding should always be done away from any sort of combustible material; in the United States, OSHA regulations actually state welding must be done 35 feet from any combustible material. Whenever dealing with a process like welding that generates a lot of heat, it is a good idea to watch the area for a half an hour or so; errant sparks can find their way to a small, hidden pile of sawdust and smolder for several minutes before they generate enough energy to catch fire. You don't want to finish your day with a welding project and leave the shop immediately afterward; you could come back in the morning to find your whole shop has burned to the ground.

Since grinding or cutting metal with abrasives can also create sparks, you do not want to connect these tools to your dust collection system. Dust collectors are filled with large volumes of moving air saturated with highly combustible sawdust. If you have ever heard of a grain silo explosion, you can imagine what would happen if you introduced hot sparks into this explosive atmosphere.

Any flammable liquid should be stored in a flammables cabinet that is kept away from ignition sources and exits. A product's label will say if it is "flammable," "inflammable" (which, for some reason, means flammable), or "combustible"; the MSDS will also have information about its flammability. If more than one person is working in the shop at a time, make sure one person is not working with flammable chemicals while another is working with an ignition source.

Most shops require a three-foot-wide (or greater) passageway to be kept clear at all times to get out of a room. You should also keep clear areas around fire extinguishers, electrical breaker boxes, first aid kits, and emergency eye wash stations. Props shops can run short of space particularly when you are under a heavy time crunch, but do not use that as an excuse to stack things you do not need in the middle of the floor where it will block you from exiting should a fire break out. Leaning long items up against a wall, or piling unsecured items on top of each other can cause them to topple or fall on you. Keeping fire egress paths clear is doubly important when your props shop is part of the same building as a theatre or studio that an audience and performers will use.

Depending on the local regulations of your municipality, any time your props will be used in a space shared by an audience, your props may need to be fireproof (aka flame proof), fire resistant, or flame retardant. Though the definitions differ depending on your local regulations, fire resistant typically means the material discourages the spread of flames, flame retardant means it will slow the spread of flames, while fireproof means the material will literally not burn. Of course, these definitions depend on the intensity and duration of a material's exposure to flame; even steel will eventually succumb to fire. Again, the specifics depend on your local jurisdiction; the rules differ wildly from town to town, and even within different buildings and situations within the same town or city. Determining whether your prop needs a certain level of flame proofing or resistance is something that should be known before the build begins as it can affect what types of materials or techniques you use. Some materials are easier to flameproof than others, while some are inherently flame retardant. For other materials, there are a number of paints or coatings you can add on top that will flameproof them.

Finally, some materials can never be adequately or satisfactorily flame proofed; you do not want to finish building a complicated and expensive prop only for the fire marshal to tell you it needs to be completely replaced or removed before the production can pass the fire inspection. Find out the rules and plan ahead accordingly.

Conclusion

When it comes to health and safety, remember this: Your goal in life is not to finish a single prop; your goal is to build props for the rest of your life. Taking shortcuts now will affect your health later on, making it more difficult or even impossible to use all the skills and techniques you learn. No prop in the existence of humankind has ever been more important than your health, so take care.

four

shop space

Figures 4-1 to 4-3: Three different types of facilities show some of the variety props shops can take. The first is the basement of Urban Stages, an off-off Broadway theatre in New York City. The second shows the combination scenery/props shop at Monomoy Theatre, a summer stock in Massachusetts. The third is the shop at University of North Carolina School of the Arts.

How you set up your props shop will have a great effect on how quickly, efficiently, and safely you will build your props. Kitchens are set up to take care of the "work triangle," that is, the three stations used most: food storage, preparation and cooking area, and cleanup; more bluntly, the refrigerator, stove, and sink. Setting up a props shop can take advantage of a similar line of thinking. You have your carpentry section, your welding section, your soft goods, your paper props/layout/drawing, your molding and casting, etc. Some work triangle examples include jointer/planer/saw and tool storage/workbench/assembly.

Keep dedicated stations for core processes and transformable stations for other tasks. Keep in mind that setting up a professional shop is different from setting up a home hobby shop; if you work for a company or have employees working in the shop, you will have to adhere to rules, regulations, and laws (depending on where you live) pertaining to ventilation, lighting, electrical power, fire extinguishers, sprinklers, signage, and more.

The general need for proper ventilation in a shop includes extraction systems at the source of all dust and fume creation; this means dust collection hooked up to the woodworking machines and fume extractors near welders and soldering stations. Spray booths and fume hoods are useful when working with paints, casting materials, and other substances that off-gas toxins when in use. A shop also needs to ensure general extraction of the dirty air. Dirty air should not be exhausted where it can reenter the shop. Ventilation also requires the constant introduction of fresh air into the shop; this can be as simple as an open window, though in most cases it involves fresh air from outside being sucked in and blown through pipes and vents around the shop. The shop should be set up so that the fresh and clean air moves from the person to the material and then to the exhaust; it is no good if the fresh air picks up the toxins and dust first and then reaches the person. Many shops have electric fans of various sizes that can be positioned to move air around depending on the task at hand. Once again, a professional shop has to adhere to applicable rules and regulations guiding the setup of ventilation and exhaust systems, and often requires a trained professional to set up and test the actual system. My words here are meant simply to remind professional shops to double-check whether their ventilation system is up to snuff.

You can find air filtration units that hang from the ceiling of a shop. These can be good in some cases for cutting down on dust in the air, but be aware they are not a substitute for ventilation; they neither introduce clean air to the room nor do they exhaust dirty air. They simply clear some of the dust out in between intake and exhaust. They also do not remove gases and fumes, just dust and particulates.

Pay attention to the floor. In some areas, you want a clean and smooth floor, such as a waxed tile floor, so you can keep static electricity from building up and to make cleaning easier. These same floors are inadvisable in carpentry and other dusty areas, where a thin layer of sawdust can turn the floor into a slippery nightmare. Concrete floors can be a killer after a full day of working on your feet. Padding and floor mats, even just a small mat directly under your feet, can keep chronic pain and fatigue in your legs from developing. Mats can also keep you dry in areas used for dyeing and other wet processes.

Poor lighting can cause eye fatigue, as well as create dangerous situations where you cannot see potential hazards. A good props shop will have adequate overhead lighting as well as area lighting that can be turned on or positioned over specific work areas. Some machines benefit by having their own dedicated lights mounted directly on them so you can illuminate the material as it comes into contact with the cutter.

You need a table to work on. A table allows you to work while standing up, which makes it easier to use tools and keeps you from working with your back bent all day. A table also gives you a surface to clamp materials or attach tools to. Your table needs to be sturdy so it does not collapse under the weight of your props, and so it can withstand any sort of pounding, striking, bending, or other forces you subject your materials to while working with them; it is no use having a sturdy bench vise to hold steel while you bend it if the whole table will move before the steel will bend.

A typical prop work table is built with sturdy 2" × 4" lumber (or larger). The top is a sheet of 4' × 8' material either left whole or cut down for a smaller shop. Plywood makes a sturdy top, while hardboard makes a smooth and clean surface; many prop makers will put a sheet of hardboard on top of plywood for their table to take advantage of both properties. This also makes it easy to replace the hardboard when it has suffered too much wear and tear to continue being useful.

Putting the table on wheels is helpful in smaller shops where you need to move things around to create space for different projects, but a way to lock the table in position is essential for many projects. Whether or not the table is on wheels, it is often helpful to have the table set away from the wall so you can work from all sides.

Underneath the table is a useful storage area, though what you choose to store up there varies greatly between prop makers and props shops. Some use it to store longer materials that do not fit elsewhere. In shops where each prop maker has a personal table, personal tools are often kept under it. Projects in process may also be kept there during the build of a show, along with drawings and notes.

Temporary tables can be made with sawhorses and sheet goods or lengths of lumber. Temporary tables are useful when a large project needs to sit for a few hours or overnight for glue, paint, coatings, or some other substance to dry. Keeping it on a separate temporary table allows you to continue working on other projects on your real table.

Props shops benefit from separating processes and creating distinct areas for certain materials and processes. Many theatrical props shops will have a "dirty room" and a "clean room." The dirty room is where dust-generating tasks take place, such as woodworking and sanding. The clean room is where jobs such as working with soft goods, gluing, and sculpting with clay happen.

Painting may also happen in the clean room to keep dust from getting on the surface before it dries, though spray painting and other tasks that release fumes and toxins will happen in their own distinct areas, such as a spray booth. A paint area needs its own sink for cleaning paint; this is often called a **slop sink** because it drains through a different system that does not lead back to the municipal water system or sewage system. Molding, casting, and sculpture often requires a slop sink as well. A props shop will often need another sink for other tasks, such as food preparation, cleaning old props from storage, and other "household" tasks. It is unsanitary to use the same sink for all the different tasks a props shop does.

Paper projects, drafting, and computer work may also happen in the clean room, though many props shops have a third room where computer equipment can be sequestered; this may be in the props shop office, where reference books, props bibles, and other important office paperwork and paraphernalia are kept.

Metalwork may have its own separate area as well, if space allows. OSHA actually requires any area where welding and grinding of metal are done to be a distinct room with separate ventilation from carpentry and other flammable dust-creating areas, or for it to be 35 feet from said areas. Many props shops will share the metal-working area that the scenery shop uses, since their own carpentry shop is typically too small to carve out a distinct area for metal. Metal working can also require larger and more expensive machines to work with, and by sharing spaces, the two shops do not have to buy the same machines.

Fire extinguishers should be located near ignition sources and at regular intervals around the shop, and should be easily accessible. First aid kits containing bandages, gauze, disinfectant, and other supplies should also be accessible. Eye wash stations and deluge showers around the shop will also come in handy (and are required in professional shops). The accessibility of items such as fire extinguishers, first aid kits, eye wash stations, as well as fire alarms, breaker boxes, and emergency cut-off switches cannot be overemphasized; they do no good if you stack material over them or store tools in front of them, even if it is "just this once."

Clamps and Clamping

Clamps are needed to hold materials together while joining them or while glue is drying between two pieces. They are also useful for securing materials to a work surface to ameliorate working on them. Finally, they can occasionally be employed to pull apart or push together materials that are too rigid to manipulate with hands alone.

Pipe clamps have two jaws on a pipe, one fixed at one end and the other free to move. Many pipe clamp jaws can fit standard sizes of pipes, giving you the flexibility to use any length of pipe you can get your hands on. **Bar clamps** are similar, but the jaws are on a bar; this keeps them from freely rotating, as the jaws can do on a pipe. Most pipe and bar clamps allow you to roughly position the jaws by sliding them, then applying more pressure with a screw vise attached to one of the jaws.

A **C clamp** (sometimes called a G clamp in certain geographic areas) is a single C-shaped piece of metal with a screw vise on one end.

Alligator clips and **spring clamps** open by squeezing the two handles together. A spring keeps them closed when they are not being squeezed. They act similarly to clothespins (which can also make useful clamps).

A **wood handscrew clamp** involves two thick pieces of wood held together with two large screws. Manipulating two

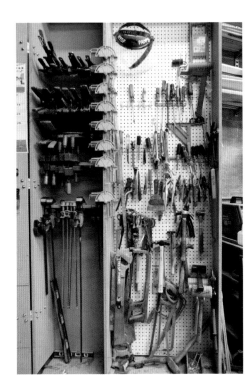

Figure 4-4: You can see clamp storage along the left side of this tool cabinet. The first three rows have a variety of alligator or spring clamps. The fourth row down has some Jorgensen clamps. The bottom row is a mix of blue quick clamps and orange bar clamps.

Figure 4-5: Bar clamps.

Figure 4-6: A C Clamp.

Figure 4-7: Clothespins are useful clamps for smaller or more delicate materials.

screws allows you to keep the two pieces of wood parallel, so you can use these clamps to place an even amount of clamping pressure over a large area. These are often called **Jorgensen clamps**; Jorgensen is one of the most popular manufacturers of wood handscrew clamps. However, Jorgensen makes other kinds of clamps as well, and other companies make their own wood handscrew clamps.

Quick clamps are similar in appearance to bar clamps. Rather than a screw vise to tighten them once in position, they have a trigger that you can squeeze to ratchet it slightly tighter.

Difficult-to-clamp areas can sometimes be held together by wrapping rope or string tightly around the pieces. If possible, you can insert a stick or garrote through the string; as you rotate the stick, the rope is pulled together even more tightly.

Holding your work is important as well. You may need to keep your material steady while retaining both hands to operate your tools. Or you may need your prop held in a specific

Figure 4-9: When working on this severed head, I mounted the skull on a wooden pole so that I could paint any side—even the bottom—without having to touch it and disturb the wet paint. *The Bacchae*, the Public Theater, 2009. Scenic design by John Conklin.

position to keep liquid and viscous materials from dripping or spilling off, or so you can quickly access all sides of it without having to touch it.

Machines, Power Tools, and Hand Tools

It is helpful to distinguish between "tools" and "machines." A tool is brought over to the material you are working on, while you bring the material to a machine. Many modern machines are powered through electricity, though not all; a metal bending brake is mounted to a bench or sits on the floor, yet it is powered by hand.

Tools are further divided into hand tools and power tools. Power tools frequently refer to those powered by electricity; tools that are driven pneumatically are often called "pneumatic tools"; these may be connected by an air hose to a large air tank and compressor, or they may have a small

Figure 4-8: A **strap clamp** (or just a regular ratchet strap) is useful when you wish to apply equal pressure around a circumference. Photograph by Anna Warren.

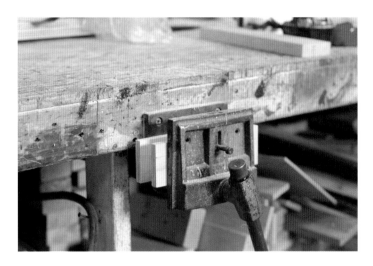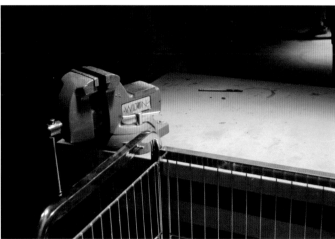

Figures 4-10 and 4-11: A **bench vise** is a type of clamp mounted to a work table meant for securely holding material as you work on it. Two main types of bench vises are the woodworker's vise (left), which is attached to the side of a work bench, and an engineer's vise (right), mounted to the top of a table. Notice how the woodworker's vise in the photograph above has two scrap pieces of wood inside; these are used to protect softer materials from being marred by the metal jaws.

compressor built in that is powered by electricity. Electrically powered tools may either be corded, which are plugged into a wall outlet, or cordless, in which case a portable battery provides their power.

A **machine tool** is a powered tool or machine that guides or constrains the cutting edge in some way. On a drill press, for instance, you clamp the material to the table and turn a wheel to move the drill up and down. The material remains in place, and the drill can only travel vertically in a line. Contrast that with a cordless drill, which can touch the material at any point and at any angle. Tools like a cordless drill are often referred to as "freehand" tools to differentiate them from machine tools. Some machine tools can guide a cutting edge over the material without any manipulation by the user (that is, after it has been set up and/or programmed).

The task you need to perform on a material can often be accomplished by many types of tools or machines, either powered or not. Choosing whether to use a portable tool or a stationary machine, a power tool, pneumatic tool, or a hand tool depends on a number of factors.

The biggest factor is whether or not you can move your material to a machine and maneuver it within the machine. A portable tool is needed when your material is too big or heavy to manipulate through a machine, or when it is shaped in a way that a machine cannot reach all the parts.

Many machines have fences, rails, and tables that allow you to manipulate your material with more precision and accuracy than with a hand tool alone. If you need precision and accuracy with a hand tool, you often need to construct jigs or use commercial attachments.

Power tools offer the advantage of speed. Ripping a long board on a table saw can be done far quicker than hand-sawing through it. On the flip side, the slow and deliberate nature of unpowered hand tools is often needed in more exacting work. A rasp can shave off just a bit of material at a time to coax a delicate curve into place, where a belt sander might remove the material before you realize you did not want to remove it. A sewing machine cannot close up the last stitch on a pillow the way a hand stitch can.

A well-equipped props shop will have a healthy mix of hand tools, power tools, and stationary machines. A good props artisan will understand when and why to use each tool or machine to perform the tasks needed to manipulate his or her materials into a prop. Never feel bad about using technology to solve a problem. On the flip side, do not feel old-fashioned for using a low-tech or even childish solution. You have to use the best solution for the problem at hand. When faced with a problem, you choose a tool to solve it. You do not choose a tool first and then try to figure out how to solve a problem with it.

Power Tools and Machines

Most machines have some sort of **table**, which is a surface to place your material. Besides keeping your material secure, the table also helps position your material in relation to the cutter (or whatever part of the machine affects your material). Many tables are configured to hold your material either perpendicularly or parallel to the cutter, though many allow you to adjust it to any angle in between. On some machines, like the table saw, you set the angle on the blade rather than with the table.

Machines may also have a **fence**, which gives another surface along the table for the material to either rest against or ride along. The fences on some machines, like a table saw, are adjustable; moving a table saw fence allows you to rip material to different widths. The fences on other machines, such as a sliding miter saw, are stationary, meant solely to hold the material in place as the cutter itself moves.

Most hand-held power tools have a **shoe**, or a metal plate that acts like a tiny, upside-down table. It helps the tool sit flat on the material so the material is fed through the cutter in the correct orientation. The shoe on a tool like a jigsaw or router

Figure 4-12: Jigs and attachments, whether bought in a store or built in your shop, can augment and extend the features of a machine. This auxiliary table clamped to the table of the drill press above is meant to position multiple pieces of material so that a hole can be drilled in precisely the same place in all of them.

allows the cutter to cut into the material perpendicularly to its surface.

Choosing Your Tools

Artisans have a wide range of opinions on how to choose their tools. Some feel the cheapest tools are good enough, while others feel only the most expensive tools are worth their time. I believe it's better to have the right tool for the job, rather than trying to improvise with the wrong tool. If that means you have to buy the cheapest one because your budget is small, so be it. It's better to pound in a nail with a cheap hammer than with the end of your cordless drill.

Prop making is built from a number of craft traditions, each with their own distinct set of tools and machines. Sometimes these tools remain necessary for certain tasks; a wood lathe is really the only way to make turned wooden spindles, legs, and balustrades. There is no hand tool or machine that can shape wood the way a lathe can. Other times, more general tools can be used in a number of different crafts. A mat knife can be used to mark wood, skive leather, and cut plastic almost as well as the specialized tools unique to each of those materials. Since it is impossible, even with the largest of budgets, to buy a unique tool for every material and technique, it is better to outfit yourself with more general tools, and buy the more specialized ones when you find yourself using a material or technique on a regular or semiregular basis.

When you are building your tool collection, you will most likely feel tempted to buy all sorts of tools you see in the store or read about. If you wish to "audition" a tool to figure out whether it deserves a place in your toolbox, buy the cheapest version that will get the job done. If you use it to the point where it wears down and falls apart, you know it will be worth it to invest in a more expensive and higher-quality version. You will also learn why it is a cheap version and which features and specifications to look for in your next purchase. If, however, that cheap tool sits around in your tool box for a year, unused, then you can feel good that you did not spend a lot of money on a tool that you don't actually need.

Types of Tools

It is useful to introduce you to some general categories and types of tools, even though more specific tools will be discussed in the chapters that deal with individual materials. This will be by no means an exhaustive list of all the kinds of tools that one might use (for that, it would be better to have a book such as *The Backstage Handbook* as reference).

Cutting Tools

A cutting tool separates a piece of material into two pieces. Cutting tools may use a blade, a blade with multiple teeth, or a cutting edge. You can also find tools that cut via abrasion or heat.

Blades are made up of many teeth, which can be shaped either like tiny knives or chisels. The type of blade you choose depends on what kind of material you are cutting, how thick it is, and what kind of cut you are making. Kinds of cuts include a rough cut versus a smoother finish cut, and a straight cut versus a curved cut.

The number of teeth on a blade is measured in teeth per inch (or **TPI**). The general rule of thumb is that you want three teeth in contact with your material at all times to keep it from chattering or catching. The more TPI a blade has, the smoother the cut will be. It will also make the cut slower and make it more likely that the blade will clog up with waste material. Every material has an ideal TPI that will make a smooth cut without clogging the blade up too quickly.

The area between the teeth is the **gullet**. Thicker materials require a larger gullet to help carry the waste material away, otherwise the blade will clog up.

The **blade width** is the thickness of the blade (though for band saws, the blade width is used to indicate the distance from the tip of a tooth to the back of the blade, which determines how tight a radius you can cut with that blade). The **kerf** is the width of the cut that the saw blade makes (in Chapter 6, we will also see how the kerf affects how you measure your materials). The **set** of a blade is the angle at which the teeth are bent away from the blade to the side. A blade with the teeth set to the sides will create a kerf that is wider than the width of the blade.

A **knife** blade is a blade without distinct teeth that cuts by slicing or splitting material. These are useful for cutting through soft foams, rubbers, paper, and fabric. You can outfit power tools such as jigsaws and bandsaws with knife blades.

A **utility knife** has a straight blade sharpened on one edge and is suitable for general craft tasks. Many utility knives

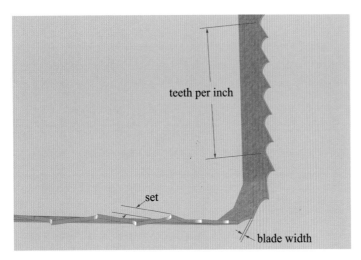

Figure 4-13: Illustration showing the teeth per inch, blade width, and set of a saw blade.

Figure 4-14: This knife is known by many names, such as utility knife, mat knife, or box cutter.

have a retractable blade that is also replaceable; these are commonly called **box cutters**. Box cutting knives are so named because of their ubiquitous use in factories and facilities where the opening of packaging is done frequently. They are alternatively known as carpet knives. These are sometimes also referred to as **mat knives**, though a knife intended to cut the thick paper known as mat board is often of a quite different design. Some utility knives with retractable blades are known as **snap knives**; on a snap knife, the blade is scored at regular lengths. When the edge gets dull, you "snap" that portion off, and you can then cut with the next section, which has remained sharp. A snap knife is also helpful because it gives you a very long but razor-sharp cutting edge; materials such as thick foam rubber can be sliced with fully extended snap knives.

Familiar to many props artisans is the X-Acto knife (actually a trade name), otherwise known as a hobby knife or razor knife. These are useful for making more precise cuts on thinner materials. The term **penknife** is sometimes used to denote the kind of fixed-blade knife that can fold into its handle for easy transport; knives made for carrying around in your pocket are

Figure 4-15: This knife serves many of the same purposes as a utility knife but is known as a snap knife, because sections of the replaceable blade can snap off when too dull to cut.

sometimes called, surprisingly, **pocket knives**. There are an endless variety of knives with names that often overlap. For the props artisan, it is helpful to have a number of knives with different forms, shapes, and blade thicknesses to accomplish any number of cutting tasks.

Some tools cut by **shearing**. These tools have two surfaces that pass each other; the material caught between these two surfaces is separated by the force. Shearing does not create chips or dust-like blades, but it can only be done on thin materials; thicker materials take a lot more force, and the edges can be deformed through the process. Tools that shear include scissors, metal snips, and guillotine-style paper trimmers. You can also find large machines such as hydraulic metal shears that can shear plate metal much thicker than what is possible with hand snips.

Some tools use cutting edges that are mounted to a rotating **spindle**. These tools include routers, shapers, and milling machines. They also include planers and jointers.

Routers are tools to **rout out**, or hollow out, part of a hard material such as wood or plastics. Routers can be scary to those unfamiliar with them, and for good reason. They are loud, fast, and the cutter sticks out the bottom with no guard or protection. If you turn a router on without holding on to it, the sudden torque can actually throw the whole router through the air. If the collet is worn down or not completely tightened, the router bit can fall or even be thrown out, resulting in a bullet-sized blade hurling across the shop at up to 24,000 rpm. But a well-maintained router in the hands of one familiar with its usage can be amongst the most versatile and useful power tools in woodworking. It can cut grooves and channels, trim edges flush, cut circles and unusual shapes, carve and engrave designs, add profiles to edges and cut moldings, and more.

A router that is turned upside down and mounted in a table is called a **router table**. A router table is used for similar outcomes as a router except the material is moved rather than the tool. A similar tool with a dedicated spindle cutter (rather than a removable router) is known as a **shaper**.

Some tools cut with heat, such as plasma cutters and cutting torches for metal, or hot-wire cutters for Styrofoam. The heat melts or burns away a thin line of material to separate it into two pieces.

Some tools use abrasion to cut. Abrasion removes little bits of material from the surface. Cutting with abrasion works essentially by removing these little bits in a tiny path through the whole material, thus separating it into two pieces.

Gripping and Turning Tools

Tools capable of gripping and turning are usually used on fasteners (you can read more about fasteners in Chapter 5). These include all manner of wrenches, screwdrivers, and pliers. They may also be utilized on materials you wish to bend or twist: materials that become plastic when heated, materials that become flexible when wet and rigid when dry, or materials that are pliable but hold their shape such as thin metals. Some types of pliers are also useful for gripping and holding hard-to-reach or hard-to-hold materials that need to remain in place while you perform some sort of task on them that would otherwise move them from position.

Figure 4-16: An adjustable wrench, also known as an adjustable spanner, is one tool that everyone working in the entertainment, live performance, or display industry should own and carry at all times. It may also be called a "crescent wrench," which is a generic term for a Crescent™ brand adjustable wrench, and is sometimes shortened to "C wrench."

Striking Tools

Tools that strike take advantage of the fact that a mass that is accelerated can exert more force than a mass which is only affected by gravity. Hammers are typically used to strike an item such as a nail or another tool when a sudden application of force is needed. A few hammer blows can drive a nail into a piece of wood; if you stood on the nail, all your weight would not be enough to push the nail all the way into the wood. A 16 oz hammer can easily impart 244 oz with each blow.

Mallets are designed to deliver a solid blow without marring the surface of your material, or to impart force to tools such as awls and chisels without damaging their handles. Peen hammers are designed to shape metal through repeated hammering. Tack hammers have their shape to make it easier to drive in upholstery tacks and finish nails. If you spend a lot of time using specific techniques with certain materials, you may find it helpful to use a hammer designed solely for that task. You should also have the right size and weight hammer for your task and physique. A small person with an overly heavy hammer will tire easily and create messier work and a dangerous situation. Using a hammer too small for the task at hand will cause endless hammering when one or two blows with a bigger hammer may have done the job.

You should not use tools not designed for striking as hammers; the back of your cordless drill was not built to drive in a nail.

Prying and Pulling Tools

Prying and pulling tools are used to separate materials and remove fasteners among other things. As with striking tools, you should not use tools such as screwdrivers or chisels for prying. The steel in these tools is formed and hardened differently from a pry bar; a screwdriver will probably bend with too much force, and a chisel may actually snap apart. Only tools designed for the purpose should be used for prying. Crowbars and pry bars come in a variety of sizes depending on the size of material you are working with and the amount of force you need; a pry bar is a lever, and as per physics, the greater the distance from your hand to the fulcrum, the more force you can apply. Upholstery staple removers are great for removing staples, while pincers are useful for removing nails; the back of a claw hammer is also a great nail remover. Many of the pliers in the "gripping" category can also be employed for these pulling tasks.

Abrading and Scraping Tools

Abrading and sanding uses sharp particles to randomly cut bits of material from a surface. Tools include files, grinders, rasps, and sanders. When you look at files and rasps, they are actually made up of hundreds or thousands of tiny cutting edges. The difference is they are designed to remove bits of material at a time to shape a surface, as opposed to removing a path of material in order to separate it in two pieces.

Scraping tools include planes and chisels, as well as scrapers. Scraping tools differ from cutting tools in that they have a single wide cutting surface that is drawn along a material at a fairly oblique angle so it shaves a bit of material off the top to smooth or straighten it.

Figure 4-17: Just a few of the thousands of varieties of hammer. From left to right: claw hammer, rawhide mallet, lead mallet, dual head assembly mallet, tack hammer, ball peen hammer, and wooden mallet.

Measuring and Marking Tools

A large number of tools exist for measuring or dividing materials, and for marking, drawing, or transferring lines, points, and profiles to materials. Chapter 6 will cover these tools in depth.

Boring Tools

Boring tools are tools that make holes in a material. This category also includes any tool that pierces or cuts the hole in the material rather than boring into it.

Drill bits act like rotating chisels, scraping away chips of material in a circular pattern. Many variations of drill bits exist, such as twist, brad point, spade, Forstner, and auger. Twist bits, the most common kind, can be used on wood, metal, and plastic. The angle of the tip and the rake of the cutting head are different for twist bits intended for use on different materials. Using wood bits on metal will quickly dull the drill bit, while using wood or metal bits on plastic can crack it or leave a messy exit hole.

A spade bit, also called a paddle bit, is shaped to quickly cut larger holes though a piece of material. A Forstner bit also cuts larger holes of various sizes, but it leaves a much flatter bottom than a spade bit, making it useful for drilling only partly through a piece of material. Both spade bits and Forstner bits can only be used on woods and some plastics and never on ferrous metals.

An auger bit has a threaded point that helps pull it into the material; it should only be used on wood and only with hand-powered drills, *never* with electric ones. I mention them here only because you still find them lying around in some shops.

Hole saws are another type of drill bit, though rather than scraping away chips of material, they are actually a blade with the teeth arranged in a circle to cut a circular path. Different hole saws are made for a variety of woods, metals, and plastics.

Piercing tools, such as awls, are thin enough to slip between grains and particles of a solid material and push them to the side to allow the tool to pass all the way through. Other tools create holes by shearing the material between two surfaces, such as hole punches, grommet punches, die punches, and leather hole punches. These tools are better for textiles because a drill bit will catch the individual threads as it spins around, wrapping them up in a huge mess.

Spreading Tools

Tools for spreading material are optimized for taking a viscous liquid or paste-like material and applying it to a surface in a controlled manner. These include paint brushes and putty knives, as well as all manner of other painting and plastering tools. While some of these tools are used for spreading adhesives, the majority of them will be discussed in Chapters 16 and 17.

Heating Tools

Heating tools take either electricity or a fuel source and convert it to heat. This heat can do a number of things. In plastics and metals, when the material is heated to a certain point, it becomes flexible and pliable. The material can be easily shaped at this point, and when it cools back down to the ambient temperature, it becomes rigid again. For plastics, a hot air gun, strip heater, or oven are the common tools for this, while with metal you would use a torch or a forge (though forges are typically rare in props shops). An oven used for plastics should never be used for heating food. The chemicals released from the heated plastic become ingrained in the surface of the oven itself and are released every time you turn the oven on again. It is the same reason you should not heat your food in the same pot used to dye fabric. No amount of cleaning will remove chemicals that have leeched into the surface. It is like trying to clean all the wood off of a piece of wood.

With the application of more heat, welding processes can occur; these happen because the surfaces of two materials melt to a liquid where the particles can intermingle with each other (a filler rod is usually necessary to add even more material for this intermingling). When the materials cool back down, they are now physically one single piece of material. With even more heat, the materials decompose to the point of essentially disappearing; tools such as laser cutters, hot-wire cutters, plasma torches, and torch cutters take advantage of this by applying this amount of heat to a thin path, which, after disappearing, leaves two separate pieces of material.

Digital Fabrication

Digital fabrication refers to a number of tools and machines that take files generated digitally (on a computer) and use them to control tools to shape material. In most cases, the operator simply sets up the machine and loads the material; the tool does all the cutting, heating, or other tasks to manipulate the material to its final shape.

Many of these tools take a drawing from a CAD program and transform it into data for a computer control (CNC) machine tool. The first CNC machines in the mid-20th century were milling machines for milling shapes out of plate metal. Since then, CNC systems have been built into a variety of tools such as wood routers, lathes, plasma cutters, laser cutters, and hot wire foam cutters. In addition to tools that cut smaller shapes from larger materials, there are also CNC machines for building up a shape by the addition of small amounts of material, known as 3D printing. These commonly work by extruding a stream of heated thermoplastic, such as ABS, into a shape (kind of like a CNC hot glue gun) or by building up layers of powdered resin which is selectively solidified by a process called laser sintering.

These kinds of tools remain fairly expensive. Larger commercial props shops may have a few of them, though most theatrical props shops borrow time on the scene shop's machines when the need arises. There also exist spaces in some cities that rent time on these machines for a props artisan to cut or print a number of shapes. You may also find companies that will mail you your object after you e-mail or upload a CAD drawing.

These tools require additional skills and training in drafting and drawing or converting drawings into the correct formats in CAD software to use them, as well as their own specific instructions for running the machines.

Figure 4-18: The cut-out portions of this headboard were cut on a CNC router, while the rest of it was cut and assembled using conventional carpentry. *Henry IV*, Playmakers Repertory Company, 2012. Scenic design by Jan Chambers.

They still require all the other work of making a prop; determining the needs of the prop, or the parts of a more complicated prop, choosing the materials you will use for each part of your prop and how you will finish these materials to give the correct appearance, and looking at your resources, both time and money and the capabilities of your tools and your own skills, to determine the best means for manipulating your materials into the final shapes and surfaces you need. Saying you know how to make a prop simply because you know how to operate one type of 3D printer is like saying you know how to build furniture because you know how to operate a table saw.

five

assemblage

Props are rarely made from one piece of material. Artisans combine a whole variety of materials and objects to construct a single prop. Some props may be made entirely of found objects assembled together.

Found Object

You do not need to limit the materials you use to things considered materials. While wood comes in a myriad of forms, like sheets, sticks, and rods, you can also find wooden beads, buttons, and knobs. Further, there are any number of already-made items made out of wood, such as finials, carvings, and toys. The same is true of all materials. In addition to raw materials, any object can be added to your repertoire of materials for use in prop making.

Take a look around you. Tables, chairs, stools, cushions, desks, and other furniture probably line the room you are in. Small objects are everywhere: cups, utensils, computer parts, speakers, bowls, coasters, etc. If you are in your home, you can go to other rooms and find vacuum cleaner attachments, bottles and containers of all shapes, disposable pens, shaving razors, tools, toys, lamps, etc. If you browse the various aisles of a hardware store, you can find hoses, pipes, connectors, knobs, and all sorts of shapes and devices in a variety of materials. Flea markets and thrift stores are full of an assortment of goods that can be appropriated, or that can be taken apart and the pieces used for your props. Items for use in your props are, in fact, everywhere, from the most expensive stores to the garbage can.

For many props artisans, it can be a matter of pride to be able to fabricate, cast, and manufacture every single part of a prop. However, for theatre, film, and television, we rarely have the time to do that. Found objects and materials in unusual

Figure 5-1: This tiny boombox began as a rectangular piece of MDF. Wooden knobs and discs were attached to make the dials and speakers; a piece of screen was cut into circles and attached on top of the discs to finish the speakers. The handle is a bent section of wire. The antenna is a piece of coated wire with half of the coating stripped away, and a bead attached to the end. The panels are thin sections of styrene glued on. The buttons were cut from a sheet of fake bricks used in model railroad-making.

Figure 5-2: This "steampunk" exterminator device is mostly a garden sprayer and respirator with a variety of hoses and other found objects attached. Prop made by Jim Luther at Childsplay Theatre for *The Borrowers*.

Figure 5-3: This space scooter was made with a regular scooter, some fabricated parts, and some buttons and switches bought from an electronics store. Prop built by Will Griffith for the Actors Theatre of Louisville.

one at a time depending on what prop you are currently building. It is far better to collect these pieces as you find them and keep a collection handy for when the need arises. The dilemma comes in organizing these parts. How do you catalog pieces that are not only disparate but possibly unique? Some prop makers divide them up by material: one bin for steel bits, one for brass things, and a third for rubber parts. Others classify them by shape: balls, tubes, rosettes, discs, etc. Many use a combination of these two methods, with containers for wood beads, plastic rods, shell cameos, and any other pieces they may have in multiple. It is, obviously, a highly personalized system dependent on what the shop has and what it uses, and a good system will allow for easy reorganizing and updating.

shapes help save time in constructing the parts of a prop that would take hours to construct from scratch. Being able to look at the items and objects that surround you as potential materials and parts rather than for what they are is an incredibly useful skill for the prop maker. Model makers use the term "kit-bashing," which means taking pieces from commercially available models, such as the tires from a car or the fuel tank from a jet, to use in a scratch-built model as a way to save time in creating complex shapes. For the prop maker, the world is their kit to bash.

Of course, when you are looking for a specific item, you will not be able to find it. It is inefficient to go hunting for pieces

Helpful items to Store and Stock in a Props Shop

This is by no means a comprehensive list, but rather a way to inspire you to start thinking of further items and materials you can stock for use in props:

Beads, feathers, glass, sequins, bottle tops, wire, wrappers, glitter, foils, coins, braids, cotton balls, glitter, popsicle sticks, buttons, wooden pieces, cans and containers, tubing, pipe connectors, plumbing parts, door hardware, lamp and chandelier parts, tassels, fringe, cord, hooks, ribbon, yarn, costume jewelry, decorative appliqués, trunk parts, handles, springs, plastic bottles, medicine containers, egg cartons, hoses, gauze, screen, dials, electronic parts, textured papers, gears, dowel, bottle caps, dried beans, curtain rings, vacuum cleaner attachments, toys and toy parts, disposable flatware, rods, pegs.

Diapering, Nurnies, and Greebles

Diapering is the old art of adding a repeated or decorative pattern to a plain surface to break it up and add interest. **Greebles** are the modern-day equivalent of diapering: small pieces of detail added to a surface to add interest and complexity. The term was reportedly coined by model makers on the original *Star Wars* movies, and used to refer to unnecessary and sometimes random three-dimensional details to make a surface look more intricate than it actually is. Other terms for this process include **wiggets** and **nurnies**.

Real items have any number of bumps, ridges, and divots that you can carve or attach to make your prop look more realistic. Some examples I've seen props artisans do over the years include scribing lines into a large surface to make it look like it is constructed of smaller plates and pieces, adding a line of bumps to look like rivets or bolt heads, covering a standard hinge with a cutout detail to make it look like a wrought-iron hinge made by hand, and attaching thin sheets of material on top to look like raised panels or doors. Cutting shapes out of thin sheets of material is a fast and common way to give your prop another level of detail. This can be especially tricky where the surface is curved and you cannot attach a rigid material.

One of the more popular materials used for this purpose in the past has been industrial felt. It gives a fairly clean edge when cut, and it can easily be wrapped around curves and nonflat surfaces. It has traditionally been soaked in shellac to harden it, though artisans today may find resin a better substitute. A more modern substitute is styrene. It comes in multiple thicknesses, giving it a lot of versatility. Also, unlike felt, it is not a soft substance that can distort or be crushed under an actor's grip.

Textured and patterned materials are useful for quickly diapering a large surface as well. With a strong mounting surface and the right kind of coating, even textured fabrics and papers can appear to be solid surfaces.

Attaching Things Together

Adhesives

Finding information about glues can be tricky. You should already have the MSDS for the glues you are using; you can use them to find out more about what the glue consists of or what its intended use is. Manufacturers will also sometimes make "tech data sheets" for their products, which may include more specifications and references on their specific adhesives. Talking directly with the manufacturers or even the distributors of specific products can be helpful when researching new adhesives. The manufacturers want you to use their product successfully, while distributors are knowledgeable about their whole product line, and regularly deal with other customers who may have been in similar situations. Finally, you can learn a lot from other artisans, either those you work or interact with in person, or through websites and forums where craftspeople of all types discuss various problems and which adhesives helped solved them (or more importantly, which ones failed).

Adhesion is the action of sticking two materials together. An **adhesive** is a sticky substance that causes adhesion. **Glue** and **cement** also refer to soft or glutinous substances that stick two materials together. Though some practitioners differentiate between the terms (using *glue* to refer only to adhesives derived from plants and animals, for instance), all three can be used interchangeably. One company may sell "epoxy cement," while another sells "epoxy adhesive," and in terms of chemical composition and practical properties, both are identical.

Adhesives form bonds in a few different ways. Some adhesives work by "drying"; that is, either the water or solvent evaporates (technically, water is also a solvent). For some materials such as wood, the water can also be pulled into the material itself to help the adhesive dry where it is not directly exposed to air. Other adhesives "cure," or undergo a chemical conversion. Any "two-part" glue falls in this category, where the mixture of the two parts catalyzes, or begins, the chemical

Figure 5-4: Panels in this throne were diapered by applying materials with cutout patterns, such as fireplace screens and grills. *King Roger, the Santa Fe Opera, 2012. Scenic design by Thomas Lynch.*

conversion. Other adhesives can be catalyzed by the addition of water or exposure to air. Some adhesives are actually two-part adhesives, but the construction of their container causes the two parts to mix as you apply the adhesive, so it acts like a single-part adhesive. Finally, some adhesives work through heat, becoming soft and/or liquid at a high enough temperature, and solid again when cooled (usually to room temperature). Others, known as thermosetting adhesives, cure through the addition of heat, and cannot be resoftened once fully cured. Different glues will form a bond through at least one of these three means: evaporation, curing, or heat. Some glues fall into more than one of these categories.

Different adhesives (or even different formulations of the same adhesive) will give you a number of different working properties that may help or hinder your particular gluing situation. The **assembly time** is the amount of time a glue lets you reposition the two materials being glued before it becomes too rigid to move any more, or where further repositioning will result in a weaker bond. This is divided further into the **open assembly time**, which falls between when the glue is applied to when the materials are closed or fitted together, and the **closed assembly time**, which is the time between when the materials are closed to when they need to be clamped. Finally, the **clamp time** (sometimes called the pressure period or press time) is how long the two pieces being glued need to remain clamped together for the strongest possible bond. The **initial tack** is the amount of "stickiness" a glue has when the two materials are first pressed together. A glue with a high initial tack will allow you to press two materials together and not have them move when you remove your hands.

Glues that harden chemically have their own set of terms used to describe their various working properties. The **cure time** is the time it takes for an adhesive to transform from a liquid to a solid.

The **initial cure** is when the glue fully hardens (sets) but has not developed all of its properties, particularly its strength. The **final cure** is when all of its properties have been fully developed. The **pot life** is the amount of time a glue remains usable while it remains in the pot, or container, it was mixed in.

This may or may not be different from the **working life**, or the amount of time a glue remains usable after it is mixed and dispensed from its pot or container. Some glues (such as epoxies) set faster when they remain in the pot than when they are spread out thinly.

Some glues have additional considerations for working with them. Two-part adhesives may require containers or stirrers to mix them up. Hot glue requires a hot glue gun; other glues may require a caulk gun or more specialized applicator. A final consideration is safety. Some glues are fast and foolproof but highly toxic. Make sure you know what chemicals you are dealing with, and what your shop is set up to handle in terms of fumes and personal protective equipment.

Besides the working properties, different glues have all sorts of variations in what kind of bond they achieve when dried. Some give a flexible bond, while others create a rigid one; some can even be sanded once dry. If you are working with a translucent material or are creating a joint where the dried glue will be visible, you probably want a glue which dries clear or semiclear. Some glues dry with a dark or deep color. One glue may create a permanent bond, while another creates a more temporary bond that can be undone at a later time. You may need to create a waterproof bond in some situations, while in others, you want a glue that can be washed off with water. Some glues can actually cure or harden while completely submerged in water, while others require exposure to air until they harden. Some glues are thick and can fill gaps, while others are thin enough that you can adhere a thin and flexible material to another without any lumps or wrinkles.

All the variations in how you work with a glue and what properties the joint can have once the glue hardens should prove that there is no such thing as a single "miracle" adhesive. Every situation is different; it is not enough just to know which materials you are joining, but also the type of glue joint you wish to create. I have put together a chart of suggested adhesives for various materials, but keep in mind when using it that selecting a glue involves many more considerations than just the materials. Common glues in the props shop like PVA and epoxy come in such a vast array of working and final properties that the different types can almost be thought of as separate products.

The glue you choose is practically useless if you do not apply it correctly. Read the directions. You need to apply the correct amount; glues like PVA only need to be applied to one side, while contact cements need to be applied to both materials. Some glues require exposure to air for a length of time or some other activation before materials are pressed together. Some glues only work when bonded with the material directly, and have a completely different strength if your material is painted or coated, or if the glue is reapplied over already-dried glue. You may need to treat, clean, or otherwise prepare the surface of your material before applying the glue. Many glues require clamping the two materials together for a length of time (the clamping time). You will save a lot of trouble if you plan ahead how you will clamp your materials together before applying the glue. It is helpful to **dry-fit** your materials, that is, to assemble them without glue to make sure everything fits.

Types of Adhesives

Up until about the twentieth century, adhesives available to props artisans were limited to those derived from nature. The earliest glues came from either animal or plant sources.

Figure 5-5: A **caul** is a piece of wood (or other material) placed between the clamp and the wood. It is usually meant to keep the clamp from marring or denting the surface of the wood, though it can also be used to spread the force of the clamp out to a larger surface area.

Animal glues—Most animal glue used today comes from horses, either the hide or the hoof. It comes in either flakes or powder, which is melted down in a double boiler; it also comes premixed in cold bottle versions. It is still preferred by many furniture makers as a wood glue, and some props artisans for its distinct properties. It remains slightly flexible when dry, so it will not crack as the furniture is abused, or the wood expands and contracts. It can be remelted with heat, so loose joints in furniture can be taken apart and reglued with ease. The ease of use of modern alternatives has largely replaced animal glues in nearly all other situations.

Casein—A paint binder derived from milk with some adhesive properties.

Starch glues and pastes—Glues derived from the starches of plants. Flour glue, wheat paste, and other similar substances are types of starch glues. It is still used for work involving paper, particularly in papier-mâché.

With the development of the plastics industry, the amount and types of adhesives available has literally exploded, with more being created even as I write this book. I will attempt to break down the different types into broad categories and list what they are good for. Though I try to stay away from specific brand names, the world of adhesives is a confusing one, made even more so by theatrical folks using brand names in a generic fashion. Hopefully, by categorizing them as such, you can see exactly what kind of adhesive your favorite brand is, and should it become discontinued or hard to find, you can determine a similar alternative.

PVA—Polyvinyl acetate, a type of glue developed in the early twentieth century. This is frequently referred to by color, coming in either white or yellow.

"White" glue is often referred to by one of its most famous brands, Elmer's. "Yellow" glue is commonly called "carpenter's glue" or "wood glue." The yellow color is actually just a dye added to regular PVA. A joint created in wood with yellow PVA is just as strong as a joint created with white PVA; the difference comes in the working properties as well as some differences in its properties when dry. Wood glue is less runny and has a higher initial tack. When it dries, it is more rigid so it can be sanded. If you find a white PVA that calls itself a wood glue, know that it has no particular advantage or disadvantage over a yellow PVA.

PVA glue comes in many other formulations for various other tasks. Some PVA dries a lot more flexibly; popular brands include Sobo and Rhoplex. PVA for bookbinders is pH-neutral, so it can be used for archival purposes. It can also be formulated to be spread over large surface areas for use during scrapbooking-type tasks or découpage work. One of the most popular brands of this type of PVA is Mod Podge™.

"Flex" glue—A general term for any adhesive that remains flexible after drying. Older prop-making texts frequently refer to Phlexglu™, which is a specific brand of flex glue made by Ford Davis of Spectra Dynamics in Albuquerque, NM, from 1979 to around the early 2000s. Often misspelled "Plexglue" or "Phlex-glue," it is a vinyl-acrylic binder/adhesive that dries clear and flexible; it was used as an adhesive, a binder for pigments, metallic powders, and any sort of textural material (sawdust, dirt, etc.), or as a texture. Modern alternatives include well-known theatrical brands such as Rosco's Flex-Bond™ and Rose Brand's Flex Glue™; you can also find these glues labeled as book binder's glues. Some of these are also vinyl-acrylic emulsions, though many are simply variations of PVA that dry flexibly; their use and compatibility with materials is very similar to PVA as well.

"Super" glue—Cyanoacrylate or CA glue (a type of acrylic resin), sometimes known as "instant" or "Krazy" glue. As its name implies, this glue is prized for its ability to make instant or near-instant bonds between two materials. In many cases, only a few drops give a strong bond, making it especially useful for smaller parts; larger quantities are extremely expensive, so it is less useful as an all-purpose adhesive. Thinner amounts also harden faster than thicker amounts. Cyanoacrylates can be viscous for some gap-filling abilities, or thin enough to run down the smallest of cracks. It works well on nonporous materials; it also works well on many plastics, though it does not dry completely clearly and it can cloud the plastic, so you may wish to avoid it on transparent plastics. It will also glue your skin together almost instantly; several variations are actually used to seal wounds in medical emergencies, though the stuff you buy in a hardware or art store is probably a skin irritant or even toxic, so don't use it to seal a cut.

"Hot" glue—Also known as hot melt adhesives, these are glues that are heated, melted, and applied with hot glue guns. Ethylene-vinyl acetate, developed in the 1940s, is one of the most commonly used thermoplastics in the hot glue guns you find in props shops. The thick body makes it useful to fill gaps and bond materials that do not fit together tightly; it also makes it useful to quickly add raised decorations to a surface. It comes in both "low" and "high" melt variety. Some hot glue guns, particularly those found in craft stores, will only do the low-melt version. High-melt glue is needed for more structural needs. The glues also come in many colors; you can use these

for all sorts of effects, such as fake sealing wax on medieval letters. Be careful of getting the hot glue on your skin; if this should happen, allow it to cool before trying to remove it. If you try to pull or wipe it off, you will simply spread more hot glue around and burn more of your skin. Keep a bowl of cool water nearby to douse your hands in if they get hot glue on them.

Fugitive glue—A special type of hot glue that is easily peeled up and remains gummy. It is also known as "snot glue" or "credit card glue" because it is the type of adhesive used to stick new credit cards to paper when they are mailed out. It requires a different gun than standard hot glue. It is useful for making temporary and removable attachments between paper, plastic, and other thin materials, while leaving no residue.

Epoxy—A type of resin usually found in a two-part liquid form. It can be as thin as baby oil or as thick as ketchup; when mixed with fillers, it can even come in putty form, which is used to fill large gaps and repair holes, as well as to sculpt small details and shapes. Most epoxies are fairly rigid when cured, so they are not useful for joints or materials that are flexible. They are especially useful for joining disparate materials, especially if one or both of them are nonporous. You can find all sorts of epoxies formulated for specific materials, such as metal epoxy and plastic epoxy. Some epoxies cure incredibly fast (frequently sold as "five-minute epoxy", though others can cure in as quickly as one minute), making them useful for emergency repairs or other situations where prolonged clamping is not an option. They are also frequently employed in woodworking as an alternative to PVA when the wood joint must remain immersed in water for extended periods of time, as they are completely waterproof.

Contact cement—This is a broad category of adhesives, encompassing those that are meant to be applied to both surfaces, allowed to dry, and then pressed together. Some adhesives are specifically made to be contact cements, while others can be used as either a regular or a contact cement depending on the materials being adhered. Many are based on either natural rubber or synthetic rubber, such as polychloroprene (also known as Neoprene). Rubber cement itself can be used as a contact cement. They are often used for applying laminate or veneer to wood. They are also extremely useful on rubber and leather. "Barge cement," originally used by cobblers, is particularly prized for its ability to adhere leather to itself and other materials despite its toxicity.

Water-based contact adhesives contain far less toxic solvents than regular contact cements. This makes them useful both for health reasons as well as for use on materials that are normally dissolved by solvents. Styrofoam™ in particular works well with water-based contact adhesives, either when you have to glue several pieces together, or when you have to attach it to another material. Water-based contact adhesives are often called **"green glue"** because of their perceived environmental benefits and because of their color. Common brands include LePage's Press-Tite Green Contact Cement and 3M Fastbond 30-NF.

Latex—Latex is derived from the rubber tree and can be used as an adhesive. Its main advantage is that it is very flexible and stretchy. Rubber cement is latex dissolved in a solvent; when the solvent evaporates, the rubber portion is left behind. Other latex-based adhesives are used as contact cements or as carpet and fabric glues. Water-based latex adhesives exist as well, such as Copydex™.

Solvent-based synthetic polymer adhesives—Solvent-based adhesives are another very large and broad category of adhesives that employ a synthetic polymer resin dissolved in an organic solvent. When the solvent evaporates, it leaves behind a very sticky substance that holds the two surfaces together. They use the same basic concept as rubber cement, but with synthetic elastomers rather than natural rubber, and a whole bunch of different solvents that achieve different properties. In fact, these types of adhesives are occasionally referred to as "rubber cements." These types of adhesives fill the store shelves these days and are often touted as "miracle" adhesives, or as glues that will "repair anything." It is helpful to break them down into further categories; these are not exact categories, mind you. Specific ingredients for these adhesives is difficult, if not impossible, to find; usually only the solvents

are listed on the MSDS, while the polymers used are usually proprietary and differ widely from company to company. Even glues made by the same company can have vastly different working properties and create bonds between a variety of materials. Many glues are specifically formulated for certain materials, such as ceramics or vinyl, so if you do your homework, you are bound to find a glue in this category that will bond your materials. I have divided them up into smaller categories to differentiate them somewhat, but keep in mind that these categories are my own invention and highly subjective.

- **Bridal glue**—Alternatively called floral and craft glue, or jewelry adhesive. These are so named because they are most commonly used in assemblage-type crafts involving flowers, fabric, beads, feathers, and other small decorative items of various materials. They work especially well when attaching items to fabric, or fabric to itself; some props artisans will even use it to hem an edge or close a seam when sewing is not an option (though the adhesive is not reversible as thread is). Most use a solvent such as acetone, which evaporates and leaves a slightly flexible material behind almost like "cold hot glue." Many of the most popular brands used by props artisans are made by Beacon Adhesives, which sells products such as Bridal Glue, Fabri-Tac, MagnaTac, and GemTac.
- **Household cement**—"Household cement," sometimes called "goop" or "jewelry cement," is like a thicker, stronger version of bridal glue, formulated and marketed for general household repairs. Their thickness allows them to fill gaps or adhere irregularly shaped surfaces together. They are especially useful on nonporous materials. Check the MSDS because they may use some pretty potent solvents, such as tetrachloroethylene; most of these solvents are known or suspected carcinogens, and the long drying time of these types of adhesives (24–48 hours) means you are producing a lot of fumes wherever your objects are left to dry. For some glues, the solvent actually interacts with the material being glued, which can make a stronger bond.

Since these glues are meant to be repair adhesives, they are usually not useful for fabricating props from scratch, though like bridal glues, they are helpful when applying small objects as details, or for constructing small hand props from a disparate array of materials and found objects. Common brand names include Amazing Goop™, E6000™, and Elmer's Household Cement™. Variations exist for general auto and machine repair, such as Seal-All™.

- **"Spray" adhesives**—Though the term *spray adhesive* is broad enough to mean any adhesive that can be sprayed, we tend to use it to refer to specific solvent-based adhesives that come in a spray can. These are a quick way of adhering thin materials, such as paper or fabric, to rigid materials such as wood or metal. There are hazards inherent in the solvents themselves, as well as the additional hazards that come from being sprayed into the air. Though these hazards mean they should be avoided when possible, their advantage over water-based adhesives is that they will not wrinkle the paper as they dry. 3M produces some of the most popular spray adhesives, such as 3M Spray 77, which some artisans simply call "spray 77."
- **Construction Adhesives**—These adhesives are frequently used for attaching paneling, molding, or other general home construction tasks. Most are a fairly thick paste that comes in a tube meant to be applied from a caulk gun. The polymers and solvents they use vary widely (some are even water-based), but the common feature is the addition of inert fillers such as kaolin, quartz, or limestone. Familiar brands include Liquid Nails™, No More Nails™, and PL200™

Polyurethane—Anyone who molds and casts with 2-part polyurethane knows it will stick to absolutely everything. I've seen it used as an adhesive, specifically for sticking foam to wood. More useful to the props artisan is the polyurethane developed specifically as an adhesive in the late 1980s, known best by its most popular brand name, Gorilla Glue™. Rather than using a two-part formula, polyurethane adhesive is activated through moisture, often by dampening the surface being glued.

The moisture in the air, or on the surface being glued (if it is a material that holds moisture, such as wood), can also be enough to activate it. As it dries, it also foams, so it will fill slight gaps, though it works best when the two materials fit closely together. I like it for adhering expanded foam to plywood.

Urea and Resorcinol glue—These are two other categories of resin glue. Though they are rare in many props shops, they are known to hardcore woodworkers. Either can come in powdered or a two-component form. Powdered urea resin is sometimes referred to as "plastic resin glue," even though many glues can technically be referred to as plastic resin glues. It is also known as urea-formaldehyde, or UF glue. The formaldehyde off-gasses as it sets, which is a long time. These glues can have a pot life of up to four hours, and a clamping time of over thirteen hours. This makes it useful for veneer and laminates because its slow setting time makes precise positioning and repositioning possible. It is also very waterproof and has no creep (the movement of two materials after they have been glued), unlike PVA. I've even seen it used for papier-mâché. This is the type of adhesive used in the manufacturing of MDF and some plywoods. Resorcinal glue is another two-component glue used for gluing lumber joints and laminates; it is used primarily in boat-building applications and for aircraft as it is completely waterproof and highly weatherproof. It has almost no gap-filling abilities, which makes it incredibly difficult to use for anything but the most precise work. It dries to a dark maroon/purple color, which makes it bad to use where it will be visible.

Silicone—Silicone adhesives remain very flexible and fill gaps well. These are usually used as bath and shower sealants and to construct glass aquariums because they make joints that are both waterproof and watertight. They come in one-part or two-part formulas, and may dry translucent or opaque. They are difficult, if not impossible, to paint over, so choose a color that you like.

Solvent welders—Though technically not adhesives, it makes sense to include them here because they are used in a similar fashion. Many plastics become soft and tacky when exposed to acetone, and if you press two of these tacky surfaces together, it will reharden into a single piece of plastic. Since acetone evaporates too quickly to be a viable glue, we have a number of adhesives that include acetone (or some other solvent) in a formulation that allows it to be used as an adhesive. PVC glue, model airplane glue, etc, work by dissolving the surfaces of the two pieces of certain plastics, letting them intermingle, and then re-solidifying as the solvent evaporates away. Check Chapter 9 for a list of common plastics that can be solvent-welded.

Removing Glues

Depending on your situation, you may wish to consider how difficult or easy it is to remove the glue you use. Some heat-activated glues can be resoftened and removed by applying heat. Glues that dry can often be removed by reapplying the solvent used, whether water or a more harsh industrial solvent. Some glues have their own special removers, such as "debonder," which will soften and break the joints created with cyanoacrylate glue. Finally, some glues can only be removed mechanically, by either cutting, sanding, or otherwise wearing away the dried glue and wherever it has soaked into the material itself.

On Choosing a Glue

The chart on the following page lists some common materials and suggestions for the best kinds of adhesives to choose. The amount and variety of adhesives you can choose is practically infinite, and I could not possibly fit all of them there. Instead, I've tried to limit them to the more general categories I described on the preceding pages. If you cannot find your favorite glue, it may be because you know it as its brand name; I've also tried to list the more common brand names in their respective categories.

The variety in materials is practically endless as well. A glue that works well on brass may not work on cast iron, but the chart only lists the more general category of "metal." This is especially egregious in the plastics category, where the chemical composition of many of its varieties means that some forms of plastic need entirely different adhesives than others. Number "two" plastics, for instance, will not chemically bond with any adhesive.

Keep in mind the scale and scope of the materials you are joining. When many bridal glue manufacturers claim that their products work on "wood," they usually mean decorative carvings, rosettes, and beads made from wood that you wish to apply to a surface. This is very different from attaching several boards together to make a giant dining room table.

Finally, remember that adhesives are not the only, or even the best, way to join two materials. While metal can be bonded with metal epoxy, in many cases you will be welding it together. Materials can be fastened mechanically, tied or sewn together, or even taped. The process of choosing your adhesive should only commence after you've decided that an adhesive is the best or only way to connect your materials.

Tape

Though tape is rarely used for permanent attachment, prop making does include a few situations when tape comes in handy. Often it is used as a temporary attaching device, such as when an adhesive is drying, and you need to hold the pieces together.

You can also find it handy to tape a drawing or template to a piece you wish to cut, sculpt, or carve. Certain tapes are great for masking areas you need to paint or otherwise treat. When carving pieces on a band saw, tape is helpful to reattach the cut-offs so that you have a flat surface to sit on the table of the saw.

Many tapes contain what is known as a "pressure-sensitive" adhesive on a backing of typically paper, cloth, or plastic. A pressure-sensitive adhesive creates a bond when you push down on it (as opposed to one that dries in the air, cures with a catalyst, or sets when a solvent evaporates). They can be either permanent or temporary. Other tapes may be activated when you moisten or wet them (such as brown packing tape) or when you heat them. You can find innumerable tapes

	Wood	Styrofoam**	Rubber	Plastic	Paper
Plaster*	contact cement PVA	contact cement PVA latex	cyanoacrylate	super glue epoxy	contact cement PVA latex
Ceramic	epoxy household cement polyurethane PVA	epoxy hot glue PVA spray adhesive	household cement cyanoacrylate spray adhesive hot glue	epoxy cyanoacrylate household cement	spray adhesive PVA
Fabric	PVA spray adhesive contact cement latex green contact cement	PVA hot glue spray adhesive contact cement latex	barge spray adhesive contact cement household cement	spray adhesive household cement hot glue	PVA starch adhesive spray adhesive barge
Glass	silicone caulk epoxy hot glue household cement	spray adhesive household cement epoxy	silicone caulk household cement contact cement epoxy rubber cement	epoxy household cement hot glue silicone caulk	spray adhesive hot glue starch adhesive
Leather	barge green glue contact cement PVA	hot glue green glue PVA epoxy	barge spray adhesive household cement epoxy	barge silicone caulk household cement epoxy	PVA spray adhesive starch adhesive
Metal	metal epoxy contact cement polyurethane household cement epoxy putty green glue construction adhesive	metal epoxy household cement epoxy putty spray adhesive hot glue contact cement PVA latex	household cement spray adhesive rubber cement contact cement polyurethane	epoxy polyurethane epoxy putty silicone household cement	spray adhesive rubber cement epoxy contact cement PVA starch adhesive
Paper	PVA spray adhesive starch adhesive contact cement UF resin	spray adhesive hot glue contact cement green glue PVA latex	barge spray adhesive	spray adhesive PVA	PVA starch glue spray adhesive contact cement UF resin rubber cement
Plastic	epoxy household cement green glue contact cement polyurethane	epoxy hot glue spray adhesive household cement	barge green glue contact cement spray adhesive epoxy household cement	solvent welder*** epoxy household cement contact cement cyanoacrylate silicone	
Rubber	barge contact cement green glue polyurethane epoxy household cement rubber cement	spray adhesive household cement epoxy	barge spray adhesive epoxy polyurethane household cement		
Styrofoam**	polyurethane green glue construction adhesive hot glue PVA spray adhesive contact cement latex	green glue spray adhesive household cement contact cement PVA latex polyurethane			
Wood	PVA epoxy polyurethane animal glue casein glue UF resin resorcinol				

Metal	Leather	Glass	Fabric	Ceramic	Plaster*
contact cement PVA	PVA	cyanoacrylate	contact cement PVA latex	PVA cyanoacrylate epoxy	PVA cyanoacrylate
metal epoxy epoxy putty cyanoacrylate polyurethane	household cement PVA spray adhesive	cyanoacrylate silicone caulk household cement	spray adhesive household cement PVA	cyanoacrylate epoxy household cement	
spray adhesive household cement contact cement PVA latex	barge spray adhesive PVA green glue household cement bridal	spray adhesive bridal hot glue silicone PVA household cement	PVA spray adhesive green glue barge hot glue contact cement bridal latex		
epoxy household cement silicone	household cement bridal epoxy	silicone household cement cyanoacrylate epoxy			
household cement epoxy	barge epoxy household cement PVA contact cement				
metal epoxy polyurethane epoxy putty household cement silicone contact cement					

*Plaster can be a very difficult material to make an adhesive bond with. Many glues work only when the plaster is fully dried, which can be days or even weeks after it hardens. Some types of glues, such as cyanoacrylate or PVA, work really well if the surface of the plaster is first sealed with a thin layer of paint or PVA.

**Most harsh solvents will eat Styrofoam away; some of the glues in the categories suggested may contain such solvents, so do a test first. Heat can also melt Styrofoam, so avoid anything but the lowest temperature hot melt adhesives.

***Solvent welders only work on specific plastics and combinations of plastics. See Chapter 9: Plastics Construction for a list of which plastics can be solvent welded.

Figure 5-6: Blue masking tape used to hold materials together while glue dries.

for a variety of needs and purposes, but there are a few which props people should definitely know about.

Gaffers Tape—A cloth-backed tape that leaves almost no residue. Used frequently throughout the various departments of a theatre, particularly by lights and audio for attaching cables to the ground (typically done by the, you guessed it, "gaffer"). "Spike" tape is exactly the same as gaffers tape except that it is thinner in width and comes in a multitude of colors; it can be used in emergency situations when you need gaffers tape but none can be found.

Masking Tape—Also known as painter's tape, this is useful for masking areas when painting that you wish to not receive paint. It is easily removable with no residue.

Double-stick tape—Great for attaching two pieces together. Notable types include carpet tape, which is fairly thick and good for bonding fabric to rigid materials. Twin-tac is a sheet of plastic that is sticky on both sides, like a double-sided piece of contact paper. It is used a lot by scenic design model makers (and in architectural modeling) as a great nontoxic alternative to spray adhesives for paper and card stock. You will also find foam-backed double-stick tape for mounting together two surfaces that may not be perfectly smooth or level.

Box sealing tape—Also called "packing tape" or "parcel tape." This is a clear or opaque plastic tape made for sealing boxes to be shipped. The clear kind is often used by props people as a quick and cheap way of covering and waterproofing something like a wine label on a bottle of wine that needs to be washed and rinsed every night.

Office tape—Popularly known as Scotch™ tape. This is similar to box sealing tape, just smaller, less tacky, and easier to tear. It is useful for assembling and attaching paper props.

Duct tape—Duct tape is a strong tape similar to gaffers tape, except that the adhesive is more permanent and the cloth back is frequently sealed with polyethylene. Hobbyists and fans of the tape have found it useful for nearly everything (except for use in actual ducts; building codes require a fire-resistant tape, and the heat from the ducts causes the adhesive to fail). Enthusiasts have expanded duct tape's repertoire to an actual building material; by laying down sheets of duct tape and alternating the direction of the strips with every layer, one can construct shapes and patterns. Items ranging from prom dresses and wallets to functioning cannon barrels have been constructed in this manner. Props artisans find it less useful other than for dire emergency repairs, as the polyethylene coating prohibits most paints from adhering to its surface, and more elegant and reliable connections and attachments can be made through proper planning and more appropriate materials rather than just by wrapping everything in duct tape.

Electrical tape—Because it is used to cover electrical wires, this tape is made with an insulated backing, usually vinyl. Besides being indispensable for any electrical work, its stretchiness, multitude of colors, ability to be written on, and clean removal from many smooth surfaces gives it a number of other uses in the props world, such as labeling, temporary attachment, and wrapping around a handle to make a quick "grip." It can make removable pin or racing stripes on a prop that has been rented or borrowed.

Floral—Floral tape (or "stem wrap tape") is a waxy tape that, when stretched, will stick to itself. It was developed

Figures 5-7 and 5.8: Brown floral tape is wrapped around a frame of different wires to simulate these pheasant feet. *King Lear, the Public Theater, 2011.*

to wrap the stems of flowers together into bundles, or to hide supporting wires in flower stems. Props people use it for flowers, both real and artificial, and for similar purposes.

You can also find a second type of floral tape that will also adhere to other surfaces.

Mortite—Mortite is actually a brand name for a type of caulking putty used for sealing gaps around windows. It is slightly adhesive but leaves little residue, and it remains soft and pliable for months or even years. Props masters and set dressers employ it to temporarily anchor and hold objects in place on stage or set.

Floral putty—Similar to Mortite, only less goopy. It is available at floral supply and craft stores.

Mechanical Attachment

Mechanical attachment is the joining together of two materials without the use of adhesives, chemicals, or heat (such as welding and soldering).

Fasteners

A fastener is some kind of object or bit of material that is attached to two or more materials to hold them all together. Some fasteners, like nails, sit inside the materials and hold them together through friction. Others, like nuts and bolts or rivets, create a barrier on the outsides of the fasteners to capture and hold the two materials in place. Fasteners can be used to add strength to a glue joint, to attach two pieces that cannot be glued or welded together, or to allow pieces to be removable in the future. I cannot possibly describe or even list all the possible types of fasteners one may come upon and the countless variations each one can take, but I will describe some of the more common types which props artisans use on a daily basis.

- **Nails**—A nail is a simple spike made of metal. It is hammered, pushed, or otherwise driven through one material, out the other side, and into a second material, holding them together through the friction of the materials around the nail.

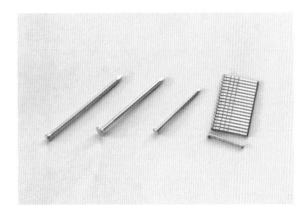

Figure 5-9: From left to right is a finish nail, common nail, box nail, and a row of brads glued together for quick loading into a brad gun.

Nails come in many forms for many tasks, such as wire nails, finish nails, brads, and box nails for carpentry and construction, as well as pins and tacks for soft goods and upholstery.

- **Staples**—A staple looks like a two-pronged nail. The top, or "crown," can be curved or slightly rounded, or bent at sharp angles. Staples come in many different widths, which refers to the distance between the two prongs. Staples can be hammered in one at a time, but most are driven from either a hand stapler, or an electric or pneumatic staple gun. They are used for attaching paper, thin lumber and other sheet goods, as well as for fabric and upholstery.

- **Screws**—A screw looks like a nail except it has a spiral ridge (known as a "thread") running down its length. Screws are driven into a material by turning it, and this thread moves it in a linear fashion. Screws come in a dizzying array of types; props shops commonly use a few such as wood screws, drywall screws (frequently employed as an "all-purpose" screw in shops), self-tapping (for both drilling and screwing through metal), and sheet metal screws. Many of these types can have different-shaped heads, such as pan head, round head, and flat head, as well as having different slots or shapes cut in the head for use with different types of screwdrivers; common ones include slotted (or flat head), Phillips, and square (or Robertson). Many other variations exist that may come in handy for more specialized tasks.

- **Nuts and Bolts**—A bolt has a thread like a screw, but it is not pointed or tapered. Rather, the other end is meant to have a nut turned on to it. The two materials being joined

Figure 5-10: Staples for staplers or staple guns come adhered together in rows. On the bottom is a single staple.

Figure 5-11: From left to right, a wood screw, drywall screw, flat head sheet metal screw, and a pan head sheet metal screw. Along the bottom is a self-tapping or self-drilling screw; notice how the tip looks like a tiny drill bit.

Figure 5-12: Top row, from left to right: A hex head bolt, washer, and nut. Middle: A machine screw with two washers and a nut attached. Bottom: A hex head lag bolt.

Figure 5-13: A corrugated fastener.

are trapped between the nut and the head of the bolt. Some bolts have heads like screws, while others have heads meant to be turned by various wrenches. A bolt may also have an unthreaded shank just below the head; if the threads cover the entire shaft, it is typically referred to as a "machine screw." Bolts have different head types, such as hex, stove, and carriage. Lag bolts actually do have a pointed tip, and are driven in like screws. Nuts come in many forms as well. With some materials, especially metal, you can drill and "tap" (cut the female portion of the threads) a hole directly in the material, so that a bolt screws directly to the material without needing a nut. The terminology differentiating various screws, machine screws, and bolts is not entirely standardized and has evolved throughout history, so if you hear someone refer to a fastener as a "bolt" when you think it should be called a "screw," that person may not necessarily be wrong. One of the biggest advantages to using nuts and bolts over screws is that it gives you a reversible bond rather than a permanent one.

- **Rivets**—Rivets are like a permanent version of a nut and bolt. A shaft with a head on one end is inserted through a hole in two or more materials. The other end is deformed so the rivet cannot be pulled back out of the holes. They are useful for joining thin sheets of materials together and in places where a nut and bolt will protrude too much from the surface of the materials. Most props artisans use pop rivets (also called blind rivets), which use a rivet gun and a special rivet that allows you to both insert the rivet and deform the opposite end without having to access the other side of your materials.
- **Corrugated fasteners**—Also known as "wiggle nails," these fasteners are meant to be driven in perpendicularly to both sides of a butt joint at once. They are especially useful for joining the four pieces of wood used in a picture frame.

Plumber's strap—Also called plumber's tape, hanger iron, or pipe strap. As its name implies, it was originally meant to hang or hold pipes and plumbing. It is an easily bent metal strap with regularly occurring holes that comes in long rolls like tape. It can strap items and objects down by driving a screw or bolt through one of the many holes. Though it has a reputation for being an inelegant solution used by lazy builders, it does have many uses in the appropriate situations.

Hook and loop fasteners—This is known almost universally by its most popular brand name, Velcro™. One side of a joint receives the "hook" part, and one the "loop" part, which are pressed together to create a strong, but completely reversible and mechanical bond. The materials used to make

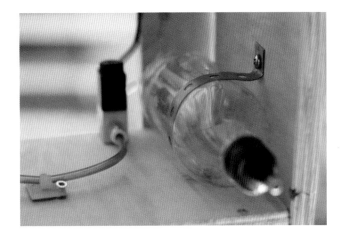

Figure 5-14: A piece of plumber's strap holds this plastic bottle in place.

hook and loop fasteners can range anywhere from a soft fabric to a hard and rigid plastic. Hook and loop fasteners are frequently used on fabrics, and can be attached by sewing it on. It can also be glued to other materials; you may also find hook and loop fasteners with self-adhesive backs so that you can apply it like tape.

Sewing, Lashing, and Wiring

Fabric can be sewn, sticks can be lashed, and metal can be wrapped in wire. You can also sew hard objects together, or sew using wire. In fact, staples were invented as a way to simplify the traditional practice of stitching papers together with thin lengths of wire.

You can find more specific information about sewing in Chapter 11. Information on lashing can be found in Chapter 10. These techniques are useful when you cannot attach two pieces with an adhesive and a readymade fastener is not appropriate. Lashing or wrapping can also double as a visible and decorative finish for a prop.

Monofilament, commonly called fishing line, is a single strand of plastic with enough strength to catch and hold a fish. Since it is fairly translucent, it all but disappears on camera or on

Figure 5-15: Jay Duckworth attaches fake leaves to a staff by wrapping floral wire around the stems.

stage, so is useful to the props artisan for when tiny bits of support are needed but no visible reinforcements can be added to the prop. Monofilament can be wrapped or sewn around objects to keep them together; it can also be strung between two points of an object to maintain a shape that might otherwise collapse.

Capturing the Object

You can hold a piece of material in place by building around it so that it has nowhere to move. Consider a picture in a frame. The front is smaller than the pane of glass, so it cannot fall out forward. The picture is sandwiched between the glass and a backing board. The frame has hardware that swings around to block the backing board from falling out the back. The picture is not glued or otherwise attached to the frame, but it is still held in place.

Magnets

Magnets are useful for constructing certain kinds of breakaway items, or for attaching a number of items together that need to be removable, but which cannot be altered with holes for bolts or residue from tape.

Rare earth magnets are the strongest nonelectrical magnets you can buy. They are found in a wide variety of shapes, sizes, and thicknesses, though you can also sand them down to a more precise size. Be sure when attaching them that your method of attachment is stronger than the magnet, or it will rip itself free. Gluing with epoxy or embedding the magnet is usually the strongest option; even if the magnet is covered over with a thin layer of material, it will still attract other magnets or steel. Be careful with these magnets, as they will snap together quickly with any other magnet or steel surface in the vicinity; if your hand is between them, they can pinch your skin off, while larger ones can crush or even break fingers.

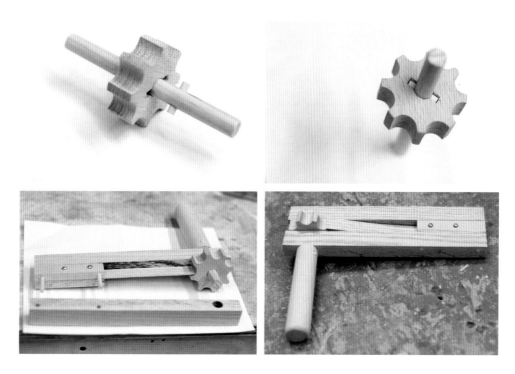

Figures 5-16 to 5-19: In the above four photographs, you can see that the wooden gear is not attached with glue, screws, nails, or any other type of fastener, yet the way the object is constructed completely surrounds the gear, preventing it from falling off.

six

measuring and marking

In this chapter, we will look at the process a props artisan uses to go from idea to reality. The starting point is our reference image. It may be a construction drawing or drafting from a designer, a sketch or doodle, a photograph, or a real object. In some cases, we have to draw or draft the prop ourselves, if it is from our imagination, or if the reference image needs to be altered. Occasionally, you may be provided with simply a verbal or written description of what needs to be built.

We then take our reference and transfer it to our construction materials. This covers a number of techniques of measuring and marking our materials so they can be cut, bent, sculpted, carved, folded, sewn, crumpled, attached, or otherwise manipulated into the shape and structure we need. We will also look at jigs, which extend our ability to transform our raw materials into props.

Construction Drawings

The prop may be drawn out, ranging from a fully realized technical drafting to the most basic of doodles, and everything in between. A **drafting** is an orthographic projection of the piece to be built. An orthographic projection, a method of representing a three-dimensional object in two dimensions, is a way of drawing the object as if you are taking a picture with an infinite focal length. In other words, it is as if you have a piece of glass in front of your object and you are tracing all the lines, except the effects of perspective are eliminated and shapes do not get smaller as they get farther away. So if you draw an orthographic projection of a box from the front, it would appear as a square. Lines that are perpendicular to the plane you are drawing will remain perpendicular rather than converging to a vanishing point as in perspective drawing.

A typical drafting includes the orthographic projections of the top, left, and front sides, though simpler props may only include the front and a side. Choosing where these sides are can be tricky on props with no definite "front" or "top," but once chosen, these projections are all at right angles to each other.

The different types of lines used indicated different things. A solid line indicates the outer boundaries of the material. A dashed line indicates a hidden line used to show the outline of something obscured by the material in front. An "X" within a shape is used where the material is cut out or hollow. Dimension lines give the measurements between the two

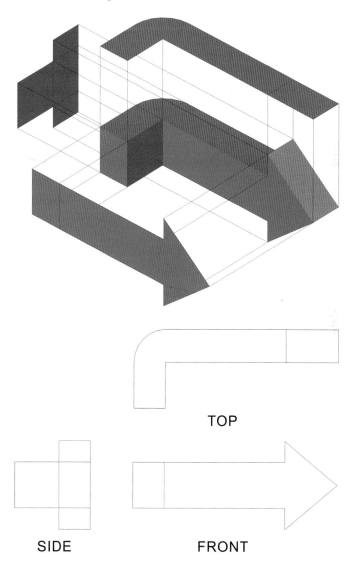

TOP

SIDE   FRONT

Figures 6-1 and 6-2: How the orthographic projection of the front, left, and top of an object is derived.

arrows used. A section line is used to indicate where a section is taken from; a section drawing shows what the object looks like if it were cut at the section line. Designers use section lines when a portion of the prop is obscured because it is on the inside or because it is behind the outermost parts of the prop. In a section drawing, crosshatching is used to indicate where

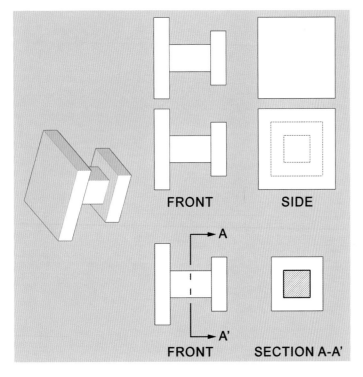

Figure 6-3: This object can be drafted a number of different ways, with three simple examples shown here. The top example shows just the front and the side; this does not really convey that much information. The middle drawing uses hidden lines (the dashed lines) to show what is behind the shapes drawn. The bottom drawing shows a **section** drawing. First, the cutting line, indicated by a heavy line with two dashes, shows where the section is taken from in the front view. The arrows indicate which direction you are looking at the section. In the section view itself, crosshatching indicates where a shape has been "cut" by the cutting line. We do not see the larger square in the section view because it is "behind" us.

you are looking at a shape that has been cut through, rather than at the outermost boundaries of the material. Break lines are used for long or repetitive sections so that the designer does not need to draw the whole thing out. Standards exist for drafting in the entertainment industries, such as the USITT graphics standards for theatre in the United States and Canada, but designers will bend these rules if it helps make the drafting clearer to read, particularly with props.

Designers will also write notes on their drafting for further clarification. Notes can indicate the materials to be used, the final look of the piece, or other needs of the prop that are not apparent from the drafting itself. Drafting is done in black and white and often does not convey any texture.

This is often used for carpentry and metal projects, where all measurements are critical for some reason, or where precision is required. **Critical measurements** are the measurements that need to be exact because of how they relate to some other element of the production. For example, a piece of furniture that is stored backstage and enters through a door during a scene change needs to be able to fit through that door. Its overall width is a critical measurement. If a box needs to hold something inside it, its interior dimensions are the critical measurement. It is important to determine which measurements are critical, and which are merely guidelines. In drafting, especially computer-aided drafting, designers have to use very specific measurements even when that is not their intent. You may wish to alter some of these measurements either to help make the prop more structurally sound, because of the materials you are using, or because it will make it either cheaper or faster to build.

Even when you have what appears to be a fully annotated drafting of a piece, you still need to think of it in three dimensions. First, there are the obvious holes in the picture; if the drafting does not show the piece from the back, do you have enough information about what the back needs to look like, or do you need to make an additional drawing? Second, when you think about a drawing in three dimensions, you may be surprised at what appears. I once had a full drafting of a wagon cart I needed to build for *La Boheme*. The drawing looked complete, and all the measurements I needed were already labeled. However, when I thought about it in three dimensions, I found that one of the handles would be floating in mid-air! When it was presented as a flat front, side, and top view, all the lines on the drawing touched each other, but that was an optical illusion; if it were to be built exactly as drawn, that one handle would not be touching any other part of the wagon. I talked with the props master, and after looking at the critical measurements, we altered the drawing slightly to make it work.

Another way you may be presented with a prop to build is with a sketch or illustration. While less exact than a drafting, it also frees the designer from having to determine exactness where it is not needed. It may provide critical measurements, or it may simply provide notes: "should be standard chair height," "must be taller than the actor," "needs to fit inside the champagne box." As you can see, measurements can

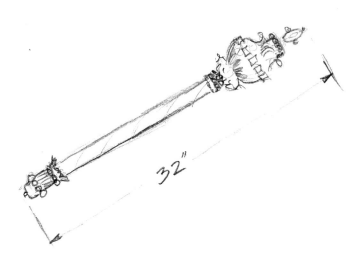

Figure 6-4: This sketch of a king's scepter gives critical measurements, overall shape, and a "feel" for what the prop should look like, but the specifics of the details and ornamentation are only hinted at with rough lines. This gives the props artisan some freedom to use found objects and applied decoration if necessary, or to carve the entire piece from scratch with whatever level of intricacy the budget and schedule will allow.

sometimes be given in relation to other elements of the production, so it is important to keep in contact with whoever is in charge of those elements while constructing that prop.

Drawings can distill the essence of what a prop looks like down to a few lines. For example, squiggly lines are often used to represent intricate detail, such as those found in Baroque or Rococo architecture. You may need to do your own research to flesh out the detail. You will also need to pay attention to whether the detail is invented, or if it is mirrored throughout other elements of the production. Often, a designer may latch onto a specific detail, such as a rosette or scroll work, which they insert into the set design, the costumes, and other props. You need to know if your specific prop will also contain that specific design detail. Squiggly lines can convey a lot of information.

Another way to convey information about a prop is through a photograph. Sometimes, it may be an exact fit; you are given a photograph, and told to reproduce it exactly. More often, the photograph is simply a guide. It may be a photograph of an object that needs alteration, such as "I want you to build this chair, but it needs to be these measurements." Other times, the prop you are building is more of an abstraction from the photograph, or a combination of elements from several photographs. It is vital to determine not just what is in the photograph, but also why is it being provided to you; what information is the designer or props master attempting to convey by giving you that photograph?

There are several ways to determine measurements from a photograph. First, you can base measurements on the prop itself by looking at the proportion of the various elements. The proportion of elements in a piece goes a long way in creating a prop that "looks right." Often, it is the correct proportions that create a more successful prop rather than finding exact measurements. If you determine the proportion of all the elements, by adding even just one critical measurement, you can then extrapolate the proper measurements for the rest of the prop.

You can also decipher the measurements from a photograph by comparing it to other elements in the photograph. If a person is holding a staff in the photograph, and the staff is as tall as that person, you know to make the staff as tall as the actor who will be holding it. If you have a photograph of a prop in a person's hands, you can use your own hands to determine the proper size.

Another way to craft the measurements you need is by using the measurements of objects that already exist. In our day and age, there are many objects which have a "standard size." For instance, chairs have a standard height for the seat, while doors have a standard height and width. Objects may also come in a variety of sizes, but still have a range of standard proportions. For example, if you are making a fantasy oversized book, it will convey itself as a book to the audience more successfully if it fits within the usual proportions of a book.

You may create a prop that replicates or is influenced by a real object. It is, of course, extremely useful to possess the real object you are building, but that is rare. More often, the real object is at someone's house, or in a museum, or in the location that inspired the set. It is likely you only have one chance to photograph or measure the object, so you have to do it right.

Start off with a front, a side, and a top view, and add any other views that may be helpful in reconstructing the object later. Even if the item is simply inspiration and not an exact replica, it is very helpful to choose which angles to photograph from and which details to include. If it's an asymmetrical object, then photographs from both sides are a must. Isometric views help to give you a guide as to how the different views join together.

Be careful about the distortions inherent in photographs. They do not reproduce reality exactly, at least as far as taking measurements is concerned. Many consumer cameras you use shoot with a wide-angle lens, which makes the center appear closer to the viewer, while the sides are pushed farther away. The front-to-back distances are exaggerated. You often have to zoom way out and step farther back to make the lens approximate that which we see with our eyes. If you have a camera with interchangeable lenses, you can take your photographs with a "standard" lens, which approximates what the human eye sees.

Taking photographs from different angles will help ensure you have the correct proportions and measurements. For instance, while a front view will make details in front appear larger than details at the back, the top view will show the correct relationship in size of the front and back.

Figures 6-5 and 6-6: Both images show the same object. The one on the top is photographed with a wide-angle lens, while the bottom image is shot with a normal focal length. Note the distortions.

Even with a standard lens, photographs have a number of distortions. If the picture is not taken completely straight on, you may get "converging parallels," that is, lines that are parallel in reality but which appear to move toward each other in the photograph. Again, this is why it is important to take photographs from multiple angles.

It is extremely helpful when photographing an object to take measurements as well. At the very least, you want to get the extreme measurements, that is, the overall width, length, and height. Remember how building a prop from a photograph is helped by having other objects to scale too? Use this to your advantage, and take pictures of the object in your hand or while standing next to it. For small objects, you can include the coins in your pocket for a quick and easy scale reference later on. If you have a ruler, include that in the photographs so when you are scaling your photographs later on, you already have an indication of how big an inch or a foot should be.

Depending on what you are building, making your own drawings from photographs (or any other information you are given, for that matter) can be extraordinarily useful. The main reason for making drawings is to determine measurements, and also to troubleshoot any problems that may arise before you begin committing your time and materials to a prop that may be physically impossible to build in a certain way. A drawing will also help you to break a prop down into simpler component parts and determine what materials and processes you can use to achieve these parts, but that will be covered in later chapters.

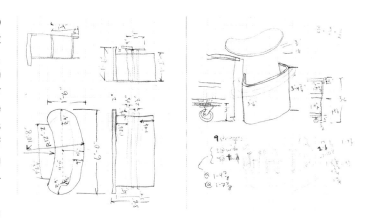

Figure 6-7: Drawing made by artisan to plan construction method.

Measuring

Props artisans utilize a number of devices for making simple measurements. A ruler is the most basic.

These come in multiple lengths, and can measure either in inches, metric, or both. Longer measuring devices, such as yardsticks and steel straightedges, are useful not just for

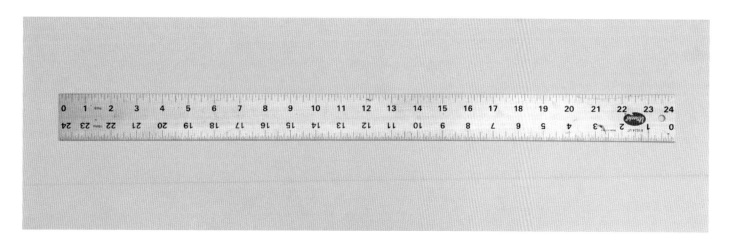

Figure 6-8: A straight edge.

Figure 6-9: A tape measure.

Figure 6-10: Calipers.

measuring, but also for drawing and cutting straight lines. Always be certain when taking your measurement that the ruler remains parallel to the edge you are measuring, otherwise your measurements will be inaccurate.

A **tape measure** is a piece of flexible steel that can measure much larger distances but still roll up enough to fit in your pocket. You can get them as large as 100 ft or 30 m (or more!), but it is rare for the props artisan to need anything larger than 25 or 30 ft, 7.5 or 10 m.

Tape measures have a little tab on the end that is used to hold the tape in place when measuring a piece of material. This tab is free to wiggle; this allows you take accurate measurements either from the outside or inside of a piece.

For fabric or other soft goods, a **flexible cloth tape** is handy. While a rigid device like a ruler or tape measure will give you accurate measurements on hard goods, a flexible cloth tape allows you to follow the folds of fabric and to wrap around contours, such as when measuring fabric for upholstery.

If you need to measure diameters or other odd-shaped pieces, **calipers** can be handy. Some calipers show the measurement that the calipers take. Others are simpler, and merely allow you to compare two measurements, or to hold the measurement next to a ruler to get a number.

When working with drawings in a different scale, a set of **architect's scale rulers** is vital. These have a number of sides with different scales; if you know the scale of your drawing, you can measure it with the proper side and find out the actual dimensions. US scene designers typically work in ¼″ or ½″ scale, while designers in metric parts of the world will work in 1:25 or 1:50. In larger works, particularly opera, designers may work in even larger scales. Of course, if the designer is drafting out the props, he or she may work in an even larger scale to fit as much information as possible on a sheet of paper.

Always check the scale before taking measurements, and use common sense; if you are building a chair from a drawing, and your scale ruler says it should be twelve feet tall, you're probably

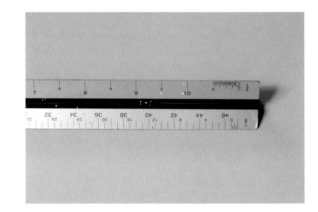

Figure 6-11: Architect's scale ruler.

using the wrong scale. Note that architect scales and engineer scales, while similar in appearance, use different numbers.

Checking rulers can be tricky since you do not really have a standard to check them against. Metal rulers tend to be the most accurate, as their manufacturing process is very precise and metal is affected by the elements the least; a wooden ruler will expand and contract with changes in humidity just like a piece of lumber. Check your measuring devices against each other and get rid of the ones that deviate from the average. Try to stick with a single measuring device on a project so at least the measurements will be internally consistent.

Tape measures can be the least reliable measuring devices if not taken care of. The little metal tab at the end is easily bent and will make all measurements inaccurate. Check your tape measure regularly by laying it over an accurate straight-edge ruler. The markings should line up. If they don't, you can bend the metal tab back into shape with a set of pliers.

To overcome the potential inaccuracy of a tape measure, carpenters sometimes "burn an inch," that is, they begin measuring from the one inch mark and forgo the metal tab altogether. This is indeed more accurate, but you run the risk of misreading your measurements. If you start your measurement at one inch, and the other end reads six inches, your actual measurement is five inches. It is very easy to forget this, especially when taking a number of measurements in a row, and a common lament heard in the props shop by carpenters is, "I forgot to burn an inch!"

Cloth tape measures can also involve some inaccuracy, as they easily stretch up to a half an inch longer over several feet. The plastic-reinforced flexible tape measures are more reliable.

A trickier measurement to come by is the volume of a certain item. You may need this if you are casting a piece and want to mix only as much casting material as necessary (for economic reasons). If you can get the piece wet, you can find the volume by submerging it in a cup of liquid. Mark the height of the water both before and after you submerge your object. The amount of water it takes to fill the cup from the first line to the second is the amount of material you will need to cast that item. If you cannot get your item wet, you can fill it with a dry material such as sand (do not pack it down).

Figures 6-12 and 13: Measuring the volume of an object.

To measure the depth of a hole or groove, you can use any number of specialized depth gauges, or just use a thin enough stick, mark the depth, and measure that. For drilling to a specific depth, some drill presses come with adjustable stops that allow you to set the depth which you drill to. But you may use a drill press that does not have a stop, or you may be using a handheld drill, or you are drilling into materials of different thickness but still want the holes to be the same depth. In any case, you can add a stop-block directly to your drill bit, but you need a different stop-block for every different diameter of drill bit you have. A quicker and cheaper option is to simply wrap a piece of masking tape around your drill bit to let you know how deep to drill.

Figure 6-14: Using masking tape to mark the depth of a drill bit.

Marking

In addition to maintaining accuracy with your measuring devices, you want to maintain accuracy with the markings you make. A dull pencil can create a thick enough line that if you cut the wrong part of it, your piece will end up slightly larger or smaller than you wanted it to be. If you use a pencil, make sure it is as sharp as possible when making your marks.

For precise work, traditional carpenters like to use sharp knives to make their marks, which essentially have no width. You can use a special marking knife for this purpose, or just a knife with disposable blades, alternately called utility knives, box cutters, matt knives, or Stanley knives. You can even use your pocket or pen knife in a pinch. Knife marks are harder to see unless you are up close (you can circle it with a pencil to solve that problem) and not every material can be marked with a knife.

The tools and machines to cut your materials also have widths. A razor blade's width is inconsequential, but the blade on a table saw or radial arm saw can be an eighth of an inch thick or more. The width of a blade is called the **kerf**. If you mark a piece of wood at six inches and cut it so the kerf is on the wrong side of your mark, your wood will be .5 ⅞" long. So the other consideration in making your marks is indicating which side of the mark the kerf should go on. This is known as the **waste side** of your mark to indicate that it is not the piece of material you are keeping; all cuts should be made on the waste side of your mark.

For layout, there are a whole class of tools for making and marking perpendicular lines. Combination squares and speed squares enable you to push one side to an edge and make a quick mark. Framing squares will also let you find perpendicular lines.

To find and mark angles, sliding bevel squares are extraordinarily useful, particularly in their ability to find an angle on one piece and transfer it to another.

For fabric, paper, and other delicate materials, plastic versions of the above tools exist (commonly sold with drafting supplies at hobby and art stores). Clear plastic squares and triangles allow you to see the material underneath while measuring and marking.

Tools for checking the squareness of an object, like combination squares or quick squares, can be checked for accuracy by drawing a line with them, and then flipping the tool over and drawing a line over the top of the first line. If the two lines

Figure 6-15: The kerf of a blade is wider than your pencil line. Mark which side of the line you should cut on.

Figure 6-16: Try square.

Figure 6-17: Combination square.

Figure 6-18: Framing square.

Figure 6-19: Speed square or rafter angle square.

Figure 6-20: Sliding bevel.

Figure 6-21: Bevel protractor.

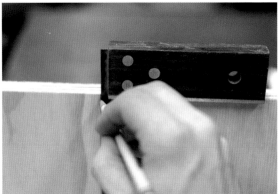

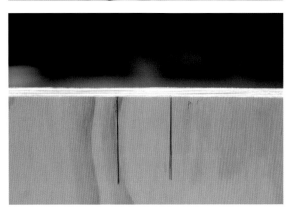

match, the tool is square. If the lines form a slight V, you have an inaccurate tool.

Making sure your pieces are square when they are supposed to be is important for a lot of constructed props. In some cases, your tools may not be large enough to check the overall squareness. If you have a box, the best way to check if it is square is to measure the diagonals. If these are equal, the box is square. If not, you may need to rack the box to tweak it into squareness.

To make circles, you can use a compass. The kind of compasses you find in elementary schools are typically low quality, and do not hold their settings for very long. Much better ones exist for the professional. You may need to draw circles that are much larger than any compass can achieve. You can try putting a nail or screw in the center and tying a string to it with a pencil on the other end. The problem with this is that string stretches and sags, and it will not keep your pencil at a consistent angle. A far better method is to use a piece of stiff material, such as a wooden stick or metal bar. On one end secure a point so it cannot move, and on the other, attach your pencil or marking tool so it is stiff and unmovable. You can buy manufactured versions of these called **trammel points**, where you only need to supply the board and the pencil.

Figures 6-22 to 6-24: Checking the squareness of your tools. The first line shows a square tool, the second shows a tool that is off-square by a bit; notice how it forms a slight V.

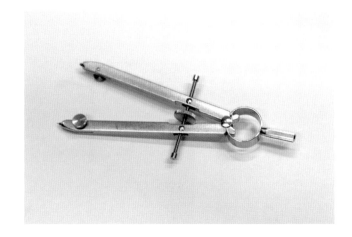

Figure 6-25: Compass.

What follows are a number of shortcuts that carpenters and others find useful to make precise and accurate shapes and marks with the tools available in the typical shop.

A divider can be used when you need to divide a piece of material into divisions of a specific length. Dividers look like a compass except that both legs are pointy, and neither holds a pencil.

Figure 6-26: To find the center of a square or rectangle, draw two diagonal lines connecting the opposing corners.

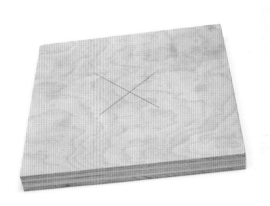

Figure 6-27: The intersection is your center point. This works for other parallelograms as well, such as rhomboids and rhombi, but not for quadrilaterals with unequal opposing sides.

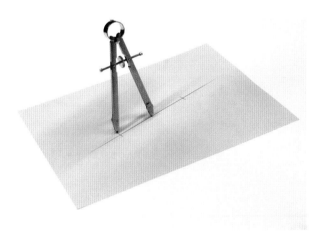

Figure 6-28: You can create a perpendicular line with a compass rather than a square. Take your compass, and from the point where you wish the line to pass through, mark a point on either side.

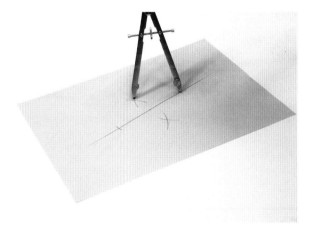

Figure 6-29: Set your compass to a larger radius. Inscribe an arc from each of these two points on either side of your line. These arcs should intersect once above your line, and once below.

Figure 6-30: If you draw a line connecting these two intersections, it will be perpendicular to your original line. You can modify this method to find the center of a line as well. If you set your compass to a radius greater than half the length of your line and draw an arc from either end point, the line connecting the two intersections of the two arcs will run through the exact middle of your line.

Whether you are drawing directly onto your material, or onto a piece of paper, you may find drafting tools to be helpful. In some cases, you may even wish to sit at a drafting table and do all your layout there.

Figure 6-32: From each of these two points, draw a small arc.

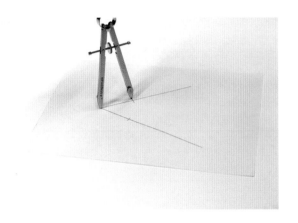

Figure 6-31: One way to bisect an angle (divide it in half) with a compass is to mark off a point along each side, keeping the compass set at the same radius.

In other cases, you may wish to work on a computer. You can print the drawings out at full-scale; from that point, you may use them simply as reference, taking measurements from them, or transfer them directly to your material. With carbon or transfer paper, you can trace your lines on top, and they will appear on your material below.

If your material is translucent or transparent, you can place the drawing below and draw directly on the material

Figure 6-33: Take the point where those two arcs connect, and draw a line connecting that to the vertex; this line is your bisection.

Figure 6-34: Another method involves laying a board along the edge of one side of your angle so the edge is flush. Inscribe a line, and then repeat with the board along the other edge.

Figure 6-35: Take the point where these two lines connect, and draw a line to your vertex. Bisecting an angle is helpful when you need to determine what angle to cut for molding that runs along the perimeter; the angles need to match for the shapes to line up with each other.

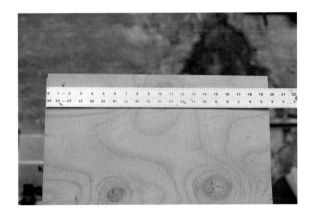

Figure 6-36: If you have a piece of material that is 20 inches long, and you need to divide it into 4 equal parts, you can use math; each piece will be 5 inches long. But if you have a board of a size that does not divide evenly into the number of parts you need, you need another method. In the following photographs, we have a board that is about 19 ¾ inches, and we want to divide it into 7 equal parts. We can try to mark off 2.82142857 inches for each part, or we can solve the problem manually.

Figure 6-37: Hold the ruler at an angle so that the 0 is at one end, and a multiple of the number of divisions you need is at the other end. In this photograph, we hold the ruler at 21, a multiple of 7. If we place a mark every 3 inches, we will have 7 equal parts.

Figure 6-38: You can now use a square to extend your marks to the edge of the board. No math needed!

on top. For some materials, you may wish to **pounce** it. Rather than tracing with a pencil, you trace with a rotary tool that leaves a trail of little holes or indentations along the material. For materials that cannot be pierced, you can still punch the holes in your paper, and then take some colored chalk and pounce it through the holes. Special pouncing bags exist for this.

An alternative to tracing or transferring your drawing is to adhere it directly to your material. You want a temporary

Figure 6-40: This ornate fan was drafted in full scale to establish proportions and solidify the details.

adhesive (spray adhesives work well here) unless that surface will be covered or removed in a later process.

If you need to enlarge or reduce a drawing, you have several options. First, you can do it on a computer or photocopier

Figure 6-41: For a cheap and quick method of transferring when you do not have access to transfer paper, shade the back of your paper with a graphite pencil or charcoal. You do not need to fill the whole thing, just the areas where the lines are.

Figure 6-39: A divider.

Figure 6-42: Trace the lines on the front over your material.

Figure 6-43: The graphite or charcoal will be transferred to your material.

Figures 6-44 to 6-46: A grid is drawn over a photograph and transferred to a piece of foam. *The Gods Are Not to Blame*, Ohio University, 2004. Scenic design by Natalie Taylor Hart. Photograph and sculpture by Debi Jolly, costume crafts and props artisan.

if it is capable of printing on paper large enough for your prop. If not, you can print to several pieces of paper and tape them together to get one large piece. If that is still not possible, you can project the image with either an overhead or a digital projector onto a surface and then trace the lines. These methods of enlargement will make everything bigger, including the lines of the drawing, which in some cases leaves too much room for ambiguity and imprecision. It is also vital to point the projector so it does not shine on the surface at an angle; known as **keying**, this distorts the image.

A grid layover is a method to enlarge or transfer an image when you cannot do it mechanically. Draw or overlay a grid over the reference image, then make a larger grid with the same number of squares, and redraw your image. If your reference image is in scale, you can use a scale rule to draw a grid in scale. Depending on the size of the image and the size you wish to enlarge it to, you may want to put a line at every inch, every couple of inches, or even every foot.

Making a Cut List

A **cut list** is a list that displays the sizes of all the pieces you will assemble together. It allows you to estimate the amount of material you will need to purchase and use for a project. You can also do all your cutting at the same time, so you do not have to walk back and forth between the power saws, or set up and reset machines, particularly if you are working in a small shop where your table saw surface doubles as your assembly table.

Figure 6-47: A cut list allows you to cut all the pieces out first. This can be incredibly efficient, especially when you need to cut many pieces out to the same measurements. These pieces have been labeled to help keep track of where they go on the final prop (as well as to distinguish them from scrap pieces that other artisans may grab for their own projects!)

For many prop projects, you may not be able to develop your entire cut list at the beginning. Sometimes it is more helpful to build a portion of your prop before taking the next step; maybe it has some tricky geometry that you cannot sketch or visualize in your head and which you'd rather see in real physical form. Sometimes, you just do not have all the parts figured out yet, and you like to construct your prop little by little before making the decisions on how to proceed.

Whether you make a complete cut list at the beginning, or develop one as you move along, you should know how to make one.

In this example, we have a box we wish to make out of ¾" plywood. It has four sides and a bottom, and is open on top. It has a 20 inch by 20 inch footprint, and is 28 inches tall. We have our first bit of information: our cut list will have five pieces of wood listed. So our cut list should look like this, right?

	Length (inches)	Width (inches)
Piece 1	20	28
Piece 2	20	28
Piece 3	20	28
Piece 4	20	28
Piece 5	20	20

Wrong! Look again; if we draw the cube out as if we would construct it, you will see that not all the pieces are the same size; you have to take into account the thickness of your materials.

This is one of the most common mistakes made by beginners (and even some experts) when making a cut list for carpentry and other constructive projects. Here is our correct cut list:

	Length (inches)	Width (inches)
Piece 1	20	27 1/4
Piece 2	20	27 1/4
Piece 3	18 1/2	27 1/4
Piece 4	18 1/2	27 1/4
Piece 5	20	20

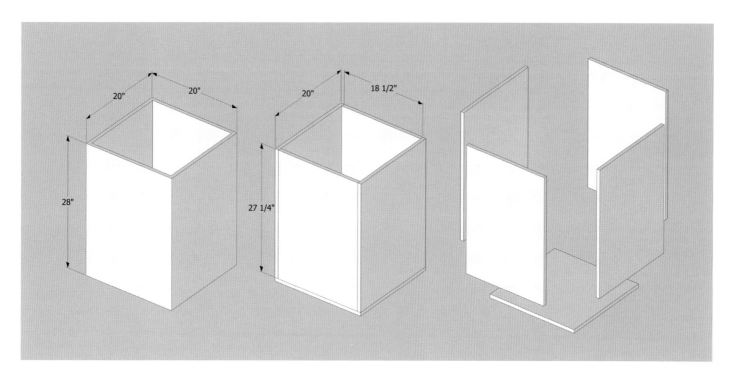

Figure 6-48: Breaking apart a box to develop a cut list.

Once you have your cut list, you can also plan out the most efficient way to make all the cuts while using the least amount of material possible. For our box example, you can lay out the pieces on a stock 4' by 8' piece of plywood in a manner that will maximize the size of the leftover piece or pieces.

Mock-Ups and Patterns

A props artisan may build a full-scale mock-up of a prop. When an actor needs to interact heavily with a prop, they may wish to use it during the rehearsal process. It may be difficult to have the real prop completed that early, so a mock-up that matches the size and weight as closely as possible may be substituted. This may also happen because the real prop will be expensive to make, and the director is not entirely sure exactly what kind of interaction the actor will have with the prop. The props artisan will make a mock-up out of a cheaper material so it is easier to change and modify while the design evolves during the rehearsal period. Often, the designer or director cannot conceive of the scale of certain props, particularly furniture. When it is mocked up in full size and placed next to actors in the rehearsal hall, they can see more clearly whether it is the size and proportion that they were hoping for, or whether parts need to be lengthened or shortened. When it comes time to construct the real prop, all the design factors (size, weight, shape, balance, etc.) will have been refined to a point where the designer, director, and actor are happy.

A props artisan may also build a mock-up for personal reasons. A drawing or photograph of an item does not fully convey all the information of a three-dimensional object, even if it is drawn up in full scale. A three-dimensional digital model will also be incomplete, because you cannot see how the item feels in your hand, how it is balanced, or what it looks like in proportion to a human being or other objects it will need to interact with. If your prop is going to be constructed out of a cheap and easily modified material, you may as well just build your prop to completion, then make modifications as you figure them out. But when your prop is built out of an expensive or labor-intensive material, a mock-up is helpful.

Building mock-ups is also a great opportunity to reuse materials rather than purchasing new materials for a disposable use. I have built many pieces of rehearsal furniture out of the lumber from previous sets that were headed for the dumpster. I have never had to purchase cardboard to use for rehearsal props because so many props and supplies are shipped in large cardboard boxes; I actually run out of room to store cardboard before I run out of usable cardboard.

Patterns are a way to record the full-scale sizes and shapes of the pieces you need to cut out. These can be developed from your mock-up or directly from the drawings. In some cases, your

Figure 6-50: Natalie Taylor Hart uses a full-scale paper cutout of a chair leg to trace multiple exact copies out on a piece of wood.

Figure 6-49: A mock-up of a saddle built out of cardboard.

mock-up may actually become your pattern; when you make a mock-up out of cardboard, you can then disassemble it into individual pieces for a pattern that you can trace onto a different material. When constructing armor or other sheet metal products, artisans will frequently use thick card stock or heavy paper to get the fit and shape right before tracing the patterns to steel. Costumers and fashion designers develop patterns on tracing paper, either altering existing patterns, developing them from their own draping, or somewhere in between. More about patterning will be found in Chapter 12.

Some tools will even let you duplicate shapes if you have a pattern cut out. A router with a flush-trim bit router, for instance, can follow the shape of a piece of wood on the

Figure 6-51: This box was small enough that it could be drawn out full-scale on a single sheet of paper. The widths and thicknesses of all the pieces were laid out exactly so when the time came to construct it, the measurements could be taken directly from the drawing without needing a scale ruler or math.

bottom and cut the same shape out of a piece of material on the top.

You can use computer-aided drafting and 3D drawing software to help you as well. These programs can let you construct a virtual mockup and even let you develop patterns or cutlists. These programs use an entirely different set of skills than what is covered in this book, and you still need the knowledge of materials and building techniques for them to be useful.

A 3D program can let you sketch up an object so you can play with the sizes and proportions of the parts that may not be clearly defined in the drawing. It can also be used to communicate to the designer what you intend to build before committing any materials.

If you draw a triangle with a base and a side of known measurements, a CAD program will give you the measurement of the hypotenuse. While this may be easy enough to figure out without a computer program, more complicated measurements

of angles, curves, and other irregular shapes can easily be automated by drawing out the object with whatever measurements you do know.

Finally, the parts you draw on the computer can be printed out at whatever scale you need and transferred to or pasted directly on the material you need to cut. You can also use the drawings to have the pieces cut on any number of digital fabrication tools at your disposal, such as CNC machines or laser cutters.

Jigs

A **jig** is a device for maintaining the spatial relationship between two or more objects. The objects may be your tool and your material, or it may be several pieces of your materials. As an example, a circle jig for the bandsaw allows you to cut a nearly perfect circle from a piece of material. A jig can be as simple as a spacer block, which holds two materials apart at a certain distance; in other words, it maintains a spatial relationship between two objects.

You can find all sorts of commercial jigs that simplify certain tasks or allow you a greater precision with your tools. If you work in several different shops, you may find certain homemade jigs that turn up everywhere you go. You can find any number of books, magazines, and online resources that have ideas for any number of jigs to make your life easier. Finally, there are the jigs you construct while building a specific project, designed solely to allow you to position the pieces of that exact project and nothing else.

Think of it this way; if your project has a repetitive task, like placing hundreds of evenly spaced tacks around the perimeter of an upholstered seat, or if it requires a certain amount of precision, consider using a jig. Being able to freehand something is not necessarily the sign of a good props artisan. Often, it is the experienced artisan who spends more time measuring, laying out, and preparing jigs before beginning a project. The novice is more likely to jump right in with a saw and make a mess of the whole thing.

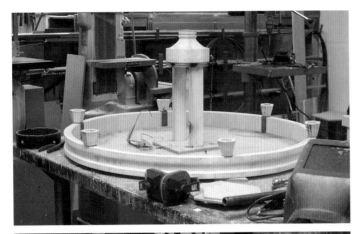

Figure 6-54: A jig holds the wheel of this carriage in place while the supports are added.

Figures 6-52 and 6.53: A jig holds the body dish of this chandelier in the center and at the required height so the arms can be welded on. *Romeo and Juliet*, Ohio University, 2004. Scenic design by Pavlo Bosyy.

Figure 6-55: This jig allows a tapered leg to be cut on the bandsaw.

Jigs for your tools can be helpful in adding precision. A table saw is really just a collection of jigs for a circular saw. It has a large flat table that holds the material perpendicular to the blade. The fence is a jig that keeps the material at a consistent distance from the blade to ensure a parallel cut. Your tools may have features that allow the addition of readymade jigs, such as the miter slot on the aforementioned table saw, or changeable sole plates on a router. Homemade jigs can range anywhere from simple devices for accomplishing a single task on a specific prop, to fully adjustable reusable jigs, such as a router table for your router.

Figure 6-56: David Schneider uses a shop-made jig to cut large arcs and circles with a router.

seven

carpentry

Carpentry is one of the oldest artisan skills co-opted by the props artisan. Every culture that exists near trees utilizes wood as a construction material in some way. The mass production of modern power tools and machines, along with the ready availability of lumber and lumber-based sheet goods, have made it possible for even the most basic of shops to quickly turn out furniture, cabinetry, and other wooden items for use on the stage or screen.

Compared to other materials, wood is cheap. The tools needed to work it are inexpensive and easy to learn as well. It is relatively strong and can mimic a wide range of other materials. For these reasons, it is a staple in practically every props shop, from bare-bones summer stock theatres to high-tech film fabrication studios.

The lumber from a tree comes in boards, planks, and sheets of all sorts of thickness, widths, and lengths. We can also buy lumber in different shapes, such as dowels, pegs, blocks, discs, rings, and any number of carved shapes and moldings. Apart from pure wood products, many materials are made from wood and wood by-products, such as plywood, particle board, MDF, MDO, Masonite, and so on.

Parts of a Board

Wood has a grain. Grain runs along the length of a board. If you run down the length with your hand, you will find that it feels smooth to rub it in one direction, and rougher to rub it in the other, like when you rub a shark. The smooth direction is with the grain, while the rough direction is against the grain. Moving perpendicularly to the grain is known as cross grain.

Wood is stronger along the grain than it is across the grain. This is extremely noticeable if you've ever split firewood with an axe. The axe readily chops the wood in one direction, sometimes with a minimum of force. Try to cut it perpendicularly, however, and you will merely succeed in putting a dent in it.

Cutting wood and wood products with power tools, or even just hand sanding, releases dust into the air. Sawdust is not only an irritant, it can also lead to asthma and other breathing problems. Wood dust is also classified as a Group 1 carcinogen by the International Agency for Research on Cancer, meaning it is *known* to be a carcinogen. Proper dust collection at the tools, ventilation in the air, and respiratory protection is vital in a shop that builds props out of wood.

Cutting Wood to Length and Width

Cutting a board along the grain is called **ripping**. You rip a board to get it to a specific width. The quickest and most accurate way to rip a board to width in most props shops is with the table saw. When you cut a board perpendicularly to the grain, it is called a **cross-cut**. Most of the time in a props shop, you would use a miter saw, a chop saw, or a radial arm saw to cross-cut a board to the length you need. A saw blade for ripping is different from a saw blade for cross-cutting in the number of teeth, and how the teeth are angled and shaped. However, you can get combination blades, which allow you to cross-cut on the table saw as well. A portable circular saw is useful for ripping or cross-cutting as well, particularly when a board is too unwieldy or large to maneuver on your stationary machines. You can mark a line along where you want to cut and freehand, or attach a straight guide or rail that the saw can follow along for greater accuracy.

You can also cut a board with a hand saw. Like circular saw blades, hand saws come with rip, cross-cut, or combination blades. While ripping a long board to width by hand can be quite a chore, cross-cutting a small piece by hand can sometimes be quicker than looking for an outlet, plugging an electric saw in, making the cut, then unplugging and rolling the cord back up.

Figure 7-1: A chair built for the Santa Fe Opera. Without the paint and upholstery, you can see how it is constructed from a number of individual pieces that were cut and shaped from boards of wood. Look closely, and you can see that some of these pieces (the legs and the arms) are actually made up of thinner pieces sandwiched together.

Figure 7-2: The parts of a wooden board.

Figure 7-4: The correct way to grip a handsaw.

The table saw is one of the most common machines found in a props shop, and is one of the most useful and versatile as well. Statistically, the table saw is also the most dangerous, so it is worthwhile to describe its safe usage.

Figure 7-3: A stop block on a saw allows you to repeatedly cut pieces to the same length without having to measure and mark each one.

A table saw has a rip fence, which allows you to make cuts parallel to the blade, and a miter track, which allows various tools to push the wood either perpendicularly or at another angle through the blade. Most saws come with a simple miter gauge, though cutting large pieces often requires building or purchasing a sliding table to ride one or both of the miter tracks. You should never use both the rip fence and the miter gauge at the same time.

If the material does not move perfectly straight through the blade, it can suddenly catch on the blade, and the force will shoot the material back at you. Be sure the rip fence is locked securely in place before making the cut, and that it is exactly parallel to the blade. Keep the material firmly against the rip fence throughout the cut by firmly holding the material against the fence at the point right before it enters the blade; never push it to the side at a point past the blade. Only run a straight edge along a rip fence; a wavy or uneven edge will cause the material to shift back and forth as it runs along the rip fence.

When using the miter track, make sure the wood is secure in whatever accessory you are moving it with.

Figure 7-5: Though table saws can have major variations, most share some basic features seen in this photograph. The blade sticks up through a "throat plate." An adjustable **rip fence** allows you to set the width of the board you wish to rip and keeps the material parallel to the blade as you feed it through. The two channels on either side of the blade are **miter tracks**, which let you run a miter gauge and many other types of jigs parallel to the blade. Below the table, in the front is a wheel that controls the height of the blade. The wheel on the left side controls the angle the blade is tilted at; on most table saws, you can tilt it anywhere from 0° to 45°—sometimes more. This saw also has a blade guard that doubles as a dust collector (you can see it in the corner—it is painted yellow and pushed aside for clarity in this photograph).

The speed of the table saw blade may also lift the material up as it moves through the blade, so keep a hand firmly pressing down on the material as well.

Kickback may happen because the wood tries to squeeze itself back together as you cut it, and it pinches the blade. Wood can be under a lot of internal stress, which is relieved as you cut it. You will hear the blade slow down and start to whine as this happens; you can also sometimes see the kerf of the wood closing up as it exits the blade. When this happens, stop your cut; do not back the wood out, but rather hold it firmly, making sure it is not going anywhere, and keeping at least one hand on it, stop the machine. Wait until the blade has completely stopped spinning before taking your hands off or attempting to remove the wood. Some machines have a large off switch that can be easily pressed with your knee. Most table saws have a safety feature called a riving knife, which is a finger of metal as thick as the blade's kerf that rises up just past the blade. This keeps the wood from closing back onto the blade. Because a riving knife is mounted to the same part of the table saw as the blade, it travels with it when you change the height or the angle. It does not need to be removed for cross cuts or blind cuts, and so should be left on at all times.

To avoid injury in the case of an inevitable kickback, position yourself to the side of the wood you are pushing through. Should the wood shoot backward, it will fly past you rather than slamming into your stomach or groin.

The other danger of a table saw is contact with the blade. For most cuts, the blade should not stick more than ¼" above the top of the material you are cutting. The throat plate (the typically red or orange oval of metal that surrounds the blade) also serves as a guide to keeping your fingers away from the blade; your fingers should never enter the throat plate zone while the blade is spinning. If you need to handle the wood within the throat plate zone, use a push stick. Feather boards are also handy attachments for keeping the wood firmly in place close to the blade. Never cross your arms over the blade while it is spinning. If you want to grab the cutoff piece of wood on the left of the blade, use your left hand, because your right hand would have to cross the blade to get it. I did just that in high school, and my right hand was not high enough; in a fraction of a second, the blade nicked my thumb and I could see straight down to the bone. Never push the wood with your hands directly behind the blade; should the wood suddenly cut very quickly, you will push your finger right into the blade. Never pull the wood from the other side. It is sometimes necessary to enlist the help of another to "catch" the wood as it comes off the end of the table saw, particularly for larger pieces. The helper should not pull, push, or otherwise manipulate the wood. They need to support the wood as lightly as possible.

Most modern table saws have blade guards, which keep anything directly over the blade from coming into contact with it. This still does not protect your hands if you reach in from the sides. You should keep all guards and safety features in place at all times. If, for some reason, you have to perform an operation

that requires removing one of the safety items, be sure to put it back on as soon as you are finished; this is true for all tools. Before doing that, though, ask yourself if you really need to remove the safety features, or if you can perform the task in another manner.

Table saws cause as many accidental amputations in the United States as doors. The vast majority of table saw injuries are due to a lack of training, or oversight by more experienced saw users.

Some larger saws now come with "flesh detection" technology. If a finger comes into contact with the blade, the saw will stop instantly before the skin is even broken. Most such devices require replacing the whole mechanism once it is

Figure 7-6: This solid wood tabletop was too wide to make from a single board, so several planks of poplar were glued along their edges. While edge-to-edge joints in lumber are the strongest glue joints and require no reinforcement, many props carpenters prefer to use biscuits, dowels, pocket hole screws, or other means to line the boards up more precisely. The clamps should be placed evenly along the edge. A clamp may cause the boards to bow as they dry, so alternate your clamps along the top and the bottom to ensure no bowing occurs. For this tabletop, I also clamped a piece of steel box tube along the edge to help keep it flat while drying. *The Last Cargo Cult*, the Public Theatre, 2009. Scenic design by Peter Ksander.

activated, which can cost over a hundred dollars. While this is a hefty cost if the flesh detection accidentally goes off while you are cutting wet wood, it is far cheaper than having to replace a finger. Personally, I think with proper training and a well-maintained saw, such detection technologies are unnecessary. However, for an educational shop or a props shop that trains interns and apprentices, such saws can relieve a lot of stress in the teachers.

It does not really matter what order you rip or cross-cut in. In some cases I will rip a board to width first because it is too wide to fit on my chop saw. Other times I will cut it to length first so I do not have to maneuver a very long piece through the table saw. Some shops do not have enough room to fit boards over a certain length through the table saw. Always check before cutting to make sure your board will not hit the wall in front of your table saw (or any other obstacle) before your cut is complete. I may also make my cuts in a certain order to maximize the sizes of my offcuts so as to waste less wood. Every situation is different.

Cutting at an Angle

You will occasionally need pieces cut at an angle, rather than just parallel or perpendicular to other surfaces. Miter boxes allow you to cut a specific angle with a hand saw. A miter saw gives you the powered equivalent of a miter box while also allowing you to choose any angle to cut the end of a board at. For cutting a long edge to an angle (sometimes known as a **taper**), you can either use a power tool like a circular saw or jig saw with a rail following that angle, or use a special taper jig (constructed or purchased) with a machine like a table or band saw.

To cut an edge or end at an angle to the face of a board (known as a **bevel**), many machines allow you to adjust either the blade or the table within a range of angles; on power tools, the shoe (sometimes called the "soleplate") can be adjusted. The **shoe** is the metal plate on the bottom of many tools that is placed on the material being cut. Routers, router tables, and shapers can also be equipped with angled cutters to cut specific angles.

You can, of course, employ any number of hand tools, such as saws, chisels, and planes, to achieve the same results, albeit more slowly.

Making Wood Thinner or Thicker

A **planer** is the quickest and most precise machine to make a board thinner. You feed your board in one end of this machine, where rollers grab it and move it under a cylindrical blade that shaves a tiny amount off the top (usually between 1/16" to 3/32"). You can also plane a board by hand, though this takes a lot more time and labor, especially to make a truly flat board. Using a hand planer for more than just the occasional small piece is not realistic with the deadlines of your typical props shop.

Since a planer shaves a board down bit by bit, planing an especially thick board to a much thinner one results in a lot of usable wood being reduced to dust. If you have a board 1 ½" thick and you need a piece ½" thick, it is better to **resaw** it so you have two pieces that can be planed down to ½" thick each (better still is to buy your boards as close to the thickness as you need). Resawing is where you turn the board on its edge and cut it along its thickness. This is typically done on a large band saw (called, coincidentally, a "resaw") with a very wide blade (2" to 3" from front to back). If your board is not too wide, you can run it through your regular band saw. In some cases, you can even resaw a board on your table saw, though this is particularly dangerous; raising the blade all the way leaves a lot of exposed teeth and makes the board more susceptible to binding. Running the board through on its edge also makes it harder to balance and keep upright.

If you need pieces that are thicker than the lumber you have, you can glue them together face to face. Coat one face completely with glue. It is helpful to squeeze the glue out in a zigzag pattern along one face, then spread it out with either a roller, paint brush or squeegee. Clamp your pieces together well, and ensure that you have even pressure along the entire

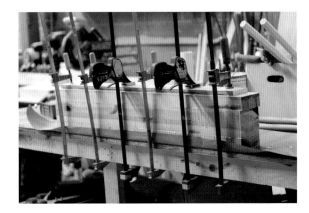

Figure 7-7: Because gluing large boards together uses a lot of clamps, multiple boards can be stacked on top of each other to share clamps.

length. You may even use weights as clamps, especially for larger pieces that cannot be clamped in the middle. The glue causes the pieces to slip and slide out of place as you tighten the clamps. Keep the pieces a little large at this point, and cut them to the proper length and width after they have been glued together, rather than trying to line them up precisely while the glue is drying.

Cutting Curves and Making Irregular Shapes

For boards and sheet goods, you have a number of options for cutting curved or irregular-shaped profiles. Among powered machines, the band saw is the most popular workhouse for these cuts, while a scroll saw is sometimes employed for finer and more intricate details. The jig saw is a useful powered hand tool; a reciprocating saw can be used too, though it is harder to control with precision. To cut by hand, carpenters find a fretsaw to be most useful; this tool is so named because it was traditionally used to cut the intricate designs and patterns known as fretwork. A coping saw is similar to a fretsaw in appearance and use.

Figure 7-8: One of the first woodworking projects I ever did was cutting a letter "E" out of a board on a band saw when I was twelve years old. Sixteen years later, I made the letters for this "hotel" sign in much the same way, by cutting MDF out on a band saw. The center of the "O" was cut with a jigsaw.

Some curved surfaces will be too large to cut from a solid piece of wood, and will require bending a sheet of wood into shape. Thin sheets of wood can take a gentle curve. For more severe curves, wood can be steamed, which makes it temporarily more flexible. Without steam, you can buy sheets of "bending" or "wiggle" boards (described later in this chapter). You can also **kerf** a sheet or board of wood. This involves cutting parallel grooves nearly all the way through the wood along the surface that needs to curve. You may also purchase sheets of lumber that are already kerfed.

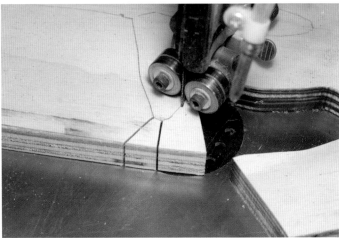

Figures 7-9 and 7-10: A band saw can cut curves and irregular shapes out of a sheet of wood. The minimum radius that can be cut is determined by the width of the blade. For tighter curves, you can make cuts from the edge to your pencil line, so as you cut, the offcuts free themselves and your blade has room to maneuver.

Figure 7-11: A jigsaw is like a hand version of the band saw. Use it when you can't fit your material on the band saw, or when you need to cut interior shapes out. When cutting an interior shape, drill a hole in the off-cut section so you can fit the jigsaw blade inside.

A scroll saw is a stationary machine with a thin blade attached at the top and the bottom to move it up and down rapidly. A jig saw is a portable hand-held tool with the blade extending out of the bottom. The jig saw sits on top of the material and cuts a horizontal line by oscillating the blade up and down rapidly. Though both of these are technically "reciprocating saws," the term *reciprocating saw* has come to refer to the demolition-type saws in which the blade extends horizontally out of the front. A popular brand is Sawzall™, made by Milwaukee Electric Tool Company, and the term *sawzall* has come to be used generically for this style.

In the past, a scroll saw was sometimes called a "jig saw." A jig saw is sometimes called a "saber saw." Either term is correct and refers to the same type of saw; some manufacturers called their portable electric saw a jig saw, while others called theirs a saber saw. Today, the companies that made saber saws are mostly out of business, so the more common term is jig saw.

Figures 7-14 and 7-15: The three raised details circling the center of this bar unit were created by laminating seven layers of lauan and wiggle wood together. *Why Torture is Wrong and the People Who Love Them*, the Public Theater, 2009. Scenic design by David Korins.

Figures 7-12 and 7-13: Each layer of this giant "cake" was made by cutting a circular "former" out of plywood for the top and bottom; the center of each circle was removed to minimize weight. Stretchers ripped from more plywood connected the top and bottom formers and gave additional points to glue and staple the wiggle wood to.

Whether using thin sheets, bending/wiggle boards, or kerfed pieces, you also need a way to hold the curve. The quickest and most common way is to cut "formers," which follow the path of the curve you wish to create; usually you cut a former for the top and the bottom, though for larger pieces you may wish to have one or two in the middle as well. To line up and connect the formers, you can attach stretchers. The stretchers will also give you additional points along the path of the curve to glue and/or fasten your curved board to.

Another way to hold a curve is to laminate (glue together the faces of) several pieces of thin board together. When you laminate two or more sheets of wood together while bent in a curve, they will maintain at least some of the shape of that curve after the glue dries and the supports are removed. The more sheets you laminate together, the more rigid the curve will be.

For shaping beyond flat or angled curves, props carpenters may employ belt sanders (hand or stationary), as well as rasps and files for more controlled shaping. Grinders with sanding discs and rotary tools (Dremels) can remove a lot of wood quickly as well.

For adding more controlled edge profiles to a piece of wood, a router is often employed. Round-overs, bull noses, chamfers, and all sorts of molding profiles can be cut into an edge of a wood with this versatile tool. Information on more complicated shaping and carving can be found in Chapter 13.

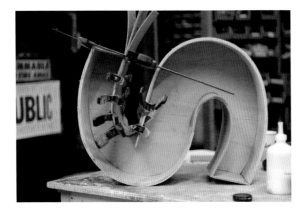

Figure 7-16: The interior curves along the spine of this "S" were too severe to make with the same wiggle wood I used for the exterior curves. I soaked and then laminated four layers of cardboard to achieve the bend.

Figures 7-17 and 7-18: David Levine uses a router in a handmade jig to cut the channels in the design on the back of this chair. *Tea: A Mirror of Soul*, Santa Fe Opera, 2007. Scenic Design by Rumi Matsui.

Lathe

A lathe is used to create pieces with axial symmetry. A lathe spins a piece of wood, and the artisan uses a cutting tool to cut or scrape away the wood, creating a surface in which all the wood along the circumference is at the same distance from the center. Lathes can be used to construct all manner of furniture legs, candlesticks, bowls, gun and cannon barrels, baseball bats, and more, so their use in a props shop is necessary to replicate many of these items. You can attempt to shape these pieces without a lathe, but achieving perfect axial symmetry is incredibly difficult. Many lathes can also be employed to turn pieces of dense foam.

Figure 7-20: A lathe in action.

Joinery

The glue used most often in carpentry is PVA. "Wood glue" or "carpenter's glue" is a type of PVA with working properties that make it suitable for woodworking. Some old-school carpenters still prefer to use animal hide glue, which needs to be heated in a double boiler. This is often best left for repairing joints that have been previously glued with hide glue. For convenience's sake, you can find hide glue in bottled form at woodworking supply stores.

Unlike other materials, when using PVA glue on wood and lumber products, you want smooth surfaces in the joint rather than surfaces roughed up with sandpaper. Sand the joint surfaces to 200-grit or higher to get the smoothest and tightest fit you can. PVA glue shrinks as it dries and will pull away from one or both surfaces unless you keep the two pieces clamped. Keep your wood joints clamped for a minimum of twenty minutes; more time will not hurt the joint. Clamp firmly, but not tightly; the wood should not be crushed or deformed under the clamps. While the clamps can be removed after twenty to thirty minutes, the glue still needs 24 hours to *set*. You can continue working on the piece, but do not place the joints under stress until the glue is fully set.

In an optimum glue joint, the PVA is applied to both sides of the joint and spread out with a cheap paintbrush, roller, or squeegee. Let it soak in for a few seconds, then clamp the pieces together. You should apply enough glue so that when the pieces are clamped, the glue *almost* squeezes out of the joint; that is,

Figure 7-19: Objects with **axial symmetry**, like these throne legs, have a top and a bottom, but no front, back, or sides. No matter which way you rotate it along the central axis, the outline remains the same. Photograph by Andreea Mincic.

you can see a bit of glue poking out along the whole joint. If you use too much glue, it will squeeze out and drip down the wood. Besides making a mess and wasting glue, the glue will soak into the wood and prevent wood stain from properly sticking. If this surface is hidden or being painted, a few drops here and there will not hurt anyone; better too much glue than too little.

With props, time is never on your side, and for many joints, you can often skip spreading the glue on both surfaces and simply squeeze the glue over as much of the surface of one side as you can. Though not the strongest joint, it is often strong enough to last through the production.

If your prop will spend significant time underwater (I'm talking about boat building, not using furniture in outdoor theatre. A little rain, or even a lot of rain, will not soften PVA), then you may wish to use a resin instead. Carpenters prefer either epoxy resin or urea-formaldehyde (UF) resin. UF glue is especially helpful for laminating thin sheets or veneers because it is thin and has a long working time. Contact cements are sometimes used when applying laminates or veneers, though their downside is that once the two sides touch, they cannot be repositioned. Both UF glue and contact cements are potential carcinogens, and so require proper ventilation and respiratory protection. Green glue (3M FastBond 30NF) is sometimes used as a less toxic alternative.

Cyanoacrylate (super glue) is useful for attaching small wooden decorations to props, or for creating nonstructural props out of tiny pieces of wood. However, it becomes far more expensive than wood glue when used in the same quantity for furniture building.

> While you want your joint surfaces *smooth*, you do not want them *burnished* (polished from rubbing). A burnished or sealed surface will keep the glue from soaking in. If you think your wood is burnished or sealed, test it with a drop of water; if it does not soak in, you will need to sand the surface to remove the burnishing or sealer.

Joinery is the range of methods for attaching two or more pieces of wood together. Joinery is a subject that can fill many other books. How you join your wood will depend on a compromise between a joint's function and economical considerations. In prop-making, we rarely have the luxury to lay out and cut more traditional joints, and since we are not creating pieces for permanent enjoyment, we really only need to worry about knowing a few joints to begin with. Joints can also help with construction by giving shoulders and edges to make lining the pieces up foolproof, or to hold a piece together before gluing. These shoulders and edges may also mean that for the joint to fail, the wood itself needs to break rather than just the dried glue or fastener.

The workhorse of traditional Western furniture makers is the mortise and tenon, which provides one of the strongest joints possible. A mortise is a square hole that runs part of the way through one piece, while the tenon is a square projection extending from the end of the other piece. Cutting a square hole requires either a specialized mortising machine, or a mortising attachment for your drill press. You can also use a regular bit in your drill press as well as a router or shaper and then square off

Figure 7-21: Joints where end grain meets end grain are the weakest and require reinforcement in addition to just glue.

Figure 7-22: Joints where end grain meets long grain are in the middle, and usually require more than just glue to hold together.

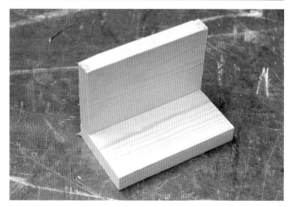

the ends by hand with a chisel. It does not matter how clean or straight the bottom of the mortise is; traditional woodworkers actually prefer to leave a gap so the tenon has room to expand and contract with humidity.

As the mortise and tenon joint requires some specialized tools and setup and careful planning, it is usually reserved for joints that need to withstand a lot of force and for shops that can devote the time and care to achieving these kinds of joints.

You can achieve some simple but strong joints with the tools you have already been using for woodworking. Half laps, halved joints, and bridles can be cut on the band saw, the table saw, with a router, or by hand. Halved joints give a lot of strength to two pieces that cross each other in the same plane. Bridles, especially t-bridles, not only give a lot of good gluing surface to a joint, but their shape helps lock the two pieces in location.

Grooves, Dados, and Rabbets

Many joints utilize a straight slot or channel cut in one or both pieces of wood being joined. Depending on the direction,

Figures 7-23 to 7-25: Joints where long grain meets long grain are strongest, whether edge to edge, face to face, or edge to face. These joints can be held together solely with glue.

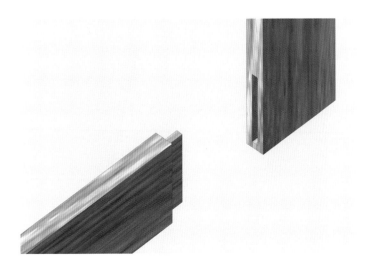

Figure 7-26: A mortise and tenon joint.

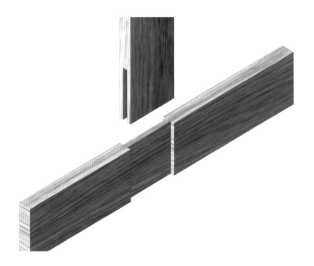

Figure 7-28: A tee bridle joint.

length, and position of this cut, it can have one of several different names.

If the slot runs parallel along the grain, it is known as a **groove**. If it runs perpendicularly across the grain, it is known as a **dado** (or, alternatively as either a **housing** or a **trench**).

Figure 7-27: A half lap joint.

If it is located on the edge or the end (so that it creates an "L" shape), then it is a **rabbet**. If it runs all the way from one side to the other, it is a **through** groove, dado, or rabbet. Otherwise it is **stopped**. You can combine any of these terms, so you may have a "stopped dado," or a "through edge rabbet."

Grooves and edge rabbets are easily cut on the table saw by dropping the blade height so it doesn't cut through the whole thickness of the board. A dado or end rabbet can also be cut on the table saw using a cross-cut sled or miter gauge (never use a sled or miter gauge in combination with your table saw's fence, as it will cause kickback. Cross-cutting with a table saw in general is much more dangerous than ripping, so proceed with caution). You can also cut slots with a radial arm saw if your shop still has one; most shops have replaced these with miter saws, which are unable to cut slots with any accuracy. A router, router table, or shaper with a straight bit are the other tools and machines that are helpful in making these cuts. For boards that are not too wide, it is even possible to turn the board on end and make the cuts with a band saw; these may not be as accurate or smooth as with the previous tools I mentioned, though a well-maintained band saw and an accurate

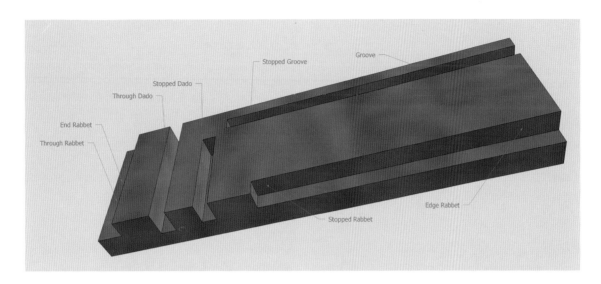

Figure 7-29: Illustrating the differences between dados, rabbets, and grooves.

Figure 7-30: Cutting grooves on a table saw with a miter gauge that runs in the miter track. There is a stop block attached to the rail so the grooves can be cut in the same spot in multiple pieces of wood, but notice how the stop block does not extend past where the wood starts to come into contact with the blade; if it did (or if you used the table saw's fence as a stop block), you would risk kickback.

fence or other jig can get it close. Making stopped, as opposed to through, grooves, dados, or rabbets with power tools and machines will leave a rounded edge; for a truly square end, you need to finish it off by hand with a chisel. You can, as with anything in this chapter, use hand tools (saws, chisels, and/or special planes) for the whole process of cutting slots and channels, but in props, we seldom have the time.

Mechanical Fasteners

Nails and staples are needed to strengthen glue joints involving the end of a board. Screws can be used with glue as well, or they can be used without glue to make a joint that can be broken down later, either for transport or to reuse materials after the production. Nuts and bolts can be used to make temporary joints as well, such as when you wish to make a "knock-down" joint so a prop can be taken apart into smaller pieces for easier transport, or if you want to attach something like a caster, which can be removed after the production and returned to your stock. Nuts and bolts are also useful for making attachments that will undergo enough stress to pull a screw

Figure 7-31: Screwing directly into wood can cause it to split, especially near the end (left). A pilot hole with a countersunk hole (center) will let you drive a screw in without splitting (right).

Figure 7-32: Countersunk screws can be hidden with wood putty.

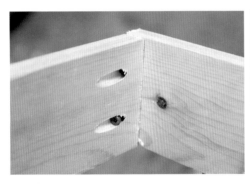

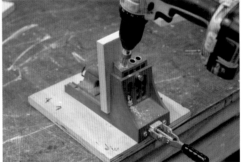

Figures 7-33 and 7-34: **Pocket holes** allow strong joints with screws that can be hidden from view. A hole is drilled at a very steep angle from the back of a board near its end. When a screw is driven into that hole, it comes out of the end and into the piece of wood next to it. Many commercially available jigs exist that allow the quick creation of pocket holes.

right out of the wood. We looked at mechanical fasteners in more detail in Chapter 5.

Splines

A **spline** is a thin piece of wood, plywood, Masonite, or other material inserted between two pieces of wood being joined.

A biscuit joiner (or plate joiner) is a specialized machine that cuts slots to hold a **biscuit**, which is an ovular type of

spline made from highly compressed wood that expands from the glue which is applied.

Cleats and Glue Blocks

When two pieces of wood need to be joined that are too thin for glue to be applied or hold mechanical fasteners, a glue block may be added to strengthen the joint. A glue block can be part of the original structure, or it is used to repair a joint that has come apart and cannot be put back together without

Figure 7-35: A biscuit joiner cuts a semicircular slot into the edge of a board. A football-shaped biscuit slides into these slots to join two pieces of wood together along their edge. Though the majority of props shops that use biscuits will employ a handheld biscuit joiner, shops dedicated to wooden furniture construction may opt for a larger tabletop biscuit-joining machine.

reinforcement. When the glue block will be visible, such as when used on the inside of a box that can be opened, they are frequently prism-shaped (a long triangle) rather than a square.

Dowels

In traditional furniture making, dowels are used to strengthen joints where screws or other fasteners will detract from the visual appeal. With the right tools and setup, dowels can be a very fast method of making joints, and so are very useful to the props artisan. You can buy pre-made dowels; these typically have rounded ends to ease insertion, and ridges along the side that allow the glue to squeeze out as they are pushed into the hole. The tricky part of making dowels is ensuring that the holes are lined up and run in a straight line. Commercial jigs exist that aid this; otherwise you need to be extremely precise with your measuring and marking. Dowel centers can be inserted into one hole, and when the wood is pushed together, it leaves a mark where the other hole should be drilled.

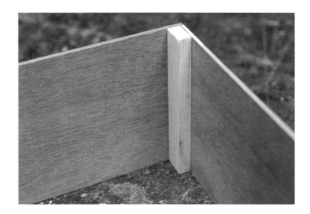

Figure 7-36: When attaching thin pieces of wood together, it is often helpful to attach each piece to a supporting glue block on the inside.

If you cannot use a jig, it can be difficult to make sure that both holes you drill are square to each other, even if you use dowel centers. In these cases, you can line both of your pieces up together, then drill all the way through one piece into the other one. You then push the dowel in from the outside. If the dowel is longer than the hole, it can be cut flush when the glue is dried, otherwise the hole can be filled. This does result in a visible joint, though some period furniture utilizes visible dowel joints in their design (and if you are painting the piece, a bit of wood putty will make everything disappear). This is known as a through-dowel joint.

Faking It

To save time and money, you do not have to make all the parts of your furniture functional. For instance, if you have a dresser with many drawers, they do not all have to actually open. Some can just be false fronts permanently attached to the face. In many cases, though, it makes sense to make everything functional to allow the blocking to evolve during rehearsals. If the director changes his or her mind about which drawer the actor should open, you do not want to hold up rehearsal to rebuild the dresser to allow this to happen. Of course, if you are building a filing cabinet with dozens of drawers and only

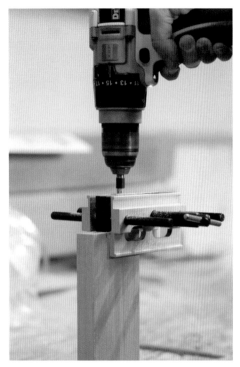

Figure 7-39: The joints on this chair are pulled apart slightly so you can see the dowels in action. This chair is **dry fit**, meaning it is fully assembled with no glue added. This is a good way to check the snugness and precision of all your joints before you make the connections irreversible. *Pride and Prejudice*, Elon University, 2012. Scenic design by Natalie Taylor Hart.

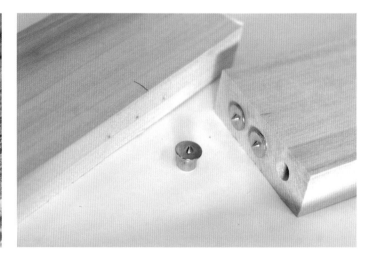

Figures 7-37 and 7-38: A commercial dowel jig allows you to drill holes along the middle of a board's end. The jig also helps keep the holes perpendicular to the end. The dowels, which are bought in bulk at a home improvement store or lumber supplier, are fitted halfway into the holes.

Figure 7-40: Dowel centers.

one needs to open, it may be too costly to make everything functional. In such cases, you can just build one drawer that can be moved to whichever opening the director decides to use, and wait until as late as possible to attach the fake drawer fronts to the rest of the openings.

Often, you need to make a large sheet of wood look thick, such as when you are making a top for a table. It may be too expensive to use a solid piece of wood with that thickness, and it will add a lot of unnecessary weight. You can give the illusion of thickness (in scenery this is called a **reveal**).

Figure 7-41: If the edges will be painted, you can simply fill and smooth them with wood putty or whatever your preferred filling material is.

Figure 7-42: Edge veneer is a very thin strip of wood that often comes with an adhesive already applied to one side. The adhesive is melted by heating it with a special veneer iron, or just a regular clothes iron, and forms a very strong bond when it cools back down.

Figure 7-43: You can cut your own veneer or thin strips of wood and glue them on yourself.

Figure 7-44: Attaching a full thickness of wood to the end is called a nose. It does make a visual difference to the top, though some real tables have this look, either from a frame or from breadboard ends.

Figure 7-45: You can attach a reveal to the bottom of your sheet of wood. This leaves the end grain exposed, so is usually only suitable when filling and painting rather than when staining or leaving bare.

Figure 7-46: This table was meant to look as though it was constructed with a through mortise and tusk tenon. The wedges and tenons that stick out of the other end of the leg are actually just applied to the surface of the leg. *Henry IV*, PlayMakers Repertory Company, 2012.

Carcass Work

A **carcass** is any type of furniture shaped like a box or a case, such as dressers, wardrobes, and grandfather clocks, as opposed to those made of just the frame, such as chairs and tables. While traditional cabinet and furniture makers have developed numerous techniques over the centuries to build this kind of furniture "correctly," the props carpenter relies on much more trickery to build these kinds of pieces quickly and efficiently.

A props carpenter saves time by building the basic box shape of the piece, either a frame or a solid piece made of sheet goods such as plywood, then layers moldings, boards, and spacers on top to make the construction appear more complex than it really is. This kind of work requires a lot of breaking down of the parts of the prop and planning it all out ahead. If you are not careful, you can make the piece too big. Suppose the piece should be one foot wide. You start by building a box that is one foot wide. Then you add a fake frame on either side out of ¾" thick boards, followed by a piece of molding on each

Figure 7-47: This pedestal began as a basic box made of ¾" plywood. I cut a square out of the center of each piece and attached a smaller sheet of ¼" lauan behind it. Molding covered the exposed plywood edges and completed the illusion that this pedestal had an inlaid panel. The bottom is made from cove molding.

side that is ½" thick; your box is now 1'-2 ½" wide. You can also easily make the piece too heavy by just stacking solid pieces of wood on top of each other to build up the profile until your piece of furniture is essentially a solid cube of wood.

Finishing Up

Though we will look at sanding and finishing in later chapters, I wanted to point out how important it is to give your wooden prop a once-over with a sander. Wood, especially rough wood, can give splinters, and you don't want to injure your actors as they use your prop. Pay particular attention to the corners. In woodworking, we call this "breaking the edges." It can range anywhere from giving the corners a slight round-over with sandpaper so that it retains its crisp look, to giving it a full chamfer or radius with a router or hand plane. It is good practice to run your own hands all over your prop before handing it off. If you encounter a rough area or get a splinter, you can give attention to it right there, rather than having an actor discover a sharp edge during a performance.

Figures 7-48 and 7-49: Front and back of a presidential desk. *Bloody Bloody Andrew Jackson*, the Public Theater, 2009. Scenic design by Donyale Werle.

The presidential desk for *Bloody Bloody Andrew Jackson* shows some simple prop carpentry in action. From the front, you see some imitation frame-and-panel work made from rectangles of thin wood attached to the face. From the back, you see that the very thick top is actually a regular sheet of plywood with a reveal covered in edge veneer. I used cleats to attach the interior shelves and the bottom, which give a stronger joint than just screwing through the sides into the end grain. It also makes it easier to line the pieces up; I can measure and mark where the shelves go and attach the small cleats there, and when I place the shelf on top of them, it simply sits in the right place. It's much less strenuous than muscling the large shelves into position and trying to hold them in place while attempting to attach them. The metal legs were removed from an Ikea armchair and modified to screw into the bottom of the desk.

Types of Wood and Buying Wood

The two major types of wood are hardwoods and softwoods. Softwood is generally used in construction, while hardwood is used in furniture construction. As a prop maker, you only need to familiarize yourself with a handful of species. With stain or paint, you can mimic any type of wood just by using softwood and one or two species of whatever hardwood is cheapest in your area. To save money, some carpenters use softwood for furniture construction as well, because the piece does not need to last for decades. If you are working on an important hero prop that will be shown close up on film, it may be worth it to have a small amount of specialty wood shipped in; keep in mind that all woods behave differently, and the first time you work with a new species, it may not cut or chisel the way you think it will.

In North America, the softwood you will typically find at lumber yards includes pine, fir, and spruce. Some areas refer to this as SPF lumber (Spruce, Pine, Fir) to indicate that what you are buying may include any combination of those three species. Other areas sell "whitewood," which is wood from a spruce tree. In Europe and England, the most common softwood used in construction is either Scots Pine (sometimes called "red" in the United Kingdom), or a mix of spruce and fir (called "white" in the United Kingdom). The exact species of pine, spruce, or fir used in construction differs between

countries, and even regions, so the pine you buy in London is different from the pine you buy in southern California.

Softwood is sold in three grades: construction, common, and clear. Clear, also known as "select," refers to a piece of lumber that is theoretically clear of knots; it is more suitable for constructing furniture pieces and other props where the wood will be a visible portion. It can be twice as expensive as common grade lumber. Many lumber yards use the terms "construction" and "common" to refer to the same grade of lumber. Construction lumber has knots and other defects, and can be more warped, twisted, and cupped than clear lumber. The dimensions of construction lumber are usually less precise than clear lumber as well.

Furring strips are very rough pieces of wood meant only as nailing surfaces on the inside of walls. Their sides are often rounded, and their dimensions are not very precise, but if you need to make "rustic" props, they fit the bill nicely.

Dimensional Lumber

Dimensional lumber is how you find your construction and clear grade softwood, as well as some hardwood boards. You are more likely to find dimensional lumber at home improvement, construction, and builder's supply stores, though more traditional lumber yards will carry some as well. Dimensional lumber is surfaced (smooth and square) on all four sides, and comes in standardized sizes. Almost everyone is familiar with boards known as *one by threes* and *two by fours*. These refer to their nominal sizes; a *two by four* actually measures 1 ½" by 3 ½".

You can buy these in a variety of standard lengths, such as 6, 8, 10, 12, 14, or 16 feet. The price per foot varies depending on length; usually, a longer board is a better value (that is, two 16' boards will cost less than four 8' boards even though you are buying 32' of wood in both cases). On the flip side, longer boards are more likely to be warped or twisted.

Purchasing dimensional lumber is the easiest and fastest way to buy wood and to start building props, but for anything but construction-grade softwood, it is the more expensive option. If you need a particularly thick or wide piece of wood, a

While the hardest hardwoods are far harder than any softwood, the terms do not necessarily relate to their hardness. Balsa is a hardwood, but it is softer than many softwoods. Technically, hardwood comes from angiosperm trees, and softwood comes from gymnosperm trees.

Names of common sizes of dimensional lumber compared to their actual measurements.

Nominal	Actual	Nominal	Actual	Nominal	Actual
1x2	¾" x 1 ½"	2x2	1 ½" x 1 ½"	4x4	3 ½" x 3 ½"
1x3	¾" x 2 ½"	2x3	1 ½" x 2 ½"	4x6	3 ½" x 5 ½"
1x4	¾" x 3 ½"	2x4	1 ½" x 3 ½"	6x6	5 ½" x 5 ½"
1x6	¾" x 5 ½"	2x6	1 ½" x 5 ½"	8x8	7 ¼" x 7 ¼"
1x8	¾" x 7 ¼"	2x8	1 ½" x 7 ¼"		
1x10	¾" x 9 ¼"	2x10	1 ½" x 9 ¼"		
1x12	¾" x 11 ¼"	2x12	1 ½" x 11 ¼"		

special type of hardwood not found in the builder's supply stores, or just want to save some money (but use more time and labor), then you will want to purchase rough lumber from a lumberyard or sawmill.

Rough Lumber

Rough lumber is wood that has come straight from the saw mill. The saws at mills are particularly aggressive and leave noticeable marks on the surfaces of the wood. Some rough lumber may even have pieces of bark still stuck to the edges. None of the surfaces are flat, straight, or square. You are supposed to surface or mill the surfaces yourself. Many lumberyards will offer surfacing of boards for an extra cost. You can get "surfaced one side" (abbreviated to S1S), "surfaced two sides" (S2S), or "surfaced four sides" (S4S), which is sometimes called "planed all around" (PAR).

Rough lumber is sold in quarters, which means if you want a one inch thick board, you would ask for a 4/4 inch board (though that measurement may vary to over or under an inch in spots). If you ask for a piece of 4/4 from a lumber yard that is S2S, it will end up being 13/16" thick. It is possible for you to get a slightly thicker board if you surface it yourself, but you cannot always count on it, especially if the board is not completely flat or has low points. Some lumberyards will surface your boards to a more specific thickness, so you can ask them to plane 4/4 to ¾" thick if that is more useful than 13/16". The widths and lengths that rough lumber comes in depend on the log it was cut from, and will vary with every visit to the lumberyard.

Purchasing rough lumber gives you far more options in sizes and types of wood for a much cheaper price, but it

The "sides" in S1S and S2S refer to the faces. S4S means that both faces and both edges have been surfaced. Some places will even let you get S3S, which means that both faces and one edge have been surfaced. You may also be able to request "surfaced 1 edge" (S1E) and "surfaced 2 edges" (S2E), as well as combinations such as "surfaced 1 side and 1 edge" (S1S1E) or "surfaced 1 side and 2 edges" (S1S2E).

The names and measurements of various sizes of rough lumber in the "quarters" method, along with their actual measurements when surfaced by the saw mill or lumber-yard.

Nominal	Measurement	Surfaced 2 sides (S2S)
2/4	½"	5/16"
3/4	¾"	9/16"
4/4	1"	13/16"
5/4	1 ¼"	1 1/16"
6/4	1 ½"	1 5/16"
8/4	2"	1 ¾"
12/4	3"	2 ¾"
16/4	4"	3 ¾"

involves more time in picking out your boards and surfacing them all. Purchasing rough lumber from a lumberyard and having them surface some or all of the sides is a nice middle ground; it is more expensive than buying rough lumber, but can be cheaper than buying dimensioned lumber, and particularly useful if you need especially thick or wide hardwood boards, which are less common at places that sell only dimensioned lumber.

You always want to "pad" your lumber needs and add a contingency for waste. Like buying fabric, the amount of lumber you need to buy is dependent on the widths and lengths you can find in the lumberyard. While you can improvise and revise your order when picking out your own lumber at the lumberyard, ordering wood over the phone can be even trickier. Tell them what thickness you need, and ask them what widths they have. Figure on losing up to a half an inch in width once you surface the edges, and determine the lengths and number of boards you need from there.

The cost of rough lumber is calculated in **board feet**. A board foot is a measurement of the volume of the wood. Take the length, width, and thickness in inches, and use the following formula:

(Length × Width × Thickness)/144 = Board Feet.

So a piece of wood 1 inch thick that measures 12 inches by 12 inches is one board foot.

Often, a thicker board will have a higher price per board foot than a thinner board; a lumberyard might sell 4/4 poplar at $3.20 a board foot and 5/4 poplar at $3.35 a board foot. In some cases, especially wide boards may cost more; a poplar board that is over 10" wide costs $3.55 a board foot at this imaginary lumberyard (real lumber prices vary greatly depending on where you live and can change rapidly over time, so these prices are for illustrative purposes only).

You can also order rough lumber just by asking for a certain amount of board feet at a certain thickness, known as "random width and lengths" (RWL). You have no guarantee of having boards at a specific length or width, though they are generally never less than 3' long or 2 3/4" wide. This can be the fastest and most economical way to purchase a lot of hardwood.

Using Rough Lumber

If you do not purchase your rough lumber surfaced, you will need to flatten the faces and get the edges square and straight before cutting your board into individual pieces.

You flatten the first face, or the "working face," on a machine called a **jointer**. You surface the opposite face on a planer, which will also shave your board to the thickness you want. Next, you surface one of the edges on the joiner; the flat face runs along the joiner's rail, ensuring that your edge is square to both faces. Like the planer, the jointer cuts a small sliver of wood off as it passes over a rapidly spinning head that holds two or more knives. You only take about 1/16" to 3/32" off at a time, so you may have to run your board through a few times.

After both faces and one edge are surfaced, you can cut one end off your board with your miter or radial arm saw. You now have a straight edge that you can run along the rail of a table saw to cut your board to width, as well as a straight end you can measure from to cut your board to length.

Both a planer and a jointer are not the kinds of tools you want to use without someone showing you how first. They are also fairly pricey and use up a lot of space in the shop. They may not be worth the investment for the shop that only does occasional furniture building, especially since it is so easy to buy dimensional or surfaced lumber (although a planer on its own can still be a worthwhile investment if you frequently need lumber that is thinner than the standard sizes you can buy).

If you do not have a planer and jointer, you will have to plane your wood by hand, which can take a long time and is usually not suitable for prop making other than in small doses. Even with a planer or joiner, it is useful to have a stockpile of finished lumber in a variety of sizes for those projects that pop up with a tight deadline.

Wood-Based Products

As I mentioned at the beginning of the chapter, prop makers use all sorts of wood-based products other than traditional lumber. I will attempt to describe some of the more common ones.

Plywood is made from several veneers of lumber laminated together with the grain in each layer running perpendicularly to the ones next to it. This allows you to use it over long spans without having to worry about splitting along the grain.

Fiberboard is made from sawdust, wood ships, wood shavings, and other sawmill by-products adhered together with resin or some other binder. It comes in a variety of densities.

Medium Density Fiberboard, or MDF, is engineered from sawdust pressed together at high temperatures and pressures with various waxes and resins to make a highly uniform and dimensionally stable sheet good. Because it has no grain,

it lacks the strength that real wood and plywood has. It does, however, give you one of the smoothest and most uniform surfaces for painting or attaching veneers and laminates to.

Medium Density Overlay, or MDO, is a cross between plywood and MDF. The interior layers are plywood, while the outermost layer on each side is MDF. This gives it the structural strength of plywood but the clean, smooth, grainless surface of MDF.

High Density Fiberboard, or hardboard, is more commonly known by one of its most popular brands, Masonite. It is similar to MDF, just stronger, denser, and harder. It is also frequently tempered on one or both sides, giving it a super-slick surface useful for painting high-gloss treatments.

Low density fiberboard (LDF) is commonly called **particleboard** or chipboard. It is useful as an economical substrate (an underlying layer that will be hidden from view) to hold heavy textures or laminates.

Lauan, or lauan plywood, is a type of tropical hardwood (Philippine mahogany) that is useful because it comes in hard, rigid, and very thin sheets. A quarter-inch thick sheet of lauan is far lighter and practically as strong as a ¼" sheet of plywood or MDF.

Wigglewood™, Bending Lauan, Bending Board, Bending Plywood, Flexply™, or Wacky Wood™ are all names given to plywood in which multiple plies of material have the grain running in the same direction, thus making them bendable. You usually need to buy these at lumberyards, though some big box home improvement stores now carry some.

Historically, much of the lauan exported comes from unsustainable sources, with some even coming from illegal logging sites, which have driven out or even murdered the indigenous people who lived in those forests. Consider buying only lauan certified by the FSC (Forestry Stewardship Council), which comes from sustainable and managed forests.

Figure 7-50: Wiggle wood along the top and bottom of this fanciful spaceman seat allows the surface to follow a complex curve.

Homosote is useful as a substrate, or even as a heavily textured surface; a faux brick facade is easily made by carving Homosote. It is also useful as a sound-deadening material, especially when placed between a prop and its casters. Another brand known to many theatrical and film folks is Easycurve™ (formerly known as Upson Board). This compressed paper product can conform to curves like wiggle wood. The same company also makes Upsonite™, which is like a cross between Homosote and heavy card stock.

They typically come in 4' by 8' sheets, and can be bent either horizontally or vertically depending on which way the grain runs. If the grain runs lengthwise, it is referred to as "column" or sold as 4' by 8', because you can use it to wrap around an eight-foot-tall column. If the grain runs widthwise, it is referred to as "barrel" or 8' by 4', because it can wrap around a barrel that is four feet tall.

You can also find single veneers of wood that are especially "bendy." Common species include bending poplar, bending birch, and bending maple.

Paper can also be compressed and mixed with glue to make sheet goods. One of the most common sheet goods found in theatrical and film set construction is Homosote™.

Figure 7-51: Though cardboard is infrequently used as a construction material, one exception is tubes. Cardboard tubes come in a wide range of diameters, from the thin ones used to mail posters or found inside rolls of carpeting, to the larger round concrete forms seen here in this photograph. These are often referred to by one of the most popular brands: Sonotube™.

Molding

Though you can find plastic and even metal molding, the vast majority is still wood or wood-based, and carpentry uses molding the most. Molding is a strip of material with various profiles along it. The profile can be a continuous shape, or it can consist of a repeating pattern either carved or molded into it. Molding, or "trim" (or "trim molding"), is used to decorate the edges of materials and to cover the transitions between different surfaces, like between the top and apron of a table. Antique furniture design has a whole design vocabulary of traditional molding use, so it is helpful to understand a bit about the different kinds of molding and how to make or fake them.

Lumberyards, builder's suppliers, and home improvement stores frequently carry a selection of common molding types. Stores that specialize in decorative wood carvings and furniture parts will have more fanciful molding types. You can also find them at furniture and antique restoration shops. Frame

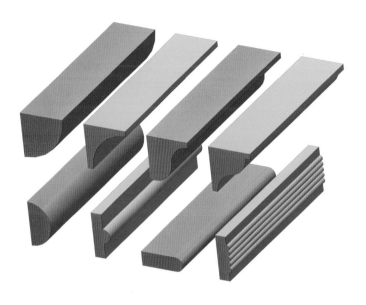

Figure 7-53: Common examples of molding with a continuous profile. Top row (left to right): Ovolo or quarter-round, cavetto or cove, cyma (cyma recta), ogee (cyma reversa). Bottom row (left to right): Half-round, astragal, bead, reeding.

Figure 7-52: The base to this chaise lounge was covered entirely in several strips of molding to make it look like it was fully carved.

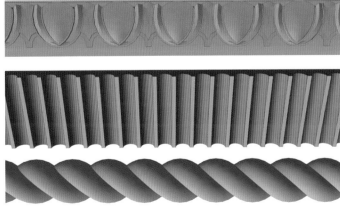

Figure 7-54: Common examples of molding with a carved profile. Top to bottom: Egg and dart, fluting, rope molding.

shops sometimes have smaller lengths of molding, and if you only need a small length, you can just knock a regular picture frame apart and use that.

You can also make your own molding. Though it's possible to make it by hand with various molding planes, most props artisans use either a router, router table, or shaper to make molding. These allow you to cut a continuous profile directly along the edge of a piece of wood. If you wanted to make a strip of molding that can be attached to a prop, it may be safer to cut it on a wide piece of wood, than rip the molding part off after, since manipulating a thin strip of wood along a router or shaper blade is a dicey proposition. You can purchase a vast variety of cutting profiles to make nearly any molding imaginable; you can also run your router over an edge more than once with different cutting heads attached to invent your own custom profiles.

A mill workshop or scene shop may have a "molder," which is a machine resembling a planer. Rather than a straight blade that shaves the top of a board, it has a shaped blade that shaves a molding profile over several passes. In fact, many machines exist that can act as both a planer and a molder depending on the blade used. Molders can make very wide molding profiles, which are rarely needed in props, but it is helpful to know that these machines exist for those rare occasions.

Carved and patterned moldings are less straightforward to automate. Unless you have a CNC router or carving machine, you are going to have to either purchase pre-made molding or carve it by hand; you can also fake it with other materials, either by stamping, stenciling, or casting. You might also use something like upholstery fringe, rope, Ethafoam, or even heavily textured paper that you can stiffen with glue or resin and paint over.

Figure 7-55: For larger and more complex molding profiles, you can piece together smaller moldings, along with spacers, plain boards, and castings, to construct something that looks like a single piece.

eight

metal

Like wood, metal comes in rods, sticks, sheets, and other shapes. You can find it in plates of various thicknesses and widths like sticks of lumber, but if you built objects out of solid metal, it would quickly become far heavier than you can handle. Instead, we tend to use hollow shapes of metal, such as tubes, pipes, and "box tube," which are square and rectangular tubes that come in any width and thickness you can imagine. "Structural shapes," such as angle iron, I-beams, and channels, are also used.

We use a number of different kinds of metal for several purposes in prop-making. Steel is one of the most common. Steel is extremely economical for the strength and durability it offers. It is easily cut and shaped with a variety of affordable tools, and can be welded effectively even by beginners. You can make sturdy pieces that appear to be very delicate. Steel will rust if not coated or treated.

Aluminum is a much lighter alternative to steel for structural pieces. It is much more expensive though, and welding it

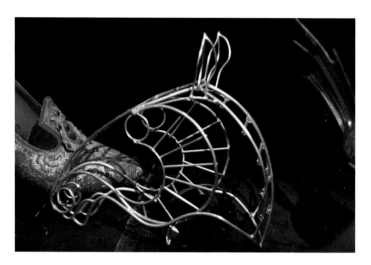

Figure 8-2: These horse heads are made of thin aluminum tubing that has been welded together. The result is a strong but lightweight head that can be comfortably worn for long periods of time. *Equus* at the John Drew Theatre, 2010. Constructed by Costume Armour, Inc.

Figure 8-1: The bottom of this wagon cart is fabricated from a number of common steel forms. The rectangular base is 1" square box tube; the supports leading to the front wheel are ½" box tube. The wheel itself is a piece of flat bar bent into a circle and connected with spokes made of solid rod. The back axle is a round tube with a solid rod inside.

requires much more expensive equipment and extensive training. One advantage is that, as a nonferrous metal, it can be cut with the same power tools as wood (though the blades themselves need to be changed).

Copper is found in foil form, wires, and tubes. Tubes can range in diameter between $\frac{1}{8}$" and 8" or even larger. It is easily cut, bent, and soldered with a minimum of skill and tools. Tube structures can be assembled for plumbing purposes or as decorative elements. It comes in sheets as well, though it is one of the more expensive metals you may use, so its appearance is often faked by coating another metal or with a paint treatment.

Brass is an alloy of copper and zinc and finds its way in a number of decorative elements, such as door hardware, cabinet knobs, candlesticks, beds, and trunk parts, that can be repurposed for props, as well as in a variety of raw shapes. It is less expensive than copper but still quite costly in any large amount. Many more shapes can be found in the form of lamp parts, which are a number of fairly standardized shapes and

Figure 8-3: This Alethiomet for the film *The Golden Compass* is made from a solid piece of brass that has been machined and engraved.

The chart below lists some of the more popular gauges of sheet metal along with the thickness, in inches, of common metals.

gauge	steel	stainless steel	aluminum and brass
10	0.1345	0.1406	0.1019
11	0.1196	1/8	0.0907
12	0.1046	0.1094	0.0808
13	0.0897	0.0937	0.0720
14	0.0747	0.0781	0.0641
15	0.0673	0.0703	0.0570
16	0.0598	1/16	0.0508
17	0.0538	0.0562	0.0450
18	0.0478	0.0500	0.0403
19	0.0418	0.0437	0.0360
20	0.0359	0.0375	0.0320
21	0.0329	0.0344	0.0280
22	0.0299	0.0312	0.0250
23	0.0269	0.0281	0.0230
24	0.0239	0.0250	0.0200
25	0.0209	0.022	0.0180
26	0.0179	0.019	0.0170
27	0.0164	0.017	0.0140
28	0.0149	0.016	0.0126

elements that can be attached together and assembled into an assortment of larger forms. Brass is easy to work with basic hand tools. Like aluminum, brass can be worked on with the same tools as wood. It is also soft enough that sheets of it can be cut with tin snips or even heavy-duty scissors. Though it can be welded with specialized equipment, such as a TIG welder, it is more convenient to solder or braze it.

Bronze is an alloy of copper and tin. It is found in many decorative objects, particularly in statuary as bronze is a popular casting metal among artists. It can be brazed similarly to brass; in fact, the term "braze welding" was originally "bronze welding."

Thickness of Metal

The thickness of **sheet metal** is given by its **gauge**, which is a measure of how much it weighs; thus, 14 gauge steel is not the same thickness as 14 gauge aluminum or 14 gauge stainless steel. The *lower* the gauge number, the *thicker* the metal. Gauge numbers describe metal up to ¼" thick. Any piece thicker than that is considered **plate metal**, which is measured in fractions of an inch. Square tube and pipe can also be described in gauge to identify the thickness of their walls.

Cylinders

Cylinders of metal come in several forms. A **rod** is a solid cylindrical bar. A **tube** is a hollow cylinder meant to construct structures and frames. A **pipe** is a hollow cylinder meant to transport liquids and gasses. The measurements of hollow cylinders are indicated by the outer diameter (OD), the inner diameter (ID), and the wall thickness. The OD is equal to the ID plus the wall thickness on both sides (OD = ID + 2*wt). Because tubes are used in fabrication, they are typically sold by OD and wall thickness. Their specifications will also indicate how much weight or force they can handle before bending or buckling. For pipes, it is more important to know how much material can flow through them, so they are sold by ID and wall thickness. Their specifications will indicate how much pressure they can be filled with before cracking or bursting. Pipes can come with threads on one or both ends to attach various pipe fittings to, such as elbows and tees. You can also thread your own pipes with a pipe threader, which is useful for when you need to cut a pipe to a shorter length.

The common system for indicating the pressure a pipe can withstand is given by **schedule**. The two most common schedules used by props artisans are **schedule 40** and **schedule 80**. A two-inch schedule 80 pipe has thicker walls than a two-inch schedule 40 pipe. The wall thickness for the different schedules differs depending on the size of the pipe; a quarter-inch schedule 40 pipe has thinner walls than a half-inch schedule 40 pipe. For added confusion, schedule pipes are not sold by ID, but by nominal pipe size (NPS); in pipes with an OD of 14 inches and up, the NPS is equal to the OD. In smaller sizes, the NPS is different from both the OD and the ID and follows its own system. PVC pipe is also sold in schedule 40 and schedule 80.

The cheapest tubing, called ERW (Electric Resistance Welded), is formed by rolling a flat piece of metal into a cylinder and welding it together down the length; this leaves a welding bead running along the inside. If you need your pipe or tube to be perfectly round on the inside, such as when you need to sleeve a smaller diameter rod inside, you will need to spend the extra money on seamless tube or pipe. Drawn over Mandrel tubing is ERW tubing, which goes through a second process to remove the welding bead and smooth the walls; the process also makes DOM stronger than ERW (as well as more expensive).

Machining and Shaping

Steel and other metals containing iron are called **ferrous** metals. Other metals not containing significant quantities of iron are **nonferrous**. Nonferrous metals, such as aluminum and brass, can be cut on some woodworking machines with only a change of blade and other settings. Ferrous metals require their own set of machines for cutting. You can tell that a metal is ferrous because a magnet will stick to it (though some ferrous metals, particularly stainless steel, are nonmagnetic).

Hand power tools can be used for cutting metal, and are particularly helpful when you cannot bring the metal to a machine. Both a jigsaw and a reciprocating saw can be used to cut any type of metal; blades exist for either steel or nonferrous metals, and these tools allow you to adjust the speed of the saw to whatever is appropriate for the metal. A handheld angle grinder can be equipped with a **cut-off wheel**. You can also buy stand-alone cut-off wheel tools, which may be electrical or pneumatic. For smaller pieces of metal, a small rotary tool such as a Dremel can also be outfitted with cut-off wheels. As with a table saw, the wheel must remain parallel to the cut, otherwise it may bind or kick back from the material. With abrasive cut-off wheels, the wheel may also shatter, sending shards of material flying off at high speeds in all directions. Always wear safety glasses or even a face shield, as well as a particulate respirator (dust mask), and be sure your material is firmly clamped down, and you have a solid grip on your tool.

A **portable band saw** is useful for making cuts on any type of metal. These were developed for contractors who need to cut pipes and other steel structural members that are attached to a building. They offer more control and give a cleaner cut than a reciprocating saw, though they can be unwieldy and heavy to use for some people. A portable **metal circular saw** is used the same way as a regular portable circular saw; however, the blades and the machine itself are different, so you cannot just put a metal-cutting blade on a woodworking circular saw.

Machines such as the table saw, chop saw, and band saw can be used to cut nonferrous metals, such as aluminum and brass, provided you use the correct blade and set the speed properly. On a table saw, the metal shavings will fly at you and produce thousands of tiny and painful cuts on your hands and arms. It is dangerous to wear gloves while operating the table saw, so if you must run aluminum or other metals through the table saw, wear heavy sleeves and use push sticks wherever possible. If you are ripping sheet metal, it may be helpful to sandwich it between two sheets of sacrificial plywood. This will also give you a cleaner cut.

For steel and thicker pieces of nonferrous metals, you have several options. An **abrasive chop saw** operates like a wood chop saw, but it has a large abrasive disc in place of a blade. This machine is loud and produces a shower of sparks, but cuts hard steel (like rebar and case hardened steel) very quickly; for thicker pieces, the abrasive wheel may not cut in a straight line, so it is not the most accurate tool. A **cold cut saw** uses a very hard blade that spins very slowly to cut steel. Many models also pump a milky-white coolant fluid over the blade while it spins to keep the steel cool and lubricate the blade. These produce no sparks when used correctly and will not cause the ends of the metal to distort from heat. In a **horizontal metal band saw**, the piece of metal is clamped to a base, and the band saw slowly lowers itself onto the material like a clapperboard. Some even shut themselves off when they cut through the entirety of the material. It can be used vertically like a wood band saw, but the table is usually too small for larger plates and sheets.

You can also cut metal by hand. A **hacksaw** is helpful for cutting straight lines or gentle curves. For sheet metal, a pair of **tin snips** is used like scissors. For thicker sheets, **aviation snips** use a compound lever action to give you mechanical advantage in your cut. These can cut aluminum up to 18 gauge, mild steel up to 24 gauge, and stainless steel up to 26 gauge. You can find three different types for different directions of cuts; they are typically color-coded. Aviation snips with a yellow handle are for cutting straight lines or very wide and gentle curves. Red handles cut to the left, while green handles cut to the right. Both red and green will also cut straight. These three are needed because sheet metal does not move out of the way when it is cut.

Figure 8-4: A metal chop saw uses an abrasive disc rather than a circular saw blade. You should not simply put an abrasive disc into a chop saw meant for wood, as they operate at different speeds, and a metal chop saw requires the material to be secured within the built-in clamp.

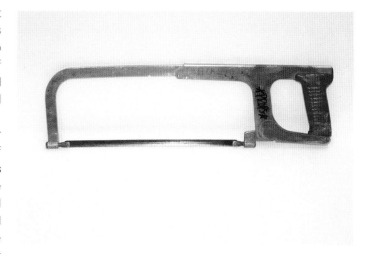

Figure 8-5: A hacksaw is designed to cut metal, and is useful for denser plastics as well. Most hacksaw blades have far too many teeth to cut wood; it would be very slow, and the small gullets would quickly clog with sawdust. For some reason, I see a lot of beginners grab a hacksaw to cut a piece of wood by hand. Please don't.

For thinner tubes and pipes, a hand **tubing cutter** is helpful. This looks like a C-clamp but with a circular blade where one of the jaws should be. You tighten this around the pipe and rotate it to score the metal. As you score the metal, you tighten it more and rotate it again. You continue this way, slowly cutting through more and more of your pipe, until finally you cut through the whole thing. It gives a fairly clean edge and ensures the end is cut squarely.

Whether you cut your round and square tubes with a pipe cutter or another type of saw, the inside often needs to be **reamed** out because of the thin sliver of metal left by the cutting. If an actor sticks his finger inside, it may be sliced open in a fraction of a second. Files work well for removing interior burrs, though for round pipe, a tool called a reamer (often found in the plumbing section of hardware stores) can quickly remove this ridge.

A **nibbler** cuts sheet metal without distorting it. It punches a thin section of metal, rather than shearing it in a single place. A hand nibbler requires a lot of work and leaves a wide kerf, because it is punching lots of little bits of metal to create a cut line. Much quicker is a pneumatic nibbler, which punches many times a minute; even though you are only removing a tiny sliver of metal with each punch, the speed allows you to quickly make a long cut in your metal.

For cutting patterns into thicker plate material, some props shops use a **plasma cutter**. This blasts a jet of hot plasma through the metal, separating it into two pieces. The ends are distorted very heavily from the heat and require significant cleaning, but it is one of the fastest ways to cut irregular shapes from thick plate steel. It is also cheap (after the initial purchase of the machine) because it uses only air and electricity, and does not require any blades or consumables to run. Even if the props shop does not have its own plasma cutter, the scenic shop may have one that it will share. You can also fit a cutting head to an oxyacetylene torch.

Very thin metals can be cut with a **laser cutter**, which traces a drawing from a computer file onto your metal. These machines can cut very precise and intricate patterns, though the laser, like abrasive and plasma cutters, may distort the ends from heat. Though these machines are very expensive and still rare in props shops, you can often rent time on one from a local business, or have an outside company cut your pattern simply by e-mailing a drawing.

A **mill** uses a spinning cutter head to remove material or cut profiles into a block of metal. It cuts metal the same way a router cuts wood. One of the key differences is that on a milling machine, the cutter head only moves up and down (like on a drill press); the table underneath the cutter, where the material is clamped, moves from side to side and front to back. It's important to note that though they look similar, a drill press cannot be used as a milling machine; a milling machine's head is designed to withstand the horizontal forces placed upon it, while a drill press' head is only strong in an up-and-down direction.

A milling machine can cut precise channels and grooves into a solid chunk of metal, as well as take the overall thickness down. Milling machines are vital for shops that produce practical and trick props, such as working weapons or mechanical effects.

Figure 8-6: A nibbler in action.

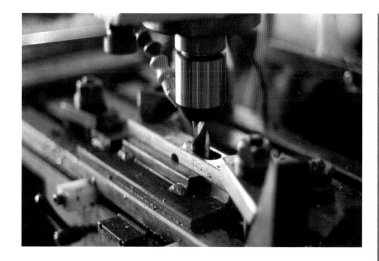

Figure 8-7: A milling machine cutting a channel along the length of a piece of square tube.

Temper describes a piece of steel's hardness. When steel is very hard, it is very rigid. It is also very brittle, and may fracture or break if bent. If steel is soft, it can bend without breaking. Temper can also impart springiness to steel; when bent, it springs back to its original shape. Tempering is done by the application of heat, and steel's properties can be altered by controlling the rate of heating and cooling. Different parts of a piece of steel can have different tempers, such as when the blade of a sword is springy but its tang is hard and rigid. Steel can also be made very hard on the outside but soft and malleable on the inside; this is known as **case-hardened steel**.

A **shear** is a gigantic piece of machinery that operates like a pair of tin snips, only on a much grander scale. It will quickly and cleanly cut a piece of sheet metal in a straight line (some can even shear sheets of thin plate metal).

Machine cutting, shaping, and drilling of metal often benefits from the use of coolant, lubricant, or cutting oil. Most metals change temper as they are rapidly heated or cooled, which affects their properties; cooling fluid minimizes this. It also lubricates the edge of the cutting tool as it works on the material, which extends its life. For drilling, a few drops of WD-40, 3-In-One Oil, or lithium grease can be applied to the surface of the material and reapplied periodically as you drill. Many companies make **metal cutting fluids** for use with saws. Some of these come in paste versions as well, which are helpful for applying to a blade on a portaband or horizontal band saw. Some horizontal band saws and cold cut saws have their own fluid reservoirs that disperse fluid as you cut. Regular motor oil is useful, but avoid the kinds with detergents and other additives as these can corrode parts of your machines. Even water is often better than nothing; the reason it is rarely used is because it causes rust if not dried off, and modern cutting fluids are so much better. Cast iron and brass should be machined, drilled, and cut *dry*.

Shaping Metal

Files are used to cut, smooth, or polish metal by hand. You can find an endless variety of types, sizes, and shapes for a number of uses, but they fall into a few basic categories.

A file can have either single-cut or double-cut teeth. In **single-cut**, the teeth run in parallel lines to each other. In **double-cut**, a second line of teeth is cut at an angle across the first lines, making a series of X shapes. Double-cut files remove material more quickly but leave a rougher edge. Single-cut files are used for sharpening tools, finish work, and draw-filing. They are also the best for smoothing sheet metal edges.

The shape is chosen for the kind of surface you are filing; most of these shapes taper to a smaller width and thickness at the end opposite the handle. Flat files are the most common general-purpose shape, used when you need to remove material quickly or if you are working a flat surface. Round files are good on curved surfaces or when you are enlarging a hole; small round files are often called rat-tail files.

The grade of the teeth determines the coarseness or fineness of the file. Three of the most common grades, in order of coarsest to finest, are **bastard**, **second-cut**, and **smooth** (there are other less common grades at the extremes, such as rough-cut and dead-smooth). The length of the file will also influence the coarseness of the file.

A **needle file** is a very small file used for smaller materials where a smooth finish is needed. A **diamond file** has a coating of industrial diamonds adhered to the surface rather than teeth cut in. These are used for much harder substances, such as stone or very hard alloys of steel, and produce a very fine finish. **Rifflers** are files that come in a number of shapes and profiles, often either curved or coming to a point. These are used for extremely hard-to-reach places or filing unusual shapes.

The grade and cut of the file you choose depends on what you are filing and whether it is a rough or finishing cut. For instance, on steel, you can use a large, coarse double-cut file to begin your rough-cutting. For your finishing cuts, switch to a second-cut or smooth single-cut file. For harder steel, you may wish to start with a smooth file and finish with a dead-smooth file. For softer metals, such as aluminum or brass, start with a bastard file and finish with a second-cut or smooth file.

Though files are typically sold without handles, do not use one until you attach a wooden handle to it. Some newer files come with plastic handles or removable "quick-change" handles.

The proper way to hold a file is with the handle against the palm of your dominant hand, thumb on top, and the front of the file held in your other hand with the fingers curled under. Hold it firmly and flatly against your material, but do not force pressure down, or you will bend the file. Do not go too fast or you may rock the file and end up with rounded corners rather than a flat surface. Of course, if you are filing a round surface, rotating the file as you push will help keep a flat surface from developing. Only cut on the push stroke; lift the file

Figure 8-8: The proper way to hold a file.

off the material when you bring it back toward yourself; diamond files, however, can cut on both the push and pull stroke.

In **draw-filing**, you move the file perpendicularly along our material. A single-cut smooth file works best. Draw-filing is helpful to smooth surfaces and edges and make them true.

Use a **file card** regularly to keep your file clean. Do not store your files all together in one drawer or box; as they rattle around and bump into each other, their teeth become dull or even damaged. Hang them up separately.

An **angle grinder** equipped with the proper grinding wheel can quickly grind away material to give irregular and rounded shapes to a piece of metal. A **bench grinder** is a stationary machine with a grinding wheel (or two wheels). It is also useful for grinding metal, but for more free-form sculptural effects, a handheld angle grinder is easier to manipulate and reach different parts of your material.

You use different grinding wheels depending on what material you are working on. Aluminum oxide wheels work best on all types of steel and some bronze, while silicon carbide wheels work well on brass, aluminum and other nonferrous metals; it is also the preferred grinding material for stone and rubber. A solid grinding wheel will remove material quickly but leave a rough surface. A flap-wheel disc removes material more slowly and leaves a smoother surface. A grinding wheel

Figure 8-9: A bench grinder is used to remove the burrs from a freshly cut bar of steel.

is disposable and self-sharpening; as you use it, the abrasive material wears away, exposing the next layer of sharp abrasive material as well as making the wheel smaller. Eventually, the entire wheel wears away and you have to replace it with a new one.

As with sandpaper, the **grit** of your wheel corresponds with its coarseness. A lower number indicates a coarser grit. A coarser grit will remove material more quickly but leave a rougher surface. The numbers do not correspond with sandpaper; a 100 grit aluminum oxide grinding wheel is actually considered a fine grit, whereas 100 grit sandpaper is considered very coarse.

Drilling puts holes in metal. Different metals require the drill to spin at different speeds. Generally, the larger your drill bit, the slower your speed should be. Aluminum is typically drilled at a high speed, brass at a medium speed, and steel at a low speed. Feed the drill bit into the material at an even and continuous pace. If you go too slow, you will dull the drill bit, and if you go too fast, the bit may jam or even break. You should let the bit cut at its own pace; if you find yourself having to force the bit through the material, it is a sign of a dull bit that needs to be sharpened or replaced, or that you need to apply more cutting fluid.

A **center-punch** resembles a nail-set or an awl and is meant to place a divot in the center of the hole you wish to drill. This gives the bit something to bite into and prevents it from walking all over your piece before it starts digging into your material. Place the point of your center-punch on the center of the hole you wish to drill, and give it a strong blow with a hammer.

You need to use twist drill bits for drilling through metal. You can also find hole saws made for cutting through metal if you need to drill very large holes. Other bits such as brad point drill bits, paddle (spade) bits, and Forstner bits will not work.

Most metal, particularly smaller pieces, need to be securely clamped when drilling; if the bit catches in the hole, it can grab a free piece and spin it around rapidly. The piece of metal will smash or slice your hand before you can even react. Pay particular attention as your drill bit is about to come through the other side of your material. The tiny burr created as it exits can easily get caught in the fluting of the drill bit and spin the whole piece out of control. Use a drill press and clamps as much as possible. If you are using a portable drill and the piece you are drilling into is unlikely to move, the drill itself may spin around. Many electric drills have a second detachable handle that extends perpendicularly out to the side of the drill. Use this whenever possible, and proceed with caution as your drill bit begins to exit the back of your material.

Drilling requires lubrication. Steel, in particular, should never be drilled dry. You may need to reapply oil in the middle of drilling a hole if it burns away from the heat or otherwise disappears. Information about the specific lubricants to use depending on your metal can be found in the lubrication section of this chapter.

With a **metal lathe**, you can make pieces with axial symmetry. A cylindrically shaped bar of metal is spun in the lathe, and cutting tools can reduce the diameter equally around the center, much like turning wood on a wood lathe.

Forming Metal

Metal can be bent in ways wood cannot. You can bend thin pieces of wood, to a certain degree. It will usually snap back to its normal position if it is not fastened down though. If you wanted a bent piece of wood to retain its shape, you generally need to steam it, which is quite an involved process. Metal, however, can be bent by hand. Many kinds of metal will stay bent. You can take a piece of thin metal rod and bend it at a right angle or even completely in half, something that is nearly impossible in wood.

Most metal bends more easily when heated, especially steel. It is helpful to have a machinist's vise, which can hold one end of the metal as you push down on the other end. If you are bending rods or bars, a long pipe sleeved over the end will give you more of a mechanical advantage. Bending requires leverage. Of course, the table that holds your vise needs to be sturdy and hard to move, otherwise you may end up pushing it around the room rather than bending your steel.

For long curves, it is helpful to make a series of smaller bends along the length of the curve. For sharper bends, you can bend it in one spot. For very sharp bends, it may be better to hammer it over a hard surface. Most machinist vises have a small surface for hammering angles into pieces of steel. For larger and heavier pieces, or for more subtle curves, you may find it helpful to hammer over an anvil.

Figure 8-10: The bends in the branches for this tree were achieved "cold"; that is, no heat was applied.

Figure 8-11: All the curves on this three-quarter hilt rapier were achieved by heating with an oxyacetylene torch and bending into shape.

Figure 8-12: An **anvil** is a hard block of metal that allows a worker to strike repeatedly against it without deforming it. The horn on the front gives a surface to form a variety of bends. Prop makers find them handy when shaping metal through hammering. Anvils are also the primary tool for protecting road runners from wily coyotes.

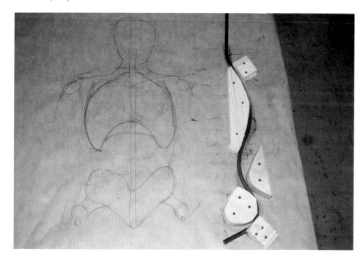

Figure 8-13: To make this series of curves, the end of the rod was first held in place between two jig blocks. After the first bend was made, another jig block was added to act as a fulcrum for the second bend. This continued down the line until the resulting shape was achieved. Photograph by Natalie Taylor Hart.

For more specific bends, constructing a jig can be helpful. For instance, if you need to bend a semicircle, you can cut the shape out of a piece of plywood and attach it securely to a strong surface. Fix the end of your metal into one end, then bend it around the circumference of the plywood shape.

Countless metal-bending machines exist for a myriad of needs, and plans to build your own are out there as well. They come in two varieties: horizontal and vertical. Choosing one depends on what you need to do; whether you need to do sharp bends or gentle curves, whether you want to bend tube and pipe or just flat stock, how big or thick of a piece you need to bend, and so on. Many metal-bending machines use interchangeable dies that allow you to accomplish many different kinds of bends in an assortment of materials.

Figure 8-14: To bend this circle of steel, a circle of plywood was cut and attached to the table. A flat bar of steel was placed against it and a jig block attached to secure it in place. The bar was bent by hand around the circumference of the plywood little by little, with jig blocks added along the way. The two ends of the bar were welded together where they met.

Figure 8-15: A Hossfeld Universal Bender is a horizontal-style bending machine. With a number of interchangeable dies, it will bend tube, pipe, flat stock, angle iron, and several other types of shapes; the bends can range from sharp angles to gentle curves.

A **ring bender** is a smaller device used by jewelers to bend various shapes of metal into different size circles. If you are bending conduit or thin-walled pipe, it is helpful to use a **conduit bender**, sometimes called a "hickey." This tool lets you bend soft curves without crimping or crushing the pipe. For a thin-walled tube, you can also fill it with sand and plug the ends before bending to avoid any kinks or crushing.

As with wood, metal can be **kerf-bent**; a series of cuts partly through a piece of metal allows it to be bent more easily. Once bent, some artisans will weld the gaps shut to make a continuous length of metal that resists further bending.

Sheet Metal

Sheet metal is metal that is thin enough that it can be bent, folded, curved, or otherwise manipulated much as paper is manipulated in *origami* and other crafts. In fact, many of the layout and patterning techniques used for folding paper and cardstock can also be used to make a suit of armor out of sheet metal (see Chapter 12). Sheets of metal are cut with tin snips

Figure 8-16: Anna Warren uses a vertical hydraulic tubing bender at the Skylight Music Theatre. These are sometimes called "bottle jack" benders (a bottle jack is used to raise cars and other heavy equipment). Photograph by Anna Warren.

or other types of cutters, pieces are folded and bent, and they are attached together. The edges are often folded over because it is difficult to dull down such a thin edge no matter how much you sand or file it. As for attaching, the pieces can be folded together, riveted, soldered, or brazed. Thicker sheet metal may even be welded, though it is easy to burn right through if you are not careful.

A major property of sheet metal that is unique among materials is its ability to be hammered. Hammering sheet metal not only distorts it into a new shape, it also compresses and stretches the metal. Shields and armor are frequently made by hammering sheet metal, as are trays, plates, and platters.

Figures 8-17 and 8-18: These art deco footlights were made by bending a sheet of aluminum. The photograph on the left shows a homemade brake for making the bends. The metal is secured underneath the piece of wood. The steel box tube is attached to the table by a hinge; when it swings up, it pushes the metal with it, creating a sharp and clean bend. *Sleep No More*, New York City, 2011.

Figures 8-19 and 8-20: This steel sheet was hammered into a dish, and then a smaller bowl shape was hammered in the center to create a buckler. Since hammering stretches the metal, adding the smaller bowl did not decrease the overall circumference of the whole shield.

Welding

A second difference between metal and wood is how you join the pieces together. With wood, you use glue and create joints by fitting various shapes together, such as mortise and tenons, or dowels and holes. You can also use fasteners such as screws and nails. Metal can be assembled with screws, bolts, and rivets, but to fabricate a single piece from several smaller pieces, you weld it together. Though many methods of welding exist, the basic concept is that extreme heat causes the two separate pieces of metal to melt, mix together, and cool back into a single solid piece.

Welding Safety

Welding brings up its own special safety considerations. You are dealing with a process that uses a lot of electricity to generate much heat, radiation, and fumes, so you need to protect yourself and others in the vicinity.

It is difficult to be electrocuted while welding in normal conditions, but it can happen. Watch out for water near your welder, your workpiece, on your clothes, or under your feet. Do not touch the electrode with bare skin or wet gloves. Make sure the welder and the workpiece are insulated from each other. Inspect your welder to ensure the cable insulation has not worn away to expose bare wires.

Sparks made by welding can cause fires. Always keep a fire extinguisher handy when welding. A cup of water or spray bottle is also handy for cooling your hot metal, particularly when you are using wooden jigs that can catch fire when the metal heats up enough. Remember that hot metal looks like cool metal. Never grab a piece of metal with bare hands without knowing how hot it is. Sparks that roll off to hidden places can find a pile of dust or other combustibles and smolder unnoticed for quite awhile before eventually catching fire; whenever you weld, you should stick around for a good half an hour afterward to catch any of these secret fires. You do not want to go home immediately after welding, as the shop may catch fire when nobody is around.

The arc of your weld is bright enough to blind you, which is why you should always wear a welding helmet when welding. Besides protecting your face, a dark lens protects your eyes from the bright light of the welding action. Welding lenses come

The American Welding Society (AWS) has standardized names for the various welding processes used in the United States. ISO 4063 standardizes the names of these processes for the rest of the world. I have placed these side by side so you can quickly look up the alternate names for a specific welding process. Throughout this chapter, I use the term that I have encountered most frequently in various shops throughout the country.

AWS		ISO 4063	
GMAW	Gas metal arc welding	MIG	Metal-arc inert gas welding
GTAW	Gas tungsten arc welding	TIG	Tungsten inert gas arc welding
SMAW	Shielded metal arc welding	MMA	Manual metal-arc welding (also knownas "stick welding")
FCAW	Flux cored arc welding		Self-shielded tubular-cored arc welding
OAW	Oxyacetylene welding		Oxy-acetylene welding

Figure 8-21: Basic safety gear for most welding processes include a protective jacket made of leather or heavy flame-resistant cotton. Leather can get hot, particularly in the summer, but cotton will not protect you completely from the larger globs of molten metal. As a compromise, you can wear leather sleeves, a leather bib, and/or a leather apron over a cotton jacket. More expensive jackets can be found with sleeves and other parts made of leather, while the back is mostly cotton.

The gloves in this picture are thick leather "gauntlet cuff" gloves. The longer cuffs keep errant sparks from flying up your sleeves. They inhibit a lot of hand movement, though for MIG, FCAW, stick, and torch welding, that is fine. For TIG welding, most welders prefer thinner leather gloves for extra dexterity; because TIG produces practically no sparks or flying bits of molten metal, gauntlet cuffs are not needed.

A welding helmet protects your face from flying sparks and UV radiation, while a dark lens protects your eyes from light and radiation while allowing you to see the weld. The lens is dark enough to prevent you from seeing anything when not welding, so you need to flip the helmet up. Auto-darkening lenses let you see out in normal light, but switch to a darker shade as soon as you start welding. If you do a lot of welding on a daily basis, the constant flipping up and down of a helmet with a passive lens can lead to neck fatigue and repetitive motion strain, so an auto-darkening lens, though more expensive, may be preferable. It takes a slight fraction of a second for the lens to darken once welding begins, and this tiny fraction of exposure can lead to eye damage over time. Better (and more expensive) auto-darkening lenses darken much more quickly than cheaper ones, so if you do a lot of welding, investment in the best safety equipment you can afford will pay off in the long run.

You will also notice a box of disposable welding respirators in front of the worker; the one she is wearing is hidden under her welding helmet. Ideally, some form of fume extraction will happen as close to the source of welding as possible. Overall ventilation in the welding shop is also vital.

in a range of shades numbered 9–13. The standard is #10, which covers most situations a prop maker deals with. Some auto-darkening welding helmets come with a variable shade lens, which allows you to choose how dark your shade gets. Though it is harder to see through, a shade too dark is better than a shade not dark enough, which will damage your eyes over time.

The UV rays will also burn your skin just like a sunburn; wear a welding jacket and gloves. Welding jackets are usually made from leather or a heavy cotton; avoid wearing synthetic fibers because these will melt to your skin and burn you if they come in contact with hot metal or an errant spark. Make sure all your skin is covered; I've seen people weld while wearing shorts, which leaves them with sunburns on their legs and knees after just a few minutes of welding. Watch for places where sparks can catch; pants and shirt cuffs are a likely culprit, as are pockets. If other people are in the shop while you are welding, try to weld behind welding shields or curtains, which will block the bright light. You can use anything opaque to help block the direct light from the arc; sometimes the only thing you can do is reposition yourself so your body is between the light and others' eyes. Always warn when you are welding in case somebody might catch a glimpse of your weld; a simple announcement of "Welding!" a second before you start the weld is sufficient.

Fumes and gases form while welding. The electrode or welding wire releases toxins as it decomposes from the heat (welding wire and filler rod actually have their own MSDS). Any coatings, paint, or other impurities on the material will also release fumes during welding; you should remove these from your joints before welding as much as possible. Use proper ventilation. A fan blowing near your welding area can be helpful, but do not aim it directly where you are welding if you are using MIG or TIG; you will blow the shielding gasses away. You can buy portable fume extractors that you can set up as close to the source of the fumes as possible. Some materials require you to wear a respirator while welding. Welding in confined spaces is particularly dangerous; try to position yourself so you are not between where the fumes are being created and where they are exhausting to. You should particularly avoid welding

galvanized steel or any metal with zinc coatings. When the coating burns off, the fumes can cause immediate poisoning (known as "welding shivers") and is carcinogenic to boot.

Be cautious of gas cylinders when you are using a process that requires a shielding gas. These cylinders should be secured upright and chained to a support. Do not touch the cylinder with your welding electrode; if an arc is created, the cylinder may explode.

Techniques of Welding

With any welding process, the most basic idea is that you heat both pieces of metal until they melt into a small **weld puddle**. You introduce your filler material, which also melts and joins this puddle. The metals mix around and become one. You move this weld puddle along the joint, which solidifies behind you as you go. All of this is much easier said than done. Welding demands practice, as not even a video, let alone a book, can adequately describe the rhythm and feel one must develop in one's hands to make a successful weld. What follows is information to help

Figure 8-22: The five basic types of weld joints. From left to right: butt, corner, lap, tee, and edge.

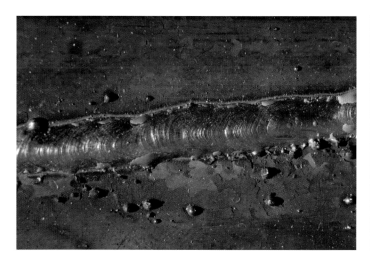

Figure 8-23: A successful weld should look like what is known as a **stack of dimes**.

Figure 8-24: Besides ensuring all your settings are correct and your surface is properly prepared, you also need correct technique. **Operator speed**, or the speed at which you move your welding gun along the surface, affects the weld. Many beginners move too fast, which results in clumps of filler material that does not penetrate the base metal, as seen in the above photograph (this weld is also not quite a straight line, another beginner mistake).

you get better welds, but it's important to have hands-on practice, and recommended to have a more experienced welder guide you, at least in the beginning, so you can avoid developing bad habits that become harder to break later on.

It is very helpful to practice on scrap steel and to test the strength of your joints afterward by abusing your prop with more force than you think the actors will use.

A **stringer bead** is a steady movement along the seam. A **weave bead** is a side-to-side movement along the seam. Use weave beads to cover a wider seam or when you are welding thicker metals. Since weaving brings the torch back into the weld puddle, it makes the metal hotter and increases penetration, which could burn a hole through thinner metals.

The weave pattern for a weave bead could be a simple straight diagonal side to side, or it can be a series of semicircles (akin to frowning or happy faces; some welders also call this "making rainbows"). On really thick metals, you may even do a series of cursive "e"s, or loops. Even on a stringer bead, you may find it necessary to do a very subtle whip as you move forward.

A weld only goes so deep into the surface of the metal. For a solid joint, you need complete **penetration** of the metal. With steel less than 3/16" thick, you should leave a gap of 3/32" to $\frac{1}{8}$" between the two pieces. This allows the weld to penetrate deeper. With steel between 3/16" and $\frac{5}{8}$" thick, you should grind a bevel (known as a **vee**) on the edge of each piece of metal along the joint. When the two pieces are placed together (also with a slight gap between them), the two beveled edges will form a vee-shaped groove that can be filled with the weld. On pieces $\frac{1}{2}$" or thicker, you will want to bevel and weld the edges on both sides of the joint; this is called a **double vee**. Grinding a vee or double vee into the metal makes what is known as a **groove weld**.

The opposite of a groove weld is a **fillet weld**, in which you weld directly on top of the metal. Fillets are useful where the two pieces are perpendicular (or close to perpendicular).

Figure 8-25: Left: A stringer bead. Center: A zigzag weave pattern. Right: A "cursive E" wave pattern. Many other weave patterns exist.

Fillet joints are obviously faster because you do not have to grind a bevel or groove into the metal before welding. The sides of steel box tube are slightly rounded, so when you butt them together, they already have a groove.

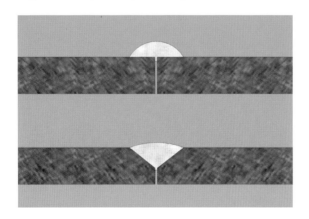

Figure 8-26: On a butt joint, a fillet weld (top) offers far less penetration than a groove weld (bottom).

A **butt weld** connects two pieces on the same plane. It usually requires a groove weld as a fillet weld will not offer enough penetration.

A **flange weld** is used with sheet metal. The edge of each piece is bent up to form a small flange, and the two sides are butted together. When welded, this flange will melt almost entirely away, leaving a fairly flat weld on the surface.

A **lap weld** is used when the two pieces overlap. It needs to be welded on both sides otherwise it may bend (and ultimately break) out of shape. A fillet weld is typically used here.

A **tee joint** is where one piece of metal joins another piece of metal at or near a perpendicular angle. A **corner joint** is a tee joint located at the ends of both pieces. These also may require welding on both sides to keep the joint from bending. Fillet joints are mainly used for tees and corners, though groove welds may be employed on particularly thick pieces.

A **plug weld** is used on overlapping pieces where you drill through one of the pieces and weld inside that hole rather

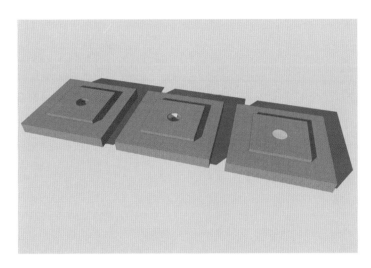

Figure 8-27: In a **plug weld**, a hole is drilled in one of the plates. A weld is built up inside this hole. Start the weld in the center of the hole to penetrate the face of the back piece, then work in circles to draw the edge of the hole into the welding puddle. Continue until the hole is completely filled with metal. The weld can be ground flat if needed. A plug weld is useful where you cannot use a fillet weld along the sides of the piece, either for decorative reasons or because it would prevent another part from fitting.

than along the edges. It is less strong than other types of welding joints, but it is one of the cleanest welds.

Welders recognize four distinct positions that your material can be in when you weld:

- Flat—The work surfaces are parallel to the ground.
- Vertical—The work surfaces and your weld line are perpendicular to the ground.
- Horizontal—The work surfaces are perpendicular, but the weld line is parallel to the ground.
- Overhead—Same as flat, but you are welding on the bottom of the work surfaces.

On pipes or curved surfaces, it is necessary either to step through different positions, or to rotate the material as you weld. Flat is the easiest position to weld in, and it will aid you to position your prop so you can weld flat whenever possible. In other positions, there is the possibility of dripping or of the weld falling out. In the overhead position, you have the additional hazard of sparks falling on top of you.

On a vertical surface, the weld puddle will drip or run down because of gravity. Start at the bottom and work your way up. Begin slowly, making sure not to heat the metal to the point that it will run down. Once you build up a little "shelf", you can work your way up the weld line. The molten weld puddle will be held in place by this shelf of cooled material directly underneath it.

A more difficult method is to start at the top and work your way down. You cannot let the weld puddle get too big or it will run down the joint on top of the unheated metal. The trick is to use the pressure from the shielding gas coming out of your nozzle to suspend the puddle. This can be done with MIG, TIG, and torch welding. With flux-cored or stick welding, you can use the filler rod or wire to hold the weld puddle up.

With horizontal welding, it is again helpful to create a little "ledge" along the bottom as you go to keep the puddle from spilling down. Something you want to avoid is having the top part melt too quickly and run down to the lower part before the lower part has heated; this will cover the joint with melted filler rod that has not penetrated into the material itself. Direct the heat at the lower piece, and when that is hot, swoop the heat, and the puddle up to the top piece.

With fillet welding, the torch or electrode should be held at an angle that bisects the angle of the two pieces being joined; on a tee joint, the torch or electrode would be held at 45° to either surface. It is easiest to weld flat, where the sides are each held at 45° angles. This is rarely practical, and it is more likely that one piece will be parallel to the ground and the other will be standing vertically upright. As with a horizontal weld, you want to avoid the metal from the top piece from overheating and flowing down over the joint before the bottom piece has a chance to melt. Aim your heat at the bottom piece, and when you have a puddle going, pull it up to the top piece. Continue along the joint in this manner, oscillating in semicircles as you would with a flat weld, but with more time spent on the lower piece.

On TIG and torch welding, you are holding the heat or arc source in one hand and the filler rod in the other. In **forehand welding**, you hold the torch or electrode at about a 45° angle and point it in the direction you wish to weld. The filler rod moves in front of the torch along the joint. Move your heat in an oscillating semicircular pattern so that the weld puddle first fills the bottom of the weld joint, then is pushed up the sides and melts the edge. At the beginning of the weld, you may need to hold the torch or electrode vertical above the joint and heat the metal for a second or two until it begins to melt; only then can you drop it to an angle, introduce the filler rod, and begin the weld.

In **backhand welding**, you work the weld in the opposite direction. The torch or electrode is pointed backward, and the filler rod is introduced into the welding puddle. This is useful on thicker metals (usually over ¼") as it heats the material more than it heats the filler rod.

The metal you weld must be free from contaminants such as paint, dirt, oil, and coatings. A grinder can remove hard coatings quickly, while a sander can take paint and dirt off quickly. A wire brush is useful for removing rust and corrosion without destroying too much of the metal itself; you can use a wire brush by hand or get wire brush attachments for drills to clean more aggressively. If you are arc welding, the ground clamp needs to be touching bare metal as well; if it sits on a coated or painted portion of your material, you may be unable to form an arc.

Metal tends to deform as it is heated, and with welding, you run the risk of bending the metal out of shape. You can combat this in a number of ways. If you can lay out your entire workpiece, you may be able to clamp it all firmly in place to keep it from distorting while you weld. Otherwise, you may wish to tack weld all the joints in place before going back to fully weld each one. A **tack weld** is a small temporary weld meant to hold the joint in place rather than be structural. Basically, you form a puddle on one side of the joint, drag it over to the other side, and stop; you just made a tack weld.

A pattern cut out of thin wood or drawn on your welding surface can help make sure every piece is the right size and remains in the right place as you are welding. For more repetitive tasks, a jig that holds the pieces securely in place can be a great help; remember to cut away enough of the corners where you will actually be doing the welding. For some welding projects, jig blocks are useful. A **jig block** is a small piece of material (usually a scrap of ¾" plywood around 1" by 3"). Jig blocks can be stapled or nailed directly to the surface of the table (or floor). When jig blocks are placed on both sides of a piece of metal, it cannot move side to side. Strategic placement of jig blocks around all the pieces of what you are welding can hold them securely in place until welding is complete and the pieces have cooled.

If distortion still occurs even when you have clamped and/or tack welded all your pieces in place, you may need to let your welds cool before starting the next one. You can also make extra welds on the opposite sides of your joints to create a distortion in the reverse direction.

Sometimes you may need to do more than one "pass" with your welder to build the weld metal up level with the surface of the base metal. This first weld is known as the "root pass." Subsequent passes are known as "fill passes."

Figure 8-28: Jig blocks hold these two pieces of half-inch box tube in position for welding.

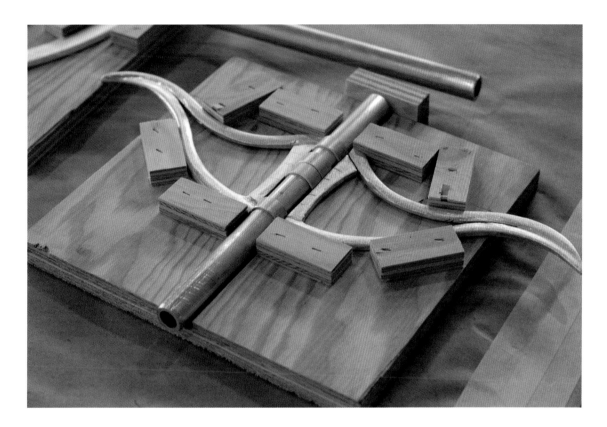

Figure 8-29: A more complicated arrangement of jig blocks holds these aluminum pieces in place for welding.

Types of Welding

Arc welding uses electrical power to create an arc between an electrode and the metal that creates enough heat to melt the metal. Common arc welding techniques used in props shops include MIG welding, flux-cored arc welding, TIG welding, and stick welding. Some shops also do torch welding. Many other forms of welding exist, but these are not used by the prop maker.

MIG Welding

MIG welding, short for metal inert gas welding, sometimes known as gas metal arc welding (GMAW), is one of the most common forms of welding found in props shops, particularly for steel. The electrode is a metal wire that is fed continuously through the welding gun. You connect a ground clamp to part of your material. When you pull the trigger on your gun, the wire emerges; it touches the material and arcs, completing the circuit through the ground clamp. When it arcs, the wire melts, becoming the filler metal. The welder is connected to a tank of inert (or semi-inert) gas, which is fed through the nozzle to shield the arc from oxygen. The use of a metal wire and inert gas gives this process its name, "metal inert gas."

You can find wire in a number of thicknesses. A props shop will generally use anything between .023 inches for light work

Figure 8-30: A typical MIG welding setup. The main box has a power switch, a dial to control voltage, and a dial to control wire speed. The wire itself is stored inside. A hose connects the air tank to the welder. In the front, one wire runs to the ground clamp (seen here sitting on top of the box), while a hose runs to the gun. The gun has a copper nozzle to direct the gas; a red trigger controls whether the wire moves.

The voltage controls penetration: Too little voltage and the wire may just be sitting on top of the material. Every welding machine will have a "sweet spot" for the thickness of metal and the thickness of the wire you are using. It is helpful to turn the voltage a little high if you are unsure where it should go since you can always dial it back.

A good weld will sound like a "sizzle of bacon." A loud popping sound might mean the gun is too far away or the wire feed speed is too slow.

and .030 for more heavy-duty stuff. Your specific welding machine will have its own limitations of how thick or thin the wire can be.

Some props shops do just fine with a small MIG welder that plugs into a standard 115 V outlet. Larger welders give you much more flexibility in the range of thicknesses you can weld and produce far superior joints, but they need to be plugged into 220V outlets.

MIG welding requires an inert shielding gas. As you weld any metal, the heat causes reactions with the surrounding air. The air in the room causes the welds to be weak or otherwise low quality, and may make it more difficult to weld. By blowing an inert gas over the surface as you weld, you shield the molten metal from the air in the room and your welds turn out better. Argon produces clean welds, but is expensive. Carbon dioxide (CO_2)

Figure 8-31: Natalie Taylor Hart MIG welds two pieces of steel held in a jig to position them at a specified angle.

gives more penetration and is cheaper. Most shops use a mix of argon and CO_2 to take advantage of both gases. A mix of 75% argon and 25% CO_2 works well, while some shops use a 50/50 mix to cut costs. When MIG welding aluminum, pure argon is ideal.

Stickout is the distance the wire sticks out of the tip of the welding nozzle. A good stickout is 1/4"–3/8". Keep a pair of diagonal cutters with your welder so you can snip your wire to the correct stickout before welding.

Hold the nozzle perpendicular to the direction of the joint at a 45 degree angle. Simultaneously tilt the nozzle 10–15 degrees in the direction of the weld so you can push the puddle along.

MIG welders can be used to weld aluminum as well with the correct filler wire and shielding gas. The soft aluminum wire often gets tangled traveling from the machine through the hose to the nozzles; many MIG welders used for aluminum will have the spool located directly in the welding gun. This makes the gun heavier, but decreases the chance of a "birds-nest" of aluminum wire forming. For thin aluminum plate, TIG is a better option.

Stainless steel can be welded with MIG welding, provided you have the correct filler wire. The preferred method is TIG welding, as it offers far greater control for precision work, particularly when welding thin sheets of stainless steel.

Flux-Cored Arc Welding

A subset of MIG welding is flux-cored arc welding. The metal wire surrounds an inner core of flux. As the flux burns in the arc, it generates its own shielding gas, which is enough to protect the weld. Some MIG welders can do flux-cored arc welding simply by disconnecting the air tanks and replacing the wire with a spool of flux-cored wire. Without a shielding gas, the welds do not look as pretty, but with practice, they can be just as strong. The big advantage of FCAW is that it can be used outdoors in windy conditions where you don't have to worry about your shielding gas being blown away from the weld.

TIG Welding

TIG welding is short for Tungsten Inert Gas welding. It is also know as gas tungsten arc welding (GTAW) and is sometimes referred to by one of its early trademarked names, Heliarc® welding. It uses a nonconsumable electrode made out of tungsten and, like MIG, requires a shielding gas to be fed through the nozzle. The filler material is a rod held in the other hand and fed to the arc manually. Some welds on some materials do not require any filler material.

TIG welding requires argon as its shielding gas. Helium can also be used, as can an argon and helium mix. Do not use the argon/CO_2 mix from your MIG welder on TIG; the CO_2 will contaminate your tungsten electrode after only a few seconds of welding, making further welding impossible until you clean it.

TIG is the preferred method for welding aluminum and stainless steel. It is popular for welding magnesium and tin. It can also weld many copper alloys, such as brass and bronze; with the proper filler materials, it is one of the few welding processes that can join different types of metal together, such as bronze to steel.

Figure 8-32: The steel for this wall sconce was far too thin to weld successfully with a standard MIG welder; a TIG welder allowed fine enough control to get extremely small but strong welds, and the lack of filler rod kept the welds from visually disturbing the look of the piece on stage.

It also does not produce the spatter that MIG does, though because of the UV radiation the arc produces, you still need to cover all of your exposed skin with protective clothing.

The greater control and precision of TIG allows you to weld much smaller and thinner pieces of metal than with MIG. You can, in fact, weld all your steel with TIG, but it is a much slower process and more skillfully demanding, so it is rarely economical or more efficient to do so.

Most Common Filler Rods	Type of Metal
ER70S-2	Mild steel
ER308	Stainless steel
ER4043	Aluminum
ERCuSi-A	Copper, Brass and Bronze to themselves and to steel.

Many TIG machines will also allow you to stick weld; the box itself is the same, and you simply switch the TIG electrode with a stick welding electrode holder and unhook the gas. Many of the smaller hobbyist TIG machines, which can only run on DC power, will not let you weld aluminum, which requires AC power.

Successful welding of aluminum requires the material to be *perfectly* clean and the surface to have all oxide and coatings removed. The tungsten electrode needs to be free of contaminants as well. It is a good practice to keep an entirely separate set of electrodes and wire brushes for dealing with aluminum, because using any of these on steel (even just once) will cover them with contaminants, making aluminum welding difficult, if not impossible.

TIG is also useful for welding stainless steel. Stainless steel distorts readily under the heat of welding. You have to either weld quickly to minimize the heat, or place your steel on top of heat sinks, such as a block of brass or aluminum. This will draw the heat away as you weld. Welding stainless steel is also tricky because every defect and inconsistency shows up readily on the shiny surface, with no way to polish it out or cover it up as with carbon steel.

Stick Welding

Stick welding, or SMAW, uses a consumable welding electrode connected to the welder. This type of welder is often nicknamed a "buzz box," while the electrode is a "stinger."

Years ago, stick welders were vastly cheaper than MIG and TIG welders, making them popular in theatre. These days though, you can find MIG welders almost as cheap as stick welders, and MIG welders produce better welds. The electrodes in stick welders use a flux, which is a chemical cleaning agent; this flux needs to be cleaned off after you weld. Use a chipping hammer and a wire brush to chip off the slag and brush away the dark oxide that has formed. Otherwise, these impurities will be covered by the next weld, preventing a solid weld from forming. (MIG and TIG use a shielding gas rather than flux, making it unnecessary to clean the welds afterward.)

Many TIG welders can double as stick welders, though, so it can still be useful to learn.

The electrodes, or "sticks," come in a variety of grades and diameters. A smaller diameter requires less current. Your **arc length**, or the gap between the electrode and your material, should be no more than the diameter of your electrode. In other words, with a 1/16" diameter electrode, keep the electrode 1/16" from the material while welding. This is quite tricky at first, because the electrode melts as you weld, so you will be slowly but constantly lowering the electrode as you move along the joint.

To start the weld, use what is known as a "scratch start." The arc is struck as soon as you touch the electrode to the material, so scratch it on the surface as if you are lighting a match. Do not lift it too high once the arc is struck, or you will lose your arc.

Angle the electrode away from the direction you are traveling as if you are slightly dragging it (10° to 30° is sufficient). The one exception is when welding vertically; you want the tip to lead the weld rather than follow, because the rod helps hold the puddle in place. If you look at your weld from a front view, the electrode should be perfectly perpendicular to your material when welding a flat butt joint. If the two pieces you are welding are joined at an angle and you are making a fillet joint, the electrode should be held at an angle that bisects the angle of the materials. In other words, for two pieces joined at a right angle, hold the electrode at 45° to both of them.

E6013	One of the most common types used when learning stick welding. Nicknamed "farmers welding rod" because it is a good general-purpose rod for a variety of mild steel types.
E6011	Aggressive rod producing deep welds even on rusty and painted metal.
E7018	Popular for more structural objects and for cleaner welds.
E7024	For quickly welding thick steel (over ¼" thick). Not for overhead or vertical welding.
E308L	Common choice for regular 18-8 stainless steels.

Electrodes are sold with a four-digit code to indicate their strength, composition, use, and other properties.

Always check with manufacturer recommendations and tailor your welding rod choice to the machine you are using. Other people's "favorites" may work differently on their welder.

Torch Welding

An oxyacetylene torch runs on a mixture of oxygen and acetylene gasses. As with TIG welding, you hold the torch in one hand to heat the metals and feed a filler rod in with your other hand. Steel is the most common metal welded with this process; it is also possible to weld aluminum, but it is far more difficult than the other methods, and the results are usually awful.

Each of the two gasses is stored in its own tank with a valve to control its flow. These tanks will also have a regulator attached that controls the maximum amount of gas flowing from the tank. Hoses connect the tanks to a welding torch. A red hose indicates acetylene, while green means oxygen. The welding torch has two of its own control knobs to regulate how much acetylene and oxygen enters it. The two gases mix inside the torch and exit the end.

You can get different tips for your welding torch for a variety of options in both heating (for bending) and welding different types and thicknesses of metal; there are also tips used for cutting metal.

Oxyacetylene welding uses the same filler rod as TIG welding, with ER70S-2 being the most popular for mild steel. If you run out of rod, you can use steel coat hanger wire; just unbend/unwrap it and snip off the kinked bends.

Welding goggles are needed when using an oxyacetylene torch. These protect you from the bright light of the flame, though they are not nearly as dark as the viewport of a welding helmet.

The order in which you turn on your gas and strike a flame is important. First, make sure both tank valves are closed as well as both valves on the torch. Open the acetylene valve on the torch. Turn the acetylene regulator on the tank until the gas is coming out at the correct working pressure, then shut off the acetylene valve on the torch. Repeat this with the oxygen regulator and valve on the torch.

Next, *crack* open the torch's acetylene valve. Spark a flame with a flint striker while wearing your gloves (a match or lighter places your hands too close to the flame to be safe). With the gas lit, slowly open the valve even more until you have a slightly roaring flame which is not producing any smoke. This is an "acetylene flame."

As you slowly open the oxygen valve, a white jet of flame will begin to form near the torch's tip with a feathery edge. This is a "carbonizing flame." Add more oxygen until the feathered edge disappears and only the white cone of flame is visible. This is a **neutral** flame, so named because neither the acetylene nor the oxygen will chemically alter the material it heats. This is what you want to weld with.

Adding more oxygen to the flame creates an "oxidizing" flame that will burn the metal, but is used when cutting metal.

When turning the torch off, close the oxygen valve on the torch first, followed by the acetylene valve. Otherwise, you will get a surprising "pop."

When done for the day, you also need to bleed the hoses. After the torch is off, turn both the tanks off. Reopen the oxygen valve on the torch so the gas can run out, and then close it. Repeat with the acetylene side.

Welding Troubleshooting

Porosity refers to tiny air bubbles left in your weld. A porous weld reduces its strength. This can result from the arc length being too long or because your material is dirty.

Excessive spatter may be caused by having your amperage too high for your electrode, or from using too high a voltage. Your arc length may also be too long.

Incomplete fusion occurs when your filler metal has not fused with your base material. The weld has solidified, but it is basically sitting on top like dried glue. Your heat may be too low, or your material may be too dirty. This can also occur from poor technique, particularly from moving too quickly,

so be sure to practice on scrap material if you think your welder's settings are correct. These problems may also cause a lack of penetration, where the filler has fused with the base material, but not by enough. You may also get shallow penetration if your material is too thick and you have not beveled the edges enough to provide access to the full thickness with your welder.

On the other hand, *excessive* penetration happens when you have too much heat or you are moving too slowly. With enough heat, you may even **burn through** your metal and create a hole. This happens especially with thinner metals, where even a fraction of a second can be the difference between a solid weld and a molten mess. You can sometimes fill these holes by incrementally depositing tiny weld beads followed by a brief pause to let the metal cool. With patience, you may eventually cover the entire hole.

When welding with any of the gas processes, make sure the gas is turned on and the tank is not empty.

One final note on welding: While it is certainly capable of creating some of the strongest joints in metal, it may not always be ideal for whatever reason. Metal can be joined with adhesives and mechanical fasteners just like any other material. Sheet metal is particularly difficult to weld, but you can get very clean and strong results by riveting it together, for example. Always consider alternative means of fastening if welding is proving difficult or less than ideal.

Brazing and Soldering

Soldering and brazing both involve melting a filler metal to join two pieces of metal together. Unlike in welding, the base metals themselves do not melt. The melted filler metal will readily flow onto the surfaces of the base metals to form a thin film (called **tinning**) that bonds at a molecular level to create a strong connection. Soldering and brazing are essentially the same process, but at different temperatures. In soldering, the filler metal melts below 800°F; in brazing, it melts above 800°F.

Most solder is a mix of tin and lead; they are typically named by the percentage of tin and lead used, with tin being the first number: 60/40 solder is 60% tin and 40% lead. Other commonly found solders include 50/50 and 63/37. Using lead-containing solder carries the same risks and harm as using lead in any capacity in your shop. Lead-free solders are becoming more and more available these days. They are a bit harder to use than the ones with lead, but if you are just learning to solder, you will never know the difference. They may seem more expensive as well, but once you factor in the costs of the additional safety infrastructure and ventilation needed for working with lead, they are actually far cheaper. Besides the hazards of working with them, solder with lead should not be used on items that will come into contact with food or beverages, or on items that will be handled frequently.

Lead-free solder still contains toxic metals, and all solder, regardless of content, requires strong ventilation from the metal fumes released during use. Your best option is a fume extraction unit or table that can suck in the fumes as close to where you are creating them as possible.

Preparation

Brazing and soldering requires a **flux**, which is a paste or liquid applied to the joint before brazing. When heated, the flux will dissolve the oxides left on the surfaces of the metals being joined, which inhibit good connections. It will also prevent new oxides from forming as the metal is heated. Lastly, the flux will also break down the surface tension of the liquid solder and help it to flow more easily into the joint.

Flux comes in three forms: liquid, gel, and paste. Flux is categorized by its contents and aggressiveness. The most aggressive kind will clean the surface of contaminants, but when you are finished soldering, you will need to clean it off; otherwise, it will continue dissolving the metal, and any contact will transfer corrosive chemicals to your skin. The least aggressive kind does not leave any residue behind, but it will not clean the surfaces, so you need to clean any corrosion or oxides off before soldering. Use the least aggressive flux you can get away with.

Some solder comes with a flux-core, which melts with the solder. For small electronics soldering, this is often sufficient and a separate flux is not needed. For anything larger than attaching a single-strand wire, a flux will help immensely. Lead-free solder often requires a flux specially made for lead-free solder.

For successful brazing and soldering, the joint needs to be a tight fit. The two pieces should be clamped securely so that they cannot shift or move around while you are soldering. It is even better if the joint is mechanically joined before soldering. For instance, you may wish to tightly wrap two pieces with fine copper wire to hold them together and just solder or braze over the whole thing.

The surfaces in the joint you are creating must be clean of grime, dirt, residue, and oxidization. Anything short of perfectly clean will make soldering practically impossible. Fine steel wool, either #000 or #0000, is handy in removing the outermost layer of oxide. Even a flux that cleans your metal may not remove all kinds of dirt and grit. The flux should be applied to the joint immediately before brazing or soldering.

When finished, if you used an active flux, you will need to remove or neutralize it to stop it from corroding your metal.

Soldering with a Soldering Iron

Hold the soldering iron with your main hand and the solder in your other hand. It is often easier to snip a section of solder off the roll rather than try to hold the entire roll. First place the hot soldering iron on the metal you are going to solder. Then bring the solder down to touch the tip just above where the iron is touching your surface. Let the solder flow down the tip into the seam.

Figure 8-33: As with welding, you can lay out your design and attach your pieces directly on top so they do not move and shift as you solder. With small pieces, masking tape may be all that is necessary to hold your material.

The solder will be drawn onto the heated metal almost like magic. If the base metal in your joint is not heated, the solder will not penetrate it; you are simply depositing beads of solder on the surface that are easily broken off. You are not using the solder like a glue; the heated material is what draws the molten solder into the joint through capillary action.

When it does draw itself into the joint, remove the heat and let it solidify. Only when it is completely hardened should you attempt to move your material.

As with welding, when soldering a long seam, you want to get a bead going and move along the length of the seam at a continuous and even rate.

If you deposit too much solder in a spot, you can remelt it with your iron and draw the excess away; it is easiest to pull it directly onto your soldering iron tip and redeposit it on a piece of scrap metal or a wet sponge. You may also wish to remelt the solder along the seam to clean up the appearance and smooth it all down. Be careful with smaller joints, as you can inadvertently melt all the solder and reseparate the pieces.

Solder comes in different thicknesses, which are useful depending on the size of the pieces and the seam you are soldering. Use solder that is thin enough to easily flow into the joint without accidentally applying too much, but thick enough that you do not have to continually unroll solder from your spool.

Brazing and Soldering with a Torch

Brazing is typically done with an oxyacetylene torch as many irons cannot get hot enough to melt the filler rod it uses. Almost any metal can be brazed, as well as many combinations of metals that cannot be welded together. Soldering can also be accomplished with a torch, such as a self-contained propane torch or an air-acetylene torch.

For brazing, the flame of your oxyacetylene torch should be carbonizing slightly. Heat the metal to a low red heat than begin brazing the same way you would torch-weld; the one difference is that the material itself should not melt.

For torch soldering, first add flux to the joint, then heat the area around the joint with the torch; do not touch the flame to the joint itself as you will burn away the flux. Dip your solder wire in flux (unless you are using flux-cored wire). When the material is hot enough, remove the flame, and touch the solder wire to the joint. Use the torch to draw more solder along the joint until you have soldered the full length.

An alternative method is to cut little bits of solder wire, and lay them along the joint. The material and the solder should all be fluxed. Heat the whole thing with your torch, and let it all just melt together.

In **sweat soldering**, the pieces being joined are first coated with solder (tinned) near the joint. When the material is heated with the torch, the solder in both sides melts and flows together. This produces a very neat joint.

Finishing Metal

Any place where you have cut the metal should be checked for sharpness. Corners and edges in particular can be very sharp and should be ground, filed, or sanded down smooth. As with wood, you should check all over your prop for sharp or jagged edges before handing it off to the actors; unlike wood, you should check more cautiously, because if you just rub your hands all over the edges, you may slice your skin open on a razor sharp piece before you even feel the pain.

If you will be painting the metal, it will need to be clean and free of oil and grease. You should prime it with an appropriate metal primer as soon as possible, because rust and oxide begin forming right away.

Polishing metal involves first smoothing it all down to an even, matte finish with a grinder, sander, file, or wire wheel. You can then polish it to a shine with a cloth wheel and a polishing cream. Cloth wheels can be fitted to a power drill or be mounted on a bench grinder.

Alloys

An alloy is a metal made of two or more elements mixed together. We rarely use metals in their purest form, as these do not have all the properties we need, and they may also be expensive. When purchasing steel, stainless steel, and aluminum, you need to specify which alloy you want, as the alloys of each of these metals can have vastly different properties, appearances, and prices. What follows is a description of the most common alloys of metals you may wish to use in the props shop.

Steel

Basic steel classification has been developed by the American Iron and Steel Institute (AISI) and the Society of Automotive Engineers (SAE) to standardize the naming of the different alloys among manufacturers. Each alloy has a four-digit number that identifies the percentage of carbon and other materials present in the steel.

All steels are technically "alloys" because they contain a mix of iron and carbon, but for purposes of standardized classification, steels with less than 0.5% manganese and 0.5% silicon are considered **carbon steels**, while others are referred to as **alloy steels**. The most common and one of the least expensive forms of carbon steel is often called **mild steel**. The vast majority of work you do with steel in props is with mild steel, which some call "plain old steel." Mild steel is easy to cut, bend, and weld, and is the least expensive form of steel.

Mild steel encompasses any of the low-carbon steels between AISI 1006 and AISI 1026. The two most common stock alloys carried by suppliers are 1018 and 1020. This steel is commonly available in sheets, round rod, and square or rectangular bar. Structural steel parts, such as square box tube, angle iron, I-beams, and the like, are also found in this range of grades.

Other useful alloys for the prop maker include the following:

AISI 1045	One of the strongest mild steels sold by suppliers. It is useful for shafts and moving parts that may withstand more stress than lower carbon steels, though it's slightly more difficult to weld and form.
AISI 1215	"Fast cutting steel". It resists distortion when being machined on high-speed machine tools, such as lathes and mills its hardness makes it more likely to break when folded, rather than bend.
AISI 12L14	The same as AISI 1215, but with lead added to make it even easier to machine.
AISI 5160	One of the strongest types of **spring steel**. Spring steel bounces back to its original shape when bent or flexed. It is most commonly used to manufacture stage combat sword blades, which requires blade-to-blade contact at high speeds without the metal snapping or deforming.

Merchant quality is the lowest-quality and cheapest type of steel. These are designated with an M before the grade, such as M1044. Merchant bar is used for decorative items and nonpermanent pieces, which is what the majority of steel props are. The basic or standard quality of steel is known as special bar quality (SBQ), and is the quality assumed when there is no prefix to the four-digit grade.

The American Society for Testing and Materials (ASTM) has its own classifications of steel. Their classifications are not tied to the steel's content, but more to its intended purpose and specifications. ASTM A108 is a general-purpose low-carbon steel, and can include AISI grades from 1045 and below (though not every AISI grade below 1045 meets ASTM A108 specifications).

ASTM A36 is the standard for structural steel. It can be up to five times as expensive as ASTM A108. ASTM A615 is frequently referred to as "rebar" (short for "reinforcing bar").

Their shape and strength makes them useful for reinforcing large plaster molds or castings.

Tool steel is meant to withstand the various situations a tool might find itself in. It may need to maintain a sharp edge when cutting, or resist impact. While various alloys can be used as tool steel, most tool steels are defined by their own naming system, which consists of a letter followed by a number, such as W1, O1, S7, A2, H13, etc.

Steel is manufactured through either cold rolling or hot rolling. **Cold-rolled steel** has tighter tolerances, better properties, improved finish, and more straightness than hot rolled steel. It is also much harder to cut. **Hot-rolled** steel is less than half the price of cold-rolled steel. Complex shapes such as I-beams can only be formed by hot rolling, as cold rolling is limited to simple shapes like bars and rods. Be sure to specify what type you want when ordering.

When ordering steel, you also need to indicate the finish you want. **Plain oxide** is the most common and the cheapest. A gray oxide coats the surface, along with the occasional rust. Suppliers may also call this an **unpolished mill finish**. The coating usually needs to be cleaned, wire-brushed, or even ground off for many operations. It may also need to be removed before painting since it can affect the paint from underneath over a long enough period of time. Plain oxide is usually sold with a coating of grease to keep it from rusting. This needs to be washed off. The quickest and most convenient way to do this is to set up all your bars of steel on saw horses when it is first delivered to the shop. Using a rag, a bucket of water, and some cleaner, such as dish-washing

"High speed steel" (HSS) is a marketing term used by tool makers to indicate their product uses tool steel. You cannot buy HSS; you need to specify the specific type of tool steel you want.

Figure 8-34: A good source for wide plates of tool steel is old circular saw blades. These can be cut and formed into all manner of axe, hatchet, and halberd blades when such a weapon actually has to split something on stage or screen. This executioner's axe had to split a melon in half every night, so the blade was cut from an old table saw blade. *Measure for Measure*, the Public Theatre, 2011. Prop constructed by David Hoffmann-Schneider.

detergent or general household cleaner, wash it all down, then wipe it dry with a clean rag. Many shops prefer a cleaner called "Simple Green" or even "Industrial Simple Green" (which is purple, not green); use gloves with these cleaners, as they contain toxins that are absorbed through the skin (check the MSDS for any household cleaner you use, because they are often more toxic than you may suspect). Cleaning steel is a wet and messy process, so do it in an area where a little water won't hurt.

In a **precision ground finish**, the steel is made uniform in diameter and the overall straightness per foot is improved. This finish is useful for shafts and other parts where precision and accuracy in size are vital.

For shiny steel, you can purchase the steel **polished**. If you are buying hot-rolled steel, you also have the option of an **oiled and pickled** finish; this steel is cleaned with hot acids and then coated with oil to prevent rust. The terms **black** and **bright** are sometimes used to differentiate between unpolished mill finishes and polished or pickled finishes.

Steel can also be bought **painted** or **plated**. Painted steel comes in all sorts of colors; the paint has to be removed to allow welding, or it will burn off and release toxic decomposition products. KleenKote™ is a specific type of pre-primed steel that can be welded without first removing the paint; the coating also makes it easier to clean off welding spatter. Though more expensive, it saves time and labor, which can help balance the cost. Plated steel can include products such as copper-plated steel and galvanized steel. Be wary that galvanized steel will release noxious and toxic fumes if welded, so avoid welding it as much as possible.

Stainless Steel

Stainless steel is a set of steel alloys that do not corrode, rust, or stain in the presence of water as carbon steel does.

Only three of the over 150 types of stainless steel are really ever used by prop makers. Type 304, also known as 18/8 (18% chromium 8% nickel), is the most common grade. Type 316 is the second most common grade. It is more corrosive-resistant than 304, but can be two to four times as expensive per unit. Type 410 is the third most common; it is less resistant to corrosion and only comes in a dull finish. 410 is often used for kitchen knives and other flatware.

Aluminum

Alloys of aluminum are distinguished by a four or five digit number, such as "6061." Sometimes they have a suffix of a letter and a number that indicates the temper, such as "6061-T6." "EC aluminum" is pure, unalloyed aluminum.

The most common aluminum alloys used in the props shop are 6061 and 6063. 6061 is a medium-strength alloy that has been extruded into a variety of structural shapes such as channels and angles. 6061-T6 is by far the most common type of aluminum you will work with in a props shop. 6063 is also extruded; the square and rectangular tubes you can buy are made from 6063 aluminum. 1100 is the most common alloy for aluminum sheet and plate stock. It is easily worked and welded; it is also the lowest-strength aluminum alloy.

While **aircraft aluminum** can refer to any number of alloys used in the aviation industry, most prop makers use the term to refer to 7075. This is the highest-strength aluminum alloy available. It machines extremely well and can achieve one of the finest finishes. It is also the most expensive alloy and is very difficult to weld. Nonetheless, it is very popular in the film industry for sword and knife blades used for on-screen combat.

It looks like steel when filmed and it is easy to shape, polish, and repair (though it dents far too readily to be used on a daily basis as in theatre; a blade made from aircraft aluminum would only last for a week of stage combat fighting).

The variations of steel, stainless steel, aluminum, and other metals I have mentioned are certainly the most common alloys found in props shops, and they should cover nearly any prop you may have to build. Know that there are dozens, if not hundreds, more alloys out there, each with their own special properties, and if you come across a project where none of your typical metals are working, it may be worth checking out what else your supplier has, or what is available online.

nine

plastics construction

What is a plastic? The dictionary says it is an organic polymer that is in a resin form or a form derived from a polymerized resin. Great. What's a polymer?

A polymer is a long chain made up of a monomer, which is either an atom or a molecule. If a monomer was a bead, a polymer would be a beaded necklace. It is the fact that it is a long chain that gives plastics their range of unique properties and appearances.

Polymers exist in nature; some examples are natural rubber (latex), tar, collagen, spider silk, casein (milk protein), ivory, tortoise shell, horns, tree sap, various waxes, hair, starch, wool, shellac, and cellulose. Some of these are useful as adhesives, binders, and coatings, such as shellac, animal glue, and casein paint, while others such as ivory and tortoise shell have been used historically to carve decorative and functional items. The introduction of synthetic polymers helped bring about stronger and better glues, coatings, and paints; it also led to the creation of all sorts of construction materials, textiles, casting resins, and other products with properties never before seen in

A **resin** is any liquid that hardens or sets to a hard material or coating. Before synthetic polymers, resins were mostly plant secretions, such as amber, rosin, and frankincense, or insect secretions like shellac (which comes from the lac beetle). Today it includes materials such as epoxy resin, acrylic resin, polyurethane resin, polyester resin, and styrene resin. All plastics begin as a resin. Some are cast into sheet goods and other building materials, such as styrene resin, which is turned into High Impact Styrene Sheets. Others can be suspended in an emulsion to be used as coatings (such as polyurethane varnish), glues (PVA or "white" glue), and paint (acrylic paint). Others are sold directly as a resin, which can be useful as a casting material (polyester resin) or an adhesive (epoxy resin).

human history. At the height of the synthetic polymer boom in the 1930s, this large group of materials took on the name of *plastics*. The term plastic was given to these materials because many of them exhibit plastic properties; that is, they can be molded, shaped, or otherwise deformed (usually with heat). Other materials can exhibit plastic properties, such as clay, or even metal at hot enough temperatures. For added confusion, some plastics do not actually exhibit plastic properties.

Plastics are divided into thermosets and thermoplastics. When **thermosets** are cured, set, or hardened (usually through heat), they will not soften again. A thermoset material is like a lump of bread dough. When it is baked long enough, it is turned into a loaf of bread. It cannot be cooled down to turn back into dough. Thermosets include plastics like epoxy adhesive and casting resins.

Thermoplastics become fluid and plastic whenever they are heated to a certain point, and can be reshaped repeatedly without changing their chemical nature (though repeated heating and cooling will eventually lead to degradation). These include many of the plastics found as sheet goods, such as acrylic, ABS, and styrene. A plastic can come in both forms: polystyrene sheets are thermoplastic, but polystyrene foam (such as Styrofoam™) is a thermoset.

Plastics comprise such a wide variety of materials that to attempt to describe them all in even one book, let alone one chapter, would be foolish. Even if it were possible, there are so many new materials being developed all the time that even the most comprehensive guide would be outdated by the time it is published. It is that reason that also makes them so exciting for theatre work; with their endless iterations and unique properties, you can solve any number of props problems by finding the right material. That being said, there are a number of tried-and-tested products that have become a staple in most props shops.

The number of basic plastic materials, such as polyester, vinyl, and acrylic, is itself fairly large and growing all the time. You can also form **copolymers** from two or more polymers to make a new material (ABS plastic is a copolymer of styrene, acrylonitrile, and polybutadiene). Two plastics can also be combined into an **alloy**, which is a blend or mix of two or more plastics (common alloys include polycarbonate mixed with acrylic, or acrylic mixed with PVC). In an alloy, the two plastics are joined mechanically, as opposed to a copolymer where they are joined chemically.

These plastics can be made to exhibit any number of variations and modifications by using heat and pressure, or by catalyzing them in the presence of other chemicals. They can also be treated with any number of additives, such as plasticizers (chemicals that make them softer and more flexible), colorants, fillers, flame retardants, and antioxidants. The emerging field of nanoparticles is also increasing the types and variations of plastics materials. Nanoparticles can be used as coatings, or mixed with polymers to make nanocomposites with new and useful properties. Polymer clay such as Sculpey™ is actually a nanocomposite of PVC and clay particles, though it has been in use long before "nanotechnology" became such a hot buzzword. The methods by which they are processed and finished can also vary, and the final forms that you can purchase them in are numerous. In other words, the range of plastic materials you can choose from is far too broad for any one person to fully understand. Some plastics also have multiple chemical and technical names that are used interchangeably, as well as brand names that may be used generically. All in all, plastics can be a confusing and dizzying world, so this chapter will first describe some of the most common ones used in props making.

Working with plastics in props can involve a lot of experimentation; new materials are introduced all the time, and new types of familiar materials are invented as well. Prop makers have found a number of plastics especially useful though, and I will introduce them here. Where appropriate, I will list some of the forms these plastics may take, including casting resins, adhesives, textiles, paints and coatings, and sculpting medium. The actual use of these materials will be covered in their appropriate chapters. The rest of this chapter will be devoted to working with plastic materials used in construction. These plastics are versatile, easy to work with, economical in price, and readily available from a number of stores and suppliers in sheets of various thicknesses, as well as rods, tubes, bars, and other shapes. They also come in thin films, foams, rubbers, and foam rubbers.

Names and Descriptions of Plastics

Acrylic is one of the most common thermoplastics used in prop making due to its versatility, wide variety of colors and forms, and price. The full technical name is polymethylmethacrylate, or PMMA. Transparent and translucent varieties are sold under the brand names Plexiglas™, Lucite™, Perspex™, and Altuglas™. It has essentially replaced the use of glass on every theatrical stage and many film and television sets as well.

While the spelling of "Plexiglas" is the proper registered trademark, the spelling "plexiglass" is used far more frequently, often as a genericized term to refer to any brand of transparent acrylic. While most people use the terms plexiglass and acrylic interchangeably, it can be important when ordering your materials to be specific in the brand you wish to purchase, as they may have slightly different properties.

Figure 9-1: Cast acrylic ice cubes are mounted on a circle of mirrored acrylic using clear acrylic rods.

Acrylic is also used for paint and as many types of coatings (acrylic "gesso", modeling paste, matte medium, etc). It can also be spun into a fiber and is often used to make fake fur.

Polycarbonate is another transparent plastic that, like acrylic, is used in fabrication. Polycarbonate is more impact resistant and less brittle than acrylic, but it is also more likely to scratch. It is used where strength or structural support is needed. It does not let through as much light as acrylic, and it will yellow over time with exposure to sunlight (UV rays). It can also be two to three times as expensive as acrylic, and it contains Bisphenol A (BPA), which interferes with the body's hormones. Common brand names include Lexan™, Makrolon™, Makroclear™, and Tuffak™.

Polystyrene (often shortened to **styrene**) comes in a number of forms that are useful to prop makers. Most artisans use a variation known as either high-impact styrene (HIS), high-impact polystyrene (HIPS), or just "high-impact plastic," which is a thermoform plastic sheet popular in model-making and vacuum forming. You can sometimes find garage sale signs made out of styrene sold at more general department stores.

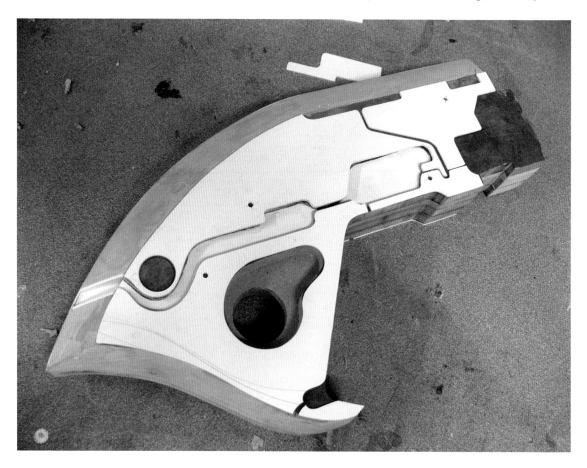

Figure 9-2: This gun stock has raised details created by applying thin sheets of high-impact styrene. Photograph and prop by Harrison Krix.

HIPS sheets come in a number of thicknesses, with the most popular ones ranging between .020 to .125 ($^1/_8$") of an inch.

It is also highly useful as a foam, and comes in two major varieties: expanded polystyrene foam (EPS), also known as "bead-board" or "white foam," and extruded polystyrene foam (XPS), known commonly by its most popular brand name, Styrofoam™, or more generically as "blue foam" or "pink foam." These are extremely popular as a sculpting medium, and will be covered in further detail in Chapter 13.

ABS, or acrylonitrile butadiene styrene, is a copolymer of styrene, acrylonitrile, and polybutadiene. It is similar to styrene sheets, but the butadiene makes it stronger and more impact resistant. You can buy it in sheet form, or as plumbing parts (similar to PVC, though where PVC is white, ABS is black). It is also used in extrusion-based 3D printers (the kind popular with hobbyists).

PVC or **vinyl** encompasses a large number of various materials used by prop makers. The word *vinyl* actually refers to one of the compounds used to make PVC, though we typically use the term to refer to PVC in textile form or as a soft film used for making dolls and figurines. Most prop makers associate PVC with the hard plastic commonly used in plumbing pipes and connectors that are useful for erecting quick frames and skeletons, or wherever tube shapes are needed. CPVC (chlorinated polyvinyl chloride) is an even stronger version of PVC.

PVC can come in sheets of closed-cell foam; popular brand names are Sintra™ and Komatex™. It looks and feels more like styrene sheet than your typical foam.

Polymer clays, which include brands such as Fimo™, Sculpey™, Premo™, Cernit™, Formello™, Modello™, and Kato Polyclay™, are actually PVC mixed with clay nanoparticles such as kaolin.

Kydex™ is an alloy of acrylic and PVC which comes in a thermoplastic sheet. It is frequently used as a replacement for leather to make gun holsters, as well as for making faux stage armor that needs to withstand stage combat.

Cellulose Acetate Butyrate (CAB), sometimes known as butyrate, is a glossy transparent or translucent copolymer derived from cellulose (usually from trees) rather than petroleum

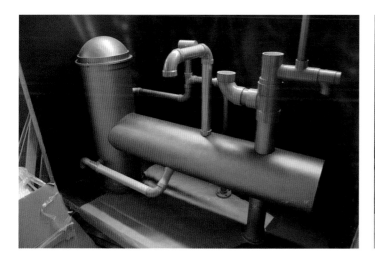

Figure 9-3: PVC pipes and connectors were used to create this whimsical plumbing-type contraption for a holiday window display at a retail store.

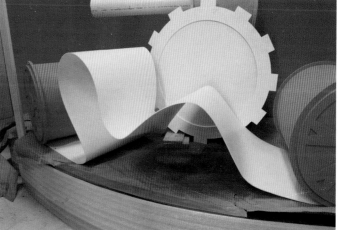

Figure 9-4: This long sheet of styrene was heated with a hot air gun and manipulated to appear like a flowing piece of ribbon between two spools in this holiday window display for a retail store.

Figure 9-5: These fire hydrants were made by vacuum-forming Kydex. The company offers Kydex props, which have been in use for over 20 years without cracking or deforming. Props created by Costume Armour, Inc.

or petroleum by-products. Common brand names include Tenite™, Uvex™, Excelon™, and Spartech™.

Polyethylene is the world's most produced plastic, though it is not as popular in the props world for fabrication. The two major variations are high-density polyethylene (HDPE) and low-density polyethylene (LDPE). Another common type found in many theatrical shops is ultra-high-molecular-weight polyethylene, or UHMW, which is used as glides and to reduce friction along moving parts.

HDPE is used to make milk jugs, plastic bags, and paint buckets, among other things. Because it is a thermoplastic, it can be used for vacuum forming; some prop makers cut apart milk jugs to form small parts.

LDPE is used for films and packaging materials. Saran™ wrap is made from LDPE (prior to 2004 it was made from polyvinylidene chloride), as is Tupperware™.

It can also be turned into a foam; one very popular brand of polyethylene foam found in props shops is Ethafoam™ backing rod

Polyethylene-based plastics are so chemically resistant that modern science has not invented a solvent glue to bond these plastics. This also means that no paint will bond to them. You may think you have found a glue or paint that sticks, but it is merely sitting on the surface and will eventually peel or flake off. Using polyethylene buckets for mixing and applying paints and adhesives is preferred for their ease of cleaning.

Polypropylene is the second most produced plastic in the world. It is also used infrequently for prop making because of its inability to hold almost any kind of paint or adhesive. It does find use as a clear film to make blood packs among other things. The foam version, expanded polypropylene (EPP), has the advantage of flexibility and high impact resistance, so it is frequently used as a cushioning material (and to make radio-controlled airplanes).

Polyester is another grand category of materials that finds use in the props shop. The thermoform version of polyester is actually called polyethylene terephthalate (PET or PETE), though it has nothing to do with regular polyethylene. Prop makers rarely fabricate items from PET as it is more costly than other plastic sheet goods and requires metal tools to machine it (acrylic, styrene, and PVC can be cut and machined with either wood or metal working tools). However, the plethora of disposable items made with PET, such as soft drink bottles, are often repurposed by prop makers to quickly create complex shapes.

Polyester modified with glycol is known as **PETG**. PETG is a popular transparent plastic for use in vacuum forming and other thermoform processes (it has a lower melting temperature than PET). It is far less likely to crack or craze as acrylic does when bent.

Unsaturated Polyester Resins (UPR) are also common in a props shop. Polyester resin is one of the most popular laminating resins for fiberglass. It was used almost exclusively as a casting resin during the 1960s and 1970s, though it has been surpassed in popularity by polyurethane casting resin. Polyester resin is also mixed with various fillers to make auto-body filler, such as the highly popular Bondo™.

PET fibers are used to make textiles, such as "polyester," "Dacron," and "terylene." As a film, it is used as the base for Mylar™ and similar materials.

Two biodegradable forms of polyester deserve mention. **Polylactic acid** (PLA) is a biodegradable thermoform plastic derived from renewable resources and gaining popularity in 3D printing. The other is **Polycaprolactone** (PCL), which melts at around 140°F (60°C), making it possible to mold and shape with your bare hands. Popular brand names of polycaprolactone include Friendly Plastic™, InstaMorph™, Shapelock™, and Polymorph™.

Polyurethane comes in a vast assortment of forms that will be covered in other chapters. Fabrication with polyurethane sheets, rods, and bars is rare. However, machining solid blocks of polyurethane is popular. Polyurethane is one of the most popular casting resins, and many prop makers pour their excess resin into a square mold to have such blocks on hand for future products. Polyurethane is frequently shortened to **urethane.**

Polyurethane resin can form pieces ranging from a hard plastic to a soft rubber; it can also create foams ranging from a hard rigid foam to a soft and squishy foam. You can also buy sheets and blocks of these various thermoset versions of polyurethane. Flexible polyurethane foam (FPF) is one of the most commonly used foam rubbers for upholstery, mattress padding, and carpet cushions. It is also ubiquitous in the puppetry world, where it is often known as **polyfoam** (see Chapter 12 to read more about how to work with polyfoam).

Other popular formulations of polyurethane include varnishes, adhesives (Gorilla Glue™ and Excel™), and fabric (Lycra™).

Acetal, also known as polyoxymethylene (POM), polyacetal, or polyformaldehyde, shares characteristics with UHMW. It is an incredibly hard, dense, and slick plastic that is used to reduce friction between moving parts, such as a stage wagon on a track. It is often referred to by one of its most popular brand names, Delrin™.

Rayon is largely thought of as a textile, but its manufacture also produces some films that have proved useful to prop makers over the years. It can also be transformed into a thin transparent film called **cellulose acetate** (also known as "Safety Film" because its predecessor, cellulose nitrate, tended to explode). Acetate is the plastic base for movie films and Scotch tape, and it is also used as "transparencies." An older trade name is Rhodoid™.

As rayon is manufactured, one of its preliminary stages is known as **viscose**. Viscose can be turned into **cellophane,** a transparent sheet form frequently used as candy and food wrappers (the kind that crinkle as you open them). In some countries outside the United States, Cellophane™ is actually a trademark. It differs from cellulose acetate in that it will not dissolve in acetone.

Buying Plastics

Sheets of plastic come in common lengths and widths, such as 12", 18", 24", and 48". Hobby and craft stores will sell smaller and thinner sheets (under ¼") of materials such as styrene, acrylic, and PVC. Model train and car shops will also carry these materials. Home improvement stores will often carry larger and thicker sheets of plastics such as acrylic and polycarbonate. Full sheets of plastic are usually 48" by 96" and often need to be bought at plastic fabrication shops; these can be found in many areas, though they are often tucked away and poorly advertised, so some searching is necessary. You can get nearly any kind of plastic shipped, but larger sizes can make shipping costs exorbitant. It can be hundreds of dollars cheaper to buy a full sheet locally rather than online, and many shops will also cut your sheets to length and width for a nominal fee.

A **film** is a thin section of plastic between 0.5 and 10 mil. Anything thicker than 10 mil is called a **sheet**. A **mil** is a thousandth of an inch, so 10 mil equals 0.01 inches (for comparison, 1/64 of an inch is 0.015625 inches).

Plastics Fabrication

Plastics fabrication shares many techniques and machines with both metal and wood fabrication. They can be cut with many of the same tools that cut wood, such as a band saw, table saw, and jig saw, but they use blades that are designed more for metal and veneer. They are not joined through joinery as with wood, but with welding, adhesives, and/or fasteners. Finally, they have their own unique properties, which will also be addressed here.

Figure 9-6: You can cut acrylic sheet less than a quarter of an inch (0.236" to be exact) thick by **scribing** it. Acrylic can also be cut with a mat knife, but because it is more rigid than styrene and PVC, scribing is often quicker and cleaner. Make a cut with a scribing or other pointed tool along a straight edge; you may need to score it four or five times to get the cut deep enough.

Cutting Plastic

Thin sheets of plastic such as styrene can be cut easily and cleanly with a mat or hobby knife.

For thicker pieces or for faster results, you can use woodworking tools such as the table saw, chop saw, band saw, and jig saw. You do not want to use a wood or combination blade to cut plastic with your table or chop saw; use one with a relatively large number of uniform teeth intended for finishing cuts on plywood or veneers. Triple chip ground teeth are ideal. On a ten-inch blade, the recommended teeth for pieces up to ¼" is

80, while 60 is fine for pieces thicker than ½". A rake angle between zero and positive 5° is usually recommended, though some blades have a slight negative rake angle if you are having problems with your plastic melting in the saw. You can also

Figure 9-7: Place the sheet so that the scribed line is directly over a dowel (at least ¾ inch); push down, and the sheet will snap along the scribe.

Figure 9-8: You can also place the scribed line over the edge of a work table to snap it. Scribing requires a piece at least 1 ½ inches wide.

purchase blades specially made for cutting plastics to take the guesswork out of what properties your blade should have.

On a band saw, use a blade with 10 to 15 teeth per inch. Most wood-cutting blades have too few teeth for cutting plastic. If you use a blade designed for cutting metal, do not use it for plastic if it has already been used to cut a piece of metal; the metal dulls the blade in a way that makes it less desirable for cutting plastic.

Saber, jig, reciprocating, and hand saws are also highly useful. Again, metal-cutting blades (or specialty plastic-cutting blades) are ideal for optimum cuts. Choose blades with at least 14 teeth per inch for sheets thicker than $^1/_8''$ and 32 teeth per inch for sheets under $^1/_8''$. On both band saws and electric hand saws, a raker set blade is best.

One of the most important things to remember when using power tools and machines to cut plastic is that the plastic cannot be allowed to vibrate or "chatter"; this will cause cracking or even shattering. With a band saw and table saw, use a zero clearance throat insert when possible. Make sure the plastic is held firmly in place as close to the saw as possible. If you are using a tool where the plastic sheet remains stationary, clamp it to the surface it sits on. Make your cuts as close to that surface as you can get; cutting where the plastic is hanging out in mid-air will surely cause vibrations as the teeth of the blade hit against the plastic. Thin pieces of plastic are especially prone to vibrating, which is why it is suggested to cut them with a knife or scribing tool. If you absolutely must run them through a table saw, you can eliminate vibrations by sandwiching the plastic between two pieces of sacrificial plywood.

When cutting, it is important to hold the plastic firmly down and proceed steadily. Feed it through the blade too fast, and you will cause chipping; too slow, and you will get burning and melting. Because many of the plastics we use have relatively low melting points, using tools with high-speed rotational cutters, especially routers, may melt and deform the edge as it cuts.

If the blade or bit heats the plastic up too much as it cuts, it may cause the chips to melt and stick back to the plastic. If these chips stick to both sides of the kerf, they can actually weld the plastic back together; you finish your cut and realize that the two pieces are still connected. This is known as **chip welding**.

If you find your tools are heating your plastics too much, you can direct a stream of compressed air at the blade or bit as you cut. You can also lubricate the cut with wax, mineral oil, or any lubricant that is plastics safe. Mild soapy water also works in a pinch.

Drilling and Machining Plastic

Special plastic bits have tip angles between 90° and 60°, as opposed to regular bits, which are 120° (plastic bits are much more "pointed"). The cutting edge also must have a 0° to 4° rake angle; regular drill bits will gouge the plastic (causing chipping) rather than scrape them as plastic drill bits do. If you use a regular drill bit, it may shatter or crack the plastic, and even break a piece off if the hole is near the edge. There are special plastic drill bits you can purchase; if it's unreasonable to purchase these, make sure to drill slowly.

Hold the plastic down firmly. If you push the drill bit through too fast or with too much force, it may cause chipping on the back. For a truly clean hole, place the plastic on top of a piece of sacrificial MDF or other lumber and hold the two firmly together so that as the drill bit exits the back of the plastic, it immediately enters the wood, leaving no room for chips or burrs to occur. For thicker pieces, you want to **peck drill** through the plastic. This means what it sounds like; you periodically raise the drill bit out of the plastic as you drill so that you can clear the chips and keep the bit from heating up too much.

Machining acrylic is similar to machining brass or copper. Machining can generate enough heat to soften the acrylic and make it gummy. If a coolant is desired, use only detergent in water; others may contain chemicals and solvents that will attack the plastic. Using a router on plastic is possible, and even preferred in some situations because of the clean edge it can produce. As with other fabrication tasks, making sure the plastic is secured well to prevent chattering is a must. Router bits for wood work well, though they need to be sharp; if the bits have been previously used on wood, they may not be sharp enough. Bits over ½" work the best. Run the router at the highest RPM that the bit will allow. The speed you move the router along the plastic (or the plastic along the router, if it is a table router) has a big effect on the quality of your cuts; too slow and the plastic will soften and melt, too fast and it will chip and shatter. Don't force the router through though; if you can't rout through the material fast enough to prevent burning, you will need to make several passes, cutting off just a bit of the material at a time. If you are routing through the middle of a piece of material, do this by sneaking up on the depth.

Joining Plastic

If you attempt to screw some plastics, the plastic may crack or break. However, you can drill a hole wider than the screw and put the screw over a washer to hold it in. It can also be bolted this way. When bolting, drill the hole slightly larger to allow for changes in size from temperature; metal and plastic contract and expand at different rates and amounts, so a tight fit might cause cracking under the hot stage lights or the rays of the outside sun. You can tap thicker plastics as well, but again, tap it a bit larger than the bolt you are using. When screwing through, you usually want to completely drill out the hole rather than allowing the threads to cut into the plastic, as this can cause cracking. Because the threads are not actually gripping the plastic, use screws with flat heads, or screws with washers.

Solvent Welding

With solvent welding, you take a solvent that dissolves your plastic and place it between the two pieces on either side of your joint. The plastic softens from the solvent, and the two pieces of plastic start to intermingle and mix together. When the solvent evaporates, the plastic hardens again, but now it is effectively one piece of plastic.

Plastics that can be solvent-welded include acrylic, polycarbonate, styrene (including copolymers of styrene such as ABS), and PVC. Some adhesives only work on similar materials, such as welding acrylic to acrylic, while others are designed for disparate materials, such as welding PVC to ABS.

Plastics that cannot be solvent-welded include polyethylene (including LDPE, HDPE and UHMW), polypropylene, teflon, acetal (Delrin), nylon, and some other exotic plastics.

To test whether your particular plastic can be solvent welded, take a solvent like acetone (nail polish remover) or methyl ethyl ketone (MEK) and dab it on a scrap of the material. If the plastic becomes tacky, it can be solvent welded; otherwise you need some kind of mechanical fastener. Remember that solvents are particularly hazardous; the liquid is absorbed through your skin, and the fumes have both immediate and long-term effects with the first breath. Always wear the proper chemically-resistant gloves and the correct type of respirator when working with them.

Because solvent welding does not actually deposit any adhesive, glues made of pure solvent (known as "water thin" solvent adhesives) require the two pieces to fit together as tightly as possible, with their edges free of saw marks (but not polished). Pure acetone evaporates too quickly to be useful in most cases, so many solvent adhesives have additives to retard the drying time, or use other solvents such as methylene chloride (MDC) and MEK. A great way to apply the solvent cement is with a hypodermic needle or eyedropper that is emptied along the edge of the joint; capillary action pulls the liquid into the joint. In other words, the glue pulls itself into and along the whole joint as much as it can. The joint should be clamped snugly together the entire time, but it should not be squeezed together tightly as when you clamp wood glue joints. Be particularly careful of dripping the solvent on the surface of the plastic as it will almost immediately begin to soften and deform it.

"Bodied" adhesives allow some gap filling, and a longer working time. The body comes from some plastic, such as styrene, dissolved within the glue. This body acts as a filler rod does in metal welding to add material to fill the gap.

Solvent welding plastics require a full 24 hours to cure before you can touch them, and 48 hours to cure to full strength (technically, they cure to 85% strength in the first 24 hours, 90% in the next 24 hours, and take a few more days to get to full strength). Many plastics adhesives claim a 20–30 minute "setting" time and seem strong enough to move after that; they are not. You should wait until at least the next day to even test the bond.

In addition to choosing between a water-thin or bodied adhesive, you want to make sure to choose a solvent adhesive that dries clear when gluing together transparent plastics.

Welding

Some plastics can be joined using heat, including plastics that cannot be solvent-welded together. These plastics can be welded with flames, but the flame will most certainly burn through the plastic before it welds it.

Hot air welding (also known as hot gas welding) involves blowing compressed air over a heating element in a tool known as a hot air welder. It requires a welding rod to be melted into the sheet joint to make a bond. Hot air welding can only be used to join two pieces of the same material, and the welding rod needs to match as well (one exception is welding acrylic to PVC). Common plastics that can be joined with hot air welding include polyethylene (both LDPE and HDPE), polyproplyene, PVC, and ABS.

If you work with films or packaging plastic, you may be familiar with an impulse sealer or other type of heat sealer. These use a metal bar that can heat up for a second or two to weld thin plastic without burning through it. These also work mainly with polyethylene or polypropylene bags, as well as other films like Cellophane and Mylar, and most can deal with films up to 6 mil thick.

A speed tip welder is a plastic welder used to weld tight corners and irregular profiles. This welder resembles a soldering iron in design and use, except that it has a hole to feed a welding rod through. Some artisans have been known to use a regular soldering iron; without a welding rod, you can only weld thinner films or make tack welds to hold the plastics in place until you can get a more sturdy weld on it. Some people even use a fabric iron on occasion. One of the drawbacks of using a direct heat source like a soldering iron or fabric iron is that you may burn through the plastic before a weld is made. Also, the plastic can melt onto the metal surface, where it will stick and continue to burn and give off fumes whenever the iron is turned on. Heating and melting any plastic will release fumes that you need to remove through ventilation; use the appropriate respirator on yourself. PVC, in particular, creates very hazardous fumes during welding.

There exists a whole range of tools to get higher-quality welds or for joining more exotic types of plastics, but these machines are too costly for the more general-purpose props shop. Laser welding is particularly prized for its ability to create an optically perfect (completely invisible) weld on acrylic and polycarbonate. In many cases, if you buy your plastics from a local source, they may also do fabrication, and laser welding is a common service they provide.

Other Adhesives

Multipurpose glues are "sticky" glues, which adhere the plastics together rather than solvent-welding them. Contact adhesives and two-part mixes fall in this category. Some glues that claim to work well on plastics have solvents in them that eat into the surface of the plastic a bit to give the glue a bit more "grip." For the plastics that cannot be solvent-welded, these glues are not much better. They are handy for attaching plastics to other materials though. Super glue (cyanoacrylate) can be used to join some plastics, particularly acrylic.

Pressure-sensitive adhesives, or tape, is often enough to join pieces of plastic. Double stick tape is especially useful, particularly when you are attaching the face of one sheet to the face of another. Some plastics come with a pressure-sensitive adhesive already applied, such as UHMW tape.

Shaping Plastic

Besides the uniform smoothness of its surface, the other great advantage in using plastics is the ease of shaping them with a relatively little amount of heat. Many thermoplastics become pliable around 300°, which can be achieved with a variety of tools. Heating metal requires the use of forges or torches using tanks of fuel. Wood can be bent with steam, but only up to a certain point, and it requires the piece to be positioned in a clamp for several hours. Plastic, on the other hand, can be blown with a hot air gun, bent, and be cooled and stiff within a few minutes.

Always use good ventilation when heating plastics. In theory, plastics become shapeable at a lower temperature than when they begin to decompose; for example, high-impact styrene sheets become formable at 325°. Tests have shown they begin decomposing and release toxins at temperatures as low as 390°. Always heat your thermoform plastics with the minimum amount of heat possible, and do it in a well-ventilated area.

You have a few options for heating and shaping plastic. A strip heater is a great tool to heat plastics to give an angled bend in a straight line. Good ones will keep the plastic away from the heating element itself. Bend the plastic in the direction

One of the toxins released when polystyrene is heated is styrene vapor. The EPA calls styrene "a suspected toxin to the gastrointestinal tract, kidney, and respiratory system, among others." It is also a possible carcinogen. Further, most tests on the substances released when plastics are heated use pure forms in ideal conditions; real plastics have all sorts of chemical additives, and heating plastics in the props shop is done unevenly and with much variation. You literally do not know what is in the chemical soup created when plastics are heated to their decomposition point, and thus, there is no respirator cartridge you can use to protect yourself. If you smell something, you are breathing fumes. If you see smoke or fumes, you are releasing fumes. If you get a headache while working, you are breathing fumes. Adequate ventilation and fume extraction are key if you wish to work with plastics and heat.

Figure 9-9: Colored acrylic rods were bent by blowing a heat gun onto a single spot for a few seconds. After fully cooling in a few minutes, they maintained their bend indefinitely.

Plastic	Temp. for thermoforming (Fahrenheit)
Acrylic	240–340
Styrene (high impact)	325–350
ABS	300–350
Acrylic PVC (Kydex™)	350–365
Polycarbonate	350–425
Expanded PVC (Sintra™)	300
PETG	230–350
Cellulose Acetate Butyrate	335–390
Polyethylene and Polyethylene foam	325–425

away from the heat; the heat should be applied to the hill of the fold, not the valley. A heat gun can be used for more irregular shaping and deforming, or for bending rods, tubes, and sticks. Be careful with the heat gun—you can burn a hole right through your plastic in just a few short seconds if the gun is too close or if you stay in one spot too long. If you need to heat an entire sheet, an oven could be used, though it should never be reused for food cooking after that. Material that is more than ¼ inch thick may require heating on both sides of the fold.

For sharp bends in thicker plastic, you can cut a V-shaped groove about ¾ of the way into the interior side of where your bend will be. After you make the bend, you can seal the groove with a water-thin solvent adhesive.

Jigs, formers, and clamps are vital for bending your plastic to the correct shape and holding it there. Often, when you bend a heated piece of plastic, it will try to spring back to its unbent shape; you need to hold it firmly in position until it fully cools. Jigs and formers also help line up your pieces and allow you to get bends with precise measurements and shapes, which is particularly helpful when you need to bend multiple copies of the same shape. If you use any kind of jig that involves pressing or clamping the plastic, be aware that if a heated por-

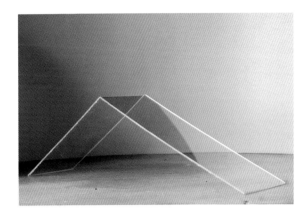

Figure 9-10: If you do not have a strip heater, you can still make long clean bends with a heat gun.

tion of plastic is pushed or pressed into another material, it will pick up the texture of that material. To avoid this, cover the former with a thin and smooth piece of material, such as cardstock. Formers do not necessarily need to be complicated; draping a plastic sheet over a pipe will give a gentle curve with the radius of that pipe, for instance.

Figure 9-11: Fashion a jig similar to a sheet metal bending brake, or clamp several pieces of plywood on your acrylic, leaving exposed the area that will bend. Make sure the thickness of the plywood doesn't prevent you from bending your acrylic all the way.

Figure 9-12: This ensures that only the area you want to bend will bend; even if the acrylic in surrounding areas heats up to the softening point, the plywood keeps it from deforming. It also helps guide your bend to keep it perpendicular and straight.

Figure 9-13: This piece of acrylic is bent using a quick handmade jig that approximates a sheet metal bending brake.

Figure 9-14: This simple jig holds an acrylic piece in position while it cools back down. It ensures that multiple pieces will have the same distance between their two ends, as well as the same angle of bend. The jig also helps keep the two ends parallel to each other, as this kind of bend can easily introduce a twist to the plastic.

Figure 9-15: Press forming of thermoform plastics requires that the shape of the two molds on top and bottom match each other. This rudimentary press former imparts a series of curves to a strip of acrylic.

Vacuum Forming

The thermoplastics we shape through heat can also be vacuum formed. Vacuum forming involves heating a sheet of plastic until it is pliable, draping it over a shape, and then using a vacuum to suck the plastic tight against the form until it cools and hardens. In "straight" vacuum forming, you suck the plastic into a negative mold. In "drape" forming, you suck the plastic over the top of a positive form known as a **buck**. As you can imagine from this description, the pieces you make with this method tend to be one-sided, and cannot have any undercuts.

You can buy vacuum-forming machines, though it also remains a popular do-it-yourself machine among hobbyists and small shops. The machine itself consists of a table surface, called a **platen**, with a hole in it that leads to the vacuum. Any type of vacuum pump can be used, even a hand-operated one, and some machines are made so that a standard vacuum cleaner can be hooked up to it. Many tables have multiple small holes so that the air can be pulled out regardless of the size or shape of the buck placed on it. The plastic is clamped into a frame. This frame helps hold the plastic taut as it is stretched over the buck. The frame also serves the purpose of sealing the table surface so that a true vacuum can be formed between the buck and the plastic. With vacuum forming, it is vital that the plastic be brought straight down over the buck, otherwise it will stretch the plastic on one side and make it thinner. To facilitate this, many vacuum formers have a track for the frame to travel in so it can be slid straight down onto the buck without any guesswork.

The final element of a vacuum-forming machine is the heating element itself. Some prop makers simply repurpose a kitchen oven, as it can fit a small-to-mid sized sheet of plastic and easily generate the heat needed in an even manner (do not use an oven that you also prepare food in; the toxins that may be released when plastics are heated can leach into the oven and will leach into any food you cook in it afterwards). Other vacuum formers have their own heating elements. Because the plastic sags in the frame when it is heated, the heating element is typically placed above the plastic. Some machines place the heating element directly above the table so that the track which moves the framed plastic down over the buck can also bring the plastic up to the heating element.

On a buck, the details are on the outside; when you vacuum-pull a sheet of plastic over it, those details will be on the inside. The details on the outside will be softened by the thickness of the plastic; the thicker the plastic, the softer the details. You may need to reduce the size of your buck and exaggerate the details if you are pulling a particularly thick plastic. At other times, you may let the details be softened on purpose, as this can create a slicker and more "mass-produced" visual appearance.

Plastics popular with vacuum formers include high-impact styrene, ABS, PVC, Kydex®, PETG, CAB, acrylic, and polyethylene, though any thermoform plastic sheet can be used. Styrene is one of the most popular because it is easy to use by beginners and is readily available in a variety of thicknesses depending on the strength needed. For general use,

0.06" thick material is a good starting point. For larger pieces, such as torso-sized armor pieces, 0.08" offers some advantages in strength. Pieces that need even more strength can use plastic up to 0.93" thick, though keep in mind that the thicker your plastic, the softer your details will be. You also need more heat and vacuum power. The stronger your vacuum is, the stronger your bucks need to be. Bucks made out of a rigid foam, such as polystyrene foam, can be crushed under the force of plastic being sucked on top of it. Bucks are commonly made from rigid polyurethane foam, plaster, reinforced plastic (fiberglass), wood, and aluminum. If the model is made from a softer material, such as clay or polystyrene foam, the top will need to be reinforced with something like epoxy or fiberglass. Keep in mind that the plastic sheet is hot when placed on the buck, so bucks made from a material that will melt or burn will also need to be coated or reinforced with a different material.

Keep in mind too that the taller your mold or buck is, the thicker your plastic needs to be; the plastic is stretched over the buck, and as it is stretched, it thins out. If you start out with plastic too thin for a tall buck, it may tear as it is sucked down, or leave you with a very thin and fragile object.

Leave the vacuum running for a few minutes after the plastic has sucked down over the buck until the plastic has cooled enough to maintain its new shape. To prevent your plastic from sticking to your mold or buck, you can lightly sprinkle the mold's surface with baby or talcum powder. After the plastic has cooled, a blast of compressed air between the plastic and the buck will also help break the suction that may make it hard to remove. You can also remove the plastic as soon as it has cooled enough to hold its shape; it may still be warm enough to have a little "give" that allows it to flex without distorting.

Transparent Plastics

Transparent plastic sheets have some additional considerations. Scratches on the surface are more noticeable than in

Figure 9-16: This vacuum former built by Harrison Krix has a frame and platen that can use sheets of plastic up to 14" × 14". The box on top contains heating elements to heat the plastic. The frame is on four drawer slides, so it can travel up and down between the heating box and the platen. It also has a handle for easy maneuvering. The platen is another box; the top has many holes drilled in it, while the bottom has one large hole to connect the vacuum cleaner hose to. Photograph by Harrison Krix.

Figure 9-17: This suit of armor is created entirely from vacuum-formed plastic. Armor constructed by Costume Armour, Inc., for the original *Man of La Mancha* on Broadway.

opaque plastics, and when present, cannot be filled or covered over. When you cut or machine transparent plastics, the edges become foggy or white, so knowing how to make them transparent again is helpful. The most common plastic sheet goods used in the props shop are acrylic and polycarbonate, so the following techniques are specific to them, though they may work on other transparent sheet goods as well.

Acrylic and polycarbonate come with a protective paper sheet or film adhered to both sides. This is easy to remove (unless the acrylic is a few years old), but you want to keep the paper on as long as you can to protect the surface of the plastic from scratches.

You can cut right through the paper; in fact, it will keep it from scratching as you push it through a table or band saw, or as you move tools around on top. It also helps keep the plastic from chipping as you cut it. If your plastic is covered in paper (rather than film), you can use the surface to make your markings with pencil.

You will need to remove the paper or film from the surfaces you wish to heat, bend, or glue. You can peel away a little strip and cut it off to expose only the surface you need to work on.

If the masking paper has dried out, or if your plastic has other labels or adhesives that prove stubborn to remove, the best way to remove it is with either kerosene or WD-40. WD-40 is great for the little stickers, while kerosene may be necessary for larger areas of masking paper. In either case, let it soak for a few minutes before trying to peel it off; masking paper may need to soak in kerosene for 15–30 minutes. You can scrape it off with a tool softer than the acrylic, like a plastic spatula or HDPE kitchen tools. Clean the kerosene or WD-40 off with dish soap and water, and wipe dry with a soft cloth.

For cleaning acrylic and polycarbonate, never use a cleaner with ammonia, like Windex or 409. Dish soap and water is fine for many situations. For more heavy-duty cleaning, special plastic cleaners, such as Brillianize, the Novus 3-step cleaner, or even Pledge will help you out.

For minor scratches on acrylic, you can use special scratch removers made by the same companies that make the above-mentioned plastic cleaners. A minor scratch is any scratch you cannot feel with your fingernail. The minor abrasives in toothpaste are also mild enough to remove these scratches. If you are able to feel the scratches with your fingernail, you will need to sand and buff it out. Start with a coarse sandpaper, and work your way up to the finer grades. For example, you might start with 150 grit followed by 320, then 400, then 600, and finally end with 800. Use a buffing wheel on your drill and some plastic buffing compound. Do not press too hard, or you will burn the compound into the plastic. Scratches in polycarbonate *cannot* be sanded and buffed out in this manner.

 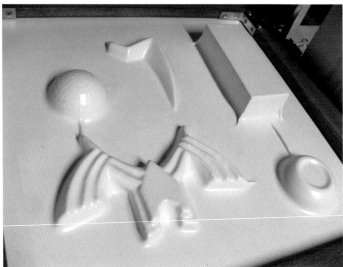

Figures 9-18 and 9-19: Objects of various shapes and sizes are placed on a platen. A sheet of styrene is vacuum-formed over them. When cooled, the original objects can be removed and the plastic pieces can be cut apart with the tools mentioned earlier for cutting plastic. Notice the lines that extend from some of the corners; this is known as **webbing** and occurs when a severe or sharp angle in your buck causes the plastic to fold onto itself and stick.

You can avoid webbing by raising your objects off the table and allowing the plastic to partially curl underneath it, or by manipulating the webbing with a push stick while the plastic is still soft. You do not have to worry about it if all the webbing is isolated to the off-cut areas of your plastic sheet. If you wish to manipulate the webbing but the plastic has already cooled too much, you can heat that section back up with a heat gun. In fact, a heat gun is useful for selectively heating any portion of the plastic while it is being vacuum-formed to further manipulate it. This is useful if a section hasn't sucked completely over part of your mold or buck. Photographs by Harrison Krix.

When you cut transparent sheet goods, the edges are foggy and cloudy. If you want to get the edges to be as clear as the other surfaces, you need to first remove all the saw marks, and then polish it to make it shiny. Remove saw marks by scraping the edges with a scraping tool or a razor blade (hold the razor blade perpendicularly on edge, and drag it along the edge). You can also try 60 or 80 grit sandpaper or various files. Whenever you sand plastic, always wet sand, as dry sanding will generate too much heat. In wet sanding, you apply a lubricant (usually water) between the sand paper and the material's surface; make sure to use sand paper intended for wet sanding.

The result of scraping and sanding will give you a uniformly smooth but matte edge (known as a **dressed edge**). To get a glossy and completely transparent edge, you will need to polish and buff it.

To polish, continue wet sanding with ever-increasing grits of sandpaper up to around 600 grit. Rub the edge with a damp, soft cloth to remove all the dust. You can then buff it with a clean muslin wheel and fine-grit buffing compound in a polishing wheel or attached to the end of a drill. Follow that with a clean, soft flannel wheel. You can also buff it with a clean cloth and a bit of toothpaste.

Figure 9-20: The blue protective film for the acrylic sheets on this gun cabinet is left on through the whole construction process. *Why Torture is Wrong, and the People Who Love Them*, the Public Theatre, 2009.

Figure 9-21: A piece of acrylic that has just been cut shows the saw marks that will need to be scraped and polished.

Rubber, Foam, and Foam Rubber

Rubber originally referred to a stretchy and bouncy material made from natural latex. Today, it applies to many of the plastics that share the properties of rubber; a more correct term is **elastomer**, which refers to any polymer with elastic properties.

A **foam** is a material that has air (or any gas) trapped in a solid. A foam can be either an open-cell foam or a closed-cell foam. Open-cell foams are like a net, where the pores form an interconnected network that can be filled with air or liquid. A sponge is an open-cell foam. In closed-cell foams, the trapped air is completely encased within the solid material; you can't fill them with water. This makes them more rigid, dense, and dimensionally stable. Some foams share properties with elastomers and have earned the nickname **foam rubber**.

I will now step through some of the more common rubber, foam, and foam rubber materials here. Many hard and rigid foams are used as sculpting mediums, so they will be discussed in more detail in Chapter 13. Softer foams and foam rubbers are often used with flat patterning methods, so their use is discussed in Chapter 12. Some foams and foam rubbers can be bought in liquid form and poured into a mold to make a cast piece; their use is discussed in Chapter 14. What follows is more of a general overview of these materials' properties and how to work with them.

Latex is a liquid from a tree that dries to a sticky and stretchy substance. A process known as "vulcanization" turns it into the more durable material we call **rubber**. Liquid latex remains an extremely useful material for prop making and special makeup effects, though a certain percentage of people have allergic reactions to latex. Rubber is used for all sorts of cushioning, padding, and elastic straps. It is most easily cut with a straight edge and sharp knife, or a pair of tin snips.

The word *rubber* is also used to describe a number of synthetic materials that exhibit similar properties to vulcanized natural rubber.

Neoprene, or polychloroprene, is a family of synthetic rubbers and foam rubbers. Neoprene began as a trademarked name but has since become generic. It is more likely to be used as a casting material; it is also used to make chemically resistant gloves for handling toxic materials. Nitrile butadiene rubber (NBR), or just **nitrile**, is another synthetic rubber used for protective gloves.

EPDM (ethylene-propylene-diene) is a dense rubber used as an alternative to natural rubber for fabricating cushions, padding, and other parts on a prop that need elastic properties. It can be bought from a materials supplier, but it is easier to find in pure form in rolls for waterproofing roofs, or in sheets for lining artificial ponds.

Polyethylene foam is found in many items that can be reappropriated by the props artisan as raw materials. Most "pool noodles" are polyethylene foam, as are many yoga and exercise mats. Ethafoam™ is a brand of polyethylene foam that most props people recognize in its backing rod form (used to fill gaps between the concrete slabs in a sidewalk). Ethafoam rod is like pool noodles in a vast range of different diameters and lengths. When Ethafoam rod is cut in half, it can be placed along and around curves to simulate curved molding pieces. Polyethylene foam can be thermoformed at the same temperatures as plain polyethylene.

Ethylene vinyl acetate (EVA) is thermoplastic copolymer of ethylene and vinyl acetate. Most low-temperature hot-melt adhesive and hot glue is EVA. It is also a common foam rubber. EVA foam is often called "craft foam," "fun foam," or Evalite™ and can be found in a variety of thicknesses, sizes, and colors at hobby stores; it is also used as yoga mats and floor mats (including those multicolored interlocking puzzle-piece kinds), which are basically the same as plain sheets of EVA. It is especially useful for making lightweight and flexible fake armor and large character heads and masks. EVA foam can be molded and shaped with a heat gun like other thermoplastics; it can even be shaped on a vacuum former with some success. It remains squishy and flexible and will deform under pressure though. Because it is the same material as EVA, hot

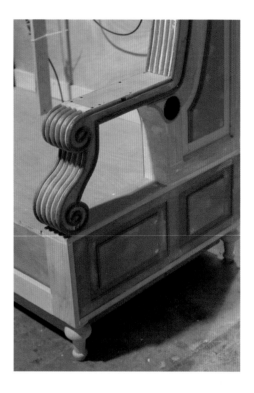

Figure 9-22: Ethafoam strips (in gray) added to the arm of this ornate bench give the appearance of fanciful carving without too much time spent on labor.

melt glue works well to join pieces of EVA foam together; the heat will slightly melt the surface of the foam and allow the glue to intermingle, creating a strong bond.

Polyurethane foam comes in both soft and rigid varieties. Soft polyurethane foam, sometimes called **polyfoam**, comes in sheets, tubes, rods, and blocks, and is the most common material used for upholstery foam. Puppet makers love it as well. Rigid polyurethane foam, often shortened to just urethane foam, is prized as a sculpting medium because it is much denser and can hold finer detail than polystyrene foam. It is, however, far more toxic. Rigid polyurethane foam is most easily found in taxidermy supply shops, as they use it to build the shape of the animals underneath the fur.

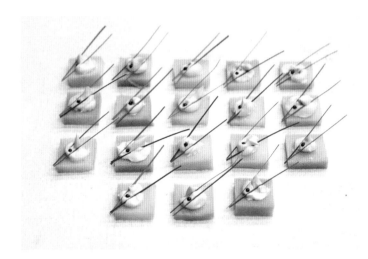

Figure 9-23: Polyurethane foam rubber was cut into squares to make a quick base for these fancy *hors d'oeuvre. Timon of Athens*, the Public Theater, 2011.

More dense and rigid foams can be cut on a band saw. For softer foams and foam rubber, you may need to use a knife-edged blade. If the foam is too soft and the band saw teeth are too large, the teeth can actually grab the foam and pull it down into the band saw. Most foams can be cut with a foam cutter, which looks like a jigsaw, but with a really big throat and a rigid piece behind the blade. For smaller or more precise cuts, a utility knife is good. The kind with the "snap-off" blades are great because you can extend the blade all the way for a long but thin cutting edge. Cutting foam quickly dulls these blades, but a few drops of sewing machine oil on the sharp edge will help lubricate your cuts and make them cleaner.

ten

structure and framework

Fabrication refers to cutting, and occasionally bending, several pieces of metal to assemble into a whole. The cutting apart and assembly of plastic pieces into larger structures is known as plastic fabrication. We fabricate wood as well, though the terms *carpentry* and *construction* are used instead. The three previous chapters dealt with the fabrication of wood, metal, and plastics, respectively. We can now look at some techniques and principles that apply to all three for fabricating objects as robustly as possible. We will also see that we can fabricate structures and framework that are not ultimately seen, but which give the outermost surface its shape and strength.

Shape versus Surface Treatment

"The camera only sees the last coat of paint." Even if the outermost surface is not paint, this old art director's quote holds true, whether it is a camera or an audience looking at your prop. For props, the appearance does not necessarily dictate what the prop should be made out of. Visual appearance is but one of many needs; the structure of your prop needs to fulfill other needs, such as weight, strength, rigidity (or flexibility), etc. You can build a structure and cover or skin it with another material to make it appear to be built out of something else.

A prop that appears to be solid may end up being too heavy if you built it solid. For most props, you want to build some kind of structure or framework that can support the outermost surface or skin to keep it lightweight and to cut down on the amount of materials you need. There may also be times when your prop needs to be hollow so some other object can fit inside.

Because faux painting and texturing techniques can make your materials appear like totally different materials, you open up thousands of possibilities to construct an item that will not break or fail no matter what material it needs to look like.

This chapter will look at some ways to make fabricated objects stronger or more rigid for your underlying structure. It will then look at ways to create more organic and curvy shapes

Figure 10-1: In this simplified example, this giant skull prop can be sculpted out of a solid piece of foam, or it can have an interior structure with only thin sections actually sculpted out of foam.

Figure 10-2: This sedan chair is made out of a steel frame with sheets of lauan attached on the outside. The steel creates the shape and the structure; the lauan is simply a skin to hold three-dimensional details and paint.

Figures 10-3 and 10-4: Even materials that do not seem like they can hold any structure can often benefit from a bit of reinforcement. For this chair, a welded metal frame was integrated into channels routed into the back of an intricate Chinese design cut out of wood. The back was filled and sanded smooth, and when the chair was fully painted, the metal was invisible. *Tea: A Mirror of Soul*, Santa Fe Opera, 2007. Scenic design by Rumi Matsui.

through fabrication, using formers and stringers. Finally, it will look at skeletal frames for creating extremely organic shapes that may only require a thin skin of material for a surface.

Compression

Let's start by thinking of a cookie. It's always a good way to start. You want to keep the cookie off the floor. You can either place it on a table or tape it to the wall. The cookie on top of the table will basically sit there forever until your cat knocks it off. Otherwise, the table itself would need to fall apart and crumble, and the cookie is nowhere near heavy enough to cause that to happen.

The cookie taped to the wall, however, will fall as soon as the tape stops sticking and peels off. The tape may not peel off itself; it may pull the paint off the wall and drop the cookie, or the outermost crumbs stuck to the tape may separate from the larger cookie, causing it to drop.

The cookie example is analogous to attaching a leg to a platform. If you screw and glue the leg to the side of the platform, it will only hold as long as the screw and glue do not fail. If you place the platform on top of the leg, the leg itself would need to be completely crushed for the platform to hit the ground. This kind of leg is known as a **compression leg**, because it relies on the compressive strength of the entire length of the leg rather than just the strength of the joint or fasteners. You can build stronger props if you take advantage of compression strength wherever possible. It is not just legs; in our cookie example, the only force acting on the cookie is gravity. With props, force may be applied in many directions, such as when someone sits on a prop, pushes on it from the side, or lifts in the air. Compression in the direction of the length of a beam is the least likely way for a material to fail. Whatever direction the force comes from, your prop will be stronger whenever it relies on the compressive strength of your materials rather than just the joints.

Spanning a Gap

A platform does not just rely on how you attach the legs; you also do not want the floor between the legs to break or sag. Now, for a platform, you may simply add as many legs as you need to keep the floor nice and solid. Of course, this wastes materials; you want to use as few legs as you can get away with. In props, you are not always dealing with platforms and legs; there are any number of situations where you need a length of material to hold its shape, and you can't always just add as many legs as it takes. We need to learn some ways to make beams and surfaces rigid over a distance.

A **wale** (sometimes called a waler or whaler) is a ridge or a stripe spanning a length meant to stiffen, straighten, or otherwise help support a flat surface or a surface made of a number of beams, studs, or posts (the ridges on corduroy fabric are also called "wales"). A very thin piece of wood or metal added to a surface for strength or support is known as a **cleat**.

Any shape or span that you want to strengthen can benefit from a ridge running along the length where it is weakest. You can see this in armor and shields, where ridges are added along the middle of long curves; this is done not just for decoration but because it adds strength. You can also see it in small plastic items, such as the cases for your cell phones and other gadgets. Take them apart, and you can see the small ridges added at curves and sides to give it strength and structure.

The strength of adding a ridge comes from the fact that it gives a small amount of material pointed perpendicularly to the surface of the main material. A board such as a 1" by 4" laid down flat is easy to bend up and down in the middle. If you turn it on its edge, it will flex back and forth. If you attach a flat board to a board laid on edge (creating an "L" shape), it will not flex

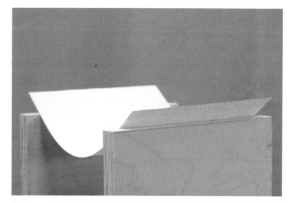

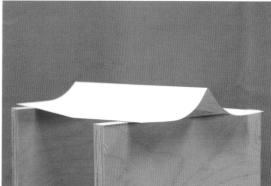

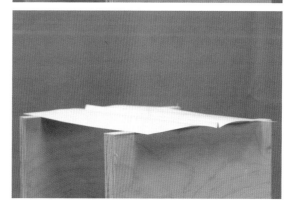

Figure 10-5: A wale placed along the back of a stud wall helps stiffen and straighten the wall.

Figures 10-6 to 10-8: Top: A piece of paper sags under its own weight. Center: With a single fold, it can span the same distance without sagging. Bottom: With three folds, it spans the distance without sagging and remains flat. These folds form a ridge, which is used frequently in manufacturing to stiffen an otherwise flexible material while retaining a low profile.

in either direction. Theatre carpenters call this type of beam a "strongback."

A beam has to support its own weight in addition to the weight of whatever is placed on top of it. A beam weighs more than an I-beam or a piece of hog's trough, so the *additional* weight a beam can support (the weight of whatever is placed on top of it) is actually less than the additional weight an I-beam can hold. It also means all the legs and beams supporting *that*

beam need to be stronger. You can see in new home construction: wooden I-beams now replace much of the structure that solid beams used to support. They impart the same amount of strength with far less material (making it cheaper) and far less weight, which ultimately means you need less structure to support the whole house in the first place.

As you add material, the weight of an object increases faster than its strength; if you scale up the size of an object,

Figure 10-9: Top left: Two lengths of lumber joined perpendicularly form what is often known in theatrical carpentry as a "strongback." Top right: A similar configuration rolled from a single piece of steel (or other metal) is known as "angle iron." Bottom left: Three lengths of lumber joined in a U shape may be called a "hog's trough." Bottom right: Three lengths of steel are typically joined (by welding, bolting, or riveting) together in an "I" shape; this is called a "plate girder." When the shape is rolled from a single piece of steel as in this diagram, we call it an I-beam.

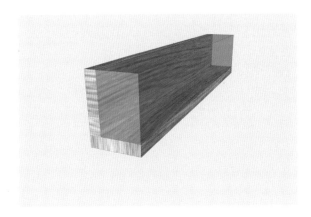

Figure 10-10: A piece of strongback has nearly as much strength and rigidity as a beam with the same outer dimensions, but it uses far less material, making it cheaper, easier to work with, and lighter in weight.

Figure 10-11: A section of truss. A truss is essentially a solid beam with all the nonstructural material removed to make it lighter.

even if you use the same materials and maintain the same proportions, you will reach a point where it gets too big to support its own weight. This is why an ant can lift fifty times its own weight, while a human can only lift the same amount of its own weight (and that's with proper training and exercise).

Engineers have figured out that within a beam of material spanning a gap, some areas provide structure, while other areas do nothing. This is important because we want to keep the weight down as much as possible, both to make it easier to lift and because heavier props need proportionally more strength, and also to save money on materials used. If we remove these extraneous areas from a beam, we are left with a truss.

Notice too, how a truss is made up of a series of triangles.

Triangles

Many of us are taught at an early age that a triangle is a strong shape, and looking around any prop or scene shop, you may see carpenters adding diagonal braces to tables and platforms to give them some more strength.

You can see why; even a triangle made of parts attached by flexible joints cannot change its shape.

A square, on the other hand, can fold up. Even if the joints are extremely rigid, the leverage you get when you push on the top of a square creates a lot of force on the joint at the bottom of the square, making it more likely to fail.

In order to keep this from happening, we can add a diagonal beam from the top corner of one side to the bottom of another corner. This creates a triangle in our structure. In construction parlance, this diagonal member is known as a **brace**.

In many cases, you do not need a diagonal brace to run the whole length of the square. Look at a theatrical flat: The same principle applies to the keystones placed in the corners. These are the bare minimum needed to keep the rectangular shape from collapsing.

You will also notice that the keystones and toggles on the middle beam are made of thin plates attached on top of the beams on both sides of the joint. These introduce another means to strengthen joints.

Figure 10-12: This table for *Henry IV* at PlayMakers Repertory Company has sturdy legs, but it will still collapse if pushed or leaned on from the end. We added diagonal metal rods connecting the top to the legs to brace the table and keep that from happening.

Gusset Plates, Toggles, and Scabs

A **gusset plate** is a sheet of material used to strengthen and/or join two or more beams together (not to be confused with a gusset used in sewing, which will be covered in Chapter 12). It is kind of like a very short stiffener or waler used for a single joint.

A wooden gusset plate used to strengthen an end-to-end butt joint (usually for making a long beam out of several smaller beams) is known as a **scab**. If it is made of metal, it is known as a **fishplate**.

Grain

Some materials consist of long strands, fibers, or other directional particles that we call **grain**. When you think of materials with a grain, you usually think of wood first, though other

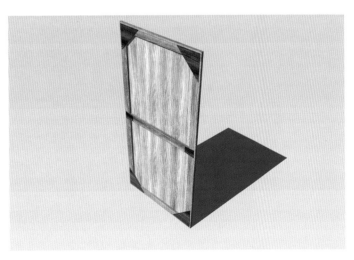

Figure 10-13: Image of back of theatrical flat.

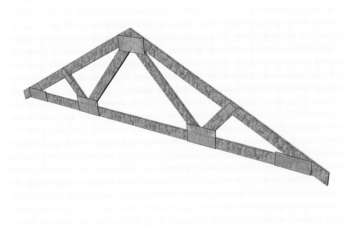

Figure 10-14: A section of roof truss illustrates several uses of gusset plates (shown transparent here for clarity). They quickly reinforce joints that otherwise do not have enough contacting surface area.

Figure 10-15: On top, a fishplate joins two 2" by 4"s. At the bottom is a scab. For more strength, a scab or fishplate can be added to both sides of the joint.

materials have grain as well: paper, fabric, stone, and even some metals that have been forged or extruded. A material with a grain exhibits different properties along the grain than across it; usually, it has more strength in the direction of the grain.

Fail Points

You can buy bolts that are rated to withstand forces and weights up until a certain point, after which they break. If money is no object, should you always buy the highest-rated bolts you can? The answer is no. In engineering, you calculate all the forces an object or structure will need to withstand, and you figure out under which circumstances it will fail. Say, you have a platform on a leg, and you need it to hold 2000 pounds. The leg is designed to hold 20,000 pounds. If the bolt connecting the platform to the leg is rated to withstand 30,000 pounds, then on the off-chance that a force greater than 30,000 pounds lands on the platform, the bolt will hold, but the leg will break. The leg is far bigger and complex, and thus more expensive to replace.

Figure 10-16: Imagine the tiny chair is a force that can break a bar of material in half (known as "fracturing"). The grains of orzo pasta show a material without any grain; that is, the individual particles are positioned randomly. In order for the chair to pass from top to bottom and split the material, it can travel in nearly a straight line.

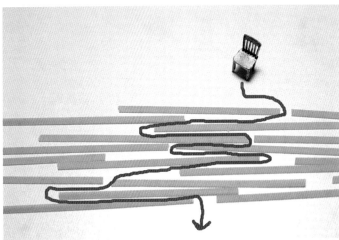

Figure 10-17: Now imagine these pieces of linguine show a material with grain. In order to split it in half, the chair would have to take a fairly circuitous route. This is why materials are stronger across the grain.

If the bolt was rated at 15,000 pounds, then it would break instead, and the only thing you would need to replace is the bolt, which only costs a dollar or two.

In props, we are not engineers, and so we should not be constructing anything whose failure can endanger a lot of people (in some locations, you need a license to perform actual engineering). Still, we do have to build chairs and tables, and they need to withstand a certain amount of weight and force without breaking. Whenever possible, figure out how and where the prop might fail, and see if you can construct it in a way where you only have to fix a cheap and easily replaceable part, like a bolt.

It's for this reason that industrial shops have lots of little window panes rather than one giant window pane. If a piece of metal hits the window and cracks it, you only have to replace a single tiny window pane, rather than a single large window pane that still has a lot of perfectly usable glass.

The same is true of parts that will wear out over time. This is why we often put pads on the bottom of a piece of furniture. When furniture moves around a stage floor, either the furniture or the stage is going to wear down and eventually show damage. You do not want the floor to wear down as you would have to repaint or refinish it. If the furniture legs wear down, they will start to look ugly and get shorter every time you re-sand them to look nice. If you put a pad on, however, the pad will wear down; when the pad wears down too much, you simply replace it with another cheap and tiny pad. Perhaps your prop is dragged across the ground every night. You can screw on plastic glides so when they wear out, you simply unscrew them and screw on new ones. If you attempt to glue them on or make them integral to the prop, you will have a tougher time replacing them later on.

Rigid versus Flexible

Is papier-mâché stronger than fiberglass? Fiberglass is used in all sorts of applications, such as outdoor sculptures or large television props. Anyone who has felt fiberglass knows how strong

"Tech out" is a phrase that comes from technical directors to describe the initial planning and engineering they do when they receive draftings and drawings from a designer. A designer may give the TD a drafting of a wall. Usually, a theatrical wall is made up of a series of flats joined together, with wales to hold it all together and braces or jacks to keep them from falling over.

So before the technical director makes the cut list for that wall, he or she needs to figure out the number and location of all these other pieces that make up the frames of the flats, the wales, and the jacks. So when a TD "techs out" this wall, it means he or she is making a new drawing to precisely determine all these hidden structural pieces. As props people, we can borrow this phrase for larger props (particularly furniture and oversized sculptures) that require an internal or hidden structure and cannot simply be either hollow or cut from a solid piece of material.

it is. But papier-mâché can be stronger in some circumstances. Upon impact, the papier-mâché will flex a little bit, whereas the rigidity of the fiberglass does not allow it to. Flexing absorbs some of the energy, and the material bounces back to its original shape. With rigidity, the material will either break or it won't; there is nothing in-between. Think about this when you have to build a prop that will be subject to strong forces or impacts. Is it worth trying to make it as rigid and unbreakable as possible? Or is there a way to put some flex in it so it has a bit of "give"?

Cushions and padding serve a similar purpose. Rather than allowing one object to impact another suddenly, a cushion will absorb and spread out the impact. Cushioning certain sections of a prop where an actor needs to strike it will help keep the actor from being injured as well as protect the prop itself. Stunt weapons for film and television are often made from a single piece of cast foam rubber so the entire weapon is essentially a shaped cushion; this both protects the actor during rigorous stunts as well as keeps the weapon from breaking apart.

As you can see, choosing the proper materials for your prop can be a complicated balancing act. The strength of your prop is dependent not only on the type of material you use, but also the shape and configuration the material is used in. The weight of your material will affect how strong your prop needs to be. You also have to consider the kind of forces that will be applied to your prop and their directions. Finally, you need to determine whether you need your prop to be absolutely impenetrable, or whether it makes more sense to have it bend or even fail at certain points.

Figure 10-18: The curves on this structure are made from identical curved shapes (formers) cut out of plywood to which a piece of bending ply will be attached. The formers are connected with stringers that are flush against the outside to provide additional places to staple the bending ply to.

Making Strong Shapes

All of the previous information is useful if you are making boxy or flat props. Of course, that is not always the case; we also need to make all manner of curved, flowing, and organic shapes. What follows are some methods for constructing structurally sound shapes that can have skins, laminates, or sculptural material placed over.

Formers and Stringers

A **former** is a structural member that is cut at a profile to establish the shape of a surface. Simple curves (a curve that bends along one axis) can be created by cutting two identical formers and connecting them with a series of **stringers**, or boards.

Armature

When you are manipulating rods of metal rather than sheets, you are working with an armature. Armatures are typically created as a rough skeleton for sculptural materials. We will look at the use of armatures for this purpose in Chapter 13. While it is certainly useful for that purpose, the same principles can be

Figure 10-19: These four plywood formers have a curved shape cut in them so when the wiggle wood "hood" is lowered onto them, it will follow that curve. You can also catch a glimpse of the formers and stretchers making up the curve of the "bumper" of this car. Actors Theatre of Louisville, 2007.

Figure 10-20: This bar looks a bit tricky, but it follows the same idea. The top former, rather than following the inside curve, follows the outside curve, and the outside of the skin is attached to it. *Why Torture is Wrong and the People Who Love Them*, the Public Theater, 2009. Scenic design by David Korins.

used to create a wireform mesh approximating the shape of your prop. This mesh can then be covered in a skin of fabric, papier-mâché, fiberglass, or some other flat material or laminating substance.

Traditional materials used to create a mesh framework for props include cane, bamboo, and wire. Less organic-looking structures have been made out of PVC and ABS pipe as well; the plethora of connectors allows one to quickly assemble a shape.

Cane and bamboo have a certain amount of flex to them, though if they are soaked, they become pliable enough to make very tight curves. Wire is easily bent with heat, and if thin and soft enough, can be bent by hand even without heat. To hold the frame together, artisans will typically tape, tie, or lash the pieces together. Wire can also be welded or soldered together.

Chicken Wire

Constructing the frame for particularly complicated shapes out of individual lengths of bamboo or wire can be time consuming. One common prop shortcut to this approach is the use of chicken wire, also known as poultry fencing. Chicken wire is a wire mesh made of thin, flexible galvanized wire with hexagonal holes; it's kind of like a pre-made wire mesh framework that just needs to be bent into shape and trimmed at the edges. It is economical, easily shaped, and cut, and can expand or contract in any direction for greater flexibility in constructing skins.

Using chicken wire in conjunction with a wooden frame of formers and stringers helps define the shape more precisely and gives a stronger structure underneath. Before the adoption of fiberglass and plastics by prop makers, larger and more organic shapes were almost exclusively built through this combination of wood formers, chicken wire, and a few layers of papier-mâché.

This method of prop making is often looked down upon because it is seen as less sophisticated than modern materials or because the props made in this manner are often poorly done—theatres that can only afford to build props out of chicken wire and papier-mâché also tend to be theatres which cannot afford to hire skilled props artisans. Chicken wire need not be sequestered to the realm of amateur-hour, though. Some sophisticated props, such as the topiaries in the film *Edward Scissorhands*, were constructed out of chicken wire. Many contemporary parade floats are constructed in this manner. In the right hands, it remains one of the least toxic and economical choices for large organically shaped props. Many other sizes and styles of wire mesh are available in arts and crafts stores for smaller and more intricate shapes.

A good set of wire cutters is necessary to work with chicken wire. Sharp edges are created when you cut the edge, so wear thick gloves whenever possible. Cut your edges as cleanly as possible, and fold them over onto themselves when you staple your piece to your wood frame. Stapling the chicken wire to a wooden frame is usually how forms are made. Multiple pieces of chicken wire can be joined together by interfolding the open edges, or by "sewing" them together with thin wire. You can sew any number of other objects or materials to them with wire as well.

Knots and Tying

Frameworks of bamboo or wire are often lashed together with rope or string, so it is helpful to demonstrate some lashing techniques. Before we get to lashing though, I should describe the knots you will need to know before lashing. These basic knots are also highly useful for many other aspects of both prop making and general stagehand work.

The **working end** of a knot is the end of the rope (or the active part if you are tying a knot in the middle of a continuous length of rope. The **standing end** is the unused length of rope that comes before the position you wish to tie your knot. A **bight** is a curved section, and a **loop** is a full circle made by passing the working end over or under itself.

Figure 10-21: On the left, an overhand knot (the kind used to tie your shoes) is a simple twist of rope. You make a loop with the working end passing over the standing end, and then bring it around back and pull it through the loop. A square knot (center) is made by tying a second overhand knot in the opposite direction; wrap the standing end *behind* the working end, and then bring it around front and pull it through the loop. A granny knot (right) is made by making two overhand knots in the same direction, and is what is commonly made by those without a knowledge of knots. Notice the difference in how the square knot and granny knot look; a square knot is a stronger knot.

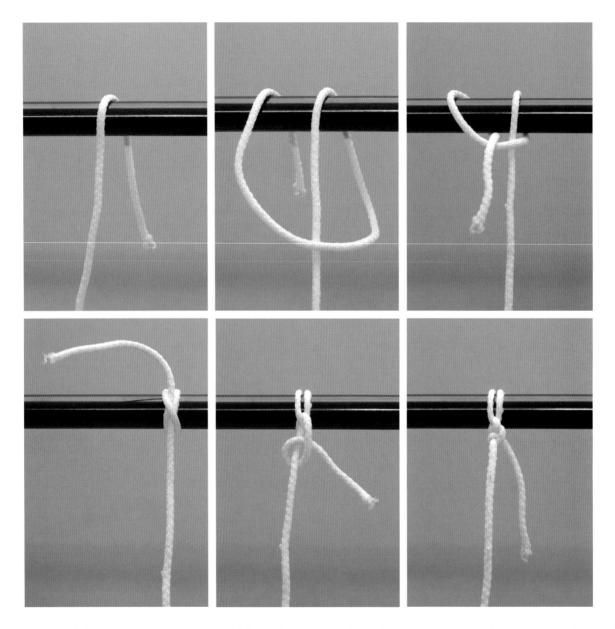

Figures 10-22 to 10-28: A clove hitch is useful for tying a rope tightly to a pipe or other bar. 1. Pass the working end over the pipe or bar you are tying your clove hitch to. 2. Bring the working end back out, cross over in front of the standing end, and pass it over the pipe on the opposite side. 3. Remaining on that side of the standing end, pull the working end through the loop you just made. 4. Cinch the rope tight, and your clove hitch should look like the photograph. 5. To secure your clove hitch, add a half hitch. 6. Two half hitches will complete the knot.

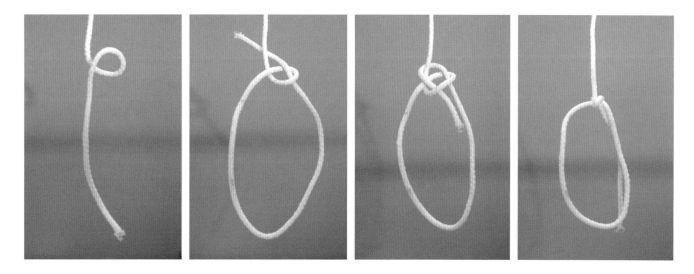

Figures 10-28 to 10-31: A bowline is a general knot for making a loop; this loop can be used to lift things. 1. Start with a small overhand loop. The rope between this loop and the working end will form your bowline loop, so leave enough length to make the size of the loop you want. 2. Pass the working end through the back of the loop and under the back of the standing end. 3. Bight the working end around the standing end, and pass it back through the loop in the direction it came. 4. Pull everything tight, and you have a bowline.

Lashing

There are many ways to lash poles together, and I will show you enough to get you started. Lashing is perfect when you are constructing a skeletal structure out of bamboo or other poles. It can be useful for joining poles or even square tubes together for other reasons, either because you need a slightly flexible joint, or you want to make a connection without drilling, welding, gluing, or otherwise destroying the poles.

Figures 10-32 to 10-37: Diagonal lashing can be used for poles that cross anywhere from 45° to 90°. 1. Tie a clove hitch diagonally around both poles. 2. Begin wrapping the rope around both poles diagonally in the other direction. 3. 3 to 4 wraps should be fine. Keep the wraps lying next to each other rather than on top of each other so that it will be easier to pull them tight. Bring the rope around the back of the rear pole, and start wrapping diagonally in the other direction. 4. Again, 3 to 4 wraps should do it. Remember to keep everything pulled tight. 5. The **frapping** turns are wraps that tighten everything up. Loop the rope around the back of the rear pole and back out front. Wrap it around the lashing, keeping in front of the rear pole and behind the front pole. This loop should only be going around the ropes connecting the two poles and not the poles themselves. Wrap 2 to 3 of these loops to frap it as tight as you can. 6. Finish with a half hitch around the rear pole. You can tie two half hitches for extra strength.

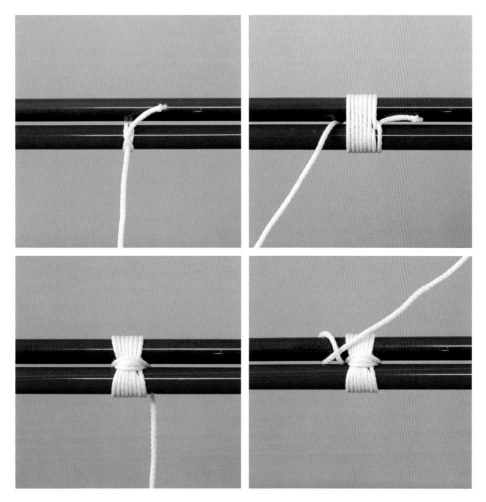

Figures 10-38 to 10-41: Sheer lashing is good for joining adjacent poles (up to 45°), and also for reinforcing long poles. 1. With the poles side by side, tie a clove hitch around 1 or both. 2. Wrap the rope around both poles tightly, keeping the wraps from overlapping. Make around 4–8 turns, or enough so that the lashing is as wide as the diameter of your poles. Pass the rope through the center of both poles. 3. Make 2–3 frapping turns around the lashing between the two poles. This will be (and should be) difficult if you pulled your lashing tight enough. 4. Finish off with 1 or 2 half hitches, or a clove hitch, to secure it.

eleven

fabric

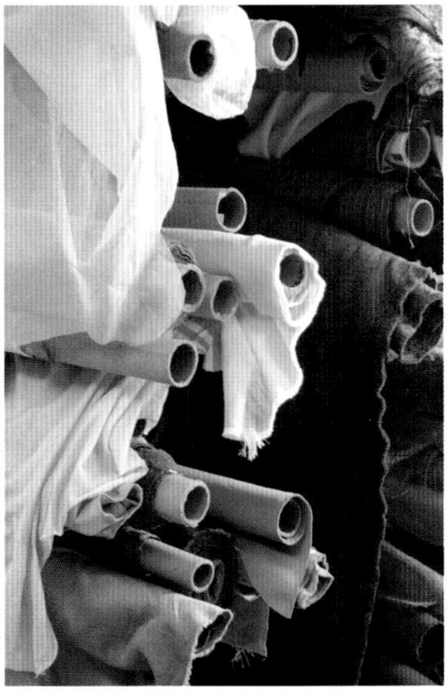

Figure 11-1: A **bolt** of fabric is one complete roll straight from the factory. The length of a bolt depends on what kind of fabric it is, though many are around 40 yards long. Pictured above is a number of partial bolts in a fabric storage area.

Fabric is a flexible sheet of material. Props people use it for everything from upholstered furniture, curtains and drapes, bags and sacks, to dead animals, tents, flags, and parachutes. When you include leather, you are also talking about all sorts of handle wrappings, whips, straps, restraints, and anything else you may imagine.

Textiles

Textiles are made from interlacing fibers or yarns together. The three major classes of textiles are woven, knit, and non woven.

Woven fabric involves interlacing two sets of yarns, threads, or fibers at right angles to each other. In a piece of fabric, the long continuous strands are known as the **warp**. The strands that cross to form the width of the fabric are the **weft**.

Because the strands in woven fabrics run perpendicularly to each other, woven fabric has a **grain**. This grain allows woven fabric to be torn in a straight line either lengthwise or crosswise. Plain weaves are the easiest to tear, while satin weaves are the hardest; twill weaves fall in the middle. Unless the fabric is made with an elastic fiber, woven fabric is not very stretchy along the grain. It is stretchy along the **bias,** though. The direction of the grain and bias on a piece of fabric will affect how it drapes and stretches.

Knit fabrics differ from woven in that each row is made of loops that intertwine with the loops in the previous row. This method makes knit fabrics far stretchier than woven fabrics. As with weaves, yarn can be knit in a variety of different ways to create different styles and patterns of fabric. Knit fabrics also have a grain.

Knitting by hand with yarn allows you to create three-dimensional shapes out of a fabric without any seams.

Nonwoven fabrics are those in which the fibers are bonded together by chemical or mechanical means, or through the application of heat or solvents. **Felt** is the most common nonwoven fabric in the props shop, formed by matting and pressing many short fibers together until they become tangled into a continuous piece. It comes in a variety of densities and thicknesses up to 2". It is useful for cushioning, particularly when a prop is held against the skin (such as inside the handle of a shield) and as padding, such as

You can also weave larger strands of material to make your own flexible sheets. Wicker baskets and furniture are made by weaving strands of reed, cane, rattan, and other plant materials. Cane and reed are woven to create cane seats and cane-backed chairs.

Most woven or knit fabrics have the same parts. The **selvage** is the factory-created edge on either side of the width of the fabric. The **crosswise grain** runs from selvage edge to selvage edge. The **lengthwise grain** runs in the direction you unroll the fabric from the bolt. The **bias** runs at a 45° angle to both the crosswise and lengthwise grain.

Figure 11-2: The selvage, or factory edge or a piece of fabric.

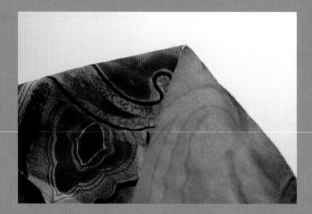

Figure 11-3: The loud pattern is the "right side," while the pale pink is the "wrong side."

Fabric has a **right side** and a **wrong side**. The right side is the side meant to be seen. Some fabrics are reversible, and either side can be the right side. Some fabrics appear at first glance to be reversible, but on closer inspection the right side and wrong side have slight differences; be sure not to get these mixed up as you construct your prop. It may help to mark matching sides with a piece of masking tape or some other removable mark. On occasion, a designer may decide he or she wants to use the "wrong side" as the visible portion. As I talk about stitches, seams, and hems in this book, I use the term "right side" to refer to the visible portion, so just be sure to reverse your thinking and call the "wrong side" the "right side" once the designer makes that decision.

inside a box or between casters and the body of a piece of furniture.

Purchasing Fabric

The sheer range of varieties of fabrics makes it difficult to shop for them online, from a catalog or over the phone. Catalogs and websites cannot convey the tactile feel of fabrics. The way they drape over large objects (called the **hand**) and how they feel when you crush them in your hand will ultimately affect the properties of your prop. Most fabric shopping, other than for utilitarian cloth like muslin and duvetyn, is done by visiting a local fabric store and collecting a **swatch**, or a small representative piece, cut from the full roll of fabric. The type and price

Figure 11-4: Several types and thicknesses of felt.

is usually written on the swatch, or on a card attached to the swatch, and these swatches are shown to the designer, who chooses one. You or your shopper can then return to the store and purchase. Small swatches will not convey larger patterns, so it is also helpful to take a photograph to show the scale and the "repeat." Some designers will go with you to the fabric store if they can spare the time, particularly when a lot of fabric purchasing decisions need to be made at the same time.

Fabric and craft stores will often carry a variety of fabrics useful for lightweight items like curtains and flags to heavier fabrics for upholstery. Upholstery suppliers may also carry a range of thicker fabrics intended for upholstery. Theatrical suppliers carry a wide range of fabrics for film, theatre, and television, particularly large, seamless rolls of canvas, muslin, and scrim. You can also find companies that will digitally print a custom design to a number of fabrics such as cotton, silk, and linen.

Fabric Math

Fabric is sold by the yard. Many types of fabric come in widths such as 40", 54", 60", or 72" wide, though some can be as wide as 110". Obviously, one yard of 110" wide fabric will give you far more fabric to work with than one yard of 40" fabric. This can get tricky if you figure out how many yards of fabric you need assuming a 54" wide roll, and when you get to the store and find the fabric you love, it is on a 72" roll.

You have to factor in the grain, any kind of direction a fabric has, seam allowances, and hems. Unlike cutting out a bunch of shapes from a piece of plywood, you cannot just nest all your pattern pieces as close together as possible to use the minimum amount of fabric.

If the fabric has a repeating pattern that you need positioned specifically for each piece you cut, you will have to factor in more fabric needed. If you can measure the **pattern repeat** (how long and wide the pattern is before it repeats), add that length and width to the size of every piece you need to cut out.

In most fabrics, the design runs top to bottom along the length, with the selvage edges as the sides. However, you may want a design that is wider than your fabric, such as when you need to upholster the back of a long couch. In **railroaded** fabric, the design is laid out so the selvage edges are the top and bottom, and the width can be as long as you want.

Marking and Cutting Fabric

Cutting fabric has its own special considerations. When laying out your patterns or making your measurements, you need to consider which way the grain runs; remember that most fabrics have a grain and stretch and drape differently depending on which direction the grain is running. If the fabric has a pattern or design, this will also affect how you cut it, particularly if you want the pattern to "match up" when it is joined by a seam. A nap or pile will also make a fabric directional. If you rub your hand with the nap, the fabric will look lighter than if you rub your hand against the nap. If you sew pieces together with the nap running in different directions, it will look like you made it from different fabrics.

When tracing a pattern or marking out where you want to cut, you want to ensure the fabric is not stretching in any direction; the best way to do that is have a table or surface large enough to lay the full piece of fabric out flat. An ideal cutting table is at least 45" wide (the common width of most fabrics) and six to eight feet long. You should be able to stick pins into the table surface to hold patterns and fabric in place. Some shops use thick cork sheets, while others wrap muslin or paper around a sheet of fiber wall board such as Homosote™; the advantage of this is that either the surface or the substrate can be replaced when it gets too dirty or worn down to use. A cutting table can be improvised by placing a covered sheet of Homosote onto a regular table or even sawhorses.

Make your marks on the wrong side of the fabric. Marking fabric is typically done with chalk (tailor's chalk is specially made for this purpose, though regular school chalk can work on some fabrics). Tailor's pencils and regular pencils can also be used. Fabric-marking pens and other types of ink-writing utensils can be used as well, though some may bleed through and show up on the front of your fabric.

Use scissors specially made for cutting fabric. It is important they are used only for cutting fabric; even cutting something as innocuous as paper will dull your scissors, which leads to ragged edges and more effort exerted cutting fabric. Never, ever, borrow someone's fabric scissors to cut anything but fabric. Most shops that work in multiple materials will specifically mark which scissors are reserved solely for fabric. Cuts with the scissors should be done with the fabric laying flat on the table rather than holding it in the air while cutting. Tailor's scissors are actually designed with one edge flat so it can run smoothly along the table's surface. A **rotary cutter** is like a pizza cutter made for fabric. These cuts are best done on a self-healing cutting mat. It is easy to slice your finger if you roll these without taking care where they are going. Nonetheless, they are great for making long straight cuts along a straight edge or for detailed curved cuts. Using a razor or knife will pull the fabric as you cut, making a less accurate edge.

Laying Out Stitches

When you are learning how to stitch and sew, it is helpful to practice on scrap pieces of fabric first. Be sure to practice on similar fabrics, because different weaves and different weights can cause different fabrics to behave differently.

Threads, such as woolen yarns or cotton threads, may have directions or piles to them; if you run the thread through your fingers in one direction, it will feel smooth, while running it through in the opposite direction can feel rough. Make sure the thread feels smooth when you run your fingers in the direction away from the needle to prevent snagging and other sewing mishaps.

When laying out and drawing your pattern or measuring the size of fabric you need, you leave a **seam allowance** for the edges that will be sewn. This is the distance between the stitching line (or lines) and the edge of the fabric you are sewing. Most prop projects use a seam allowance between ¼" and ⅝".

For most seams, you will be laying the right sides of the fabric together. If you are sewing any sort of three-dimensional piece, you will essentially be constructing it inside-out. Line up the stitching line on both pieces of fabric and pin them together. Place the pins at a right angle to the stitching line so they are easy to remove as you stitch and so they do not let the two pieces slide out of place.

Types of Seams

A **plain seam** is the most basic seam used. Other types of seams can be used as well depending on the type of fabric you are using, whether you want some decorative effect or when both sides will be visible.

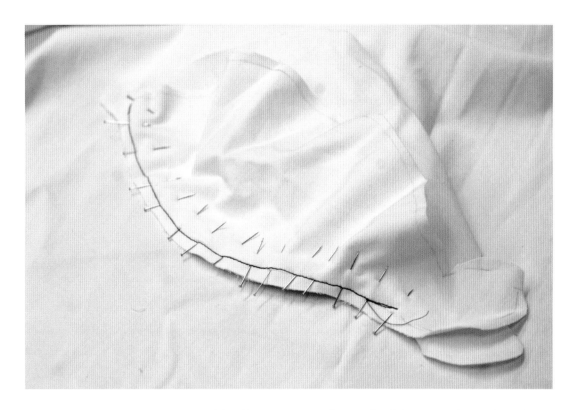

Figure 11-5: These two pieces of fabric have been pinned and stitched. The pins are perpendicular to the stitch to prevent the two pieces of fabric from shifting along the stitch line. The fabric on the outside of the stitch is the seam allowance.

Figure 11-6: After finishing a stitch, it is helpful to press it open with a hot iron. First, press the seam as sewn from both the front and the back. Then, lay the fabric out flat with the seam allowance facing up. Use the tip of the iron to coax the seam allowance apart, and press the seam open. You can then flip the fabric over, and press from the other side for an even flatter seam. Besides giving you a crisp and flat seam, pressing your seam open strengthens your stitch. When pressing curved seams, use a **tailor's ham** (also known as a dressmaker's or pressing ham); this is a tightly stuffed curved pillow (shaped like a ham).

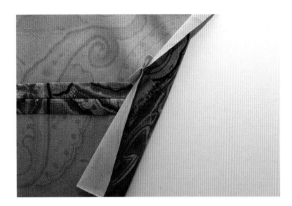

Figure 11-7: A plain seam.

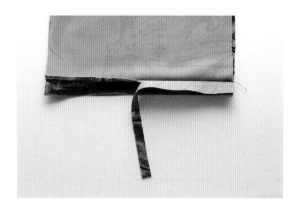

Figure 11-8: A **flat-felled seam** starts off like a plain seam with a seam allowance of 5/8". Cut *one* of the allowances to 1/4".

Figure 11-9: Lay the fabric out wrong side up. Fold the longer seam allowance over the shorter, than tuck it under the shorter. Press and pin in place.

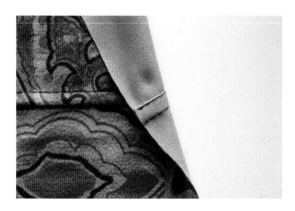

Figure 11-10: Run a second stitch as close to the fold as possible.

Figure 11-11: With a **French seam**, put the *wrong* sides of the fabric together and make a plain seam with a seam allowance of 5/8". Trim both allowances to 1/4". Lay the fabric flat with the right side up, and then fold it over so that now the wrong sides are together. Run a second stitch just to the left of the entrapped seam allowances so that they are completely encapsulated.

Figure 11-12: The end result will have a little "flap" on the wrong side of the fabric along the seam.

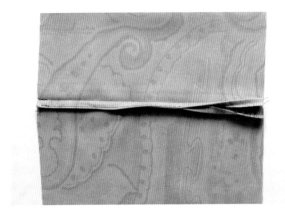

Figure 11-13: A **mock French seam** is used where you wish to match a French seam but cannot. For instance, French seams are difficult to sew around tight curves, so you may wish to switch to a mock French seam. Lay the right sides together, and stitch a plain seam with a 5/8" seam allowance. Tuck the raw edges in toward the center of the seam allowance "flap," and sew this shut as close to the edge as your machine will allow you.

Seam Allowances

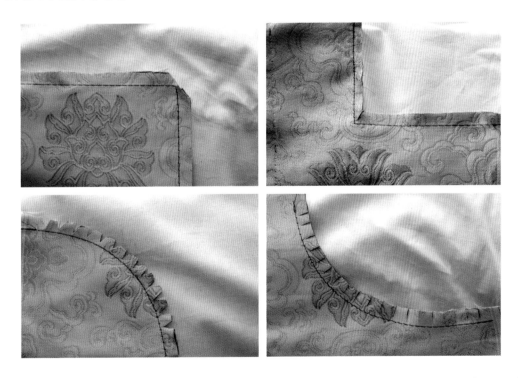

Figures 11-14 to 11-17: Seam allowances need to be cut or notched when a seam is curved or creates a corner. On an outside corner, the seam allowance is cut off at an angle as shown on the left. On an inside corner, a slit is cut. On a concave seam, V-shaped notches need to be cut to allow the seam allowance to bend and to keep it from getting too bulky. On a convex seam, slits are cut, though notches can also be used to reduce the bulk (note that these pictures show the opposite because the fabric is the wrong side out; when you sew a convex line, it becomes a concave seam after turning the fabric out to the right side). A seam allowance can also be trimmed to keep the seam from getting to bulky. Always be careful not to cut the seam itself.

Machine Stitching

A sewing machine is vital for constructing soft goods and fabric props. Besides saving time with plain stitches and seams, it can automate many tasks that will otherwise take a lot of setup to do by hand. While sewing machines can vary greatly, most share some basic parts and adjustments.

The majority of sewing machines one finds in a props shop, costume shop, or home studio create a **locking stitch**. A locking stitch requires two threads; one comes from the spool above, another is wound in a **bobbin** usually located in a compartment below the sewing machine needle.

The path a thread takes from the spool to the needle is fairly convoluted; it passes through a number of guides, take-ups, and tension regulators so that by the time it reaches the needle, it can be fed at a consistent rate with a constant tension. Most sewing machines will have an instruction manual that details how to feed the thread from the spool to the needle; it is important to follow this exactly or your stitches will not be made correctly. Once you gain enough experience, you can figure out how to feed the thread through most common machines on your own.

The speed at which the fabric travels through the machine is usually controlled with a foot pedal; as with an automobile, the farther down you push the pedal, the faster the machine pulls your fabric through.

A **domestic sewing machine** is the kind you find in most homes. Though most can only handle lighter-weight fabrics, they are easily configured to perform a number of stitch types and processes. An **industrial sewing machine** is engineered to quickly and easily perform one kind of task, such as straight-stitch only. They are also far more robust than domestic sewing machines, and can plow through several layers of heavy upholstery fabric with no problem. A **walking-foot machine** is a type of industrial straight-stitch machine that feeds both the top and the bottom of the fabric at consistent rates. These can be very useful for shops that regularly do furniture upholstery, and they can be outfitted with feet for zippers or welting in addition to straight stitching. A **commercial** or **semi-industrial sewing machine** is kind of in the middle, offering some of the versatility of the domestic machine with the robustness and speed of the industrial.

Basic Hand Stitches

While sewing with a machine is certainly the fastest way to join fabric, it is still helpful to know hand stitches. Not every seam can be closed on a machine; making three-dimensional objects in fabric, for instance, will require at least the last seam, or last few inches of a seam, to be closed by hand. Hand stitching is also necessary for fabric that is already attached to materials which cannot be maneuvered through a machine, or when you have to make a stitch on location or on stage far from any sewing machine.

When hand stitching, you must maintain the proper tension on the thread manually. You want the thread to be as tight as possible within the stitches, but you don't want to pull it so hard that the fabric bunches and puckers. The seam should remain flat and unstretched.

Finishing the Edges

An unfinished or raw edge of fabric is likely to unravel and become more ragged as time goes on. To prevent that from happening, prop makers will either hem or serge the edge. A **hem** is one or more folds sewn in place so the unfinished edge is no longer seen; the stitch also acts as a way to stop further unraveling.

A **serge** is done by a machine called a serger. It simultaneously stitches a number of threads in parallel lines (called an "overlock stitch") to the edge while cutting the excess fabric off to create a nice clean edge. The multiple stitches keep the edge from unraveling, but unlike a hem, none of the fabric is folded. It creates a different look from a hem and can be used as a decorative edge, especially when a contrasting thread is used.

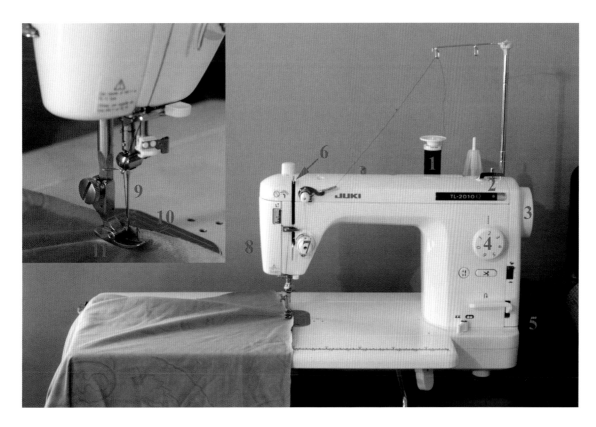

Figure 11-18: 1. The **spool pin** holds your spool of thread. 2. The bobbin winder holds a bobbin that needs to be filled with thread. You run the thread from the spool pin to the bobbin winder (your machine's instructions will indicate the path the thread must take), and when you press the foot pedal, it will spin the bobbin and fill it with thread. Most machines can detect when you are using the bobbin winder and will not run the needle up and down, and will also automatically stop when the bobbin is full. 3. The **balance wheel** or **hand wheel** allows you to manually run the machine either forward or in reverse. 4. The **stitch length regulator** sets how long each of your stitches is. For machines that allow zigzag stitches, blind hems, or other types of stitches that incorporate side-to-side movement, you will have a second dial called the **stitch width regulator**. 5. The **power switch** is typically located on the side. As with other machines, turn the sewing machine off when making adjustments to the needle or changing parts out. 6. The **thread take-up** pulls the thread up and down rapidly; be careful with this part as the machine runs. 7. The **upper tension regulator** controls the tension on the thread as you sew. Different thicknesses of fabrics, different types of seams and stitches, and different weights of thread all call for a different amount of tension on the thread. Too much tension, and the fabric will bunch up or the thread will break; too little tension, and a bird's nest of tangled thread will form on the bottom of your fabric. It is good practice to run a piece of scrap fabric through when you are drastically changing the fabric, thread, or type of stitch you will be doing next. This scrap fabric should be the same as the real fabric, and the other variables should be as close to the real stitch as possible so that you can home in on the correct tension to use. 8. Around the back is the **presser foot lifter**, which raises the presser foot so you can lay your fabric down. Always stitch with the presser foot lowered. 9. The **needle** pushes the thread through the fabric. Different machines take different needles, and each machine has a number of different needles it can use for different situations. 10. The **throat plate** or **needle plate** is a metal plate underneath the presser foot. It usually has markings to let you accurately create seam allowances of various widths 11. The **presser foot** holds the fabric down. Most machines allow you to hook a variety of different kind of feet on for different types of stitches and fabrics. Below the presser foot (hidden here by the fabric) are the **feed dogs**. These toothed strips grab the fabric and pull it forward as you sew.

Figure 11-19: Though this large upholstery panel was mostly machine-stitched, Natalie Taylor Hart needs to finish it with a few hand stitches in places. Hand-stitching techniques are a vital skill if you want to do any work with fabric and other soft goods.

Figure 11-25: A **running stitch** is a simple stitch for joining two pieces of fabric, and for gathering and mending. The needle goes in and out, making even, alternating stitches on each side of the fabric. A **basting stitch** is like a running stitch but with larger stitches. It is used for temporary stitches because it is easy to pull out.

Figures 11-20 to 11-24: A **sewing knot** is a quick knot at the end of a piece of thread to keep it from being pulled through the stitch as you hand-sew a seam. Wrap the thread once around your middle finger. "Roll" the bottom of this loop (where the thread crosses itself) by rubbing your thumb forward against your middle finger. Grasp the thread just in front of the spaghetti mess of raveled thread with your main finger and thumb, and carefully pull them back over the knot and toward the end of the thread. This should pull the mess into a more compact knot; be careful not to pull too hard as you may pull the knot apart.

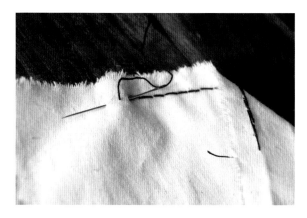

Figure 11-26: On a **back stitch**, the needle goes into the back and travels forward two stitch lengths. It comes out and travels back one stitch length, and then goes back in and travels forward two more stitch lengths.

Figure 11-27: A **whip stitch** is useful for creating a hem. The thread moves forward going in and out equally in a zigzag pattern. This leaves a row of diagonal stitches along both the front and the back.

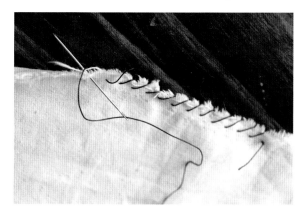

Figure 11-28: An **overcast** stitch is a whip stitch done over the raw edges of two pieces of fabric to keep them from unraveling.

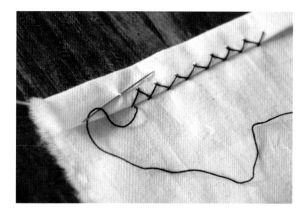

Figure 11-29: A **cross** or **catch stitch** is used on hems or facings. The needle moves backward, catching two threads on the hem, and then crosses over itself and moves backward to catch two threads on the fabric. This creates an almost invisible seam from the front and gives the seam some movement.

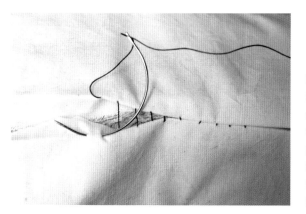

Figure 11-30: A **slip stitch** is useful for closing up two fabric panels from the front. The needle goes in the crease of a fold, slides along the inside for one stitch length, and then exits back out the crease of that fold. Insert the needle in the crease of the other panel directly opposite where the needle exited from the previous panel. A curved needle is helpful on this stitch. As you pull the thread taut (but not too tight), the thread will become practically invisible. If you were to open this seam up, you would see that the thread is doing exactly the same thing as the thread in a running stitch.

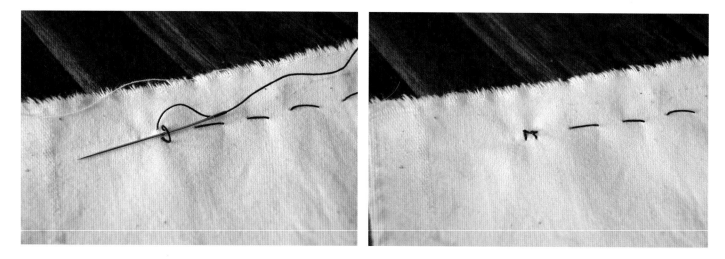

Figures 11-31 to 11-32: One method to finish off a seam and lock the thread is to make a very tiny stitch perpendicular to the seam. Before you pull this stitch taut, pass the needle underneath it. Do another one of these for more strength; start the next one directly on top of the previous one, or even slightly behind it. Pull everything taut, and snip the thread as closely to the fabric as possible (I've exaggerated the sizes of the stitches in the photographs above to show you what's going on; you can make the stitches as small as you are able).

Figures 11-33 to 11-34: A **rolled hem** involves rolling the edge of the fabric on the wrong side so that the raw edge is completely hidden. This is easiest to do on a sewing machine with a rolled hem foot; as you feed the fabric through, the foot automatically rolls the edge and stitches it in place. A rolled hem is useful for lightweight and delicate fabrics. We frequently sew rolled hems on the edges of napkins and similar small items.

Figures 11-35 to 11-37: With a **turned hem**, you make the seam allowance twice as wide as what you want your hem to be. Fold the seam allowance in half onto the wrong side of the fabric. It may be helpful to place a stitch where you wish to fold, as the stitches act like a guide. If needed, press this fold in place. Fold this over again. The raw edge will be tucked underneath; if you stitched a line for the first fold, these stitches will now be at the top of the fold. Press the folds, pin it in place, and stitch it together. Many people use a **top stitch** here; you turn the fabric so the right side is up, and stitch the hem. Since this stitch is visible, using a top stitch gives a more visibly appealing look. In the photographs, two parallel top stitches were used as a decorative accent. Turned hems are the most common and simplest hems to stitch.

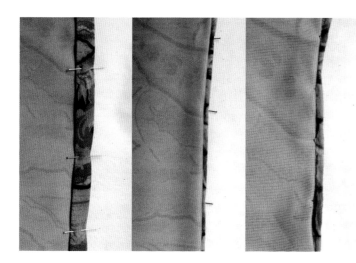

Figure 11-38: With a **blind hem**, begin by folding the unfinished edge under, the fold it under again to the width of your seam allowance. Press this flat and pin in place as shown in the fabric on the left. Now fold the seam allowance under, but leave 1/8" to 1/4" poking out like in the fabric in the middle.

Set your sewing machine to stitch a blind hem. On the fabric on the right, you can see that the machine will run about five or six stitches along the bit of the fold that is peeking out on the right, and then it will zigzag over and catch the fold on the left for one stitch.

Using a blind hem stitch foot on your sewing machine makes blind hems infinitely easier. You can stitch one without it, but you just have to go slowly and measure carefully to make sure the straight stitch remains along the outer fold while the zigzag stitch actually catches the inner fold.

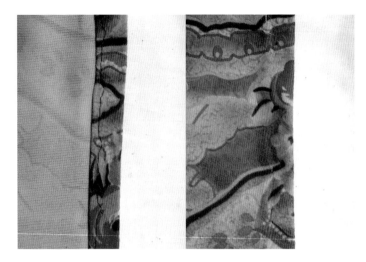

Figure 11-39: When you are finished stitching, unfold the seam allowance out from underneath the fabric and press it clean. On the left, you can see what the stitch looks like from the back. On the right, you can see that the stitch is virtually invisible from the front; it is even less noticeable if you use a thread color that matches your fabric.

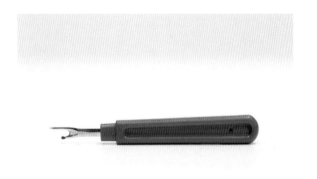

Figure 11-41: If you make a mistake or need to remove a stitch and the thread cannot be pulled back out, a seam ripper can cut apart the stitch without ripping the fabric.

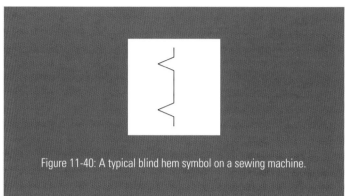

Figure 11-40: A typical blind hem symbol on a sewing machine.

Upholstery

Upholstery is the act of wrapping fabric around various materials to provide padding and cushioning for furniture. It can include padding that is integral to the furniture itself or removable cushions and pillows.

The art of upholstery can fill several books and much of it is beyond the scope of this book. Much of the upholstery done in props is in reupholstering existing furniture pieces with new padding and fabric. Since this book is dedicated to the construction of new props from scratch, information about reupholstering will be left out. Instead I will introduce some of the basic terms and techniques and demonstrate more of the "prop" methods (as opposed to the "real" methods) so that a beginner can upholster a simple piece in a pinch.

Many times when building an upholstered piece from scratch, the upholstered parts will be built as stand-alone pieces that can be attached or removed from the furniture itself. A drop-in, or slip, seat for a chair is one of the most common examples. This allows you the convenience of finishing the furniture in the wood shop while the upholstery is happening in the soft goods shop. This also gives you the option of making the piece easier to modify in the future for new productions; the upholstered piece can be removed and reupholstered

Figures 11-42 and 11-43: This chair was transformed by removing the seat, upholstering it, and reattaching it. *Timon of Athens*, the Public Theater, 2011. Scenic design by Neil Patel.

and the furniture part can be repainted or restained without getting paint on the fabric parts.

The shape and padding of a cushion is typically built up in layers. For props, a typical "sandwich" of upholstery material may include a piece of foam rubber wrapped in batting, covered in muslin, and then covered in the upholstery fabric.

The foam rubber (most upholstery foam rubbers are polyurethane) may be lightly adhered to the surface of the furniture or to a thin piece of plywood for later attachment. If you need to screw on the seat from underneath, this wood should be thick enough so that the screw does not poke through the top. Trace the shape of this wood onto the foam and cut it out. Thinner sheets of foam can be cut with razor knives or snap-blade knives. Thicker pieces can be cut with electric knives (sometimes

called "turkey carvers"). Shops that do extensive upholstery work may wish to spring for the rather pricey foam rubber cutters, which resemble a jigsaw but with a much longer blade that has a fixed plate on the bottom.

Piecing together a few smaller pieces of foam is alright as long as they butt up to each other without a gap. If you need to glue foam together, use barge or contact cement; both of these glues require ventilation, respiratory protection, and proper gloves.

You can also cut the foam a little larger than the base so it wraps around the top edge, but you do not want it to wrap all the way around to the back.

Batting is a fluffy fibrous material that comes in rolls and can be cut into individual sheets; it is similar to the fiber fill material used to stuff plush toys and pillows, except that it is more cohesive, almost like a sheet of felt, but far less tightly packed. Most batting is made from polyester (Dacron™ is a popular brand name often used to refer to any brand of batting). Cotton batting can also be used, but it is more expensive. Batting should be cut with fabric scissors; tearing it will pull and deform it. Some upholsterers like to lightly adhere the batting to the foam rubber with spray adhesive. Wrap the batting around the edges; if you need the bottom edge to have a sharp corner, cut it so that it does not continue to wrap around to the back. If you want it to have a rounded corner, wrap the batting to the back and staple it in place.

The final layer is the upholstery fabric itself. The fabric used for upholstery is usually thicker and more durable than fabric for clothing, though in props you are free to choose whichever kind you want. Pay attention if your fabric has any kind of design, stripe, grain, or other directional characteristic. Besides making sure everything is aligned correctly, you want to plan out which part of the design will be centered in the seat

(also remember that floral designs "grow" upward). Mark the center of each side of your plywood, and then mark the center of each side of your fabric (you can cut a notch if a pencil or chalk mark does not show up). Start by stapling in the center of the front, and then pull taut and staple the center of the back (or vice versa). Pull it snugly but not overly tight; make sure the shape it creates in the cushion is not uneven or lopsided. Add a staple in the center of the right, followed by one in the center of the left. Now you can work from the center to the corner of each side, making sure the fabric remains taut as you go. Stop a few inches from the corners so that you can fold and cut the corners. Fold the fabric diagonally at the corner and stretch it taut. Staple it in place. Cut the excess fabric diagonally across the corner. Miter the fabric at the corner by folding in each side up to the corner. Staple in place. Then staple the rest.

A pneumatic upholstery staple gun offers the most power to reliably drive staples into the hardest of woods. They can also fire finer gauge staples than other guns, which is handy if

Figures 11-44 and 11-45: For many folds, the corner will have two pleats; fold these so they are as close together as possible. All other pleats and folds along the edge should be on the bottom of the piece you are upholstering. The kinds of corners you make will depend on the fabric you are using and the thickness of the padding you have, as well as the shape of the piece; in some cases, you can pull the pleats completely out, while in others, you will need a more defined fold.

you are building up a lot of layers that would get bulky with thicker staples. Electric upholstery staple guns work well too, and have the advantage of not needing access to an air compressor. Hand-powered staple guns work in many situations, but for hardwoods, thick fabrics, or multiple layers, you may find they do not drive the staple all the way in and require going back to hammer them down. Many upholstery staple guns have a nose (where the staples come out) that projects out about an inch. Some long nose staple guns can extend up to two inches or more. This is useful for getting into tight or recessed areas, which happens a lot in upholstery.

It may be helpful to either pin the fabric in place first or to add staples halfway (these are known as "sub-staples" or "staple-baste") so they are easily removed. Hold the staple gun above the surface so the staples are only driven partway in. This will allow you to make minor adjustments with everything tacked in place; you can remove the pins or sub-staples as you staple everything in permanently. An **upholstery tack puller**,

Figure 11-46: It is not just furniture that may need to be upholstered. This car from Childsplay Theatre in Arizona uses many of the same materials and techniques used with furniture upholstery.

while obviously useful for removing tacks, is also great for removing staples.

You may add cambric, a black fabric for covering the bottom of a furniture piece to act as a dust cover and to give a finished look. Fold the raw edges of cambric underneath and staple in place.

In some cases, you may wish to add a muslin layer over the batting, which is then covered by the upholstery fabric. This extra muslin layer gives a few advantages. It holds all the batting and padding in place, so if you ever wish to reupholster your furniture, you do not have to worry about those layers shifting or moving around after you remove the upholstery fabric. It also pulls everything tight and creates the shape of the cushion, so that when you go to add the actual upholstery fabric, you can concentrate on making sure all the lines are straight, all the corners are neat, and nothing is wrinkled without also having to worry about stretching it all tight. It also gives you practice with a cheap fabric before you attempt the real thing, and it lets you see what the shape of the final cushion will be, giving you a chance to make minor adjustments without having to remove the good upholstery fabric. Obviously, the disadvantages are that it adds material costs and labor time.

Edges

Not every piece of upholstery can be stapled out of view; some pieces of fabric end on the face of a surface, so you need another way to secure it in place that won't show the raw edges of fabric or a row of staples.

Trim is a narrow strip of decorative material that covers the edge of the fabric, hiding the staples and creating a clean line along the transition between the fabric and wood. **Gimp** is a type of fabric trim commonly used in upholstery. For a cleaner edge with the fabric, upholsterers will fold under the raw edge before stapling or tacking it down or covering it with gimp. **Upholstery tacks** are decorative nails with wide heads placed to hold down the edge of the fabric; when they are also

Figures 11-47 and 11-48: This armchair shows how gimp that matches the color of the fabric hides the stapled edges and appears to be an integral part of the fabric. *Cendrillon*, Santa Fe Opera, 2006. Photograph by Anna Warren

used as a decorative embellishment, they are sometimes called **nailhead trim**. They can be hammered in individually or you can buy strips of decorative tacks that are applied many at a time.

Tacks can be used over the gimp as well. When this is done, you can actually staple the fabric to the furniture first; the staples will be covered by the gimp. If tacks are not used, the gimp is traditionally stitched onto the fabric, but many a props person has been known to simply glue it on with hot glue or fabric adhesive.

Piping is a decorative round edge sewn into the seams to conceal where two pieces of fabric come together. Piping is typically made by wrapping piping cord (just a plain cotton cord sold at fabric and upholstery shops) with a continuous bias strip made from your upholstery fabric.

A piping foot on your sewing machine is helpful for sewing the bias strip around the piping cord because you want the stitch as close to the cord as possible.

You may also make "double-piping," which is two pieces of piping running next to each other.

Tufting is where the upholsterer pulls a thread through all the layers of upholstery: the fabric, batting, stuffing, and through the back. This secures everything together and keeps the interior material from shifting and sagging. In button tufting,

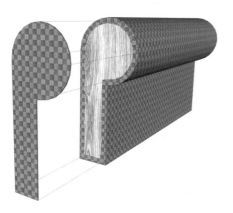

Figure 11-49: With some upholstery projects, you can wrap a very thin panel of lauan or even heavy cardstock in fabric, and then attach this over the top of an area where the edges of many other pieces have been stapled so as to cover them all up.

Figure 11-51: This headboard is paneled with piping and square pattern button tufting.

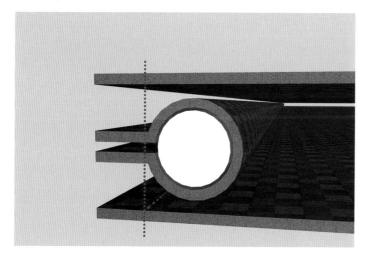

Figure 11-50: The piping is placed inside the two pieces of fabric you will stitch together, with the piping's stitch lined up where you want the stitch on the two pieces of fabric. The red line in this picture shows where you will place your stitch to join your two pieces of fabric with your piping.

a button, usually covered in fabric, is attached to the end of the thread to secure it. Tufting is frequently done in patterns to add a decorative touch. Common tuft patterns include diamond, square, cross-diagonal, hexagonal, and bead-string.

A **pleat** is a fold in fabric held in place with stitches. Pleating is a series of pleats. A pinch pleat is a series of narrow short pleats, often found at the tops of some curtains, made by "pinching" the fabric together. A French pleat is formed like a pinch pleat but with softer, less defined folds. **Gathering** is fabric that is folded or bunched together. Curtains and drapes can be gathered by using fabric wider than the rod it is on. Fabric can also be gathered by sewing parallel stitches along one edge.

Leather

Leather is different from fabric in that it is the actual skin of an animal rather than a textile made up of individual fibers. Popular animals used in leather include cattle and pigs. Other animals such as crocodiles, snakes, and kangaroo, are used to make leather, but these rarely prove economical to use in props and are more likely to have their appearance faked.

Leather must be tanned prior to using, which stabilizes the skin to keep it from rotting away. The most popular process for the leather destined for crafts is **vegetable tanning**. Vegetable-tanned leather is the only kind that can be carved, stamped, embossed, hammered and, in some cases, molded into a shell (see Chapter 15 for more specifics on that). Other tanning methods give more of a finished look to the piece, but these cannot be altered.

The thickness of leather is measured in ounces; one ounce is roughly equal to 1/64". **Tooling leather**, the most popular type of vegetable-tanned leather for crafts, can range anywhere from 3 to 10 oz, though most artisans prefer a skin between 8 and 9 oz.

Cutting Leather

Leather can be cut with a sharp knife and straight edge, rotary cutters, or a sturdy pair of scissors; the size and style of cutter you use depends on the thickness of the leather you are working with.

Skiving leather means making it thinner by shaving or paring down the back of the leather. A scalpel, razor, or other sharp knife will also suffice in a pinch for occasional skiving needs.

Stitching Leather

With tooling leather, it is very difficult to hide seams, stitches, and raw edges. Many of the techniques developed for leather do not attempt to hide any of these, and in fact, most leather work is designed to take advantage of this and show it off; often, it is the stitching in a leather object that makes it attractive and interesting.

Figures 11-52 and 11-53: This leather camera case was constructed from vegetable-tanned tooling leather that has been saddle stitched together with waxed sinew.

Unlike sewing fabric, the holes need to be punched ahead of time. A diamond-shaped awl works best, though in a pinch, any kind of awl or even a small drill bit will work. You do not want the thread to be loose in the holes; it just needs to be big enough to get the needle through. If the leather is thick enough (over 8 oz or so), you may wish to gouge a stitching channel with a stitching groover so that the threads are flush with the surface of the leather. A stitch marker can be used to mark evenly spaced depressions for your holes; this is basically a wheel with evenly spaced spikes protruding, so if a stitch marker is not available, you can improvise with other means of marking equidistant holes.

Cut the holes in the face side. Then glue the two pieces of leather together. Barge and other contact cements developed for leather and vinyl work best. Now you can finish punching the holes through the back side. The edge can be sanded or shaved down carefully to make it smooth and even.

Leather is sewn with a thick sinew or a multi-ply linen thread (anywhere from 3 to 7 cord depending on the thickness of your leather and the strength you need). Cotton, polyester, and nylon are other popular choices for stitching leather; the important aspect to keep in mind is that the thread should be thick enough for leather. Both the needles and thread need to be waxed to help them pass through the holes and also to hold them in place. Some thread for leather is sold already waxed, or you can wax your own thread. Needles can be waxed regularly while stitching to help as well. Beeswax is a popular wax to use in this case. Leather needles are generally larger and stronger than sewing needles for fabric.

The saddle stitch is one of the strongest stitches for leather. It requires two needles. Cut a length of your thread and attach each end to a needle. For waxed sinew and some thread, you simply have to pull a little bit through the eye of the needle and twist it around itself; it should hold without a knot. Some artisans start a saddle stitch with up to 3 backstitches, and others don't use any. Insert one needle through the first hole (or the third if you are backstitching first). Pull the thread exactly halfway through. Now push each needle through the next hole

so that they cross each other. Continue this way down the seam; you are basically doing a running stitch with each needle on opposite sides. When you get to the final hole, backstitch through at least two holes, and then cut the sinew or thread as close to where it exits from the hole as you can. There is no need to knot; the backstitch should keep everything from unraveling.

The thread should be drawn snug when sewing, but you shouldn't be straining to pull it tight. You are more likely to tear the thread if you do this.

You want to make sure you have enough thread or sinew for the seam you are making without running out in the middle of the stitch. Since you are running two threads down the seam, you need at least twice as much string as the length of the seam. You are also going in and out of the holes, so you need to add extra; this will depend on the thickness of your two pieces of leather and how far apart your stitch holes are. Your thread may need to be as much as 7 times as long as your seam. It is okay if it is too long; you are trimming it at the end, and thread is cheaper than having to redo a seam. As you gain experience in leather, you will get better at estimating how much thread you need for the thicknesses of leather you use.

Working with Other Types of Leather

Besides vegetable-tanned leather, prop makers also use **garment leather** and **upholstery leather**. Garment leather can be sewn and constructed much like fabric with some minor adjustments. The seams cannot be pinned together, so you will have to use pattern weights (small flexible weights you can place around your seam lines) or clamp the leather together (paper clips and small clamps work well). Less bulky seams can be sewn with domestic sewing machines, though heavier seams may need an industrial machine. Use special leather sewing machine needles, and switch them out as they dull down.

A walking foot is helpful too. For thread, avoid cotton because it will rot next to the leather; use nylon or polyester thread instead, and stick with upholstery weight threads.

Pressing the seams open on garment leather can be difficult, if not impossible. You often need to stitch the seams open.

Artificial leather is a cheaper and easier-to-use alternative for some props. **Pleather** (plastic plus leather) is a general term for some artificial leather, while Naugahyde™ is a popular brand of pleather. **Bonded leather** is another artificial leather that contains some real leather particles.

Real **fur** is basically leather with the hair still attached. Prop makers might use it for making a fake animal, as well as for fur rugs, throws, and other decorative accents. Fake fur (or **faux fur**) is often acrylic fibers attached to an underlying fabric. Real fur is worked in the same way as leather; fake fur is worked in the same way as fabric. In both cases, it is better to cut them with a sharp razor or knife from the back. If you cut them from the front with a scissors, you will be cutting

Figure 11-55: Acrylic and other fake fur can be shaved in parts to make it appear more realistic.

the fur as well, creating a noticeable edge. Leave the fur uncut, and you can brush and comb it over the seams to conceal them.

Fibers

Fabrics are made with an endless number of different fibers, and the fibers used will affect how the fabric looks, feels, how it drapes and moves when manipulated, and how you can alter it. How the fibers are put together affects the properties of the fabric as well. When choosing fabric for a prop, it is helpful to know where your textile is coming from, what its characteristics are, what it is like to work with, etc. If you are making period props, you may find that modern synthetics do not have the same look and feel as natural fabrics. Of course, time and budget constraints may prevent you from using exactly the fabric you want (synthetics are usually cheaper, and fabrics vary greatly in pricing: anywhere from $2 to $200 per yard and more). As with your prop as a whole, you must consider the

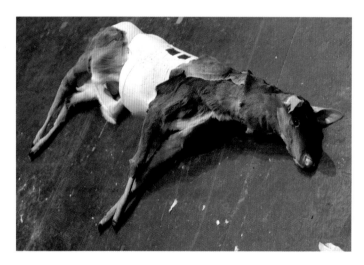

Figure 11-54: Real fur has coloring differences, direction, and variations in length that are time-consuming to duplicate with fake fur. *As You Like It*, the Public Theatre, 2012. Scenic design by John Lee Beatty.

needs and means of your fabric parts: not just how it looks, but how it flows (or doesn't) in the wind or drapes over an object, how stiff it is, whether you can glue or paint it, whether it needs to block light or let it through, its strength when sewn or pulled, and what you have to do to wash it.

A piece of fabric may be made with a single type of fiber, or it may be made of a combination of different fibers to utilize the strengths and properties of each type while minimizing the disadvantages.

Most raw fibers are spun into long strands of **yarn**. Yarn is interlaced together to make various fabrics. A thin type of yarn is known as **thread**, commonly used to sew two or more pieces of fabric together.

Plant Fibers

One of the most-produced plant fibers in the world is **cotton**. It is used to make a number of fabrics, such as muslin, canvas, and denim. It is not very stretchy, and easily wrinkled. It is also easily cut by pins inserted through it, which causes holes.

Figure 11-56: This rustic pillow for a prison scene is sewn from burlap.

Flax, which is used to make **linen**, is two to three times stronger than cotton, and is also strong when wet, making it easy to steam and dye. It wrinkles much more easily than cotton, and can even crack when folded.

Other plant fibers commonly used by prop makers include jute, hemp, and rattan. **Jute** is used to make burlap; both burlap and **hemp** fabric are very rough and natural looking, making it a popular fabric for rustic bags and sacks. **Rattan** is commonly used to make wicker. **Sisal**, a leaf fiber, can be used to make burlap like jute. Jute, hemp, sisal, and Manila hemp (or just "Manila") are also used to make "natural" rope and twine.

Animal Fibers

The hair or fleece of many domesticated and wild animals are another long-used source for textile fibers. The most popular by far is **wool** from sheep. The hair fibers from other animals are also used in making textiles. Cashmere comes from the Kashmir goat. Angora comes from the Angora rabbit. Mohair comes from the Angora goat. Other popular hair fibers come from alpacas, camels, llamas, and vicunas.

Wool is strong, flexible, and elastic. It gets weaker when wet, but it is easily tailored and shaped with steam. Wool is further divided into **worsted** yarns, which are smooth, tight, and uniform, and **woolen** yarns, which are spun from shorter fibers, making them loose and fuzzy.

Silk is another popular and useful fiber derived from animals. The fiber is taken from the cocoon of silkworms (not from spiders as is commonly believed) and is the strongest natural fiber, while also being lighter than wool, cotton, and linen. It is resistant to wrinkling, stretchy to a point, but weak when wet. Its biggest advantage is the astonishingly vivid colors you can get by dyeing it. An affordable choice for many props shops is to buy white silk in bulk and dye whatever you need for each individual production. It is also easy to compact, making it useful for a magician who wants to hide a large piece of it or for a trick curtain that needs to be sucked down a small hole.

Most directors want their flags and banners made of silk because of how delicately it waves through the air.

Synthetic Fibers

Synthetic fibers have an incredibly diverse range of properties and come in a wide variety of forms. Some can mimic more expensive natural fibers. Many are used in combination with natural fibers to impart better characteristics, such as making cotton less likely to shrink when washed. Some synthetics have special forms the prop maker should be aware of.

Acetate is a thermoplastic, so it can have designs permanently imprinted and embossed directly onto it. **Polyester**, one of the most popular synthetic fibers in use, can also be found as a soft fiberfill used to stuff plush toys and pillows, as well as batting for cushions and upholstery.

Spandex is a stretchy fiber made from polyurethane. A popular brand name is Lycra™. **Olefin** fibers, which come from polyolefins such as polypropylene and polyethylene, are used to make brands such as Tyvek™ and Thinsulate™.

Metallic fibers are rarely used alone, but can be found woven with other fibers to make many types of fabric. For example, precious metals are used in lamé, cloth of gold, and in brocades.

A **microfiber** is made of extremely fine filaments, finer than even the finest silk. Microfiber yarns are made from most of the major generic fibers.

Types of Fabric

As mentioned at the beginning of the chapter, fabric is made from fibers that are either woven, knit, or nonwoven.

The pattern of how the weft crosses the warp in woven fabrics affects its properties, and can be broken into three main categories: plain, twill, and satin. In a **plain** weave, the strands simply crisscross each other alternately. Plain weave can also be known as tabby weave, linen weave, or taffeta weave. Examples of plain weave fabrics include chiffon, organza, and taffeta. One variation is **basketweave**, in which a bundle of two or more strands form the simple crisscross or checkerboard pattern.

A **twill** weave has a repetitive diagonal pattern; types of twill include chino, denim, gabardine, tweed, herringbone, and houndstooth. The diagonal pattern gives the front and back a different look. The pattern also makes twill softer, easier to drape, and more wrinkle-resistant than plain weave.

A **satin** and **sateen** weave has a sheen. It is one of the easiest weaves to drape.

Fabric with a **pile** has an extra set of strands woven in to create a set of raised loops. If these loops are cut to form strands that stick out, we call that a **nap**. Fabrics with a nap include velvet and velour.

Nearly all upholstery fabrics are woven; common choices include plain, basket, satin, and pile.

In addition to the three major ways of making textiles, there are some minor methods that are useful to the prop maker. **Braiding**, or **plaiting**, involves twisting three or more strands together in a variety of patterns. Braiding is rarely used to make a wide sheet of cloth; rather, it is used to make ropes, decorative trim on larger items, or wrapped around handles to create a better gripping surface.

Crocheting is similar in theory to knitting. The practical difference comes from the fact that crocheting uses a single specialized crochet hook. Knitting requires two or more straight knitting needles. Crocheting interlocks each loop to the loops next to it, while knitting works a whole row at once.

Macramé is related to knitting and braiding but involves joining the strands through knotting rather than twists or loops. Knitting, crocheting, braiding, and macramé do not need to be limited to making fabric; the prop maker can also glue them to rigid surfaces to create a repetitively patterned texture.

Lace is a textile that uses holes to create patterns. Laces are useful for many types of period curtains and tablecloths, as well as items such as doilies.

A **net** is a piece of fabric made by weaving or knotting strands into an open grid.

Figure 11-57: Lace can be attached to surfaces and stiffened or coated to make textural effects or fake grillwork.

Decorative Varieties of Fabric

While an endless variety of fabrics can be made through the choice or one or more types of fiber and the means of interlacing these fibers into sheets of cloth, further variety can be found though a number of decorative additions. You can buy fabric that already has many of these decorative additions, or you can apply them yourself in some cases.

Dyeing is the act of coloring a yarn. Dye can be used to make fabric in any number of colors. Switching between different colored fibers within the same piece of cloth can make all sorts of patterns. Dyeing your own yarn or fabric will be covered in Chapter 17.

A **print** is a piece of cloth with a design or pattern printed on it, often in a repeated manner. Doing your own printing will also be covered in Chapter 17. Prints are most often found on plain-weave fabrics, as other weave patterns and knits have an inherent texture that affects the appearance of a print.

Embroidery involves making decorative patterns or pictures by stitching tread or yarn into a piece of fabric. **Cross-stitch** is one type of embroidery. Embroidered fabrics are used in many period props, such as banners, tapestries, napkins, linens, and curtains, as well as accents on bags, purses, and other fabric goods. Custom embroidery can be time-consuming to do on large portions of a prop, so it can be helpful to find fabrics that mimic an embroidered look.

A **brocade** is a richly decorative fabric made with different colored threads (usually silk). It looks as though it is embroidered, but the designs are actually woven in. It sometimes has gold or silver threads woven in as well.

Damask is the appearance of a raised design on a fabric. It is accomplished by switching back and forth between two or more kinds of weaves when manufacturing the fabric; one type of weave appears to stick out (the foreground), while the other appears to recede (the background).

Both damask and brocades are commonly used in upholstery and draperies, such as curtains and tablecloths.

Figure 11-58: This box edge seat cushion is covered in a damask fabric.

Fabric for Theatre, Film, and Television

Backstage and off-camera technicians have adopted a number of fabrics for a variety of purposes. Here are the names and descriptions of some of the most common.

Canvas is a heavy-duty plain-weave fabric. The cheap stuff we use is made of cotton, while the more expensive artist canvases you see in art stores are made of linen. Canvas is sold by weight (ounces per square yard) or by a graded number system; the numbers run backward, so #12 canvas is lighter than #4 canvas. There are two main kinds: plain and **duck**. The threads in duck canvas are more tightly woven than in plain. Canvas is useful for making tents and bags, particularly for military-style props.

Muslin is a cheap, plain-weave cotton available in white, cream, or unbleached. The different weights find a wide variety of uses in the entertainment world. Thinner muslin is used to make patterns and mockups of upholstery and other fabric goods. Muslin is also the main fabric used for cloth-mâché.

Duvetyne, sometimes called **commando cloth**, is a twill fabric with a velvet-like nap on one side. It has been prized in theatre since the 1930s for its near-perfect light-blocking abilities and matte finish. It is often used as a skirt around the bottom of furniture pieces to hide casters or other stage mechanisms from the audience's view.

Burlap is a coarse-woven cloth made from jute or sisal. Burlap is the "go-to" fabric for rustic and primitive-style props.

A **gauze** is a thin and translucent fabric with a fairly loose and open weave, and is often found in the first aid cabinet. Plaster-impregnated gauze is useful for wrapping molds to make them rigid. In theatre and film, gauzes are often fashioned into a **scrim**. **Bobbinet** is a type of gauze with hexagonal holes rather than square. Most **Tulle** (pronounced "tool") is actually bobbinet. The structure of Tulle allows it to hold a fairly stiff shape while remaining lightweight. Layers of Tulle are often used under fabric to give it a shape, and it is also commonly employed to create party decorations and wedding veils. **Cheesecloth** is a very loose and open weave gauze whose primary use in the props shop is to filter and strain paints and other materials, rather than as an end product itself.

A **sheer** is a lightweight fabric that is translucent; it is typically used for curtains though prop makers may find other uses for it. Sheers are often made of silk, rayon, and nylon.

twelve

patterning and draping

Patterning is the construction, fabrication, or assembling of an object by cutting (and sometimes bending or folding) two-dimensional surfaces according to a pattern or template, and then attaching the edges of these surfaces together to make a three-dimensional object.

Patterning techniques for props come from several crafts and industries. Costume and fashion have methods for patterning with fabric and textiles to make clothes and accessories. Sheet metal workers have methods for drafting and cutting flat patterns into steel to fold and bend into all sorts of tubes, duct work, and other shapes. The packaging industry uses dielines to create templates for cutting and scoring sheets of card-stock and plastic that are folded into boxes and other packages. Paper crafts develop a number of ways to fold paper to create complex shapes. Even pure geometry has developed a way to fold and unfold three-dimensional shapes as a way to study their surfaces. We can use all these means and methods separately—using costume design techniques to make things from fabric and sheet metal techniques to make things in metal—but the real breakthroughs happen when you combine these various techniques and use them for all sorts of materials.

Fabric Patterning

Fabric is unique with pattern making because it is not rigid like other materials. When a fabric object is constructed, it will not hold a specific shape unless it is stiffened or completely stuffed, such as upholstered cushions. Most fabric items are designed to move in a certain way and to change depending on the underlying structure. Clothing, for instance, is designed to let your arms and legs move while remaining close so that it does not fall off or drag on the ground. The pattern for a burlap sack is designed so that when you throw a severed head inside, the inside can expand to accommodate the head, and the sack can be carried so that the head does not roll out of the opening.

Pattern-makers use two methods to create shapes from fabric: the seam and the dart. The **seam** is simply sewing two

Figure 12-1: Wrapping fabric around a solid object shares techniques between costume patterning and upholstery. The goal is the same: to take flat pieces of material, cut them, and sew them together so they make a "skin" (no overlapping material) over the three-dimensional shape.

pieces of fabric together to create a single piece (see Chapter 11 for a discussion of various seams). A **dart** is created when you remove part of a piece of fabric and sew it back together to create a new shape. Think of a circle of fabric. If you cut a pie-shaped piece from it to make a Pac-Man shape, and sew it back together, you create a cone. A dart is usually a triangular, or pie-shaped, piece of fabric. Even if you just cut a slit into a piece of fabric, you need to use part of each side as your seam allowance, so that the fabric will be pulled tighter. In fact, you do not even need to always cut the dart out; in many cases, you can create a dart by pulling the fabric closer together and stitching the fold shut.

A **gusset** is a small piece of fabric added into a seam to expand the fabric; it is typically shaped like a diamond or triangle.

Further refinements to a pattern include folds that are sewn in place, such as nips, gathers, and tucks.

When working with a limited or expensive fabric, the costumer will refine the pattern by constructing the garment out of muslin first. By pinning the muslin to the dress form rather than

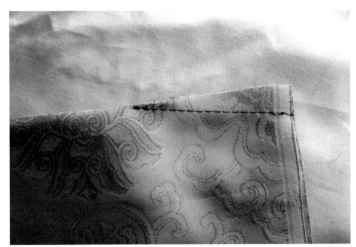

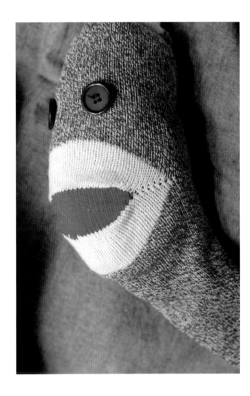

Figure 12-4 : A sock is typically made with a tube of fabric; the fabric at the heel (distinguished here by a different color) is a gusset. Adding it expands the fabric along the bottom, imparting a convex shape to the sock.

Figures 12-2 and 12-3: Sewing a dart pinches one side of a piece of fabric to create a slight curve.

sewing it, she or he can mark where changes need to be made so that the pattern fits properly.

Sewing machine companies rarely publish books that might be useful for a props person, such as patterns to make dead geese. If you have a hard sculpture of what you are attempting to replicate in fabric, you can work the same way as

you would on a dress form; cut pieces of muslin, pin them to the form, put a nip here, a tuck there, and soon you will have a pattern to use on your real fabric.

Lay these fabric pieces onto paper, and trace the shape. You can note on the paper the directions of the grain lines, notches for lining up two pieces, and seam and hem allowances. The patterns can now be traced onto the correct fabric.

To advance in patterning skills, you need to work with patterns until you begin to see how shapes are created through the manipulation of flat surfaces. Books and the Internet are filled with sample patterns for everything from messenger bags to stuffed animals. You can also take things apart by the seams to study how the pieces are cut and laid out (known as "reverse engineering"). It is helpful to develop your ability to see a pattern not as a specific thing, but as a collection of shapes that can be altered to create different shapes. For instance, a pattern for a gunny sack can easily be scaled down and flipped over to make a black hood for a Guantanamo prisoner.

You can also find many readymade patterns, which shortens your experimentation time. Sewing centers and fabric stores have loads of pattern books for draperies, backpacks, animals, and doll bodies (which can be scaled up to human size). Searching online will lead to many more patterns, both for sale and for free, such as helmets, gauntlets, armor, phonograph horns, and numerous other objects.

Soft sculpture is the use of nonrigid, aka "soft," materials to create a three-dimensional shape. You can think of it as taking upholstery to the extreme. It commonly uses textiles and soft foams and foam rubbers; perhaps the easiest way to explain it is stuffed or plush toy animals. You cut pieces of fabric into different shapes, sew them together, and when you fill it with stuffing, or foam, or what have you, the fabric takes on a three-dimensional shape. You can use soft sculpture to create objects as mundane as pillow cushions, stuffed animals, or even realistic-looking animal carcasses.

You can experiment with just sewing together pieces of fabric and seeing what shapes they make, but the most effective way to create a pattern is by starting off with a three-dimensional object. Most artisans like to create a pattern from muslin, because it is cheap, readily available, and easy to work with. Pin pieces of muslin around your object so that the muslin remains flat and tight to the surface. You can cut away the excess if it gets in the way. You have a lot of flexibility in where you place your seams. In a way, it is a lot like laying out your seam lines when creating a mold. You want to place your seams where they will be unnoticeable, like between two different colored or textured areas, or you want to place them where they become part of the design.

When making the pattern, be aware that the final fabric hand, the thickness and stiffness of the fabric, and the weave or knit will affect how it drapes and patterns. Making a pattern out of muslin for a fabric that is very different from muslin is problematic. Sometimes it is necessary to pattern directly with your real fabric.

Figure 12-5: The face for this scary scarecrow man was draped with a few pieces of burlap, and then further manipulated through a combination of selectively stiffening portions with PVA glue and using stitches to gather and tuck the fabric into position (making it a hybrid of a patterned prop and a shell prop). *Measure for Measure*, the Public Theatre, 2011. Scenic design by Scott Pask.

The fabric "hand," or "handle," is how a fabric feels to the touch.

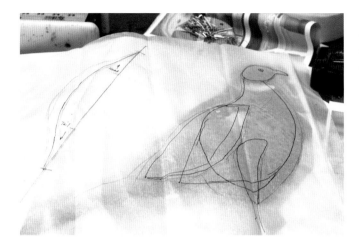

Figure 12-6 : The shape of this pheasant was made by breaking a photograph of the bird into individual components. Each component, such as the legs and the wings, were simple two-piece patterns; that is, the same shape was cut from two pieces of fabric, stuffed with batting and sand, and sewn together. *King Lear*, the Public Theater, 2011.

Figure 12-8 : You can develop flat pattern pieces from existing three-dimensional objects by wrapping them in tape. Masking tape works well for small objects, while gaffers or duct tape works well for larger ones. Wrap the tape snugly, and make sure it lies as flat as possible against the object. Wrap at least two overlapping layers, running the tape in perpendicular directions in each layer. Making sure the tape does not actually stick to the object is vital if you wish to remove it afterward. Plastic cling wrap works well for smaller objects, while garbage bags are useful for larger ones.

If you are creating a symmetrical piece, you can create the pattern for one side, and then flip it and trace it onto more fabric to make a mirror image for the other side.

Computers can automate much of the patterning process. Starting with a three-dimensional model, a program can flatten all the surfaces and break it apart into individual pieces that you can print out and trace or transfer to your flat materials. Programs that develop pattern pieces for fabric can factor in the stretch and sag of fabric, the compression/extension of fabric over complex shapes, and other distortion of fabric. Some programs deal with stretchy fabrics and can calculate what shapes various pieces create when under tension.

Figure 12-7: The components (see Figure 12-6) were then sewn to each other so they were free to move. This approximated the shape closely enough that when it was covered in feathers, it looked (and moved) like a dead pheasant. *King Lear*, the Public Theater, 2011.

Figure 12-9 : Masking tape allows you to draw potential seam lines on the object. When you are happy with where your seams are placed, you can cut them out and remove the tape shell from the object (taking care not to cut the object underneath).

Figure 12-10 : If the pieces still have a shape, you will need to cut further darts and seams until they lie completely flat. Once the pieces are flat and you are happy with your pattern, you can trace it onto fabric, leather, or whatever material you are making your prop out of. This process is similar to how costumers make a "duct tape mannequin" to drape costumes onto a dummy with a person's exact measurements.

Surface Developments

The sheet metal industry was one of the first crafts that needed to figure out how to take draftings and transform them into flat patterns that could be drawn onto sheet metal. These sheet metal pieces could then be cut out, folded, and assembled to become the three-dimensional piece pictured in the drafting. Basically, every surface on a shape is unfolded or unrolled until you have two-dimensional patterns. In the terminology of the sheet metal industry, you **develop** the surfaces of a three-dimensional shape to create a flat **template** to construct it from scratch. These patterns are known as **developments**, or sometimes **stretchouts**.

Complicated patterns can be simplified by breaking them down into more basic geometric solids. A geometric solid is formed when a two-dimensional shape such as a square or circle is given three-dimensional form. Geometric solids fall into several basic categories: cube, cone, cylinder, prism, tetrahedron, pyramid, polyhedron, and sphere.

The **net** of a geometric solid is the arrangement of its surfaces in a single plane (or a flat piece of paper), joined along their edges so that they can be folded into the faces of that solid. This allows you to construct models of polyhedra out of thin cardboard. Most polyhedra can have several possible nets depending on which edges you wish to be folded and which you wish to join.

Many shapes can be made through a combination of the basic geometric solids. More shapes can be made by **truncating**, or cutting off, a portion of the shape.

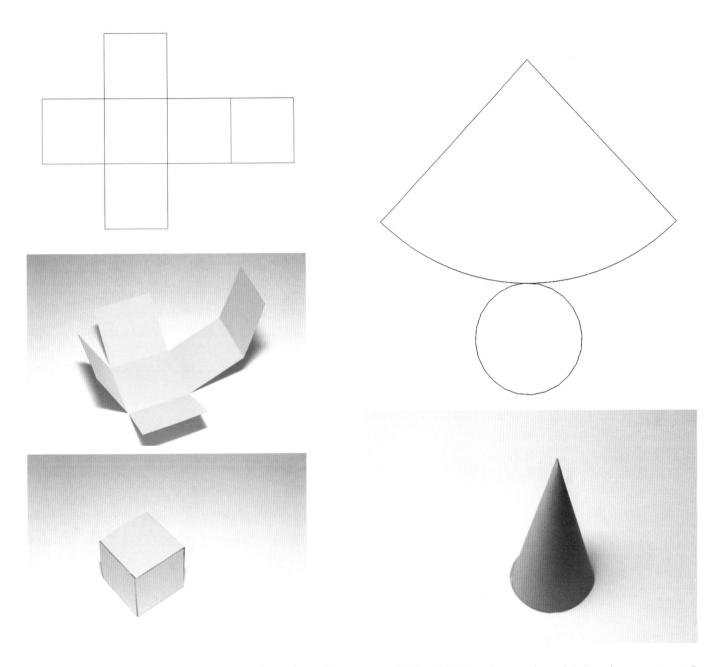

Figures 12-11 to 12-13: A cube has six faces, each a square. One of the possible "nets" of a cube is the arrangement shown on the top. When you cut it out of a piece of paper and fold the edges as seen in the middle, you can make a cube like the one on the bottom.

Figures 12-14 and 12-15: To make a cone from a flat piece of paper, you must roll one of the faces up rather than leave it lying flat.

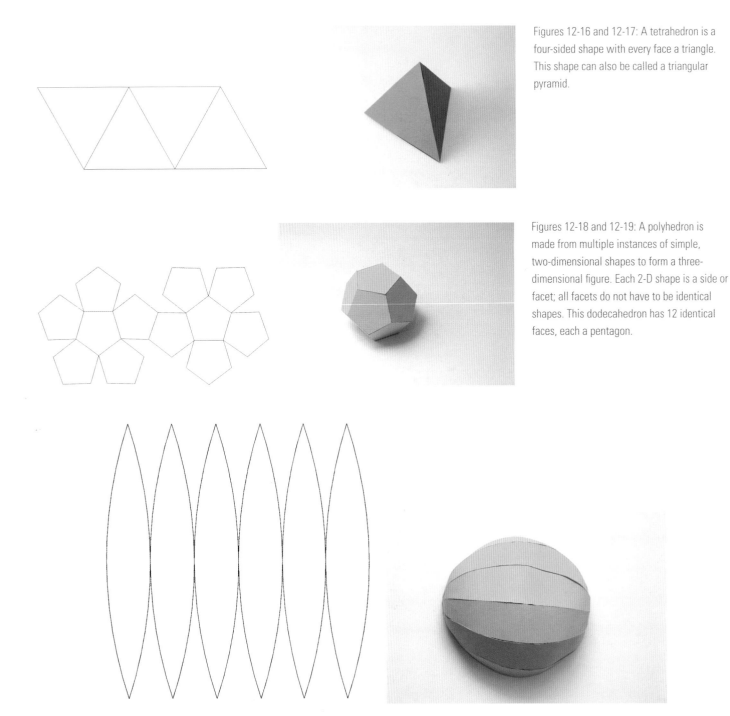

Figures 12-16 and 12-17: A tetrahedron is a four-sided shape with every face a triangle. This shape can also be called a triangular pyramid.

Figures 12-18 and 12-19: A polyhedron is made from multiple instances of simple, two-dimensional shapes to form a three-dimensional figure. Each 2-D shape is a side or facet; all facets do not have to be identical shapes. This dodecahedron has 12 identical faces, each a pentagon.

Figures 12-20 and 12-21: A sphere has complex curves and an infinite number of faces, so it can only be approximated from a flat sheet of material. One method involves using a number of "gores" (or "lunes"). This is how globes of the Earth are made. The more gores you use, the closer the final shape appears as a sphere. When working in sheet metal, a spherical shape can be hammered out of a single sheet without cutting gores; a full sphere can potentially require only two separate pieces.

Figure 12-22: Fabric with some stretch to it can better approximate a sphere or spherical shape. This ball only needed four gores.

If you are simply making solid pieces, it is usually easier to machine or carve these pieces from a single block of material. Knowing how to develop a three-dimensional object into a template is useful if your piece needs to be hollow or open to show the inside, or if it is made out of a transparent material that would reveal any structure on the inside. Open boxes, buckets, and megaphones all benefit by being

Figure 12-24: The acrylic on top of this boat is simply a sideways cylinder. It required two circles and one long rectangle, which was rolled around the circles' edges. The acrylic bars inside were added later to reinforce it. *Idiot Savant*, the Public Theater, 2009. Design by Richard Foreman.

built out of a flat piece of material that is folded or rolled into a geometric solid.

It is also useful when working with materials that do not come in solid blocks, such as fabric or sheet metal. A flat template is also useful for packaging and constructing objects out of printed material. A template can be stored on a computer and printed out whenever needed; it can also print graphics and text directly to a surface that is folded and assembled into a three-dimensional solid, obviating the need to make stickers, decals, or stencils. Some of these props can even be shipped flat between different venues of a production and only folded into a three-dimensional prop during the performance.

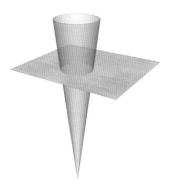

Figure 12-23: An inverted cone that is truncated parallel to the base creates a shape reminiscent of a bucket.

Paper Patterns

Paper craft is the collection of techniques that involve cutting and folding designs onto paper, cardstock, or any laminar (flat) material that can be folded. Do not confuse paper craft with *origami*, which is the Japanese art of folding a design from a single piece of paper (or *kirigami*—like *origami* but involving cutting and/or gluing the paper as well). In *origami*, portions of the paper overlap each other. Of course, the skills of *origami* can be very useful for a props artisan in various situations, but they will not be discussed here.

Thick materials such as corrugated cardboard, foam core, or heavy cardstock may need to be scored at the folds to give a clean bend. Convex folds will show gaps, as will the seams where two surfaces join. To make sure there are no gaps, the seams need to be cut at a beveled angle, covered with tape, or filled with a putty, body filler, or paste. They may also be ignored if the object will eventually be covered with another substance or material, or if the pattern is just meant to be a mockup or rehearsal item.

Items made from paper in this manner, such as envelopes, juice cartons, etc., often use tabs or extra lengths of material that overlap on the joints to hold an adhesive.

The Japanese term for paper craft, *pepakura*, has been popularized with the spread of computer programs that will automatically create a pattern from a three-dimensional computer model. These complex paper models are a far cry from the simple blocky shapes whose patterns were found on the backs of cereal and cookie cartons during the mid-twentieth century.

While these paper items can be used as a pattern to cut pieces out of stiffer material, they are also used as an end product. A variety of stiffening and coating methods have been developed by *pepakura* hobbyists to turn a paper object into a smooth and stiff, yet hollow, object. First, seal all the seams on the outside with either tape or some kind of resin. Then, if your piece is meant to be hollow, you can fill the inside to stiffen it up. Water-based or plastic resins can be used. Materials such

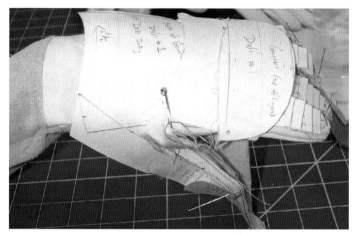

Figures 12-25 and 12-26: Heavy paper or cardstock is often used to make patterns for rigid materials. Paper lets you quickly cut and assemble three-dimensional objects from patterns so that you can test out how they fit or what shape they make. If you make a mistake, you can simply start over with a new sheet of paper rather than wasting valuable material. When the pattern is perfect, you simply have to trace it onto your sheet of metal or other rigid material and be confident the resulting shape will be correct. Photograph and gauntlet by Debi Jolly.

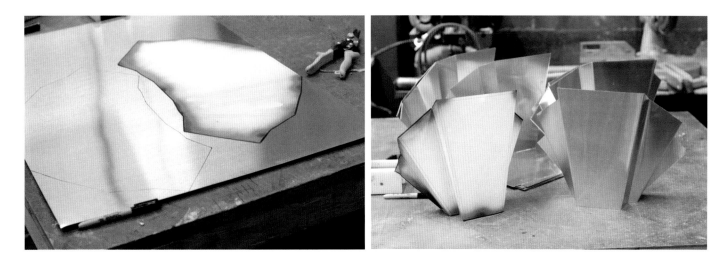

Figures 12-27 and 12-28: A simple pattern for a footlight is created on paper and traced to a sheet of aluminum. It is cut out and folded along the same folds indicated on the paper, making it a perfect duplicate of the paper pattern. *Sleep No More*, New York City, 2011.

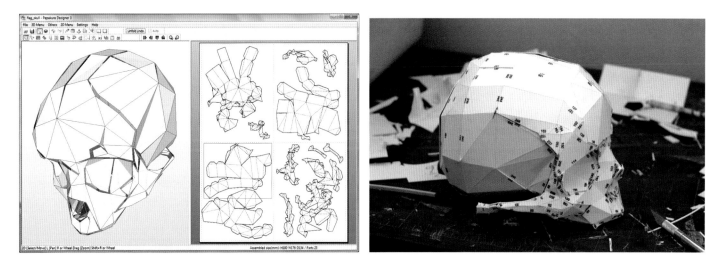

Figures 12-29 and 12-30: Computer programs exist to take a three-dimensional file and automatically transform it into a *pepakura* pattern, complete with tabs and numbers to match both sides of a joint, that can be printed on standard sizes of paper.

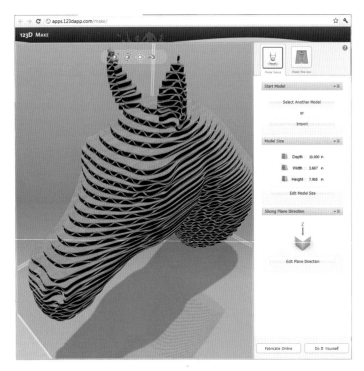

Figure 12-31: Computer programs exist that can transform three-dimensional digital files into all manner of flat drawings that can be printed and cut out (or sent to a CNC machine); these do not necessarily have to be outer surfaces formed by folding and cutting the material, but can be solid objects built up from numerous slices of materials, like the program pictured here that turns an object into stacked layers of corrugated cardboard.

as plaster or papier-mâché will soften and distort the paper unless it is sealed first with PVA glue or shellac.

The outside surface of the paper is then covered with resin or a thicker material such as auto body filler. This is not put on too thickly, as the shape and details are already defined by the paper; rather, it is put on as thinly as possible to turn the flat surfaces and sharp folds into more gentle curves. To make a smooth, curved surface like this involves a lot of sanding and refilling along the way.

Soft Foam Patterning

Soft foam and foam rubber are often patterned and assembled to create three-dimensional shapes. We covered different types of foam and how to work with it in Chapter 9. In Chapter 11, we looked at upholstery, which touches on some of these techniques as well. Flat foam patterning has developed from both paper craft and puppet-making techniques, and we will look at both of these.

Thinner foam rubber, especially EVA foam, has been used as a material for flat patterning just like paper and sheet metal. The patterns are typically created on paper, and then traced to the foam and assembled. EVA foam can be adhered with hot melt glue. Because EVA and other foams have thickness, gaps will be present at any convex joint. The foam will need to be beveled at the correct angle to fit together snugly (which can be extra complicated if the foam is rolled in any way). Most filling materials are rigid, which defeats the purpose of using flexible foam as a construction material, though not every joint needs to be flexible. You may also be able to ignore the gaps if you will be covering the foam in fabric or another skin. The thickness of EVA foam gives it another advantage in that it can be used to add raised details by cutting small shapes to apply on top of the larger surfaces.

Puppet makers work with soft polyurethane rubber, often nicknamed polyfoam, a lot. Polyfoam can be even thicker than EVA foam, which introduces some additional techniques for shaping and patterning it.

Soft foam can be cut and then glued together, as its thickness gives enough surface area to make a strong glue joint. It is sometimes helpful to use spray adhesive to attach a knit fabric on the unseen portion of the foam to give it reinforcement, particularly when using stitching to create shapes.

Figures 12-32 and 12-33: The foam puppets in the first picture show how foam can be shaped by pulling and pinching, either with glue or stitches. Contrast that with the second picture, where the foam is shaped by cutting and carving. Puppets constructed by Rebecca Akins for Childsplay Theatre in Arizona.

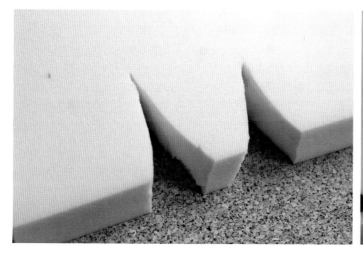 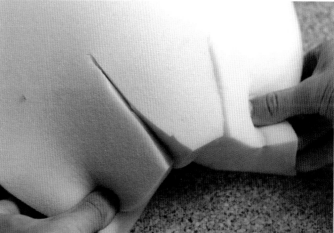

Figures 12-34 and 12-35: As with fabric, multiple dart closures will create a curve in soft foam.

thirteen

sculptural materials

The word *sculpture* comes from the Latin *sculptura*, which means "to carve or cut stone." These days, it encompasses far more materials and techniques. Carving stone is probably one of the last techniques you would ever use to make a prop.

In sculpture as an art, students are taught to respect their materials and not to camouflage them as something else; it is considered aesthetically dishonest. The same is not true in prop making; you often need to sculpt something out of one material and use a surface treatment to make it appear like another material. Sculpture for the props artisan is more concerned with the shapes one can create; all the other needs of a prop must still be considered (weight, materials cost, labor time, rigidity, or flexibility, etc.).

The media used in sculpture can be divided into two groups. Rigid and mostly permanent materials like wood, metal, and foam are carved (or cut) directly, or beaten into shape. Impermanent and plastic materials, like clay and wax, are easily altered in shape by adding and subtracting material, or by "smooshing," pulling, smearing, and stretching it around.

Machining refers to creating a shape in a single piece of material through cutting, milling, drilling, and turning with machine tools. Machining is often done on metal or solid blocks of rigid plastic. Tools such as drill presses, lathes, routers, and shapers can be used to "machine" wood or lumber products. "Machining" implies you are making parts with great precision that are often intended to fit together with other parts or create some kind of mechanism.

Though both machining and sculpting involve cutting away material from a solid piece and may share similar tools and techniques, we maintain distinct terms to differentiate the goals of each process.

(In this case, I am using the word *plastic* to refer to a material's ability to be formed, and not to the group of materials made of polymers, such as acrylic, styrene, vinyl, etc. For more information about this distinction, check out Chapter 9.)

The first group is considered "carving materials." You form a shape by cutting away the material. If you wish to build up an area on a foam sculpture, you need to attach another piece of foam; it will always remain a distinct piece of foam, connected by glue or hardware. The second group is called "modeling materials"; when you add more clay to a clay sculpture, it becomes a bigger lump of clay. You cannot distinguish the new clay from the old. When you model something out of a material, you have to do something to it to make it permanent. Some materials become rigid and hard when heated. One of the oldest such materials is clay; when you bake clay in an oven or kiln, it becomes harder and more durable, and resists further manipulation. Other materials become pliable when heated, and firm back up when they cool down, such as thermoplastics. Other materials become hard through exposure to air. Newer modeling materials such as epoxy putty

Figure 13-1: This mandrake root from *Harry Potter and the Chamber of Secrets* was created by sculpting.

harden by **curing**; when you mix the two parts together, you have a modeling substance that chemically hardens before the day is done.

Some modeling materials are not meant to make a final product. They may be intended to construct a shape that will be molded and cast in another material (see Chapter 14 for further information). They may also be used to make a *maquette*, which is a small-scale model used as a three-dimensional reference for either a larger sculpture or for an animator making a film. A props artisan can also coat a model in a substance that hardens and protects it. I've seen props that, once you break through the outer surface, have moist oil-based clay inside.

Some materials overlap the two groups of carving and modeling. Steel can be carved (and engraved), but when it is

Do You Actually Need to Sculpt?

When you are creating your prop, you often need to decide whether you are going to carve detail into the surface or whether applying a detail will work better. For example, your prop may have an area that is full of repetitive ridges. You can carve all those ridges in, or you can find a material that already has inherent ridges, such as a fabric, and apply it to the surface.

In very low-budget theatrical situations (this may be scoffed at by the film and television crowd), three-dimensional details may sometimes be simply painted on. But if you remember the lessons from Chapter 2, as long as the needs of the prop are met using the resources available to you, this can be a viable solution.

Figure 13-2: Carving a bas-relief into a sheet of Styrofoam with a rotary tool.

heated, it becomes more plastic and can be bent and deformed. Thinner steel can even be bent without heat. Pencil rod, which is a term for a thin rod (usually a quarter of an inch), is easily bent without heat and commonly used to make skeletons or skeletal-type sculptures.

Step-By-Step Guide to Sculpting

While sculpting is frequently portrayed in the movies as a single artist finessing the details of a nose or ear on a large block of uncarved marble, real sculpting is far more methodical. You begin by gathering your research and reference materials. You develop your reference into something that is useful for the materials and techniques you will be working with, whether that means a full-scale photograph, a scale drawing, or something else. When you begin sculpting or carving, you progress from an overall shape to fine details; you start with the basic outline, either by cutting away large chunks of material or by adding together big lumps of the material. You next shape all this material into a more refined form, progressing from aggressive tools to more subtle tools. Only at the end, when everything is in place, do you begin adding in details, texture, and refining the surface.

Reference

Reference and research is extremely important to making your sculpture. If you are building a sculpture from a designer's drafting, hopefully you have been given the front, side, and top views. If you only have a sketch from a single viewpoint, or if you are making a sculpture from your own sketch, it may be helpful to draw out the other sides ahead of time. Gather as many photographs and illustrations of the object you are trying to create, from as many different angles as possible. At the very least, a picture of the front, the side, and the top will make your job easier. If it is asymmetrical, you will want to photograph all the sides. Be aware that photography introduces lens distortions at the edges; use as long a lens as possible (zoomed in all the way) with the object in the center of the frame.

Even with adequate drawings, it is often helpful to gather additional reference material. For instance, if you are sculpting a small horse, photographs of real horses may help illuminate details or how parts fit together, which are not apparent in your drawings. Even if you are sculpting a completely imaginary object, you can find pictures and reference from real-world objects that your object is inspired from to help you fill in the gaps in your drawings.

Lay a grid over the photograph or drawing to create a reference for scale (see Chapter 6 for more information about enlarging a picture using a grid). If the object is small enough and your printer large enough, you can print the picture out in full-scale. Likewise, you can print it out piecemeal and assemble for a full-scale reference. If you are developing your

Figure 13-3: Sculpting from a full-scale reference. Photograph by Natalie Taylor Hart.

reference picture from scratch, or it is simply not in your computer, you can draw it out in full-scale as well.

You may do one of several things with a full-scale reference image. First, you may keep it next to your sculpture and visually compare it as you proceed. Rulers or calipers can help you check measurements and proportions more precisely.

A second option is to print the picture out and mount it to a stiff board or stock; cut out and remove the picture itself so you are left with a hole the exact size and shape of your sculpture. You can pass this hole over your sculpture as you progress; when the sculpture fits through it with no gaps, you have successfully built your piece to its outer extremes.

Third, you can use a full-scale reference picture to build up material directly on top of, or to carve away material directly underneath.

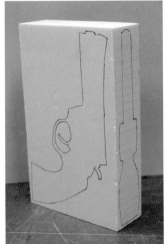

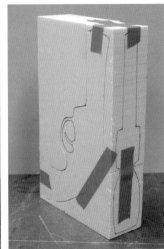

Figure 13-4: Carving away wood directly underneath a drawing. Photograph by Natalie Taylor Hart.

Developing the Basic Outline

To sculpt in the fastest and most efficient manner possible, you want to build your basic shape first. This will help you establish all the proportions first. You wouldn't want to start carving the intricate details of the ears on either side of a block of material only to find out later that they do not line up with each other.

If you are making a subtractive sculpture, draw the furthest outline of your object on the three sides (front, side, and top) of your object. Cutting around this outline will make the removal of material go the fastest.

If you are cutting the object out on a band saw (or any stationary saw with a table), a good tip is to save the offcuts and temporarily reattach them so you retain a flat surface from which to cut the other sides out.

Larger chunks of material that will not fit on a stationary machine can be attacked with hand-held saws, powered either electrically or with muscle. Polystyrene foam can be cut with a

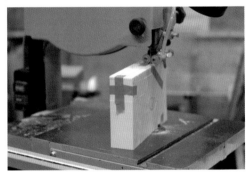

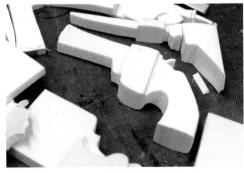

Figures 13-5 to 13-8: After you cut one face out of a block of material, you can reattach the off-cut pieces with tape or toothpicks. This gives you a flat surface to keep the material square as you cut the shape out of another face.

hot wire cutter, which is a long wire kept in tension and heated through electrical resistance; some can be long enough to require two people to operate, with one person at either end. If you are creating a large chunk of material by attaching a number of smaller chunks of material together, it can be helpful to assemble these chunks first without glue, draw the outline, than disassemble and cut each piece individually before gluing them together.

For large or complicated shapes, prop makers sometimes find it helpful to draw out various "slices" of the sculpture showing the profile at that point. You can cut these slices out of a sheet of material and attach them to a central framework. Fill the spaces in between the slices with your sculpting material. The slices serve as reference points so that you basically "connect the dots" while sculpting.

For an additive sculpture, it is easier to build up your basic shape bit by bit rather than starting with a giant lump or block of material. Add little balls of material to your shape until you have a rough form. Protrusions can be added a little bit at a time as well. It is much easier to build up your shape this way than to try and make it appear from a big cube.

More delicate sculptures require some kind of underlying skeleton or armature to support the material. This is particularly true with human and animal figurines, where outstretched limbs can easily fall off due to the weight of the clay.

What exactly is released when you use a hot wire on extruded polystyrene foam (Styrofoam™)? The 2010 MSDS for Styrofoam™ states: "Under high heat, non-flaming conditions, small amounts of aromatic hydrocarbons such as styrene and ethylbenzene are generated." The Consortium of Local Education Authorities for the Provision of Science Services (CLEAPPS), at Brunel University in England, has also tested and found that styrene fumes are released when using hot wire cutters on polystyrene foam. Styrene is an eye irritant and can cause nerve damage; you begin to get dizzy after enough exposure (also an indication that you do not have adequate ventilation). CLEAPPS suggests that with adequate ventilation around handheld cutters, exposure can be kept to 10% of the MEL (maximum exposure limit). Large, table-top or two-person wires may require local exhaust ventilation, which suggests having a risk assessment done by a qualified professional. The 2010 MSDS for Styrofoam™ also states that a respirator with an organic vapor cartridge will protect against styrene fumes. Finally, the International Agency for Research on Cancer (IARC) classifies styrene as a Group 2B carcinogen, meaning it is possibly carcinogenic to humans.

Figure 13-9: For this three-foot tall garden gnome, my wife and I cut out the front and side profile from plywood, and then added slices indicating the top profiles. Some of the slices have been fit in but are still waiting to be drawn and cut out. *Broke-ology*, Lincoln Center Theatre, 2009. Scenic design by Donyale Werle.

Figure 13-10: Pieces of foam are placed between the plywood slices. Wherever possible, we pre-cut the foam to a rough shape on the band saw before placing in the plywood frame to save time. *Broke-ology*, Lincoln Center Theatre, 2009. Scenic design by Donyale Werle.

Figure 13-11: Making the sculpture match the proportions and dimensions of our reference material was a simple matter of sculpting the foam flush with all the slices. *Broke-ology*, Lincoln Center Theatre, 2009. Scenic design by Donyale Werle.

Other times, you may simply wish to use an armature as a way to define the shape and proportions first. Many sculptors utilize **armature wire** to build a skeleton. This is basically thick wire that is easily bent but holds its shape well. Really, any kind of wire or rod will work, but if you do a lot of sculpture, you will appreciate the reduced effort it takes to shape armature wire.

When the shape is ready, some sculptors use epoxy putty to hold the wires together. For larger sculptures, the wires can be welded together as well. You can also lash the wires together, either with wire, tape, or string.

As some substances, particularly clay, will slide or rotate on a piece of wire, you may also find it useful to wrap a much thinner wire in a spiral around your thicker armature wire. This creates a gripping surface that will better hold the clay in place.

Armature wire is not the only way to build a skeleton. You can build more rudimentary or sturdy skeletons out of wood, pipe, or rod. It need not be elegant.

A quick way to add an underlying shape to your sculpture is by wadding and crumpling up material. Aluminum foil is useful in this case, as it is cheap, readily available, and it holds its shape when crumpled. You can form a rough shape with a wad of aluminum foil and then proceed to add clay or whatever sculpting medium you choose on top. The same process can be used on wadded up paper. You can hold the shape together by wrapping either tape or wire around it. This also gives you some control over the shape you form. These methods work well for more free-form sculptures, for sculptures that need to remain lightweight, and for when time is of the essence.

Choosing a sculpture medium involves deciding between rigidity and bendability, between hardness and softness. A soft and pliable material is easier and faster to shape and carve, but also easier to distort as you place your hands on it. One way prop makers take advantage of the properties of both types of materials is by modeling the rough shape or structure with a harder material and then laying on the details and more organic shapes with a softer material. The harder material can go on top of an armature or skeleton, or it can serve as the underlying structure itself.

If you work with a material that can be hardened in the oven, you can lay down the basic shape and then fire it so that as you add further details, you do not further manipulate the underlying shape. Prop makers have also cut the underlying shape out of wood and then added details and shapes on top with a more pliable substance. If you work with a material that sets after a period of time, like epoxy putty or a thick resin, you can build your sculpture in stages; begin by roughing out the shape you need, and then let it set. Add another layer of shape and detail and allow that to set. Continue in this vein until you have the level of detail you need. Working in this fashion means if you accidentally drop or bump your sculpture, you will not ruin the sculpting you have done previously. It is particularly helpful when working on sculptures seen from all sides; imagine taking a few hours to sculpt the back of a figurine out of clay. You turn the sculpture around to begin sculpting the front. You need a better grip, so you put your hand on

Figure 13-12: This procedure works in reverse as well; you can sculpt the bulk of your piece in a soft material that is easy to carve, and then lay a harder material over the top that lets you carve more precise and sharp details. Natalie Taylor Hart carves some hardened Bondo™ (polyester resin auto body filler), which was laid on top of XPS foam.

Figure 13-13: The rough shape for this bird head was first cut in a piece of wood. The finer details were then added on top with a self-hardening modeling substance that was easier to shape and carve than the wood.

Figures 13-14 and 13-15: The decorations on this cast iron bench are actually a mixture of applied resin pieces, upholstery fringe, Ethafoam, and yarn.

the sculpture, but you feel your fingers smooshing into the clay and ruining the details on the back that took you hours to create.

Some prop makers find it useful to make a waste mold of a piece in progress and then cast it into another material to continue working with a different technique; you model it in a soft material, mold it, and then cast it in a harder material. The reasons are the same. You may wish to "freeze" the progress of your sculpture and continue adding details without disturbing your basic shape and proportions. You may also want to cast it in a hard material so that you can then carve more precise details that would be obscured in a softer material. Similarly, casting in a hard material gives you the option of sanding and polishing your sculpture to a much smoother and glossier surface than you can get in materials such as clay.

You may expand all these techniques I just covered and build your sculpture out of any number of disparate materials, found objects, and appliqué. This is true whether you are building a model that will be molded and cast, or you are making the final piece directly. Your sculpture may combine flat geometric areas that are easier to cut out of materials like wood or plastic, with more fluid and organic shapes, which are easier to model in epoxy putty or polymer clay.

Sculpting Tools

For the actual sculpting and carving of your object, the tools are as varied as any. Sculpting and carving enjoys a long history over multiple cultures, and employs innumerable materials and seeks many different end results. Many artisans create and modify their own tools, so it should come to no surprise to see such a vast array of implements to choose from. If it helps, one can break down the tools between those used for plastic materials, and those used by rigid ones.

For modeling materials like clay and wax, ribbon tools are frequently used. These have a ribbon of metal at one or both ends that scrape off material when pulled. The variety of shapes the ribbons can be found in are practically infinite, and

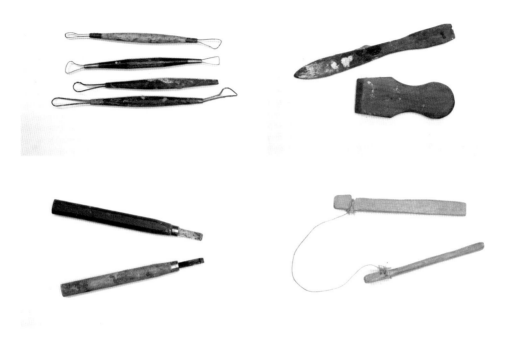

Figures 13-16 to 13-19 Top row, left to right: various ribbon tools, wooden spatulas and shapers. Bottom row, left to right: metal-tipped carving tools, wire used for cutting blocks of soft clay.

the fact that they can be reshaped by hand means the choices are greater still. Other useful implements are wooden spatulas that come in a dizzying array of shapes and configurations. Some are rounded like spoons, and others are straight like knives. Tools with various metal ends may look like chisels, but are actually designed for various sculpting and carving needs. For some materials, particularly water and oil clays, an easy way to quickly remove large chunks of material is with a wire; to save your fingers, the ends of the wires are wrapped around sticks.

For rigid materials, rasps and surforms are great at removing material quickly. For finer work or harder materials, files are used. Many of these are designed for either wood or metal, and some are even more specific in the particular kinds of metal they can be used for. The shapes and cuts of the files give them different advantages in different shapes or parts of the material you wish to file.

A surform (or "surface forming") tool resembles a cheese grater and is used similarly. The word *surform* has been trademarked by Stanley Tools, though other manufacturers make comparable tools.

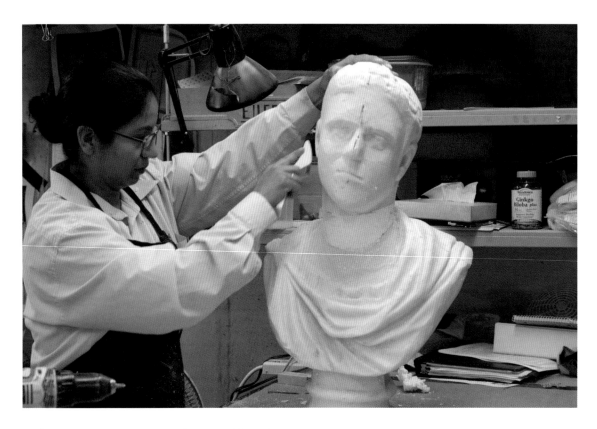

Figure 13-20: Eileen Garcia carves a cast polyurethane foam bust with a surform tool.

For larger pieces, an angle grinder is a helpful ally in removing large amounts of material quickly (though less precisely). You can use a bench grinder or other tabletop tool as well, but sculptures often demand the greater control in positioning that a handheld tool provides. Though we often think grinders are used solely with metal, you can switch out the discs for use in wood and even foam. Abrasive flap wheels, sanding discs, and wire brush wheels are popular choices. Portable belt sanders will also enable you to remove materials quickly, while other hand sanders will give you the control for more subtle shaping.

An oscillating multifunction tool is a newer type of tool that generates tens of thousands of oscillations per minute. It can accept a number of types of attachments, such as rasps, sanders, blades, grinders, and scrapers, making it a veritable chameleon of tools. It can cut a lot of time out of otherwise monotonous sculpting tasks.

Rotary tools are useful for smaller or more detailed work. Props people often refer to all rotary tools as "Dremel" tools, though that is only one brand. More powerful tools such as die grinders are available for the same kind of work. You can choose from a vast array of bits designed for various tasks, such as grinding, sanding, shaping, cutting, and smoothing, and materials, such as wood, metal, and plastics. With the right attachments, an oscillating multi-tool and a rotary tool may be all you ever need for all your sculpting projects.

Figure 13-21: An abrasive flap wheel on an angle grinder quickly shapes this large chunk of wood that will eventually become the back half of a dead deer. *A Lie of the Mind*, Ohio University, 2003. Photograph by Natalie Taylor Hart.

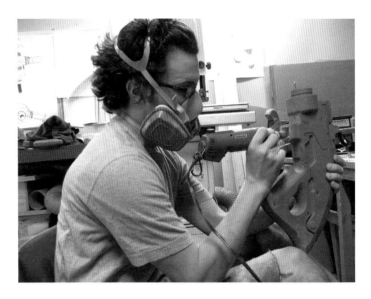

Figure 13-22: Harrison Krix uses a rotary tool to grind the opening in this gun barrel a little bigger. Photograph by Harrison Krix.

Materials

Many materials used in other processes can be sculpted, such as wood and various plastics. What follows are the materials used solely in prop sculpture.

Oil Clay

Oil clay is a popular item in props shops, sculpture studios, model shops, and animatronic studios. You may have heard it referred to a number of names and spellings, and it's easy to see why there is confusion over its name. "Plastilin," "Plasteline" (also known as "Chavant Clay"), "Plasticine," and "Plastilina" are all brand names of oil clays used by sculptors. Props artisans may use any one of these trademarked names as a generic term for all brands of oil clay. Oil clay comes in a variety of hardnesses,

Figure 13-23: A mask form sculpted out of a very firm oil-based clay.

colors, and formulations. Props artisans sometimes choose one over the other because of the specific needs of the prop being built; other times, the choice is due either to familiarity, or just on what is available at the nearest store.

Mixing a clay with oil rather than water means it will never dry out, and so its ability to be modeled will remain consistent whether it takes you an hour or a week to finish. This also means that it cannot really be a final product; it is used almost exclusively to create a model for later molding and casting.

Oil clays can range in hardness from bubble gum to blocks that carve almost like wood. Some can be heated to become softer, and others can even be heated to the point of becoming pourable. You can smooth the surface with a bit of solvent, such as mineral spirits. Many oil clays use a sulfur base, which is chemically incompatible with silicone mold-making. If you will be molding your model in silicone, be sure to use a sulfur-free clay. This is usually pretty explicitly mentioned in the packaging, so if the clay does not specifically state it is sulfur-free, assume it contains sulfur. Many props shops avoid sulfur clays altogether; they can easily get mixed in with sulfur-free clays, and there is no way of distinguishing between the two.

Wet Clay

Wet clays are clays that are mixed with water; as the water evaporates, the clay dries and becomes hard. Ceramic clays, such as stoneware, earthenware, terra-cotta, and porcelain, are meant to be fired at high temperatures (typically between 1200°F and 2300°F or 650°C–1250°C) in a kiln. We rarely use these to construct props because of the need for specialized firing equipment and other tools. They are, however, used on occasion to make breakable props, either by air-drying or with a lower temperature firing.

You can also find wet clays that air-harden. Though not as strong as their high-fired counterparts, they look similar, making them a viable alternative for a props shop that needs to produce a real clay prop but lacks the ability to fire one in a kiln.

Figure 13-24: These olives for fake martinis were sculpted with two different colors of polymer clay. Photograph by Anna Warren.

Polymer Clay

Polymer clay is more frequently used in the props shop. Though some may contain real clay as an ingredient, they are largely made of a mix of plastics, usually with PVC as a base. Many harden when placed in a regular oven (rather than a high-temperature kiln); others will harden in the air. You may recognize them by brand names such as Fimo, Sculpey, Cernit, Formello, Modello, and Kato Polyclay. Polymer clay is used a lot to make jewelry, and similar needs can be found in the props world, either for embellishment and details to props, or even for entire items. I must point out that an oven or toaster oven used to cure polymer clay should never be used to heat food again. The same is true for using an oven in any craft capacity (other than clays made entirely from flour and water or other food substances). Heating plastics releases fumes and chemicals into the oven. These can remain in there forever, and every time you heat food in there, the chemicals will propagate into your food.

Baker's Clay

Baker's clay (also called baker's dough or salt dough) is a home-made material made of flour, salt, and water. It is a useful material if you absolutely need to avoid toxic materials; it is also useful for making fake food props that are intended to look like baked goods.

The basis of the recipe is flour (avoid the self-rising kind), salt (the finer the better), and water. Various recipes can be found online, but the most common involve two parts water, half a part salt, and three-quarters water. Food coloring or powdered sugarless drink mixes can be added for color; a bit of corn starch helps maintain the color while baking. Vegetable oil can be added to increase the working time.

The dough can be mixed cold or hot. Cold mixing involves mixing the flour and salt, and then gradually adding the water and kneading until smooth. Hot mixing can be done one of several ways. Some recipes involve mixing the salt in boiling water, cooling it, and then kneading the flour into it; others involve mixing all the ingredients together and stirring them over a low heat until they dry out and cease to be sticky.

The pieces can be air-dried (which may take 2–3 days) or baked in an oven. Thin pieces may bake anywhere from 150°F to 200°F, while thicker pieces require anywhere from 250°F to 350°F. It typically takes anywhere from 1 to 3 hours to bake fully; if the pieces start to brown, they are heating up too quickly.

The pieces can be sealed with shellac or any polymer emulsion, such as polyurethane or acrylic varnish, or even just latex paint.

Polycaprolactone

Polycaprolactone (PCL) is a plastic that becomes soft and pliable at 140°F (60°C), making it possible to soften in boiling water and safely sculpt by hand without injury. You may recognize one of the many brand names, such as Friendly Plastic™, InstaMorph™, Shapelock™, and Polymorph™.

They often come in pellets or strips in a variety of colors. Their cost and workability make them more suited for jewelry and hand-sized objects, though pieces as large as masks are possible.

Drop the pellets or strips into a pot of boiling water, and wait for them to turn clear. Pull them out and begin shaping the

piece with your hands. Organic-looking shapes are easy; more refined pieces are trickier. You can do minor machining to the final piece, such as drilling or sanding, but these processes heat the plastic up and will soften and deform it if too much is done.

Joining pieces is difficult when they are cold. You can reheat the two pieces, but they will lose some of their shape in the process.

PCL also makes an incredibly strong but reversible cement for PVC parts.

Wax

Wax is a substance that is stiff around room temperature, but melts at a low temperature. It can come from animals, such as beeswax; plants, such as Carnuba wax; from petroleum, like paraffin and microcrystalline wax; as well as from minerals or through synthetic means. Jewelry wax, such as the blue wax in the photograph below, refers to any number of waxes, usually synthetic, that can be easily carved, sanded, machined, and drilled. Their low melting temperature also allows you to smooth the surfaces with heat, or manipulate the wax like a liquid in a small area with a heated tool. It is preferred, unsurprisingly, by jewelers because it allows very precise and fine detail on a small object, which can be difficult to sculpt in clay.

Figure 13-25: A figurine carved out of jeweler's wax.

Also, the fact that you need to handle and sculpt jewelry on all sides means you want a medium that won't distort from your fingers. This level of detail on such a small scale is usually unnecessary for theatrical prop making, but for small props in film and television that will be filmed up close, it is a great material to model in for later casting.

Sculptors who work in wax will often sculpt the basic figure in clay, make a **waste mold**, then cast the piece in wax, and work on the finer details. You can find out more about molding and casting in Chapter 14.

Styrofoam™ (XPS) and Bead Foam (EPS)

Another mainstay of the props shop is extruded polystyrene foam, best known by the most popular brand, Styrofoam™. Styrofoam™ is used in various applications, with different colors used to differentiate between these applications. Most props shops use the type made for construction insulation, which comes in blue blocks and sheets, and is often referred to colloquially as "blue foam." Other brands of extruded polystyrene foam used for insulation come in pink sheets and blocks, and are known as, surprisingly, "pink foam." The brand or color you use is immaterial for sculpting purposes; what you should be more interested in is the density and rigidity of the extruded polystyrene foam you can get. To avoid confusion from here onward, I will refer to any and all brands of extruded polystyrene foam by its abbreviation, XPS.

XPS can be easily shaped into many three-dimensional shapes. It can also be glued to itself to make larger pieces, with a seam that easily disappears during finishing. One of its other benefits is its light weight. Even a solid chunk twice as large as a person can be effortlessly hoisted over your head.

XPS is easily dissolved in most solvents, and even heat as low as boiling water can begin to degrade it. This precludes many spray adhesives and paints, solvent-based contact cements, and hot melt adhesives from being used on it. Most artisans use water-based contact cements, such as 3M FastBond 30NF

Figure 13-26: From left to right: white/bead foam (EPS), pink foam (XPS), blue foam/Styrofoam (XPS), dry floral foam (also Styrofoam), white craft foam (also Styrofoam).

Figure 13-27: These sheets of EPS foam are joined to each other and to a wooden core with 3M™ Fastbond™ 30NF, a popular water-based contact adhesive commonly called "green glue." Photograph by Natalie Taylor Hart.

(green glue) to adhere pieces of XPS to each other; they can also be used to stick XPS to wooden structures.

Foaming glues, particularly polyurethane glues (better known as Gorilla Glue™), are especially good at sticking

together XPS and wood; they are less useful for gluing XPS to itself because it dries to such a hard and rigid layer that the tools used for quickly carving and shaping XPS do not carve as easily or quickly through the dried glue line.

For gluing XPS to itself without affecting its ability to be sculpted, some shops use two-part foaming polyurethane as an adhesive. The XPS needs to be clamped together or weighted down because the polyurethane expands as it foams, and can push the pieces apart. When cured, it has the same density as the surrounding XPS foam, making it feel like one giant block of material as you carve.

Its light weight and ease of carving comes at the price of fragility. In nearly every case, it needs to be coated or covered with another material. I have devoted a whole section in Chapter 16 just to coatings for XPS foam.

XPS can be cut on the table saw and shaped with the band saw, an electric knife, handsaws, or any of the rasps and surform tools.

Not to be confused with XPS is *expanded* polystyrene foam, or EPS, which is the white, beady foam (appropriately nicknamed "bead foam") sold as sheets and blocks or scavenged from packing materials. EPS can come in all sorts of sizes, including blocks big enough to be used as scenic elements, so it is preferred for building especially large props. The kind used as packing material is usually less dense and rigid than the kind used in construction, but since you can get large amounts of it for free, it may be worth holding on to for the budget-conscious prop maker.

The trademark "Styrofoam" is used to refer to all polystyrene foam, extruded or expanded, which is doubly confusing. In addition to being used as a construction and insulation material, Styrofoam™ is also marketed toward the floral and crafts industry. However, this formulation of Styrofoam™ is vastly different from blue/pink foam and bead foam; it is more "crinkly", brittle, and less dense. It is available in green or white.

Figure 13-28: The type of Styrofoam™ made for the floral industry was cut, shaped, and painted to make these pieces of fake toast for *Timon of Athens* at the Public Theater. The glue helped seal the foam to make it easier to paint; yellow glue was used because it closely matched the color of the toast.

Thus, if you say "Styrofoam," someone who thinks it is a generic term won't know if you mean expanded or extruded polystyrene foam, while someone who knows it is a trademark won't know if you mean insulation or floral/craft foam.

Urethane Foam

Another foam useful for carving is polyurethane (sometimes shortened to "urethane") foam. We usually think of polyurethane foam in its two-part liquid form, useful for casting (see Chapter 14) or as a "spray foam" found in hardware stores for sealing large gaps, but you can also find it in preformed sheets and blocks ready for carving. It is not as economical or easy to find as XPS and EPS (taxidermy shops, strangely enough, often stock it), but fans like it for its greater density and ability to define more precise detail. Rather than trying to find and buy blocks, you can cast your own with two-part polyurethane foam. Some props artisans who cast objects in polyurethane foam will pour the excess liquid into a random block mold so that they have a block in stock for future carving projects.

Spray foam is a polyurethane foam that is automatically catalyzed as it is squirted out and cures as it is exposed to air. Because of its need to be exposed to air, you can only lay it down one layer at a time, otherwise it will take days to cure (the center may, in fact, never cure). It can be highly useful for selectively adding "carve-able bits" wherever you want, even around irregularly shaped supports and framework.

It is vital to keep in mind that many polyurethane foams out-gas isocyanates (among other toxic substances). These are highly reactive chemicals that can irritate the skin, eyes, and lungs, and lead to asthma or chemical sensitization when inhaled or absorbed through the skin. Eventually, you can find yourself having major reactions to even minor exposures (for isocyanates, this is typically an asthma attack) of a chemical. Sensitization can be permanent. When the polyurethane foam is fully cured (which could still be hours after it feels solid), it ceases to out-gas toxic fumes (unless burned or turned to dust). But when spraying, you need to take the same precautions as when pouring or casting other two-part polyurethane foams or resins; a local exhaust ventilation system (chemical hood) is the most appropriate precaution. Dust masks are useless, and even respirators cannot fully protect you because isocyanates have no odor or other warning signs.

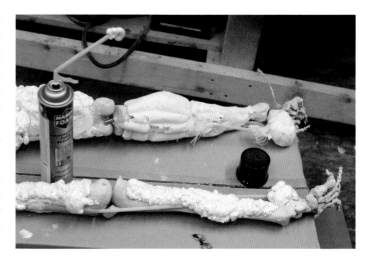

Figure 13-29: Expanding spray foam can add carve-able chunks of material to a skeleton or framework. In this photograph, we sprayed foam onto a literal skeleton to construct a corpse. The top leg shows the fully cured foam already being carved. The bottom leg shows the foam after application; it will expand in size to match the top leg. *The Bacchae*, the Public Theater, 2009. Scenic design by John Conklin.

Basswood

Basswood is another good material to hone your carving skills on, or if you need a quick and easy sculpture made out of wood. It is pretty straightforward to graduate to fancier hardwoods from basswood. Soft woods tend to be less useful for carving, as their grain is larger and harder to control. Though similar to basswood, balsa wood is considered too mushy to be a satisfactory carving medium.

fourteen

molding and casting

A prop maker molds and casts when he or she wishes to make duplicate copies of an object or when he or she wants the final prop to be made from a different material than a prototype or model is constructed with.

Molding and casting also allows an artisan to sculpt a piece out of a solid material, and then cast just a "skin" with a hollow interior. This is useful for items such as masks and armor, or to eliminate weight.

Finally, molding and casting allows an artisan to create a replica of something that cannot be used as a prop. Most commonly, an artisan will mold and cast body parts, such as limbs and heads, to create props. Using an actor's real head as a prop can be messy and is often against Equity Rules. You can also make molds out of an object that is too valuable to be used on stage, or take a mold of a piece of something larger that is fixed in place and cannot be brought to the theatre, such as a carved detail on the façade of a building.

Duplicate copies are needed when it becomes cost-prohibitive to construct matching items individually. It can also be used when a single prop has a repetitive detail, such as a carved rosette. The detail can be molded from scratch or from an already existing item, then cast and attached to the prop. They are also useful in the prop world for making breakable items, such as statues, where many copies can be produced out of a cheap, easy-to-break material for minimal cost.

Though many reasons exist to mold and cast an object, you should still ask yourself whether it is absolutely necessary in your situation. Molding and casting materials can be expensive and greatly increases the cost of a prop. It can also consume a lot of time.

When casting something, you need to know two things; what you are casting and what the final piece is made of. These two things will determine what materials you can make your mold out of. When you know those three things, you can then determine additional materials you may need, such as release agents or sealing agents. What you cast the final piece out of is decided in the same way you decide how to make all your other props; determine the needs of that prop and the resources you have available. Once you know what you are casting the final piece in, that will limit what your mold can be made out of. Further limitations may depend on what your original piece is made out of. Sometimes you need to construct the original, but at other times you are duplicating an already existing piece. Once you have the possibilities of mold materials narrowed down, the rest will depend on practical constraints, such as budget, time, and what your shop is best set up to deal with.

To figure out how you will make your mold, you need to consider a few things. Starting with the original piece, you need to consider its shape. This will determine whether it is best to use a flexible or rigid mold, a single piece, or a multi-piece mold. It may even be necessary to mold the object in several parts that are assembled together after being cast individually. The materials the original is made out of may also determine what types of molding materials are compatible for its use. Next you

Figure 14-1: The light sabers in the *Star Wars* films were carved and sculpted from an assortment of materials as well as assembled from a variety of found objects. They were then molded and cast in plastic so that it became a single piece of material, and so that multiple copies could be made.

need to know what you wish to make your cast piece out of. Your material choice is important, as is whether you wish it to be a solid or hollow piece.

After considering these factors, you should have your choice of molding and casting materials. Often, the manufacturers or distributors of these types of products will be able to guide you to the best choice, particularly when you have adequately described what exactly your mold and your cast need to do.

Getting Started

When you are first getting started with molding and casting, it is better to learn on cheap and simple materials. There are many concepts and techniques to understand in molding and casting, and you can learn these on materials that act consistently and reliably and, most importantly, are inexpensive. Such materials include plaster, latex, alginate, and papier-mâché.

Materials such as the plastic resins and silicone rubbers, though preferred by the professionals, have their own special considerations. They are more temperamental, require more safety precautions, and their chemistry can cause them to fail miserably if you do not know what you are doing. If you cannot make a plaster or alginate mold work correctly, then you will not be able to make a silicone mold or a polyurethane resin casting work correctly, and you would have wasted more money in the process. Once you can make successful molds and casts with the cheap and easy materials, then you can start trying to figure out molding and casting with the more advanced materials that require precise measurements and a knowledge of what may inhibit their curing or cause the casts to come out imperfectly.

There is a lot of information in this chapter. It is helpful to watch videos and attend workshops, seminars, classes, or even just observe other people in your shop who make molds. No two molding and casting projects will ever be exactly the same, so the materials and techniques one person uses may not necessarily be the same ones you want to use.

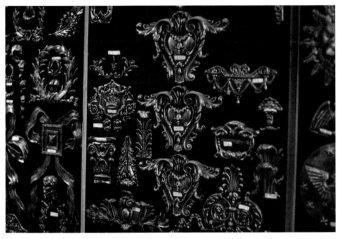

Figures 14-2 and 14-3: The shop at Costume Armour, Inc., maintains a vast mold library of ornamental details. These are cast in latex and then applied to larger props, so an incredibly ornate item such as this pipe organ can be manufactured quickly and inexpensively by applying many smaller castings to the surface.

Definitions

The object or model you wish to duplicate is called the **master**. You surround it with some other material to make a **mold**, often known as a **negative**. The mold has a void or impression in it with the exact shape and form of the master. To **cast** a piece, the void in the mold is filled with your casting material, which is usually a liquid or runny paste that hardens. You may also have a **press mold**, in which a clay-like material is pushed in by hand with rigid shapes or stamps. When the casting material is hard, it is removed from the mold, and you have an exact duplicate, or **positive** of your master. The cast is rarely an *exact* duplicate because most casting materials shrink a bit as they harden, but the casts themselves are all identical to each other. In most modern materials, the shrinkage is imperceptible on stage or on camera.

A **master mold** is a mold of a negative mold piece. These molds are made to cast more mold pieces, which are then used to cast more copies. Since molds wear down over time with repeated use, large production runs often require multiple molds to be made.

A **release agent** (sometimes called a **mold release** or **surface separator**) keeps the piece being cast from sticking to the mold or keeps one mold piece from sticking to another. Some mold releases also seal the pores of the surface as well; in other cases, you may need a separate "sealing agent" to accomplish that before adding your mold release.

Figures 14-4 to 14-6: The above was a quick press mold made in oil-based clay to cast a tongue in silicone rubber. Oil clay is great for press molds because it softens when warm and stiffens when cold. You can push a model into a bed of warmed oil clay to capture all the details, then allow it to cool (or even put it in a refrigerator for faster cooling) to keep it from distorting when you remove the model.

Negative molds can be either flexible or rigid. Flexible molds have traditionally been made of glue or gelatin, rubber, and agar compositions. Modern materials include flexible vinyl and RTV silicone rubber; a favorite with props people. We often reinforce them with an outer shell or casing, known as a **mother mold** (or "jacket"), made of plaster of Paris, fiberglass, or a thick plastic resin.

Rigid molds are commonly made with plaster of Paris. Some industries use glass and metal molds, but these are rarely, if ever, practical for a props person to make (though you can occasionally find preexisting ones for sale). Simple molds have one or two pieces, while complex ones can have many pieces. Rigid molds can be further divided into waste molds and piece molds. A **waste mold** needs to be destroyed to remove or release the positive cast inside. It is less time consuming to make and it eliminates seam lines, but it can only be used once. Waste molds (sometimes called **throw-away molds**) are frequently used so that a sculptor can sculpt the basic shape in an easy-to-shape material, then cast it in a material that allows further, more detailed refinement.

Figure 14-8: This hippo requires an eight-piece plaster mold to avoid undercuts. If a flexible mold material was used, it would have needed only two or three pieces.

A **piece mold** consists of one or more pieces that can be removed to liberate the positive and then reassembled to create another cast. Piece molds are needed when a positive has undercuts.

Undercuts

Some objects have areas that will create a recessed area in the mold, preventing it from being pulled straight out. These recessed areas are known as **undercuts**. If a rigid mold has undercuts and you fill it with a rigid casting material, the cast will become trapped in there when it hardens. If you cannot avoid undercuts, you must either make the mold in multiple parts, or use a flexible material for either the mold or the cast. Note that even flexible molds may need to be made in two or more parts if your object has severe undercuts. If your object has a hole that passes all the way through, you will also need to make a piece mold.

Figure 14-7: Plaster was poured on top of this mold to create a mother mold, which will support the flexible mold.

Types of Molds

There are four ways to make a mold. A **temporary mold** is meant to be destroyed after a single casting. A **box mold** (or bucket mold) is where you build a box or some other wall around an object and cover it with your molding material. For three-dimensional objects, you can make a two-piece box mold. The object is typically embedded halfway into a slab of clay and the first mold piece is poured over its top. When set, the clay is removed, the mold and object flipped, mold release applied, and the second half is poured. You cannot pour the material underneath the object because the hydraulic pressure will push the object up, and air bubbles will be trapped underneath as well.

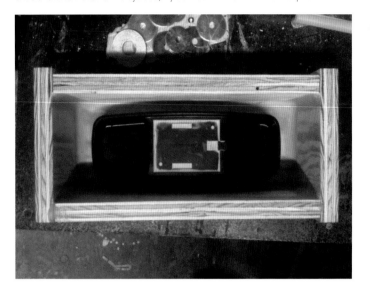

Figures 14-9 and 14-10: A box mold setup and the resulting silicone rubber mold.

Figure 14-11: In this box mold, a layer of clay is built up around the bottom. The object being cast is embedded in the clay up to where we want the seam line to be.

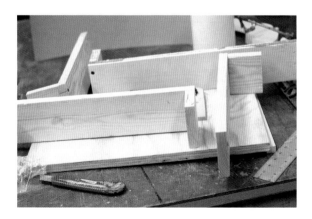

Figure 14-12: To make the box, we have four L-shaped wall pieces.

Figure 14-13: These can be clamped together as shown in the third photograph to make a box of any size.

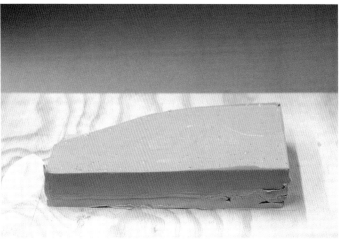

Figure 14-14: After pouring the first half, you have a block of silicone rubber on top and the clay base at the bottom. Remove all the clay, and flip the silicone rubber block upside down. Keep the model in the first mold piece, and apply mold release over everything.

Figure 14-15: Build your box back around this, and pour your second mold piece on top (shown here in a different color for clarity).

A **brush-up mold** involves brushing mold material onto a secured object. Often, the first coat, the **beauty coat**, is on thinly to capture the finest details and to avoid air bubbles. Subsequent coats are put on thicker, building up the thickness.

Figure 14-16: This safe dial is duplicated with a one-piece brush-up mold. First, it is secured to a flat surface. Photograph by Anna Warren.

Figure 14-17: One layer of silicone rubber is brushed on. Another layer of silicone rubber, colored pink, is brushed on top to thicken it up. Photograph by Anna Warren.

Figure 14-18: A rigid plastic resin paste is used to make a mother mold to support the rubber mold; it is shown in the last photograph cut in half to illustrate how it fits over the rubber mold. Photograph by Anna Warren.

Figures 14-19 to 14-22: These photographs show a three-piece mother mold that surrounds a one-piece RTV silicone mold that was brushed on. The mold was used to create a bust of Giuseppe Garibaldi out of polyurethane resin. *The Intelligent Homosexual's Guide to Capitalism and Socialism with a Key to the Scriptures,* the Guthrie Theatre, 2009.

Brush-up molds can be done in one piece (glove mold) or in multiple pieces, either by brushing on the pieces separately using a dam, or by cutting the mold when finished, usually by building up a "separation line." A mother mold can be built around the brush-up mold to help support it.

A brush-up mold made of a flexible mold material such as silicone rubber and supported by a rigid mother mold made of plaster uses a lot less flexible mold material than a box mold; because silicone rubber costs far more than plaster, you can keep your costs down this way.

In a **matrix mold**, the object is covered in a thickness of clay. A support shell is poured around it. The clay is removed, and the flexible mold material is poured in to fill the gap between the object and the support shell. The thickness of clay determines the thickness of your mold (usually around ½" for silicone rubbers). This combines the economy of brush-on molds with the speed and convenience of box molds.

Multi-Piece Molds

A two-piece mold is the easiest multi-piece mold to master. The first thing to decide is where to place the **seam**, which is where the two mold halves will join up. If you are making the mold with a rigid material, you must ensure that neither half has any undercuts. For both rigid and flexible molds, you must make sure there are no encapsulated areas that will get trapped. The seam will also create a line of material that needs to be trimmed. This material is known as **flashing**, and is caused by a tiny amount of material leaking between the two surfaces of the mold at the **parting line**, which is where they join together. With most materials, it is easy to trim away this flashing, but for areas of your cast that will get the most visual attention, you will want to keep the flashing away from there to leave those surfaces as pristine as possible. You usually want to place your seams along a line where they will be easiest to remove and noticed the least. You also may need to know where the casting agent will be poured into. Some molds and/or casting agents will also require you to place air vents in the mold.

When making a two-piece box mold, the most common technique is to build a base of oil-based clay up to where you want the seam on your object. Half of your object will be buried in this clay. Your mold material will then be poured over the top of this just as if you were doing a one-piece box mold. When it sets, you take everything out of the box and flip it all upside down. Remove the clay, and put the box walls back around your mold. You should now have a box containing half of your mold and your object, with the half that was buried in clay now facing up. Fill the box with mold material to make the second half of your mold.

It is vital to use the correct mold releases for every step. Even if you are using RTV silicone rubber, you are pouring silicone rubber on top of cured rubber; silicone rubber sticks to practically nothing *except itself*. Without mold release, you can easily create one giant block of rubber rather than two separate pieces.

Before you pour your second half, you usually want to add what are known as **registration marks** or **keys**. If you

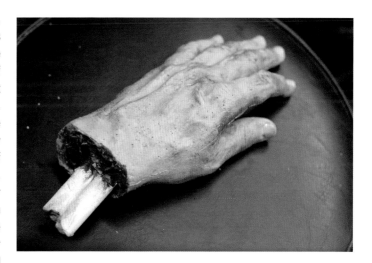

Figure 14-23: You can see minor flashing from the mold parting line on the right side of this hand running from the wrist, on top of the thumb, and up the side of the index finger.

carve a little dent in your clay base, it will become a raised shape on your first mold half. When you pour your second mold half, it will have a little dent in it. The raised shape will fit into the little dent when you put the two mold halves together, locking them in the correct position. Without it, your two mold halves will just be two flat surfaces free to slide around, and they may not line up precisely. Carve enough registration marks in your mold to ensure it locks in place; if you are doing a square box mold, one mark in every corner usually does the trick. You can find endless variations of shape, size, and style of registration marks if you watch other mold makers make a mold; there is no "correct" way to lay out and make your registration marks, but as you gain experience, you may develop better ways.

For a three-piece mold, you will bury all but the piece you wish to mold first. When that mold piece has been made, you keep the object in the mold and bury part of what is left in clay, so that only the second third is exposed. Finally, you can keep the object in the two finished mold pieces and pour your third mold piece. This process can be extended to make molds with however many pieces you need. This gets complicated

very quickly, and is rarely worth the time just to create a few props. Often, it is easier to break your object apart and make a bunch of one- or two-piece molds for each part, which are then assembled after being cast.

When doing a two-part brush-up mold, you will not bury your model in clay. Rather, you will use area separators known as **fences** or **mold dividers** along where you want to place your seam. These have traditionally been made of a thin wall of clay or thin pieces of metal (or thin pieces of metal with clay on the back to help support them). You can use stiff cardboard as well if you are making the mold out of a two-part compound or the like; a water-based material like plaster of Paris will soak the cardboard and possibly disintegrate it.

If the fence is made of clay, you can carve registration marks in just like with a box mold. If it is metal, you can glue pieces to it to make raised registration marks. Some mold makers use short lengths of metal and zigzag them along the seam, so the two pieces will only fit together the way they are supposed to.

As with a box mold, when making a three-piece mold, you will simply build two fences, one for each seam. When the first mold piece is dry, leave it on and build another fence where

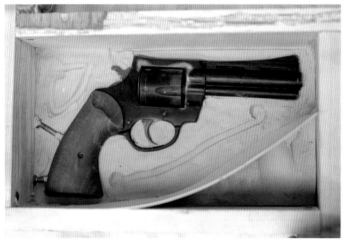 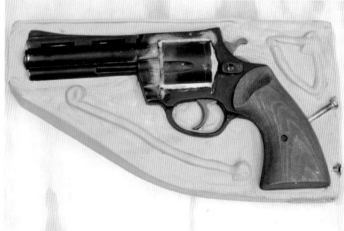

Figures 14-24 and 14-25: In the first image, you can see the registration marks carved in the clay base. In the second image, you can see how they became raised bumps on the silicone mold piece.

Figure 14-26: This helmet has a clay wall that has been built along where the prop maker wants to place the seam. Tiny hemispheres are carved in along the length to act as registration marks. Notice how the clay wall sticks out completely perpendicular to the object; this ensures the cleanest possible seam. Photograph and prop by Harrison Krix.

Figure 14-27: A layer of silicone rubber has been brushed on. It has been brushed over the clay wall as well, so the two halves will have a nice big flange where they are joined. When the rubber has set, the clay wall is removed, mold release is applied to the silicone rubber along the seam, and a new batch of silicone rubber is brushed on the other half. Photograph and prop by Harrison Krix.

the third seam will go. Finally, leave the first two mold pieces on, and simply brush the third one on.

Release Agent

If you pour plaster over a plaster piece, you will end up with one solid piece of plaster. You need a **mold release** or **release agent**, which is a thin film, usually brushed or sprayed on your model, that will prevent the wet plaster of your mold from bonding to the dry plaster of your model. Some combinations of molding and casting materials do not need mold releases, but many do. Success with molding and casting depends on knowing the right kind of mold release to use with the molding and casting compounds you are working with. A release agent is also needed when you are making multi-part molds and you need to pour a molding material on top of another mold piece.

Mold release is especially vital when dealing with any sort of plastic resin. After all, plastic resin is used as an adhesive for other materials, so you can expect them to stick to almost anything and be nearly impossible to remove once cured.

Traditionally, mold makers used fatty materials derived from plants, animals, and minerals, such as greases, metallic stearates, soaps, and waxes. Lard and tallow were used a lot, but they leave brush marks that transfer to your cast.

Waxes come from animals (beeswax), plants (Carnauba wax), or petroleum (paraffin wax). They work well on epoxies, polyurethane foam, and polyester resins. You can find aerosol spray versions as well. Waxes often work well in conjunction with PVA, which will be described later.

Green soap works well when pouring plaster against plaster, such as when you are making a two-piece plaster mold. It is also useful for other gypsum-based products and papier-mâché. Green soap is a soft liquid soap made from vegetable oils. Because of its use in the medical industry, it is often called "tincture of green soap." It may also be called "tattoo soap" because of its prevalence as a cleaner in tattoo parlors. A solution of castile soap works as well; castile soap is made from olive oil. Murphy's Oil Soap™ is another well-known product that works; the "oil" in the name refers to vegetable oil as opposed to petroleum-based oil.

Lecithin is derived from vegetable products, and some lecithin mold release sprays are approved for use with food (obviously, the casting material and the mold itself also need to be approved before you start casting food). Nonstick cooking sprays often use lecithin, such as Pam™ and Crisco™. Lecithin is useful on epoxy resin, urethane, some flexible and semi-flexible urethane foams, polyester, and polystyrene, particularly when you need to paint or coat the piece after demolding. Lecithin is useful as a release on plaster, particularly when used with clay and oil-based clay.

Petroleum jelly is a useful mold release. It is sometimes referred to by its most popular brand name, Vaseline™. As with lard, if you brush it on, the brush marks will show up on the surface of your cast. It is helpful to thin it with naphtha, mineral spirits, or mineral oil to make application easier and keep brush marks to a minimum. Alternatively, you can quickly run a heat gun over the petroleum jelly after adding it to level out the brush marks. Preformulated sprays especially made for molds can be found. It is good on polyurethane rubber, epoxy resin, polyester resin, silicone rubber, plaster, gypsum-based products, and papier-mâché.

PVA (polyvinyl alcohol) is a more modern mold release, and it is either sprayed or brushed on. Note that this is polyvinyl *alcohol* and *not* polyvinyl *acetate*, also abbreviated PVA, which is white and wood glue (I highly recommend *not* using glue to keep things from sticking to each other). PVA is effective on many epoxies, polyester resins, and polyurethanes. When the alcohol evaporates, it leaves a thin film of vinyl behind. PVA is often used in conjunction with a wax, and it usually requires a sealer used underneath. It can be built up with several applications, allowing drying time between coats. When casting plastic resins in plaster molds, whether polyester, polyurethane, or epoxy (including fiberglass work), it is often best to seal the plaster (with shellac, acrylic, or latex paint), wax the sealer, dust it with corn starch or baking soda, and then apply your PVA.

Powdered cornstarch or baking soda dusted over the surface can help in other situations as well. They help break the surface tension of the casting liquid, allowing it to flow more readily into tiny cracks and crevices. Soapy water added to the inside of a silicon rubber mold will do the same thing when casting plaster.

Silicone mold release is one of the newest types of mold releases. When it first appeared, it promised to replace all other mold releases. Silicone, after all, sticks only to silicone. It turned out not to be perfect, though. It transfers to the casting, which prohibits paint and other coatings from sticking. Since it is sprayed in a fine mist, it also travels throughout the air in the shop and gets on everything, contaminating all your surfaces and props. If you take the time to clean your cast afterward, or if your piece needs no further coloring, then silicone mold release can work great.

Any type of mold release can remain on your casting when it is fully cured or dried, particularly on polyurethane resins, which are very sticky. Dishwashing detergent and warm water will remove most wax-based release agents. Silicone-based mold releases may require acetone (not paint thinner or mineral spirits) to fully remove all the material.

Finally, thin sheets and films, such as polyethylene film (Saran wrap) or aluminum foil, can serve as effective mold releases when you do not need a perfect replication of detail between the two surfaces.

Mold releases that are applied every time will build up in a mold and need to be cleaned out periodically. This cleaning wears down the mold. Often, you can skip the application of mold release every so often; say, you apply mold release for three castings in a row, then avoid it for the fourth casting. The buildup of mold release residue can also slowly combine with residues of your casting resin, forming a difficult-to-remove encrustment (known as "carbonization"). Finally, most mold releases do not remain on just the mold. Portions will transfer to the casting surface, which needs to be cleaned prior to painting or coating. Some mold releases, such as waxes, are impossible to clean without removing part of the surface of your cast piece, and should only be used when you do not need to do any additional painting or coating to your piece.

Figure 14-28: When mixing any "two-part" molding or casting compound, you should measure each part in a separate container, and then pour them both into a third container. This ensures a better mix, since a small amount of each material will stick to the sides of their original containers. If the two parts are mixed by weight, remember to account for the weight of the container itself. In this photograph, each part was measured in disposable cups that can be thrown away, while they are mixed in a plastic bucket that is easily cleaned once the material has cured.

Thus, there is no perfect mold release for every situation. In addition to choosing your molding and casting materials based on the size, shape, and substance of your original and the form and material you want your cast to be, you also need to consider what types of mold releases are compatible with your process and whether you need to paint or coat your prop further. You need to consider all the specifics of your project at hand; choosing materials based on what you have around the shop or on what you think "the pros" use will only lead to costly mistakes. The chart included in this chapter will help you with some general guidelines for compatibility of certain mold releases with various molding and casting materials.

One trick for aiding release from your molds is to always cast rigid materials in flexible molds, and flexible materials in hard molds. It makes it easier to pop or peel the piece out of the mold. You may cast rigid materials in a rigid mold provided you have a way to pull it out and there are absolutely no undercuts, but I have seen far too many prop makers end up with a rigid cast permanently trapped inside a rigid mold; a two-piece mold or a flexible mold material is often the better choice. Many rigid materials, particularly the casting plastics, reach a point where they hold their shape but are still a little flexible; it is helpful to demold them at this point and allow them to finish curing to full rigidity outside of the mold.

Sealing Agents

If the object you are making a mold of is porous, such as plaster, stone, concrete, or wood, the surface will need to be sealed first. Sealers include shellac, paste wax, and petroleum jelly thinned with mineral spirits. Companies also make proprietary products that are nonintrusive and can be washed off the model after the mold is complete. Do not use shellac when making a mold out of silicone rubber. Plaster and some other materials can also be sealed with paint. As with mold releases, be aware that thick sealing agents will alter the appearance of your object.

| casting material | mold materials | | | | | |
| | rigid molds | flexible molds | | | | |
	plaster	alginate/agar	gelatin	latex	polyurethane rubber	silicone rubber**
Slip Clay	none*	not recommended	not recommended	not recommended	not recommended	not recommended
Neoprene	none*	not recommended	not recommended	not recommended	not recommended	not recommended
Latex	none*	not recommended	not recommended	PVA and wax	not recommended	none
Wax	none	not recommended	not recommended	none	none	none
Hot melt glue	soak mold in water for about an hour	not recommended	not recommended	not recommended	none	none
RTV silicone rubber	none (sealer recommended)	none	none	none	none	wax, lecithin
Plaster	petroleum jelly, oil soap, or wax	none	none	none	none (oil soap reduces surface bubbles)	none
Papier-mâché	petroleum jelly, oil soap, or wax	not recommended	not recommended	not recommended	none	none
Polyester Resin/ fiberglass	Wax + cornstarch + PVA (sealer recommended)	not recommended	not recommended	PVA and wax, silicon or lecithin	silicone or PVA	none
epoxy resin	Wax + cornstarch + PVA (sealer recommended); silicone	none	none	PVA, silicon or lecithin	silicone or PVA	none
polyurethane plastic	Wax + cornstarch + PVA (sealer recommended); silicone	not recommended	not recommended	Wax + cornstarch + PVA; silicone	silicone or PVA	none
polyurethane foam	Wax + cornstarch + PVA (sealer recommended); silicone	not recommended	not recommended	Wax + cornstarch + PVA	silicone	none/wax

* For absorption casting, plaster can NOT have any mold releases used.
** For silicone molds, mold release is rarely necessary, but it will extend the longevity of the silicone mold if you use it. A light coating of wax or lecithin is all that is needed.

Casting Methods

The **impression coat** or **beauty coat** is a first coat of a molding or casting material applied carefully to capture all details fully without any air bubbles. This coat can be thickened with further coats, or the entire interior can be filled at once. Sometimes, a prop maker may use a cheaper material as the interior filler, or the same material with an inert filler material added, to save money; since the beauty coat is the only visible portion of an opaque casting; what the inside looks like is of little consequence.

Gravity Casting

Many casting methods exist, some of which rely on high pressures, but for the prop maker, the most useful is **gravity casting**. In gravity casting, the casting material is simply poured into the top and left to harden. Gravity causes the liquid material to flow all the way to the bottom of the mold.

A **slush cast** is when the liquid material is slushed around so that it coats the sides of the mold cavity but does not create a solid piece. This can be done by holding the mold in your arms and swirling it around so that gravity keeps the liquid flowing along the sides; take care not to spill the casting liquid out of the sprue. Some casting materials allow you to use a brush to push the liquid up the sides of the mold; you may need to do this continually for a few minutes until the casting medium has cured enough to cease flowing down. If the mold is able to be capped on top (that is, fully closed off), then you can rotate the mold fully around to create a completely closed, but hollow object. You can buy (or build) a device that holds your mold and automatically rotates it in a pattern which ensures that all sides receive an equal thickness of casting compound. This is known as **roto-casting**. These roto-casting devices may be operated by a simple hand crank, or may run on motors.

In **absorption casting** (known as **slipcasting** when talking about clay), the material being cast becomes hard through the evaporation of the solvent (including water) used to liquefy it. As such, it begins setting on the surface where the solvent can be absorbed or evaporated, with the center being the last to solidify. If you pour it in a mold that can absorb water, then it will develop a skin around the walls of the mold; if you pour the excess liquid out after it has solidified to your desired thickness, you will now have a hollow shell in the shape of what you molded.

Plaster is essentially the only material you can use to make a mold for absorption casting. Materials that can be absorption cast include liquid clay slip and rubber, including both natural latex and synthetics such as neoprene. The plaster mold must be completely dry, which occurs a few days to a week after it has hardened. A damp plaster mold will be cold and heavy; it will be at room temperature and much lighter when it is fully dry.

Do not use any mold releases when doing absorption casting. Products such as petroleum jelly will clog the pores of the plaster and prevent it from absorbing any water; if you use latex or neoprene, it will also prevent the outermost surface from curing. As the material cures, it shrinks and pulls away slightly from the mold wall, thus releasing itself and negating the need for an additional mold release. If you are casting rubber, you can have slight undercuts in the mold as the cast material has enough stretch and give to pull away.

For a one-piece mold, you need a level surface so that the liquid material can fill the mold cavity completely without spilling over the edge. For a two-piece mold, it helps to have a sprue. As the material dries, it shrinks, and the level of the liquid casting material drops. With a sprue, that just means the excess length of the hardened sprue will get shorter. If you don't have a sprue, the mold wall at the very top of the wall may not have enough casting material. If this is a problem, you can "top off" your mold periodically as it sets in order to maintain the correct amount of liquid inside.

You can test the progression of the thickness of your casting by cutting a cross section off the very top of your piece. Once it has gotten to the desired thickness, you can empty the mold and allow it to sit for a few more hours to fully harden.

This method leaves a hole in the exterior of your casting where the mold material has been poured out. You can fill this hole once the piece has fully hardened if you want a completely solid-looking piece. Alternatively, after you empty the mold of the excess casting material, you can pour a small amount back in. Plug the top of your mold, and turn it upside down. The extra casting material you poured in should flow down and rest on top of the plug, solidifying along with the rest of the casting.

Air Bubbles

A **vent** is a passageway that lets air out to prevent air entrapment and allows excess material to escape. A **sprue** is the spout or channel where you pour your casting material. A **gate** is the passage that connects the sprue to the mold cavity. "Sprue" also refers to the excess material that solidifies in the sprue and gates that will be removed when the casting material solidifies. Not all molds require vents. Some molds are open at the top because that part of the object (usually the bottom because such molds are cast upside down) is meant to be flat; when the material is filled to the top of such a mold, it will level out, and that open area will solidify into a flat surface.

For many molds, the sprue also acts as the vent. You want your sprue to lead to the highest point of your mold, otherwise your casting material will not fill the entire mold. When your sprue acts as your only vent, it will need to be large enough to allow air to escape as the casting liquid enters.

Vents, sprues, and gates can be sculpted directly on your object. They can also be sculpted in clay once your object is being molded. You can also attach items in your box mold that will leave passageways in the mold material. For instance, a flexible tube or a dowel will leave you a nice clean tunnel when molded.

When you pour casting material into your mold, you are not filling an empty mold; you are replacing the air in the mold with casting material. If you neglect to pay attention to this, you may trap the air in your mold. In many one-piece molds, the opening you pour your casting material into is quite large, and the air has plenty of places to escape. In two-piece molds, the sprue may be rather thin. Vents may be needed to allow the air to escape through a hole that is not having material poured into it. This vent hole should exhaust to a point as high or higher than your sprue hole, otherwise your casting material will pour out of it before your mold is completely filled. If you need a vent for a low point in your mold, carve it out so it leads up to the top of the mold.

In some molds, it may help to tilt the mold while you are pouring or after you have poured to let the air out. Air floats up in casting material, so if it floats up to a point where it is walled in by the mold material, it is trapped and has nowhere to go.

Air is also introduced into your mold through the casting material itself. Most casting materials require you to stir them to activate; either stirring a powder with water, or stirring a two-part compound together. You can easily stir air into the mixture if you are not careful; keep your stirrer submerged as you rotate it to avoid introducing air in.

Air bubbles may still be in your mix. Before pouring, tap the sides of your mixing container, or vibrate it a bit to help these air bubbles float to the surface. If you have a whole film of bubbles on top, scrape it off and discard it. When you pour, pour in a thin stream, and aim for a single spot. Let the casting material flow over the mold surface rather than pouring it directly onto every square inch. Empty your container as high as you can above the sprue hole; the air bubbles have an easier time escaping the thin stream that runs from your cup to the mold than from the large mass inside the mold. Tap and vibrate the mold once it is full to shake loose all the bubbles and allow them to rise to the top.

A beauty coat is sometimes helpful to coat the walls of the mold cavity evenly with your mold material, so that when you pour the rest in, you cannot get any air bubbles to the walls. For opaque casting materials, air bubbles that are trapped inside are of less consequence than the ones that stick to the surface and cause visual defects.

Some materials are just too viscous for air bubbles to float out naturally. Many silicone rubbers are very viscous, as are some polyurethane resins too. You may need to vacuum-degas the mixed liquid before pouring it. The molding or casting material is mixed, and then placed in a vacuum chamber, which is a rigid enclosure that can suck all the air out of the inside with a vacuum pump. By letting the mixture sit inside the vacuum chamber for a few seconds or minutes (depending on the recommendations of the manufacturer for your specific material), the air bubbles will be removed.

Materials

Some materials are rigid, and some are flexible. Some can even dry into rubber or expand into a foam. Some dry from the outside in from the absorption or evaporation of water, while others cure through a chemical reaction. Some materials do not work well with other materials. Choosing what you make your mold out of and what you cast your prop in can be a complex question encompassing a number of considerations about what the original object is made out of, what your prop needs to do and what it needs to look like, the amount of time you have, the safety infrastructure of your shop, your budget, what materials are available to you, and what your expertise in the various materials are. In short, there is no one "right" material to mold and cast with.

Rigid Materials

Plaster

Plaster of Paris remains a highly economical, intuitive, and less toxic material for mold making in props shops. For one-piece and simple two-piece molds with no undercuts, even beginner artisans can grasp the concepts needed to make molds out of plaster.

Plaster has the rare ability among mold-making materials to absorb water into itself, making it almost uniquely suited for casting materials that cure through absorption, such as neoprene, slip clay, and latex. When absorption-casting, no mold release should be used as this will create a barrier for the water to be absorbed.

Different types of plaster include gypsum plaster (also known as plaster of Paris), lime plaster, and cement plaster. Props people use plaster of Paris almost exclusively, though there are many different types with very different properties.

Figures 14-29 and 14-30: A two-piece plaster mold.

The largest manufacturer of plaster in North America by far is United States Gypsum Company (USG), and props artisans often refer to their brand names when discussing different types of plaster. In the following chart, you can see a few of their plaster products and how radically different they can be. Success in using plaster involves determining exactly what you need and choosing a plaster that will fulfill those needs.

Soft and porous plasters (less dense) are useful for waste and temporary molds. Regular molds should be made out of light but strong plasters (the ones in the middle of the chart). Molds for vacuum forming (bucks) do not need any absorptive properties, but do need incredible strength to withstand the vacuum pressures. Castings usually want a plaster that is hard and has a surface that resists absorption.

Plaster is used in a liquid form (with a consistency close to cream) for molding and casting. It can also be mixed a little thicker for slush and rotational casting. As it sets, it reaches a point where it is more like a plastic material, with a consistency of butter or soft clay. During this short period, it can be manipulated, troweled, and moved by hand or with tools, and it will stay put on vertical or even upside-down surfaces. Some plasters are manufactured to go from a liquid to a solid rather quickly, while others can remain in this plastic state for quite a while. If you are casting in a slush mold or making a brush-up mold, you want a plaster that maintains a plastic state for a long time.

To mix plaster, first make sure your plaster is dry and well-sifted. Old plaster or plaster that has been stored in a damp environment will form lumps, and may be unusable because it has already absorbed moisture. Always use breathing protection and adequate ventilation when working with powdered plaster.

The ratio of water to plaster you use varies depending on what plaster you are using; most manufacturers will give the ratio in terms of weight. More water leads to a more brittle piece of plaster. Less water leads to a denser piece of plaster, which may be nice for castings, but for molds, it will be less able to absorb water when doing absorption-casting. The water should be between 70°F and 100°F. Colder water will make the

Plaster type	density (dry)	dry compressive strength	Water:plaster ratio (by weight)	set time (machine mix)
USG White Art Plaster	69 lb/ft3	2000 psi	70:100	27-37 min
USG Lab Dental Plaster	69 lb/ft3	2000 psi	70:100	6-9 min
USG No. 1 Moulding Plaster	69 lb/ft3	2000 psi	70:100	27-37 min
USG No. 1 Pottery Plaster	69 lb/ft3	2400 psi	70:100	14-24 min
USG No. 1 Casting Plaster	72.5 lb/ft3	2400 psi	65:100	27-37 min
USG Puritan Pottery Plaster	72 lb/ft3	2700 psi	66:100	14-24 min
USG Duramold	75 lb/ft3	2900 psi	62:100	14-24 min
USG Tuf Cal	85.6 lb/ft3	4300 psi	50:100	27-37 min
USG Hydrocal White	90 lb/ft3	5000 psi	45:100	25 min
USG Statuary Hydrocal	96 lb/ft3	6500 psi	40:100	25-35 min
USG Ultracal 60	97.5 lb/ft3	5000 psi	39:100	75-90 min
USG Ultracal 30	99 lb/ft3	6000 psi	38:100	25-35 min
USG Hydro-Stone	108.7 lb/ft3	10000 psi	32:100	17-20 min
USG Tuf Stone	112 lb/ft3	10000 psi	32:100	25-30 min
USG Dry Stone*	128 lb/ft3	10000 psi	20:100	5-10 min

*Dry Stone is a mix of plaster and EVA polymers, making it fully dry and paintable within two hours.

plaster set up more slowly, while warmer water will make it set up quicker; very cold water will keep it from setting altogether, while water over a certain temperature will start increasing the set time again. You do not want the plaster to set up so quickly that you do not have time to stir it and pour it before it begins hardening.

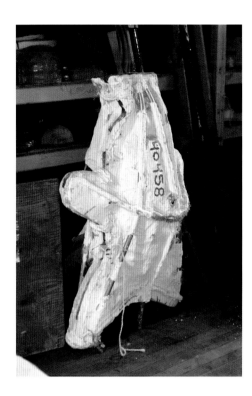

Figure 14-31: Larger plaster molds may need reinforcement; heavy wire, rebar, or other metal rods can be embedded in the plaster while it is wet. In the mold above from Costume Armour, the bars also serve as handles for easy maneuverability.

It helps to mix plaster in a plastic bucket so that the dried plaster can just be broken off by flexing the bucket. With your measured amount of water in the bucket, begin sifting the plaster in.

Once you have added your plaster, do not start mixing it yet. Let it soak for one to two minutes. Tap the sides of the bucket to loosen some air bubbles, and then begin mixing. For batches under 5 lb, you can mix by hand (wearing gloves); this helps you feel for lumps that you can break apart with your fingers. An egg beater or wooden spoon is also useful. Larger batches can be mixed with an electric drill and a propeller or squirrel cage. Stir vigorously, but do not whip it or create a vortex, otherwise air bubbles will be created in the plaster that may show up in the final piece. Make sure to break up all the lumps of dried plaster while stirring. The longer you mix, the stronger the plaster will be (and the shorter the setting time will be), which is good for casts, but reduces the absorptivity of molds. Generally, mixing time is two to five minutes (after soaking for one minute). When fully mixed, the plaster will have a creamy consistency with no lumps. Give the bucket another few quick taps, and skim the layer of air bubbles off the top. You are now ready to pour.

Pour the plaster in the lowest part of your mold, and be careful not to let it splash. Allow the plaster to flow *over* the mold's surface instead of pouring it *onto* the surface. It may be helpful to pour a little bit in, and then smear that plaster all over the surface with your hands. This informal beauty coat will help make sure plaster has made its way into the finest cracks and crevices without trapping any air bubbles. Continue pouring the rest until the mold is full.

With the "islands" or "sea level" method of mixing plaster, you do not weigh your materials. You simply start sifting plaster into the water. It will land on the water for a second, and then sink down. At a certain point, the plaster will no longer sink down, and will remain above the level of the water (forming the above-mentioned "islands"). This indicates that you have added enough plaster, and you can start mixing.

This is not a consistent method of ensuring you have the proper ratio, and you have less control over achieving the desired hardness, softness, or absorption of plaster you may need. For simple castings where consistency is not necessary, this method can save time; just be aware that mixing plaster this way will most likely not give you the properties that your plaster promises.

Let the excess plaster harden in the bottom of the bucket. Never *ever* pour wet plaster down the drain, because it will harden inside the drain and create a blockage that no drain cleaner can break. You cannot dilute it once you have poured it down a drain either because it is a chemical reaction, not a physical one. It can be helpful to have a waste bucket where you dump all excess liquid plaster and allow it to set.

You can achieve some success with brush-up molding in plaster. Rather than pouring it, let it sit for a few seconds or minutes. At a certain point, the consistency changes from a liquid cream to more of a thick paste. You can scoop this up and smear it on the sides of whatever you are molding. It will run down, but continue shoveling it on the top until it hardens enough to stay in place.

As plaster sets, it heats up. In a large enough mass, it will generate enough heat to burn the skin. It should set in about 15–30 minutes. When it is cool to the touch, it can be demolded.

At this point, though it is "set," it is still damp. Fully drying out a piece of plaster can take anywhere from 24 hours to a

Figure 14-32: Working a beauty coat of plaster over the mold piece before pouring the rest of the plaster in.

week. You can tell the difference between damp plaster and dried plaster, because a piece of damp plaster feels cool, while dried plaster feels room temperature. Additionally, a piece of dried plaster the same size as damp plaster is far lighter in weight.

You need dry plaster if you want to paint it or glue something to it. Dry plaster is also vital if you are using it for absorption-casting. You can dry plaster in a cool oven (no more than 100°F) or under lamps; you can also set up fans to increase air movement, but do not blow them directly on the plaster pieces, as this will make them dry unevenly.

Plaster also comes impregnated on rolls of gauze. These are meant for making medical casts, but they are extremely versatile for the props artisan. Cut the bandages (as they are sometimes called) into strips. Submerge the full length of a strip into a tub of water. Remove it from the water, and lay it over the side of tub for a few minutes. A "slurry" will begin to form as the plaster becomes hydrated. Lay the plaster bandage on the surface, and rub your finger over it in a circular motion so that the plaster can fully impregnate both the fabric and the material underneath. Cover the surface with a complete layer of the bandages, slightly overlapping each one with the next. On the second layer, run the strips perpendicular to the first layer.

Plaster bandages are typically helpful for making shells around a flexible mold piece.

You can find newer products that combine plaster with polymers. Their use is the same as straight plaster, but they have almost no drying time. Other gypsum-based products include fillers such as Durham's Rock Hard Water Putty™, which has been used for many decades by props people.

Flexible Materials

Gelatin

Gelatin is made from the collagen inside animal skin and bones. It can be used as a mold-making material, though you are limited to mostly plaster or wax casts. It can also be used to

Figure 14-33: A roll of plaster-impregnated gauze.

cast edible props since it is an ingredient in many foods itself (provided it is prepared and used in a food-safe environment, that is, not the same props shop where you use chemicals and make saw dust). The gelatin you buy in the grocery store, such as Jello™ or Knox™, is suitable, though you will want to alter the recipe to use more gelatin powder and less water. The gelatin is fairly fragile, though it is possible to get multiple castings out of a single mold if you are careful and allow the mold to dry thoroughly in between casts. One of the advantages of gelatin molds is that if the mold breaks, the pieces can be placed back in the double boiler, melted down, and reused, almost infinitely.

To make gelatin for molding and casting, purchase unflavored gelatin from a food or drug store, and adapt the directions to use more gelatin and less water.

Gelatin molds and casts can be placed in the fridge or freezer to harden them back up. They can be remelted for unlimited reuse. Casts made from gelatin are rarely permanent, and the stage lights used in theatres and studios, as well as the heat of the outdoor sun on location shoots, will soften and eventually melt the gelatin casts. Rather, it is commonly used to make "breakaway" prosthetics, such as the eyes torn from Gloucester's face in *King Lear*.

Alginate

Alginate is a natural polymer found in cells of brown algae, which are commonly referred to as "seaweed." It usually comes in powdered form that can be turned into a flexible mold rubber simply by mixing it with the appropriate quantity of water. Alginate is nontoxic and safe to use against skin, making it a popular choice for life casting; in fact, alginate is used by dentists to take impressions of your teeth.

Alginate begins shrinking as soon as it is mixed with water. This can be beneficial in some respects. Because it shrinks around the model you are making a mold of, it can capture extremely fine detail. However, it does not stop shrinking, and becomes unusable as a mold within 2–3 hours of setting (wrapping in damp paper towels and refrigerating may increase the life up to eight hours). You cannot make permanent molds out of alginate. Some artisans actually allow an alginate mold to continue shrinking to make a cast that is noticeably smaller than the original. This is not useful for making exact scale replicas, as the alginate does not shrink in a predictable or proportional manner, but it can be helpful in making a smaller object that generally reminds you of the larger original.

As alginate maintains a damp surface throughout its life, you cannot use a casting material inhibited by water, such as polyester or polyurethane resin.

Agar

Agar (or agar-agar) is a vegetable gelatin derived from marine algae. Like alginate, it is a polysaccharide derived from algae; alginate comes from brown algae, while agar comes from red algae. A pure agar mold is far weaker than an animal gelatin mold. It is more commonly used as the main component of a moulage compound. Popular brands include Douglas and Sturgess Moulage and Plastico. Like alginate, it is well suited to making molds from body parts, and like gelatin, it is suitable for making casts from plaster or wax. It is also reusable by reheating and melting it.

Latex

Latex, or natural rubber, is extracted from rubber trees from Southeast Asia. It is processed with ammonia and water to form a milky white or grey viscous liquid. As the liquids evaporate, it becomes a highly elastic solid; the word *rubber* comes from the substance that is formed.

Latex has long been a staple of props shops, costume crafters, and special effects makeup artists because it is an inexpensive single-component system (no need to measure and mix multiple parts). A certain percentage of people are allergic to latex, though, and others can develop allergies with repeated exposure. This needs to be considered not just for the artisans working with it, but for the actors and crew that may need to handle the finished prop. Latex gives off ammonia (and sometimes formaldehyde) fumes while drying, so work with plenty of ventilation. For larger jobs or close quarters, you can also get respirator cartridges designed for ammonia, though always be wary that people around you may not be wearing respirators.

Latex can also be slow to apply. Many latex formulations need to be brushed on. It can take up to 20 coats of latex to form a skin of sufficient thickness, and each layer needs to dry in between coats, which can take four hours. One final disadvantage is its tendency to shrink anywhere from ten to twenty percent.

Latex comes in a variety of formulations for different tasks. Many standard latex formulations can only be brushed or sprayed on. More specific formulas can be cast (through absorption casting) or slush cast. Some latex-based rug backing products or latex glues can even be used in a pinch for glove and brush-on molds. Latex varies in the amount of "solids" it contains. The higher the solids content, the greater its ability to withstand tearing.

As with other molding and casting materials, latex can be thickened with various agents.

Latex is good for making molds to cast plaster, cement, wax, low-temperature metals, and, to a limited extent, plastic resins. Because latex shrinks around the model, it captures the finest of details. Latex is often brushed on to make a **glove mold**; it is brushed over the outside in multiple layers until it forms a "glove." Remember to let each layer fully dry between applications. You can tell it is dry when the milky white areas have completely disappeared. It cannot be speeded up with a heat gun or by baking. Like a glove, it can be peeled off the model by rolling it inside out. Dust it with baby powder or corn starch first to keep it from sticking to itself.

Latex is also frequently used as a brush-on coating for flexible materials like soft foam. It gives a continuous skin to the surface to help hold paint better, but remains elastic and flexible so that it does not flake off when the foam squishes and squashes.

You can make reinforced castings with latex. Use casting latex, not molding latex. Brush one layer over the inside of a plaster mold. Repeat until you have four layers. When these are dry, brush a layer of latex, lay in a piece of cheesecloth or similar gauze (use several pieces if the shape is complicated; overlap each piece slightly, but try to keep the cheesecloth as flat as possible), and then brush another layer of latex immediately

Figure 14-34: Latex "horns" for a piece of KISS armor are cast in a plaster mold. Molds and castings by Costume Armour, Inc.

over the top of this. Let this dry, then add at least five more layers, letting each layer dry before adding the next. If you want it thicker, you can add another layer of gauze after the ninth layer, and then coat that with around three more layers. The cheesecloth has a grain and a bias; you can work with the bias if you want your piece to be able to stretch, or apply with the grain for greater strength.

Finished latex pieces can be dusted with cornstarch to keep the latex from sticking to itself.

You can vulcanize your latex for additional strength. When all the layers are completely dry, simmer your piece in hot water for around 15–20 minutes **without boiling** it. Dab the water off and let it dry while fitted back in the mold. Some latex can be vulcanized by heating it to 120°F for four hours, and others you can just let sit for 3 days.

Certain forms of latex, particularly casting latex, come prevulcanized; always check the instructions of the specific latex you purchase. Prevulcanized latex gives you a final piece with the same strength and durability of vulcanized rubber without the need for a separate heating process.

Latex is great for casting plaster because it can withstand the heat created during the curing process, and it captures excellent detail. No mold release is needed. It is also good for other hot melts, such as wax, vinyl, and hot melt glue. It often requires a rigid mother mold around it to hold its shape when casting heavier items.

Plastic resins generate too much heat and have chemical reactions with the latex to cause it to degrade with every pour. Still, with a properly vulcanized latex, you can get 20–50 pieces out, which is often good enough for props.

Latex has a limited shelf life of a year if kept in a cool dry place. It will turn a cottage cheese consistency or develop a putrid odor when it spoils, and spoilage is irreversible.

Vinyl

Vinyl is a hot melt compound that can make flexible molds. This type of vinyl is often called **hot pour vinyl** to distinguish it from other forms of vinyl, such as vinyl fabric. It can be melted at temperatures of 300°C–340°C and poured at 280°C–300°C. A popular brand is Vinamold™. The mold material can be remelted and poured again for another mold. It needs to be heated in a double boiler rather than over direct heat, and the high temperature needed requires oil rather than water as the liquid in the bottom boiler. Since silicone has appeared, vinyl as a molding compound has largely fallen out of use. The toxicity of its fumes and difficulty in melting it has also contributed to its decline in popularity and usefulness. It can, however, be useful for casting jiggly and translucent objects. It is used a lot to make fishing lures, so is often found in fishing supply stores.

Resins

A plastic resin is the liquid form of a plastic that serves as a precursor to the solid forms. For molding and casting, when we say resin, we mean the systems that involve two liquids which are mixed together and harden into a solid over time. The three that prove most common and useful to the prop maker are polyurethane resin, polyester resin, and epoxy resin.

In the two-part system, one of the liquids is the actual resin, while the other is the hardener or **catalyst**. In some cases, you can alter the amount of catalyst used to speed up or slow down the hardening time, while with other products, you must mix the two components in exact proportions.

Each of the three kinds of resins has its own properties, and within each kind, you can find a multitude of properties as well. Some resins turn into a rigid plastic, while some become flexible. Some turn to foam, some to rubber, and some to foam rubber. Some are clear, some translucent, and others opaque. Various working properties can be different as well; some set up very quickly, whereas others remain liquid for a long time to allow you to do extensive work with it, such as brushing it over a large surface.

Since these types of resins are also used as adhesives, it should come as no shock that they require plenty of mold release to keep from sticking to everything. Make sure that if the resin overflows, leaks, or spills out of your mold when pouring or curing that it doesn't run onto anything nice.

All resins are harmful and toxic in a number of ways. While in a liquid form and curing, they release irritating and toxic fumes. You need proper ventilation not just when working with them, but while waiting for them to cure. In many cases, it is best to sequester the molds to a separate room or chamber with its own exhaust (such as a chemical hood) where no one can breathe the fumes while they are curing. Remember too that the containers and mixers you use to mix them will have liquid residue left in them that will off-gas indefinitely. These should be sealed in a trash bag and removed from the room as soon as possible. The fumes are invisible and have no smell, so prop makers believe they are safe. Make no mistake, though; people have died from inhaling polyurethane fumes.

The liquids are harmful as well, and will irritate the skin on contact, possibly causing an allergic reaction. Resin allergies can be nasty things, causing rashes, open and oozing sores, and even the closing up of your throat. Once developed, it is irreversible, and you will have a reaction to even the slightest exposure. Wear the proper gloves (*not* latex or cotton gloves), as well as chemically resistant sleeves, splash goggles, and even a face shield in some cases. Respirators and proper ventilation are vital; with polyurethane resins in particular, you cannot see any vapors or smell any odor, but you are most certainly being exposed to toxins in the air. Take the same precautions when sanding, machining, or cutting cured resins to keep the particulates off of you and out of your lungs. All cured resin will contain uncured particles within that are liberated as you turn it to dust.

Many less toxic alternatives exist for polyurethane and polyester resins, and more are introduced into the market every year. Always ask yourself whether you really need the specific properties that only these resins can give, or whether a safer material will satisfy the needs of your prop.

Some resins, especially polyester and urethane, have their cure times extended or even inhibited by exposure to moisture. You want to make sure your mold is completely dry before pouring it in, especially if you are using a porous mold material that can hold water even when the surface feels dry, such as plaster. It can even be affected by using a wooden stirring stick that contains moisture; use only the driest wood, or better yet, a plastic stirring stick (polyethylene sticks, such as HDPE or UHMW, have the added advantage that cured resin will not stick as much to them).

The other big area that is exposed to moisture is the top part that is exposed to air. Humidity in the air will keep the surface slightly tacky. This is fine if the top is a sprue that will be cut or trimmed off. But if the top is the final surface, that's a problem. You can buy surface curing agents that float to the top of your resin and form a barrier against the air; in clear resins, these will cloud the surface, so they may not be desirable. You can also buy aerosols that you spray on after the resin has mostly cured; again, these form a barrier and allow the curing to complete. To avoid adding more chemicals to the mix, you can top your mold with a piece of glass or thick plastic (covered in mold release) to cut off the air; this will also give you a smooth flat surface, though it may also trap air bubbles. Alternatively, seal off the top with a piece of shrink wrap or cling wrap that is not touching the surface of the resin.

Polyurethane

Polyurethane resins have been around for awhile, but it was not until the 1980s when efficiency breakthroughs in their manufacture made them more economical to use in prop making. Polyurethanes have dominated the art and hobby market since then, resulting in a dizzying array of products; some companies can have nearly 40 different kinds of casting polyurethanes.

They come in a wide variety of strengths and hardnesses. Their forms can range from foams and rubbers to hard plastics. They can be poured, brushed, or sprayed on. They are very easy to use. Polyurethane can reproduce extremely fine detail and cure incredibly quickly (compared to other resins). Their disadvantages are that they will stick to just about everything. Mold releases are vital when using them, and it is necessary to work them into every nook and cranny. They are moisture-sensitive, and may remain tacky or bubble if the mold is a bit damp or it is a humid day. They have a very limited shelf life, and the components only really last five to six months after opening them.

They are also among the most toxic of the casting compounds used. Shops that produce polyurethane pieces on a regular basis also have the safety infrastructure in place to minimize the risks. They do not give off *any* odor while curing, so many people do not think they are toxic. Because they have no recognizable scent, you cannot use a respirator with them, because if the respirator is not sealed right, you would not be able to tell that you are breathing toxic air. You need to work with a lot of ventilation, such as a spray booth, chemical hood, or glove box. You can also use a supplied-air respirator.

Polyurethanes use isocyanates in their manufacturing, and will out-gas them as they cure. These can be off-gassing at least 24 hours after you pour it, and up to several years if it wasn't mixed correctly. The pieces must remain in a separate area as they cure. The implements you use to stir and measure the polyurethane should be disposable, because these will also off-gas toxins for quite a while, particularly because the stuff left in cups is not fully mixed.

Isocyanates can cause isocyanate asthma, which severely limits your life, and severe reactions to polyurethanes while casting have caused a number of deaths. All isocyanates have the same toxic effects, though some manufacturers switch their polyurethane to an isocyanate that has not been fully tested to avoid having to print the toxic information on the label.

Exposure to the fumes or skin contact with the resin will also lead to sensitization. This can happen after one exposure or after decades of use. Some people have worked with polyurethane resin for over 20 years with no ill effects before they develop a sudden allergic reaction to even the tiniest exposure. This means they can no longer work with or be in a shop using plastic resins without having their skin break out into rashes or even open and oozing sores.

Water-based polyurethanes are a touch safer. A few forward-looking companies are discovering ways to manufacture polyurethanes without isocyanates. Though these are so far limited to varnishes and other emulsions, it is worth keeping an eye on to see whether a viable casting alternative is ever developed.

Always use the least toxic alternative that will get the job done. While polyurethanes seem to be a miracle solution to every problem, there are often cases where the strength they give is simply overkill for a prop. Also, if you are not set up to work with them safely, you just need to avoid them altogether.

Polyurethane resins come in a range of white, off-white and brown colors. You can get clear polyurethane resins, though these are exceptionally toxic (even more so than regular polyurethane resin). You can also find black resin. Colorants exist that let you tint the liquid resin so that you can cast it in whatever color you wish. Always mix your colorants, as well as any fillers or thickening agents, into the resin first before mixing in the catalyst. Brand names of polyurethane plastic include Smooth-On's Smooth-Cast™ and TASK™, Aluminite Super Plastic Casting Resin, Por-a-Mold and Por-a-Kast, Model-Pro casting resin, TAP Quik-Cast, and Polycraft casting resin.

Polyurethane is best cast in silicone molds. For plaster molds, the plaster needs to be dry. After sealing the plaster with shellac or lacquer, apply a coat of PVA followed by paste wax that you buff.

You can also use latex, polyethylene, polyurethane rubber, or fiberglass molds. These require a liquid or paste wax, or silicone mold release. For use with plaster molds, dusting a layer of corn starch or baking soda is preferred. You can also brush a thin layer of liquid latex over the mold's surface and allow it to dry for about eight hours, though this will cause some minor obscuring of intricate details. Polyurethane adheres to everything except polyethylene.

Polyurethane rubber can range in hardness and rigidity from floppy rubbers softer than a rubber band, to rigid and hyper-firm rubbers harder than a shoe heel. They can be used as mold-making materials, or to create padding and vibration dampening, similar to commercial rubbers such as Sorbothane™.

Besides rubber and plastic, polyurethane resin can also be formulated to create foam. This is sometimes called A-B foam because it is made by mixing two parts (an "A" part and a "B" part) together. The foam will expand while it cures, with some varieties foaming only slightly and others expanding up to 20 times the volume of the liquid. The hardness and rigidity of different foam products can range from soft foam rubbers to rigid foams more dense than polystyrene foam.

Polyurethane foam can be cast or poured directly on a surface for later carving. It is stronger than latex foam. Some polyurethane foam is blown with water, making it less toxic. You can also get polyurethane foam in a canister that is mixed as you spray it (such as the brand Great Stuff™). This stuff is usually bad for casting as it needs exposure to air to cure, and anything thicker than a single layer may remain wet on the inside nearly indefinitely.

After mixing, the polyurethane will foam and rise. You should make sure it has somewhere to go and that it will not spill out over anything important; remember that it sticks to everything and is difficult to clean up. It sets in around 3–5 minutes though the actual curing will take another 30 minutes to several hours. Most foams will create their own skin, though a few need a protective skin added on top once cured.

Do not touch the foam as it is curing; you will break the surface tension of the bubbles and cause it to fail in some way.

A lightweight yet strong casting can be had by slush-casting or rotocasting a high-impact polyurethane to make a shell, and then filling it with an expanding foam polyurethane. This gives you an impact-resistant and smoothly detailed exterior with a lightweight but rigid interior.

Unless you buy polyurethane in a fire-retardant form, it will be very flammable and release many toxic gasses as it burns.

Polyester Resin

Polyester resins are the cheapest and easiest of the resins to use. While they can range between rigid and semiflexible, they do not come in nearly as many forms as polyurethanes. They also shrink a lot more than epoxies. Still, they remain one of the most popular resins for beginners and for casting clear and translucent objects. Fillers can also be added to keep shrinkage

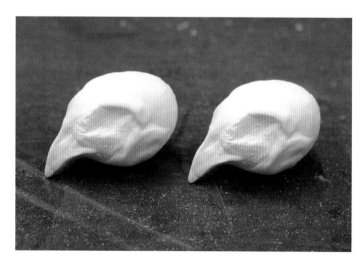

Figure 14-35: Unpainted polyurethane resin castings.

Figure 14-36: A polyurethane rubber mold.

Figure 14-37: Unpainted polyurethane foam castings.

down, though for transparent pieces, these can affect the clarity. Popular brand names include Castin' Craft Clear Polyester Casting Resin and Aristocrat Casting Resin.

Polyester resins are one of the most ,popular resins for laminating fiberglass; in fact, many types of polyester resin are labeled "fiberglass resin" (which is misleading, as you can use other types of resin on fiberglass, as well as various polymer emulsions). See the next chapter for more information on working with fiberglass

It is important not to use a resin made for laminating fiberglass for casting. Laminating resins are catalyzed hot so they can cure when spread in thin layers. If you concentrate a large amount in a mold cavity, it may generate so much heat that it degrades and release toxic fumes or even catches fire. Likewise, if you use a casting resin to laminate fiberglass, it may not get hot enough to fully cure.

Mix any fillers, thixotropic fillers (chemicals that thicken the liquid resin), and colors in the resin before mixing the catalyst. Common thixotropic fillers include silicas, a popular brand being Cab-o-Sil™. Polyester resins can be tinted with vat dyes, dry pigment powder from art stores, or any number of specialty products. A small amount of pigment can go a long way in coloring your resin, so start off by adding small amounts, Water-based tints and colors may inhibit the cure of your polyester.

Methyl ethyl ketone (MEK) peroxide is the most common catalyst used for polyester resins. It is highly explosive, though resin catalysts are typically diluted with a number of other chemicals to help stabilize them. The fumes are a severe irritant to the lungs, eyes, and skin; it can also be absorbed through the skin, leading to more severe damage, such as burns and damage to internal organs. Repeated exposure can lead to skin allergies. Using polyester resins requires adequate ventilation, fume extraction, skin, and eye protection. Likewise, used mixing containers should be disposed of out of the shop, as the unmixed portions will off-gas harmful fumes indefinitely.

Pay attention to the manufacturer's recommendations for how much catalyst to mix in. More catalyst will lead to a hotter mix that cures faster, but too much heat can cause it to shrink too rapidly and crack, break, and warp (not to mention the potential fire danger; buildings have burned down from fires started with resins that catalyzed too hot). The large masses of resin in thick castings will generate a lot of heat, and in some cases, you will have to use less catalyst than recommended to keep it from cracking. Alternatively, when you have thin parts, the recommended amount of catalyst might not be enough to generate the heat needed to cure. For especially thin parts (less than 1/8" thick at the thickest part), you may wish to use a laminating resin.

Polyester resin will not fully cure when exposed to the air and retains some "tack." Casting resins have a small amount of wax in them that floats to the surface and forms a coat against the air to allow it to cure. You can also purchase separate **surface curing agents** to mix in to achieve the same effect. There are also "resin sprays" you can buy to spray on top of a tacky surface and seal it. If you are pouring the resin into a sprue hole, of course, the tacky part will be on the end of the excess sprue material, which will be removed anyway.

Polyester resins, unless poured in a mold made of vinyl or silicone, should have a release of PVA, silicone, or wax.

The curing agents often contain MEK, so take the proper precautions when working with it. Polyester resins also release styrene vapors while curing, which are suspected carcinogens, as well as being an irritant and a narcotic. It is helpful to work in a spray booth or other type of local exhaust ventilation, and to wear the proper respirator. You should also keep the molds separated from other workers while they are curing. You can cover the molds with aluminum foil or plastic film, or keep them in an airtight container while they are curing to capture and contain the fumes.

Polyester resins are also the main ingredient in many auto body fillers. Auto body fillers, known popularly by one of the more common brands, BONDO™, are a thicker form of polyester resin, reinforced with inert fillers. They give you a runny paste about the consistency of melted chewing gum that begins to harden after only a few short minutes, finally curing to a rock-hard, machinable, and sandable chunk of material in a few hours.

Because auto body fillers and polyester resin both use the same catalyst, they can be mixed together when you want a material with an "in-between" consistency, and then catalyzed with either material's catalyst. This material is often referred to as "Rondo," which is a combination of "Resin" and "BONDO™".

Water-extended polyester is a specific type of polyester resin which you add water to as a filler; you cannot use water to extend regular polyester. It dries to a hard, white "bone-like" material similar to a hard art plaster such as Hydrocal™. The advantage of WEP is that it is far cheaper than other resins because it is up to 60% water. The disadvantage is that it tends to warp badly over time. For the life span of most props, that is not an issue, though if you mean for your prop to hold up for several years, you may wish to avoid it.

Epoxy Resin

Epoxy resin is most commonly found as an adhesive in the props shop. It is also found as a laminating resin to make water-proof fiberglass structures. It can be found as a casting resin as well, though it tends to be more expensive by volume than either polyester or polyurethane resin.

The toxicity of epoxies varies greatly, though all warrant protection of some kind. Check the MSDS to see what is in the brand and type of epoxy you want to use. Amines are the safest curing agents, though they are still sensitizing and toxic. Over half of the workers exposed to epoxy resin develop epoxy allergies; these allergies can make it difficult and sometimes impossible to work with epoxies (and other two-part resins) in the future. Even a small amount can cause rashes to break out over the skin.

When you look at the MSDS for the specific epoxy you are using, you will find that most require either a spray booth (or other local exhaust ventilation) or a respirator; be sure when using a respirator to have the correct cartridges, as many epoxies will require a combination organic vapor/ammonia cartridge. Avoid getting epoxy (or any resin) on your skin.

Epoxy also comes in a putty form, which is usually 1 part epoxy to 4 parts metallic fillers. It is typically a two-part compound that becomes like an adhesive clay when kneaded together thoroughly and hardens in about an hour and a half. You can machine, sand, and file the dried putty, though it is extremely hard. It can be modeled into shape by hand while it is curing, and it is even possible to press mold it if necessary.

Acrylic Resin

Casting acrylic resin involves high temperatures and pressures and the use of special molds. Uncured acrylic is also highly toxic, so the use of acrylic is basically avoided by prop makers. "Acrylic water" for model railroads and floral crafts is actually a thick acrylic varnish (sort of a clear acrylic "paint" with a lot of body that dries to a high-gloss finish). This is "poured," though it will take an incredibly long time to cure if it is poured in any significant volume. You can also find some brands of clear epoxy resin that are inexplicably sold as "acrylic water."

Silicone Rubber

Silicone rubber is the preferred mold material for prop makers to make long-lasting and flexible molds. If cost was not an issue, I imagine some prop makers would never make a mold out of anything else.

They are a two-component system and use either a platinum or tin-based catalyst. They can be poured, brushed, or sprayed on, depending on their viscosity. They have the best release properties out of all the mold rubbers, and most materials do not require any mold release. This makes them the best choice for production casting of any plastic resins. They have a high temperature resistance (400°F or higher, depending on the specific product), making them the only mold rubber suitable for casting low-melt metal alloys, such as tin, pewter, lead, and even, in some cases, aluminum.

They are among the most flexible and tear-resistant molding materials, making it possible to cast shapes with severe undercuts without resorting to needing a dozen separate mold pieces. This stretchiness also makes it necessary in most cases to construct a mother mold around the silicone mold so it can hold its shape; making the silicone mold thick enough to hold its own shape is usually very expensive, and often takes away the flexibility that you wanted in the first place.

The disadvantages of silicone rubbers are their high cost, especially the platinum-cure kinds. Tin catalyst silicone shrinks somewhat and has a shorter library life. Some substances, particularly sulfur clay and latex, will inhibit the cure of silicon rubbers on contact. The clay must be specifically labeled "sulfur free," or you have to assume it contains sulfur. Though more expensive, it is worth it to only buy sulfur-free clay, otherwise, you do not know if that clay you have sitting around has sulfur or not. Latex is such a strong inhibitor that even wearing latex gloves while mixing it can prevent it from curing. Though I mentioned in Chapter 3 that latex gloves should be avoided in general, this is another good reason to keep them out of your shop.

The thick viscosity of silicone means they may need to be vacuum degassed (placed in a vacuum chamber so the air

bubbles can be removed), though newer products are available that suffer less from this problem.

It is also used as a casting material. It replicates skin and flesh very well, and creates much more durable prosthetic body parts than latex. Besides molding and casting, it can be simply painted or poured onto surfaces. Thickening agents exist so it can hold onto a vertical surface without dripping while it cures (this is also what makes brush-on molds possible).

Though durable and long lasting, they will degrade over time. You can slow this by using a mold release.

Companies that produce a wide variety of silicone rubbers include Smooth-On, Silicones Inc., EnvironMolds, and Castin' Craft. Companies such as Smooth-On manufacture a

Figure 14-38: Natalie Taylor Hart builds up a silicone rubber mold around this sculpted lion chair leg.

vast array of silicone rubbers for all sorts of uses, such as budget mold-making rubbers, high-end mold-making rubbers, and stretchy casting rubbers for prosthetics and animatronic skins.

A mold release is rarely required, but one may be used to extend the life of the mold. The major exception is when you are pouring silicone rubber onto a silicone rubber mold, whether you are making a two-part mold or casting a silicone rubber piece inside a silicone rubber mold. Waxes or special mold releases made by molding and casting manufacturers are most useful.

Though silicone rubber is less toxic than other two-part molding and casting materials, the curing agents still create vapors, and the uncured liquids are irritants and can injure the skin and eyes upon contact.

Silicone Caulk

Silicone caulk is generally unsuitable as a mold-making material because it takes a long time to cure and requires exposure to the moisture in the air to harden. Some people have had limited success mixing a few drops of glycerin in to expose the insides to moisture and help aid the curing process. Mixing a bit of cornstarch in can achieve the same result. It still needs to be applied in fairly thin layers. Submerging it in a bucket of water mixed with dish soap after mixing helps keep the silicone from sticking to your gloves as you apply it to your mold; it acts more like a putty than silicone mold making. The benefit is its price in small amounts; the only way to have a more economical flexible mold material is to buy gelatin in bulk, which is a higher up-front cost.

Use only transparent 100% silicone rubber sealant. It is easiest to cut the end off the tube and remove it in one large mass rather than squeezing it all out of the nozzle. For a 10 oz tube of caulk, mix 30 drops of glycerin and 10 drops of acrylic paint. Both the glycerin and the paint help activate the silicone with moisture; the paint can also indicate that everything has

Figures 14-39 and 14-40: Some silicone rubbers are mixed in equal proportions by volume, whereas others can have a ratio up to 10:1. Always check the instructions, as even a slight variation from the required proportion can keep it from fully curing. Since most silicones are meant for mold rubbers, the two parts are often tinted different colors so that you can tell when they are fully mixed.

been thoroughly mixed. You can thin it out with mineral spirits, up to two parts silicone to one part mineral spirits.

The caulk is scooped and pressed more like putty rather than poured like a liquid. Fine details may be lost, and it is easier to trap air bubbles. It is helpful to smear a thin layer on top first, and when that is cured, add more mass in thick layers over the top.

It is hard to get consistent results with this, and it can take 24–48 hours to fully cure. This is an extremely cheap process for a temporary mold and for when castings do not need to be perfect.

Neoprene

Neoprene is a synthetic rubber that can be cast like latex. It is much less viscous than latex, making it more liable to splash or leak. It cures more quickly than latex and results in a harder piece, though it also costs more than latex. It sets through absorption casting, so the best type of mold to use is plaster. Do not use any petroleum release agents (such as petroleum jelly, aka Vaseline™. Petroleum jelly also dissolves natural latex).

Fill the mold. In one to two hours, you should have a fairly thick shell formed around the inside of the mold. You can pour out the excess liquid neoprene and let the shell finish casting. A skin may have developed on the top of the neoprene where it was exposed to the air, but otherwise, this liquid neoprene can be poured back into a container and used in a future casting. In about ten to twelve hours, you can demold your piece, and it is ready to go.

For most handheld items and masks, you only need a thickness around 3/16", as the neoprene is fairly rigid and holds its shape well.

Neoprene's shelf life is only about a year, and it evaporates quickly when not in an airtight container. You should only buy it as you need it.

Neoprene is fairly toxic while curing; you often need to work in a spray booth or chemical hood, and may even need a respirator. Check the MSDS of the specific neoprene you are using.

Foam Latex

Foam latex has long been a favorite with three-dimensional makeup artists and creature makers in the film and television world. Five different chemicals are precisely mixed. Once the foam has been poured, it also requires baking in an oven for four to six hours to fully cure. Foam latex presents the same health hazards as straight-up latex, including the potential for danger to people with latex allergies.

Silicone also comes in a two-part expanding foam. It has been developed to provide an easier to use and longer-lasting alternative to foam latex. It is used similarly to polyurethane foam, which was described earlier in this chapter.

Hardware Store Products

Plastic Wood™ (by DAP) is a mixture of cellulose products and solvents that harden into a substance intended to fill holes and cracks in wood.

Fillers for patching plaster, drywall, or concrete can often be used as casting compounds. Some are made of calcium carbonate (the main ingredient in joint compound), such as Fix-It-All™. Many of these are intended to be spread thinly, and will take extremely long to dry if cast in a thick chunk; they may also shrink while drying and are prone to cracking if a large mass is cast. For the most part, these are used "in a pinch" because they are the only things on hand or because the hardware store is the only business open, and you need to cast something immediately. Otherwise, there is usually a better choice out there.

Hot melt glue can be used as a casting compound. You can buy tinted hot glue sticks, which are useful because hot glue is difficult to paint. As it is an adhesive, a mold release is vital. Plaster is useful if you dip it in water first; hot glue will not stick to wet or damp plaster.

Figure 14-41: Foam latex also degrades over time, as seen in the handle of this sword built in 1985.

Understanding Shore Hardness

The hardness of plastics and rubbers used in prop making is measured by a Shore number, which indicates how much it is indented when a specific force is applied to it for a few seconds. Different Shore scales exist—you often run across Shore A, Shore D, and Shore OO, though others exist, such as Shore B. These scales give better accuracy within certain ranges, as no single Shore test can cover the entire range from extra soft to extremely hard. There are other scales of hardness, but the plastics and rubbers we use most in props are typically measured with one of the Shore scales. Shore A is used for flexible plastics and Shore D for rigid plastics.

The larger the number, the harder the material is. It does not indicate how strong or durable the material is, just the hardness. You want a soft material if you are making a mold that you need to flex to remove the cast; you want a harder material if you want your cast item to resist being squished.

Directly converting the different values is not possible; a plastic with a Shore A of 77 might have a Shore D of 50, while a rubber with a Shore A of 77 might have a Shore D of 24. Though there is overlap in the subjective hardness of the scales, there is no relationship; they do not measure the hardness in any kind of "unit," but rather the relative hardness in comparison with other materials measured on that scale.

Molding the Human Form

Props often requires molding parts of the human body. Severed limbs find their way into numerous shows. Many productions also require either a severed head, a bust or a full statue of a specific actor, and molding their form is the most accurate way, and often the quickest and cheapest way, to get this done. Making a mold on a person has special considerations though, both in the choice of materials used, and the methods you go about doing it.

Alginate is the preferred material for casting hands, feet, faces, and ears. It is nontoxic, easy to use and clean up, fast and comfortable for the actor, and reproduces very fine detail, such as the texture of the skin.

Flexwax™ is a brand of wax that melts at a low enough temperature to safely be used on the skin. It can be brushed on, or you can dip limbs into it if you have a large enough container. The model's skin should be cooled down with cold water first. If dipping, you should plunge the model's limb in the container and immediately remove it; let this layer solidify before dipping and removing again. Build up the mold layer by layer in this manner until it is thick enough to hold its shape (usually around ¼" thick). Flexwax molds can be remelted and reused.

For larger portions of the body, a skin-safe silicone is often a better choice. Even with a "skin safe" silicone, you should always do a small test on the model's wrist to check for possible allergic reactions. These can be brushed or poured on. As with alginate, a mold release is not necessary.

Figure 14-42: The severed head from The Public Theater's 2009 production of *The Bacchae* was cast from the actor's face. In the middle is the plaster cast made from the alginate mold taken from his face; on the right is the silicone mold taken from that. On the left is the final piece, cast in silicone rubber and mounted on a fake skull.

Figure 14-43: Casting a part like a hand in alginate is pretty straightforward. Most boxes of alginate sold at hobby and art stores will indicate on the box how many hands can be molded with the quantity inside. You need a container that will fit your actor's hand plus at least a half an inch around all sides. Mix the alginate with the specified amount of water, and pour it into this container. Have the actor pose his or her hand, and slide it inside. They should be seated comfortably as they will need to keep their hand frozen in place for about ten minutes. *Titus Andronicus*, the Public Theater, 2011.

Figure 14-44: They do not need any mold release on their hand. The alginate will not heat up either; it will just slowly get stiffer until it solidifies. It is helpful to use warm water when mixing your alginate just so that your actor does not have to plunge his or her hand into a cold and slimy bucket. When the alginate has solidified, have the actor slightly wiggle his or her fingers to break the suction, then slowly draw his or her hand out. The alginate should have enough flexibility that the hand can be drawn straight out even if he or she was making a fist. Thank the actor, and let him or her know he or she can clean up with regular soap and water. *Titus Andronicus*, the Public Theater, 2011.

Figure 14-45: The alginate will begin drying and shrinking right away; you only have about two hours to cast your material before it becomes visibly deformed.

If you are molding the actor's hand on-site, you better be prepared to pour your casting material right there rather than traveling back to your shop and casting it there. You can cast it in its final material, but often, prop makers will make a quick cast in plaster. This plaster cast is then molded in a more permanent material for future casts. This gives you the option of making multiple casts, or working with materials that require more setup. It is good to make a quick plaster cast so you do not have the pressure of the deadline where the alginate becomes unusable; it would be bad form to call the actor back for another casting session. *Titus Andronicus*, the Public Theater, 2011.

Figure 14-46: When the plaster has set, you can simply break and peel away the alginate. Plaster poured into alginate does not need a mold release; the alginate will fall away easily and cleanly. *Titus Andronicus*, the Public Theater, 2011.

Figure 14-47: This plaster cast can then be molded in your material of choice, and cast in whatever you like. Here, a silicone rubber brush-on mold is made. *Titus Andronicus*, the Public Theater, 2011.

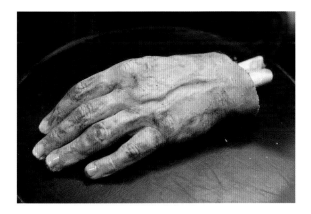

Figure 14-48: The final hand was also cast in silicone rubber. *Titus Andronicus*, the Public Theater, 2011.

If you need to cast the entire body, it may be easier to do it in pieces, cast them separately, and then attach them together.

You may also not need to do the entire body. Generic mannequin pieces can be bought to fill in the torsos and limbs, and you only need to cast the distinctive parts, such as the face and hands. If the fake body will be wearing clothes, you only need to cast the parts that are uncovered; the rest can simply be rods and stuffing.

Some artisans mold body parts directly with plaster. I do not recommend this if you are new to mold and casting. Plaster heats up while it sets, and if you put it on the body too thick, it can burn the model's skin. It can also trap body parts with undercuts inside.

In 2007, a schoolgirl in England placed both her hands within a bucket of plaster. They got stuck as it set, and the plaster heated up to over 140°F (60°C). The heat was enough to melt her fingers. Even after a dozen operations with plastic surgeons over the next two years, she ended up losing eight fingers: one hand had only two fingers, and the other, none. You should only ever apply plaster to the skin in thin layers with plenty of time to cool between applications. After the first layer, plaster bandages are a safer alternative. Putting them on one layer at a time ensures you are only adding a thin amount of plaster.

You should use a mold release of petroleum jelly or some other skin cream when using plaster on the skin. Hair can get caught in the plaster and pulled out when the cast is removed. Especially hairy people should be shaved before casting them.

Again, I recommend not molding body parts in plaster on your own; do it only when someone experienced is there to guide or observe the process.

Storing and Caring for Your Molds

Moisture, dust, exposure to sunlight, and even exposure to air will degrade your molds over time. If you wish to keep a "mold archive," that is, a collection of molds that you do not use every day but may wish to use in the future, store them in plastic storage tubs with sealed tops. Try not to stack the individual molds on top of each other in the tubs, as the flexible mold materials may deform over time and the rigid mold materials may chip as they run into each other.

Figure 14-49: A portion of the mold storage area at Costume Armour, Inc., which maintains a mold library for most of the shows they have built since the 1980s.

fifteen

shells and laminates

A skin or shell requires either an underlying shape or a mold; these materials are distinct in that they are not formed on their own by tools and machines, but by making the shape first through fabrication, patterning, or sculpting, and then wrapping, covering, or laminating materials onto or into that shape.

Some materials are manipulated into shapes in such a way that they form a hollow shell, or a portion of a shell. Think of masks, and how their construction is typically of a thin material bent into an undulating pattern that takes on the appearance of a human face.

Other materials are shaped through "coring," in which an internal support structure is covered in a skin or shell of a continuous material to give it its form.

The first group of materials in this chapter comprises flexible sheet materials that can be manipulated into shapes and made rigid or semirigid enough to maintain that shape. They may be made supple by soaking in water and then harden as they dry; others may become flexible when heated and then reharden when they cool.

The second group comprises materials known as "composites" or "laminates." A **composite** is a material made through the combination of two materials: a fibrous cloth or sheet embedded in a matrix of hardened polymer. They are called **laminates** because you apply the sheets or pieces of sheets in several layers to form a continuous skin without any seams.

Shells can be made over the top of forms, in negative molds, or on top of a skeleton or other framework. To learn more about creating forms, you can consult the chapters on constructive materials and sculptural materials. Molds have their own chapter as well.

Buckram

"Millinery buckram" is the kind impregnated with starch and used in hat making and costume crafts. Portions of the Tin Man's costume in the original *Wizard of Oz* film were constructed from buckram and painted to resemble tin.

Figure 15-1: Sample swatches of two kinds of buckram.

Buckram is still used a lot in millinery (hat-making); if you pick up a buckram hat, you can see what the material is like. It keeps its shape, but it is somewhat collapsible. Buckram starts off as a fairly stiff sheet, but it becomes soft when it soaks in warm water for a few minutes. You drape it over your form, and push the fabric into all the cracks and crevices. It becomes stiff again as it dries out. It is incredibly easy to work with as it requires no specialized tools, and it is nontoxic and very "green." It can also be resoaked for endless reuse and reworking. For hats, the buckram often serves as the underlying structure, with another fabric on top. Millinery wire is a hard but pliable steel wire covered in cloth with a bit of "spring" to it. Larger buckram shapes may collapse under their weight, so millinery wire is sewn around the edges to hold the shape. Buckram can also be further stiffened by adding additional layers, or by brushing on a coating of PVA glue or polyester resin.

With severe undercuts, you may need to pattern together several pieces.

Fosshape™ is a plastic-impregnated fabric that is used like buckram but is activated with heat rather than water. It starts to stiffen around 100°F–130°F, and is typically heated with a costume steamer, though a hot air gun can also be used. The amount of stiffness it has can be controlled with the amount

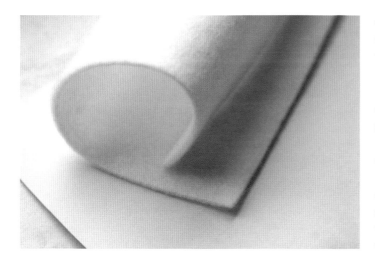

Figure 15-2: Fosshape.

of heat applied to it. It shrinks considerably depending on the amount of heat it receives, so many patterns should be made oversized. It can be stretched over forms and pinned in place to create shapes, or you can pattern and sew pieces together to create shapes. It can be sewn to other fabrics too, which is useful when you need a hidden stiffener for a loose fabric.

Leather

Leather becomes very pliable after it is soaked. You drape it over your form and work it into the cracks and crevices. As it dries, you can hammer it to further define the detail, and then burnish it to remove the hammering marks. When completely dry, it has the same rigidity as a pair of fine leather shoes.

Leather can "breathe," unlike many plastics. This gives it an advantage over many plastics when placed against the skin as with masks or armor; unbreathable materials will cause the skin to get wet with sweat and possibly overheat, while leather will allow the sweat to evaporate even when covered.

Most of the leather you find in stores is "chrome tanned" leather. This includes garment leather, dress leather, and all the other leathers with finished surfaces. This kind of leather cannot be molded, shaped, or tooled. You need "vegetable-tanned" leather.

If you drape vegetable-tanned leather over a positive mold, you can form it into a more permanent shape. The mold cannot have too many undercuts, or you will need to actually pattern the leather with seams, darts, and cuts.

Soak the leather in water for 15 minutes to 12 hours, depending on the thickness, type, and pliability needed. Drape it over the mold. It can be held by pinning it to the back of the mold. If you use steel pins, they will stain the leather, so make sure to place them in parts of the leather that will eventually be trimmed off. Be sure to leave some slack in places with deep valleys so you have enough leather to push into place.

A rounded piece of wood, known as a *sticketta*, helps shape the leather while it is damp. You need to work the leather for a while; anywhere from 20 minutes to an hour depending on the shape you are trying to create. As you press and work the leather with your *sticketta* (or whatever type of tool you wish to use), the leather will not really hold the shape. It is only through repeated pressing and working that it will begin to stay in place. Harder lines can be emphasized by using a sharper part of your *sticketta*.

Cuir bouilli, or boiled leather, is a method for making the leather harder (but more brittle). After soaking the leather in regular water, dip it in boiling water; this can quickly cook and ruin the leather, so keep it in no longer than 2 minutes. The leather shrinks and hardens when dipped in. The hotter the water, the harder the leather gets. Alternatively, you can bake the leather while it is drying; the temperature should be fairly low, around 120°F–175°F.

Leather can be pressed between two forms to make a shape as well.

Industrial Felt

Industrial felt is a heavy-duty felt made with a blend of wool and other fibers. Also known as "pressed felt," this comes in

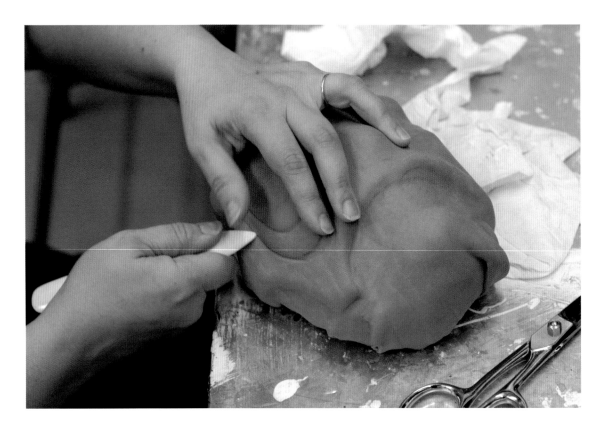

Figure 15-3: Leather mask-making involves soaking the leather, stretching it over a form, and then shaping it with a *sticketta*.

thicknesses up to 2" and a variety of densities. It has long been a favorite of props artisans for simulating cast iron and armor. Large sheets can mimic breastplates, while small pieces can be cut to resemble iron hardware on trunks and chests. It can be cut with scissors or razors (such as X-Acto knives); the denser the felt, the cleaner the edge you can achieve.

"Woven" felt, the kind used in blankets and clothes, tends to fray at the edges when cut, and so may not produce as clean an edge as industrial felt.

The traditional technique is to submerge the felt in PVA glue. Squeeze the glue out, mold it like wet leather over a form, and let it dry. Pin it in place while it is drying. It can take several days to dry. This is known as **sizing** the felt (just like sizing a piece of canvas for painting) because it causes the felt to shrink. Diluting the glue with water is helpful to make it soak more easily, and to keep costs down you can add as much as 1 part water to 2 parts PVA glue. Use a flexible white glue if you want the felt to be stiff but moveable. For added strength, you can layer two pieces of felt together. When dry, coat the whole thing with more PVA glue, shellac, or varnish.

The industrial felt you use needs to contain at least 50% wool. Unlike synthetic felt, wool fibers soak up and spread the glue evenly throughout the piece of felt, and the shrinking that occurs while drying gives it the strength and rigidity needed for a stand-alone piece.

For faster results, you can brush plastic resin (polyester, polyurethane or epoxy) on the felt rather than glue.

Celastic

One of the earliest boons to prop making was the appropriation of a material called Celastic. Celastic was used extensively in the mid-twentieth century for creating shapes. It is a rigid plastic sheet that becomes soft and pliable when soaked in a solvent, such as MEK or Acetone. It becomes hard again as it dries. It can be cut into smaller pieces for easier workability. It also adheres to itself when it dries, so smaller pieces can be attached to each other, or the artisan could build up several layers for additional strength.

"Celastic" itself is no longer manufactured, but the modern equivalent, named Formfast, shares most of the same properties.

Because you are dealing with large buckets of solvents, long chemically-resistant gloves, proper ventilation, and a respirator are vital. This process usually cannot be carried out when other people are in the shop, unless they are also wearing respirators. Working in a walk-in spray booth or outside is helpful. On the plus side, these solvents evaporate rather quickly, so once the material has hardened, it is safe to be around. While plenty of safer materials exist, none approach the "drapability" of Celastic; Celastic is also much more heat-resistant than modern thermoplastics, which can deform under the heat of the sun if used outdoors.

Thermoform Plastics

Thermoform plastics begin as rigid sheets of plastic, but become pliable and flexible (almost like fabric) when heated. They become rigid again when they cool back down. Thermoform plastics allow you to quickly form hollow shapes over

Figure 15-4 and 15-5: The clothing for the statue of Cinderella's coachmen was constructed in Celastic. Celastic sheets drape much more realistically than other materials, yet dries to a very rigid and hard material. This statue has been in use for 25 years, yet shows no signs of wear or weakness. *Into the Woods*, 1987. Scenic design by Tony Straiges, constructed by Costume Armour, Inc.

forms, in molds, or freehand in the air. This makes them popular for larger masks and mascot heads, as well as for armor, giant puppets, and any other shape that needs to be hollow or more lightweight than fiberglass.

Wonderflex™ is one of the more common brands. It is a hard plastic with a sort of screen embedded within. Fosshape is a plastic-impregnated fabric that turns into a more rigid shell when heated. It can be activated with a fabric iron or a costume steamer. Varaform™ is a version that comes as a plastic netting with hexagonal holes. It was known as Hexcelite™ when first introduced as an orthopedic tape used to replace plaster bandages in making casts for broken bones.

Thermoform plastics use heat to become soft. Some can be softened in a pot of boiling water. You may also want a heat gun or hair dryer for localized softening and to help with joining two pieces together. A conventional oven or microwave can also be used. Most of these products soften around 150°F –170°F. At the lower ends of the temperature range, thermoform plastics can be worked by hand; the adhesive in the plastic does not come off. However, it can easily be hot enough to cause discomfort over time or even burn you if you overheat a

Figure 15-6: Wonderflex.

section, so it is recommended to wear a pair of thin leather gloves or other tight-fitting insulated gloves. The material itself is waterproof. In fact, you can spray or pour cold water over a soft section to cool it down instantly and "freeze" the shape in place. Ice packs are also useful for this.

Cutting the pieces is easily accomplished with a heavy-duty pair of scissors, tin snips, or a utility knife.

It can be shaped free-hand, over a positive form or in a negative mold. Lecithin can be used as a mold release, though for many cases, a layer of aluminum foil is all that is necessary, as thermoform plastics will not be picking up much fine detail. With enough heat and pressure, you *can* make it pick up finer details and impart a texture to the surface itself.

Unlike buckram and leather, which requires stitching or adhesives to add several pieces together, thermoform plastics can adhere to themselves when heated. When you are making shapes larger than a single sheet, you can stick multiple sheets together. This means that you will have overlapping seams, even when you press them together vigorously. You can stiffen and strengthen pieces by laminating two or three layers together. Many of these plastics have a grain just like fabric, so you need to deal with both grain and bias when working with them. The sheets can be cut into small strips and shaped like papier-mâché, or you can heat a large sheet and shape it all at once.

You can get rid of the seams by sanding them or by filling with an acrylic or latex caulk. Many of the polymer emulsions used as texturing materials will stick too, such as Sculpt or Coat, Crystal Gel, Jaxsan, etc. You can paint the final piece with most acrylic, latex, and scenic paints. Larger and thinner pieces will have a slight flexibility to them, so you do not want to coat them with anything especially rigid.

Thermoform plastics can adhere when hot to a number of other materials, such as wood, leather, and metal, making it possible to embed objects. While the material is hot, you can also work it with sculpting tools or stamp textures into it to refine the surface and the shape.

If you need a smooth surface, you will need to fill the seams with a flexible filler, such as caulk. If you are coating the whole surface with another material, such as papier-mâché or fabric, you will not need to worry about the seams.

It should hold up perfectly fine under stage lights or outside, but it may begin to soften if left in a car outside on a sunny day or in a metal trailer.

Composites, Laminates, Reinforced Plastic

A **composite** is a material made of two or more different materials that remain distinct. Concrete is a composite. Most composites are made of a "matrix" and a "reinforcement." In this section, we are looking mostly at reinforced plastics, such as fiberglass and carbon fiber. These are materials made of a polymer resin (the matrix) and woven cloth (the reinforcement). Papier-mâché also belongs here (as does its less popular cousin, cloth-mâché). The matrix, whether wheatpaste or PVA glue, is itself a polymer. The reinforcement (the paper) is a fibrous material much like woven cloth.

The concept of mâché, fiberglass, and carbon fiber is similar. You laminate together strips or sections of overlapping material soaked in the liquid polymer. With enough layers, you can create a self-supporting and continuous "skin" or "shell" (though for some projects, you are creating a skin on top of a form that is left within the prop).

Releases

When making laminates in a mold or over a form, you will need a mold release just as when you are casting. Chapter 14 has information on what to use depending on the material of your mold and the resin you are using.

Both papier-mâché and fiberglass shrink a little bit as they dry. When they are laminated inside a negative mold with no undercuts, they will pull away from the mold walls as they dry, basically releasing themselves. On a positive form, it may be helpful to pop the laminate loose from the form while it is still wet and slightly flexible. Once the seal between laminate and form is broken, it can be laid back on the form to resume curing in the proper shape.

Papier-Mâché

Papier-mâché has long been used to create props for theatre. It has even been used to make permanent objects for the home. The Victorians in particular have made quite exquisite objects from this simple technique. It can be argued that up until the middle of the twentieth century, nearly all props were made of papier-mâché, wood, and fabric.

Though we often think of papier-mâché as a theatrical prop material, it has found its way into film as well. Some of the birds from Alfred Hitchcock's *The Birds* were constructed of papier-mâché, for example.

Papier-mâché can be laid down over a form, or formed in a mold. Many of us are familiar with the technique of laying papier-mâché onto a form made of chicken wire or over a balloon to make a spherical shape. One can also make quick forms by crumpling aluminum foil into a rough shape, or by crumpling up paper and holding it in place by wrapping tape or string around it. These techniques can be seen in more detail in Chapter 13.

Besides being used to create shapes, papier-mâché is sometimes used as a coating to existing shapes to give a uniform painting surface or to add texture.

Traditional binders for mâché include wheatpaste and wallpaper paste. You can find myriad recipes and variations for making your own **wheatpaste**, but a basic recipe you can experiment with involves using 2 parts water to 1 part flour. Any kind of all-purpose wheat flour will do, as long as it contains gluten. Separate a bit of the water out to mix with the flour to create a runny liquid. Bring the rest of the water to a boil. When it is boiling, slowly stir in the flour/water concoction. Let the whole thing boil for 3–5 minutes, then let it to cool. It is more comfortable to work with the paste while it is still slightly warm, but it will keep for 2–3 days if refrigerated.

Figure 15-7: Mix your flour with a bit of water to make a runny liquid with no lumps.

Figure 15-8: Some paper, like newsprint, has a grain. You can see this when you tear the paper. Tear it across the grain, and you are left with a jagged edge.

Wallpaper paste typically comes in a powder that is mixed with water. Traditional wallpaper paste contained rat poison, and modern types may contain pesticides and fungicides. Luckily, you can find "craft" versions that forego these harmful ingredients.

One of the most popular binders for mâché is the more modern PVA or white glue. This has strength and flexibility and can be used straight from the bottle or thinned a bit with water. Carpenter's glue can be used as well, though it usually dries more rigid; this does make it easier to sand though. These glues are more expensive than pastes and other homebrew methods. Variations on PVA, such as Mod-Podge, can also be used.

Other polymer emulsions can be experimented with. Acrylic media such as acrylic paint, gesso and coatings, polyurethane emulsions such as floor coating, and any number of mixed and proprietary polymer emulsions such as Crystal Gel™, Polycrylic™, or Sculpt or Coat™ are all possibilities, depending on whatever unique circumstances you find yourself in.

Some of these products will be flexible when dry, while others will be rigid. A well-made papier-mâché prop, properly

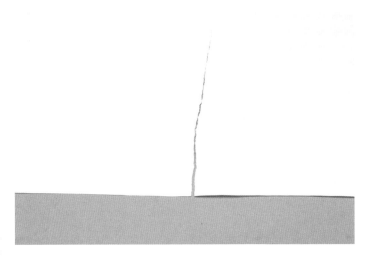

Figure 15-9: Tear it along the grain, and you get a clean and straight tear. When you are making papier-mâché with strips, you want to tear them out along the grain. Tearing is preferred to cutting; the ragged edge will blend much better into the next piece, leaving less sanding needed at the end of the process. For this reason, you will also wish to tear off any factory-cut edges on the paper.

Figure 15-10: Paper pulp is useful for sculpting features or casting intricate details.

Figure 15-12: Kraft paper is good for building up strength on interior surfaces.

sealed, can last longer than a fiberglass prop in certain situations because it will bend, rather than break, under impact.

You can turn paper into a pulp to be used in papier-mâché. Place the paper into a blender and shred it up. Mix this with glue or paste to make a material akin to clay that can be sculpted and formed in its own right.

For the reinforcing layers, prop makers have typically relied on newsprint, as it is readily available as a discarded material, rips easily, and soaks up paste well. Other suitable

Figure 15-11: Tissue paper is good for giving a surface a smooth finish.

papers include kraft paper, sugar paper, butcher paper, etc. Any unglazed paper will do; many office papers and stationery have coatings that inhibit the absorption of the water and paste which make the papier-mâché process possible. If you are using newsprint or other recycled papers with ink, the colors and patterns may show through unless you coat it completely with paint or another completely opaque coating.

When you are building up your layers with strips of paper rather than chunks, lay each successive layer perpendicular to the one before. This ensures you have grain running in all directions, which is the same concept that gives plywood its strength.

For outer layers, some prop makers switch to tissue paper or other finer materials to give a smoother coat. Tissue paper can also be used by itself to make translucent props that are lit from within. For the outermost surface, a layer of just paper pulp can be added.

If you are making your papier-mâché object in a mold as opposed to over a form, the layers are reversed. Begin with a **water coat** of fine paper; with a water coat, the paper is soaked only in water, not paste or glue. Use smaller chunks rather than long strips to keep the paper from wrinkling on curves. Overlap the pieces as little as possible so that you do not have noticeable seams. If your mold contains very fine details or texture, you may wish to begin with a beauty coat of just pulp mixed with paste. If you do not use a water coat, you will need to use the appropriate mold release so that your papier-mâché will not stick.

Continue with a layer or two of fine paper, and then reinforce the whole thing with a few layers of newsprint or kraft paper.

You may also find various commercial products that call themselves "instant papier-mâché"; these are made of pulped and powdered paper premixed with a binder. They form a thick paste that can be molded and shaped like clay when soaked in water. As with other papier-mâché objects, work in thin layers; else, it will take forever to dry. It is helpful to allow the powder to soak in water for a few hours before use so that it has time to break down. You can mix it the night before use, and store it in the refrigerator; it should last in the refrigerator up to a week before getting moldy. To keep dust out of the air, you can mix it by adding the powder and water to a sealed bag (like a Zip-Loc™) and squishing it around.

If you need additional structural integrity, you can build up a few layers, and then lay in some stiff wires and cover these up with additional layers of paper. This is akin to sewing millinery wire into the edges of buckram.

If you need to make a papier-mâché object inside a two-part mold, the easiest method is to laminate each mold half separately. When they are dry enough to demold, first trim each side to the parting line. Remove each half from the mold. You can glue the two halves together with hot glue, tape, or whatever works best for the shape you have. Now add another layer of papier-mâché, making sure that the strips of paper cross from one side of the seam to the other.

Some of the concerns with papier-mâché are that it shrinks while drying and that it takes a long time to dry. The water you add causes the material to expand, so as it dries and loses water, it decreases in size. You can minimize shrinking by using the least amount of water possible (while not inhibiting

Figure 15-13: Tobias Harding builds up a strong funnel-shaped structure with brown kraft paper soaked in Rosco Flex Glue at the Santa Fe Opera.

Figure 15-14: This bathtub was constructed of papier-mâché. The top is a piece of Ethafoam that has been attached; another layer of papier-mâché will be added to make the whole tub look like it was constructed of a single sheet of hammered copper. *Henry IV* and *V* at PlayMakers Repertory Company. Scenic design by Jan Chambers.

its ability to adhere to itself). This also helps keep drying time to a minimum. Another way to speed up drying time is to keep the thickness to a minimum—again, this should not be at the expense of its structural integrity. You can use heat lamps or an oven to speed up drying considerably. If you dry it too fast though, it can crack. Since most of the shrinking happens in the beginning, you usually let the piece air dry to the point where it can be demolded or removed from its form; in other words, when it is simply damp rather than wet. At this point, placing it in an oven (100°F–150°F) or placing it under heat lamps will be less likely to cause cracking. Even when you are not adding an additional heat source, humid or nonmoving air will increase your drying time, so even a simple fan can help out.

It is frequently necessary to waterproof a papier-mâché prop. Traditional coatings include shellac, lacquer, or linseed oil. More modern alternatives include any of the acrylic and polyurethane emulsions used for waterproofing and protecting other surfaces.

Cloth Mâché

Like paper, cloth can also be soaked in glue and laid up into a form that will dry to a hard shell. Muslin or cheesecloth are common fabrics of choice. When it is used with a flexible glue or binder, the resulting surface or shape can have more "give" than paper, which can be advantageous for props that need to be impact-resistant.

For the strongest cloth-mâché, cut strips along the bias of the fabric. Lay subsequent layers perpendicularly to the layer before.

Reinforced Plastic

Glass reinforced plastic (GRP) and carbon-fiber-reinforced plastic (CFRP or CRP) are the more appropriate terms for what we will talk about next, as "fiberglass" and "carbon fiber" technically refer to the cloth itself without the resin. When these fabrics are saturated with plastic resin, they cure into a very

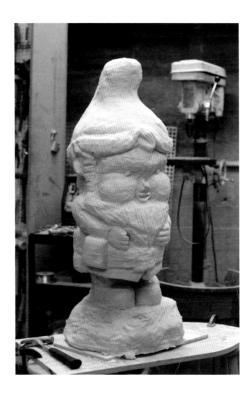

Figure 15-15: This large gnome is coated in a layer of cloth-mâché.

hard and strong shell that has all the advantages of each material and none of the weaknesses. For simplicity's sake, I will use the terms *fiberglass* and *carbon fiber* in this chapter to refer to the finished product or the technique itself. If I am talking about just the fabric before it is reinforced with resin, I will qualify it, such as "fiberglass cloth" or "fiberglass mat." Fiberglass refers to the glass fibers that can be woven into a cloth, or a mat, or just strands.

Fiberglass

Glass, in fiber form, is very flexible, yet incredibly strong. Glass appears fragile because of the defects; a sheet of glass is practically impossible to manufacture without introducing some defects. Fibers, on the other hand, can be made without defects, making them an incredibly strong reinforcing material for plastic resins. Fiberglass is also chemically stable, so it will not rot or rust. It is dimensionally stable and does not shrink during processing. It can withstand temperatures up to 1000°F and does not absorb moisture.

Fiberglass comes in many forms. Woven **cloth** is the most expensive but also the strongest. Like textiles, fiberglass cloth can be woven in many different ways, such as plain or twill, and comes in rolls of various widths. **Fiberglass mat** is a nonwoven material where the fiberglass strands are laid in randomly throughout. It is much cheaper than cloth though much less strong. It can soak up a lot of resin, and it is a little trickier to form around curves. **Chopped strand mat** (or CSM) is a fiberglass mat in which the strands are chopped into tiny lengths and held together by some kind of binder that dissolves when saturated with resin. CSM gives omnidirectional strength, but it is thicker than woven cloth. Be advised that most fiber-

glass chopped strand mat is held together with a styrene binder that dissolves only when submerged in polyester resin; epoxy or water-based resins will just sit on top of chopped strand mat rather than soaking in to create an actual composite.

A thin and delicate layer of fiberglass is sometimes laid between the gel coat and the reinforcing fiberglass to hide the texture of the fiberglass cloth. This may be called **surfacing cloth, tissue, veil**, or some similar variation of those words. Surfacing cloth has very fine fibers in a random orientation that disappear completely in the resin and become transparent.

Woven roving is a very coarse weave made of a dozen or more untwisted strands of glass woven as a whole. It is almost as strong as cloth and almost as cheap as mat. Its coarse pattern requires additional layers on top unless you want to see the texture.

Fiberglass **mat tape** is useful for the selective reinforcement of seams, corners, or edges. You can cut your own fiberglass mat into thin strips to use as tape, purchasing a roll of tape can save you time.

Fiberglass is often used to build boats, and in fact, the resin and cloth needed can be found most readily at marine supply stores.

Fiberglass used in home insulation is full of defects and so cannot be used to reinforce resin. Some people have used fiberglass insulation and resin mixed to a paste as a patch for small holes. Most insulation uses formaldehyde-based binders to hold them together, so it is best just to avoid it.

Theatrical prop makers in the United States have moved away from fiberglass since the 1980s over concerns about health and safety as well as cost. Besides the health concerns of the resins, the glass fibers themselves are a nuisance. They work their way through clothes and into skin, even after the object is finished. They are re-released into the air as you sand a finished fiberglass sculpture. The ends of fiberglass mats in particular become a hazard, as the individual strands that poke out become sharp spikes and needles when coated in resin.

Figure 15-16: Armor, such as this breastplate from the 2001 film *Planet of the Apes*, is frequently made from fiberglass. When fiberglass is laid up in a negative mold, it can have raised details and texture as seen here.

Fiberglass Resin

Fiberglass can be laminated up with either a water-based resin or the more traditional plastic resins. Resins can have different properties, so choose one that works best for your project. Some become completely rigid, while others may retain a little flexibility when fully cured. Water-based resins include products such as Aqua Form™ and Aqua-Resin™. These materials are far less toxic than plastic resins, though you still have to worry about the hazard of sanding the fiberglass itself. Many commercial shops have switched over to these products; the savings in labor and safety costs versus plastic resins are dramatic, not to mention the improvement to the health of their employees. Shops that are already well equipped to deal with the toxicity of plastic resins continue to use them because they feel the water-based versions do not have all the properties needed for their very demanding needs. For the beginning prop maker, the water-based resins are highly recommended for health and environmental reasons.

Nonetheless, I will give a quick rundown of the plastic resins here. Prop makers use two main types of resin for fiberglass: polyester and epoxy. Polyurethane resins, which are popular for casting, are rarely used; they cost a great deal more without giving any noticeably better results. They also have much shorter working times, with some beginning to set in just two to three minutes. For laminating, you want a longer working time, otherwise your resin will be getting hard before you have finished brushing it over your fiberglass.

Many formulations of polyester and epoxy may differentiate themselves as either "casting" or "laminating" resins. For the majority of "standard" fiberglass projects, the higher cost of epoxy does not bring any noticeable advantages to warrant the price. Epoxy resin fiberglassing is popular with boat builders because of its greater water resistance, so for props intended to be submerged or used outside in the rain, epoxy may be a better choice. Most of the resin you find that is labeled "fiberglass resin" will be polyester resin. Obviously, you should check the label and MSDS to be absolutely sure.

A polyester **gel coat** is a resin specially formulated to apply as a thin coating. It is meant to be used as the outermost coating. It remains tacky where exposed to the air; you can seal it with a layer of plastic sheeting, or use a "wax-type" gel coat. The wax in this type of gel coat floats to the surface and seals off the resin from the air, allowing it to cure hard. If you are laying a gel coat on the inside of a mold, you actually want it to remain tacky so the next layer of fiberglass will adhere to it. Gel coat can impart other properties, such as chemical resistance, mechanical strength, UV resistance, and weathering properties.

Resin can be thickened with calcium carbonate, or a hydrated or fumed silica such as Cab-O-Sil. Use sparingly as it slows the curing process, and too much may even prevent the resin from fully curing. The resin can also be colored with special coloring agents or even metallic powders; check with your specific resin to see what types of additives are compatible.

With polyester resin, the ambient temperature needs to be between 60° and 85°; if it is too cold, the resin will either cure slowly or not at all. The relative humidity needs to be below 60% as well; the moisture in the air will become trapped between the individual layers and can cause delamination months or years later. You cannot fiberglass in the rain.

Remember to always use the least toxic alternative for your prop. Unless you can deal with the fumes of polyester resin while working and have a sequestered environment for it to cure in, you should be using a water-based resin. Fiberglass itself is hard to deal with safely because the dust created when sanding is a skin and lung irritant. Ask yourself whether fiberglass is absolutely necessary or if you can substitute a different material or process.

Making a Fiberglass Piece

In "open molding," the fiberglass cloth or mat is impregnated with resin and layered into an open mold and allowed to set. Alternatively, drape the fiberglass mat or cloth into an open male or female (positive or negative) mold, and then spray or brush the resin on. The rigid mold form can be anything hard,

All plastic resins, such as polyester and epoxy, are particularly toxic in their uncured form. Keep them off your skin, as they are sensitizers. With enough exposure, you will develop an allergy. This can take a long time, but it can be drastic when it does manifest; you can work with resin every day for ten years, and then suddenly one day when you use it, your skin breaks out into rashes and blisters and your throat begins to close up (this differs among people; some can develop an allergy on the *first* exposure). It can take weeks to recover from one of these attacks, and afterward, even just a tiny amount of exposure will cause a new reaction.

You need to take appropriate safety precautions to reduce exposure to uncured resin as well as when you are sanding, cutting, or machining cured resin. All cured resin still contains bits of uncured resin that is released into the air when it turns to dust.

You need gloves for protection from the resin; do not neglect your sleeves, as in this type of work you can easily get resin on your forearm as you work fiberglass into a concave mold. Nitrile is usually best for both polyester and epoxy resin (though always check the specific brand of glove and resin before making a choice); avoid latex gloves, as they can absorb the chemicals in the resin, and some people are allergic to the latex itself. Some glassers like to put a **barrier cream** on their hands before putting on gloves. Never use a barrier cream in the absence of gloves. Splash goggles and an apron or some other type of coveralls are a must as well, otherwise you will be tracking toxic and irritating dust back to your home.

Resin also releases toxic and harmful vapors as it cures. Polyester releases styrene vapors; these irritate the respiratory system as well as attacking the nervous system to cause symptoms similar to drunkenness. The International Agency for Research on Cancer (IARC) classifies it as "possibly carcinogenic" to humans. Epoxy resins can differ greatly in what they contain, so check the MSDS of your specific product; even the least toxic epoxies still require gloves and respirators.

Use disposable mixing sticks and brushes for this work, as it takes far too much acetone to clean them for reuse; besides, the unmixed catalysts on them will continue off-gassing fumes indefinitely. Do not just throw them into an open trash can that remains in your shop; remove the trash from the building or seal it up (or better yet, seal it *and* remove it). Use plastic mixing bowls; flexible ones can be squeezed, which will break most of the cured resin right out of it. Polyethylene is the preferred plastic to use, as it is chemically inert and the easiest to clean. Be aware that other kinds of plastic may dissolve in polyester resin, so take care when using plastic containers or mixers that have been repurposed from food containers and the like.

such as wood, plaster, metal, or glass, but it needs a release agent and cannot have undercuts. Flexible molds supported by a mother mold allow some undercuts. Do not forget to use mold release. Petroleum jelly inhibits the surface cure of polyester resin, so use PVA (polyvinyl alcohol, *not* white glue; see Chapter 14 for more information on mold releases).

Your first coat, called the **impression coat**, will be just resin. Coat the entire surface of the mold with either a thickened resin, or by slush-casting the interior. The impression coat will take on whatever texture the mold has. If you are using polyester resin, a gel coat is used for the impression coat.

It is helpful to have all the pieces you will need cut and laid out beforehand. Cut the pieces with a sharp scissors, as a knife does not always work as well. Wear gloves even when cutting, as the nearly invisible glass shards will get into and under your skin. Do not try to make a large sheet of fiberglass conform to a complex shape; it is better to use several little pieces. For most props, you want to keep your pieces of fiberglass cloth no bigger than a sheet of paper.

Lay your pieces over the entire surface of your mold, with the edges of the individual pieces slightly overlapping each other. Mix a batch of resin and brush or roll it over the surface of all the cloth until it is fully saturated. You can tell it is fully saturated because the cloth becomes transparent. Press or roll out any air bubbles that get trapped under the cloth; a brush stiffened with previously cured resin can be helpful for this task. For larger areas, it is helpful to run a specialized ridged metal roller over the sections as you complete them to further remove air bubbles and help the layers stick to each other. Try to avoid breaking large bubbles up into several smaller bubbles as these become more difficult to remove.

Once you have one layer of the mold completely covered, begin covering with a second layer in the same manner, but criss-cross the strips over the seams of the previous layer so that the strands are running in a perpendicular direction. Do not pick up or slide the fiberglass once it has been placed down in the resin. Again, work air bubbles out by jabbing with your brush; all the pieces need to be pressed fully against the layer before it.

Two layers are often enough for handheld items, but you can continue adding more layers in this manner if you need it. Fiberglass mat or chopped strand mat can be used to add thickness over or between the layers of cloth. If you are using woven roving, you can do so after your first or second layer of cloth.

Some projects benefit from a layer of mat or surface tissue (sometimes called "veil") between your gel coat and the first layer of your cloth. This helps mask the texture of the fiberglass, which may show through on the surface of the final piece.

An alternative method for applying fiberglass is to dip the pieces of cloth directly into the resin, then squeeze out the excess, and lay it on your form or in your mold. This method is much closer to the method used to apply papier-mâché. The rest is the same; you must still overlap each piece with neighboring pieces, you need to work out all the air bubbles, and the weave in subsequent layers should run perpendicularly to the weave in the previous one.

To finish off, you can paint a thicker "flow coat" of resin over the whole piece. For polyester resins, use either a wax-type gel coat or cover the top with plastic sheeting such as polypropylene or cellophane (avoid plastics that are dissolved by polyester resin, such as polystyrene).

The texture of the surface of the mold or form is reflected in the surface of the finished object. Covering the outside with plastic gives the added benefit of imparting a smooth finish to the exposed areas. If the exposed area is a flat surface, you can cover it with glass as well while the resin cures.

When finished, let your piece cure for a few hours. Once it is hard enough to hold its shape, you can remove it from the mold. If you do this before it has fully set, it will still have enough flexibility to make demolding easy.

If you have made a multi-piece mold, you can join the pieces by carefully trimming the piece to the parting line, and then fitting the pieces together. Join them with another layer of fiberglass that you wet with resin over the seam. Try to make this as smooth as possible. Doing this, of course, means you will not get perfect fidelity, particularly if your mold has a lot of fine definition and detail.

If you are putting fiberglass over a form, you may work in the opposite direction, where the last layer is the one that is visible. A gel coat is still necessary with polyester resin as the fiberglass needs resin on both sides to help it all catalyze. You may finish with a layer of fiberglass finishing cloth, which is a finer and thinner type of cloth that will give a smoother surface.

Fiberglass is finished by rasping, filing, or sanding. It is easier to do before the resin has fully cured. The dust is extremely toxic, and any kind of abrading will release tiny glass particles and fibers into the air that you should absolutely avoid breathing in. It is often preferable to coat and sand the surface with additional material, such as plastic body filler (Bondo™) rather than trying to sand the surface smooth.

You can cut and trim the jagged edges from the cured piece with very strong scissors or a hack saw. Any individual glass strands that stick out are as sharp as daggers, and extra care needs to be taken to make sure nothing will pierce an actor's skin while handling the prop. An angle grinder can be used as well, though the dust released is a dangerous irritant; wear a dust mask, and do this only where you can extract the dust directly at the source. Fiberglass dust that gets in the air will settle over everything, and if it is disturbed months or even years later, it can still harm the lungs when inhaled. If you wish to give the edge a smooth finish, you can paint it with a heavily catalyzed resin.

You can also cast with fiberglass by mixing chopped glass directly together with catalyzed resin to make a paste. This thick paste is brushed directly on the mold. Though not as strong as reinforced glass cloth or mat, the fiberglass does help minimize the shrinkage of the resin.

Carbon fiber is another cloth that can be reinforced with plastic. It is significantly more expensive than fiberglass. Epoxy is the most commonly used resin, which also adds to the cost (though there is no reason why polyester resin cannot be used). Where fiberglass turns transparent when saturated with resin, the difference between wet and dry carbon fiber cloth is very difficult to see in all but the best of lighting situations; an unsaturated section of cloth means a weaker piece and the possibility of delamination.

Though it can be laid up by hand just like fiberglass, it really needs to be vacuum-bagged to reach its full potential of high strength and low weight. For most props shops, the proper setup is far too costly and complex, so plain old fiberglass is more than enough. Besides, carbon fiber is such a high-performance material that its advantages are rarely needed in your average prop.

Both fiberglass and carbon fiber come in **prepreg** versions, which have been pre-impregnated with resin. They require "vacuum bagging" to hold them in place, and they need to be heated to around 300°F for a few hours to cure (*never* heat plastics in the same oven you cook food in).

Figure 15-17: This helmet was laminated from two layers of fiberglass. The prop maker drew marker lines to indicate the direction of the weave on the fiberglass cloth. As he laid the second layer on, he could see that those lines were perpendicular to the lines in the first layer, indicating that the weave itself was perpendicular. Photograph and prop by Harrison Krix.

Vacuum bagging involves surrounding the material in an airtight bag, and then pulling all the air out as the resin hardens; it is like having a clamp on every inch of the surface. It is a bit more complex than can be described here, but information is easily found online and in books.

sixteen

surfaces

You still have work to do after your prop is constructed. The surfaces need to be cleaned up to make sure they are free of defects and sharp or jagged edges. If you wish to paint it (covered in chapter 17), it will need to be prepped to allow it to be painted on. If you need a smooth or glossy surface, you will need additional sanding and polishing. Any kind of texture you wish to add will need to be applied. You may also need to coat or seal it to give it additional properties, such as preventing the surface from being scratched off, making it water resistant or flame retardant, or giving it more (or less) shine.

Sanding

Many new artisans are surprised at the amount of sanding and filling needed to complete many fabrication and sculpture projects, and woefully underestimate the time it will take. In many cases, sanding and filling can take more time than the actual sculpting or constructing.

Sanding is necessary in some cases for safety reasons; a rough prop can cut or scratch an actor. Some sanding may be needed to help paint, adhesives, or other coatings stick to the surface better. Finally, sanding is often what transforms an object from a homemade-looking craft object to a realistic item that belongs in the world actors inhabit.

Sandpaper comes in different grits, indicated by number; the higher the number, the finer the sandpaper. It will give you a smoother finish, but removes less material. Lower numbers are coarser and remove material much quicker. Generally, you want to work your way up with two or three (sometimes more) different grits, from coarse to fine, to get the smoothness you need.

Don't skip grits. Do not go from 80 grit to 220 grit. The 220 grit will have to work really hard to remove the scratches left from the 80 grit. It is far more efficient to go from 80 grit to 120 grit and then to 220 grit.

The same grit number on different types of sanding devices will give you different results. For example, an 80-grit piece of sandpaper is different from an 80-grit grindstone.

Start with the most powerful tool and the coarsest grit your material and prop can handle. Obviously, you don't want to take a belt sander to a piece of doll furniture; you want to smooth large areas as quickly and efficiently as possible. As you move into the finer details and smaller areas, and your prop gets smoother, use less aggressive tools and sandpaper with a finer grit. Eventually, you will end up hand-sanding the last little bits.

With **wet sanding**, you use special wet/dry sandpaper, and you keep both it and your material's surface wet while you sand. The water keeps the dust from getting into the air. Besides being safer, this is helpful when you are sanding in between coats of paint and you want to create a very smooth and glossy surface. Since the dust is kept out of the air, it will not later settle on subsequent coats of paint as they dry. Wet sanding is more labor-intensive, and you should not use it on materials that will absorb water, otherwise you will trap water underneath your paint or coatings, causing problems later on. Wet sanding is typically used only before putting on the last one or two coats of paint or other coating.

One of the secrets for getting an ultra-smooth and glossy finish is for every layer of the process to be as smooth as possible. You can't spray one coat of metallic spray paint on a cinder block and expect it to look like a piece of sheet metal.

Fillers

Filling is the act of adding material to the gaps and crevices in your prop; these can be from using a coarse or rough material, or the result of imperfections and mistakes when making it. Also, if you use fasteners such as brad nails, you often want to cover up the little hole they make to hide them. You usually fill it with some kind of self-hardening paste-like material. The goal is to have some kind of substance that, when dried, can be smoothed to an even surface.

Most artisans do their filling before sanding, though sometimes it can be a back-and-forth process as sanding can reveal imperfections that were not readily apparent.

After a first round of filling and sanding, you can paint your prop with a coat of primer to help accentuate any remaining imperfections that need to be filled and smoothed.

To apply fillers, a **putty knife** is often used. This is a thin and flexible piece of metal with a long flat edge; they come in a variety of widths useful for different situations. It is important to keep the blade clean and free of dried bits of filler, as these will keep you from smearing out a smooth surface.

Joint compound is a calcium carbonate-based filler. Calcium carbonate is used to make other types of fillers and patch-repairing materials, such as Fix-It-All™. If you have ever done work on your house, you have probably used joint compound on your walls to smooth things out. You can use joint compound on props, though it is brittle, so if your prop flexes or bends, or is treated roughly, it can crack and break off.

Spackle was originally a trademarked product, though it now refers generically to gypsum (plaster) mixed with glues. The word may also be used interchangeably with joint compound, and its use and application is very similar.

Putty is a general term for a dough-like material that fills a crack or gap and hardens in place. **Painter's putty** has

Figure 16-2: I spread joint compound over all the surfaces of this oversized microscope so that it can be sanded to a smooth finish.

traditionally been calcium carbonate mixed with linseed oil. It is usually white and is easily painted over.

Wood putty or **wood filler** is similar to painter's putty except it has additional fillers to make it match the color of wood. It is stronger than joint compound and less toxic than more tough fillers. It is less strong when used to fill corners or edges that have chipped off, and will flake away just as readily as joint compound.

It is also meant to accept wood stains. Of course, even though it can be stained, this does not mean it will match the surrounding wood in color and tone; frequently, it does not. If you really wish to use a wood putty that can be stained over, you can make your own. Known as "cabinet makers' putty," this involves taking fine sawdust from the wood you wish to fill (not chips or shavings) and mixing it with carpenter's or hide glue to make a paste that can be pushed into the hole. You can thin this recipe with water if necessary. Wood stain pens and waxes can be used for further refinement if the color does not quite match. A brown marker can be used for really quick emergency fixes, like when the piece of furniture needs to get on stage, and the audience is already seated in the house.

Figure 16-1: A putty knife.

Caulk is used to seal gaps and joints. Most home versions of caulk are made of either acrylic or silicone and are meant to create waterproof seals that can flex as the materials around them flex with changes in humidity and temperature. Caulk is made of other materials as well; some (like the brand Mortite™) remain flexible nearly indefinitely, and are useful for other prop-related tasks, such as set dressing. While caulk is rarely needed for props, it may come in handy when you need to build objects that will be exposed to or submerged in water. Acrylic caulk is also a useful ingredient in other texturing materials as you will see later in this chapter.

Plastic fillers cure to a much harder finish than the above putties, and they shrink a lot less. They can often be machined and drilled without cracking or flaking away, making them much better fillers for corners and edges. They are, however, more toxic than most putty, as they can contain plastic resins, solvents, and more. A long-favored brand name in the entertainment world is Dap™ Plastic Wood™. **Plastic auto body filler** is extremely popular with many props artisans. The most ubiquitous brand by far is Bondo™, whose trade name is used generically as both a noun and a verb because of its popularity. It is made to stick to metal, though it adheres to nearly any kind of rigid surface. It is about the consistency of organic peanut butter and can be smeared or troweled onto any surface, though thicker portions will run or drip off vertical and upside-down surfaces.

It gasses off the same toxins as other resins, making it necessary to work with adequate ventilation and respiratory protection; ideally, it will be left to cure in a separate environment so that other prop makers in the shop are not exposed to the fumes. When sanding the cured plastic auto body filler, the dust is also a hazardous sensitizer and should be kept out of the air, out of your lungs, and off your skin as much as possible. It is best to use a sander hooked up to a vacuum or dust collector while working in a spray booth or other well-ventilated area. Wear gloves and sleeves as well as a dust mask. Though highly useful, many shops are not equipped to work with it safely. It has a very noticeable odor that will indicate that you do not have enough ventilation and respiratory protection.

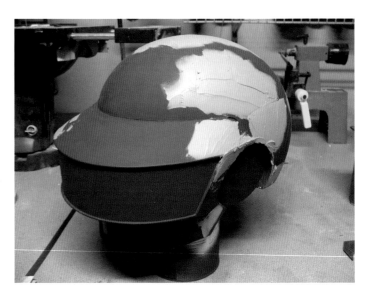

Figure 16-3: This helmet has been sanded, filled, and then primed. Further imperfections were then recoated with plastic auto body filler as shown here. Photograph and prop by Harrison Krix.

As plastic fillers adhere well to metal, a plastic putty knife is a better tool to apply it with. Cheaper disposable plastic putty knives are great because cleaning the hardened plastic filler can become laborious.

A **skim coat** is a thin layer of filler spread over an entire surface to give it a smooth or level look. While it is helpful to apply the skim coat as smoothly as possible, little imperfections here and there are alright; the skim coat material is meant to be easily sandable, which will get rid of those imperfections.

Some of the fillers already mentioned can be used as skim coats, though as props are handled more than the walls of your house, joint compound may be too fragile. Some filler materials do not make good skim coat materials, because they behave poorly when spread into a thin layer. Many of the texture compounds listed in the next section can do nicely as skim coats; really, a skim coat is just a layer of smooth texture as opposed to a layer of some other texture. A good skim coat material will

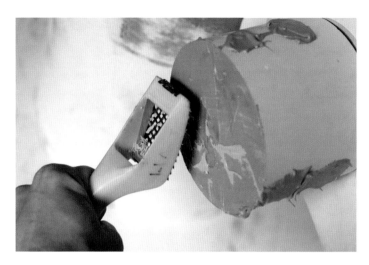

Figure 16-4: When plastic auto body has cured for around five minutes, it ceases to be spreadable, but is not yet rock hard. You can rasp or surform it down easily to save time sanding later on.

Figure 16-5: The texture on the bottom of this Medusa head came from the spray paint itself; by leaving the foam unsealed, the solvents in the spray paint ate away portions of the foam. This is also a useful technique for adding a rocky or stone-like texture to foam. It must be done in a very well-ventilated area and requires a respirator as well (this is true for using spray paint in general).

not be so runny as to drip and ooze down the surface as it dries. It should also not dry so hard so as to make sanding too difficult. When you have divots, dimples, holes, and other inset imperfections, you will never get a smooth surface unless you sand all the way down to the lowest point of deepest recess. Of course, if you are applying the skim coat to a horizontal or flat surface, a runnier material may help, as it will "self-level." Make sure to check the instructions of your filler, as some specifically state they will not work when applied in thin skim coats.

Texture

Texture on the surface of your prop can be achieved in three ways: It can be intrinsic to the material your prop is built out of, it can be added on top of your prop, and it can be removed from the surface material of your prop.

Some textures can be difficult or time consuming to replicate through faux means, and building the prop out of materials that already contain those textures is a good solution. Using reclaimed or old lumber for an ancient wooden prop or rusty steel for a metal one is often used in the prop-making world. If you consider that only the visible portions need to showcase the texture, you can build the structure and interior of your prop out of standard construction materials, saving the more interesting (and probably less structurally sound) materials for the outermost layer. Taking this idea to the extreme, your prop may actually only need a "skin" of the textural material. Rather than adding a plate of heavy steel to your prop, you can build it out of wood and adhere a sheet of thin steel to the surface; the end result will look the same.

Likewise, fabrics and leather are materials that can be glued to the surface of your prop to give a look which is labor-intensive and artistically tricky to achieve with paint alone. Using a damask or other embossed fabric, for instance, you can simulate old embossed metal with the right paint treatment.

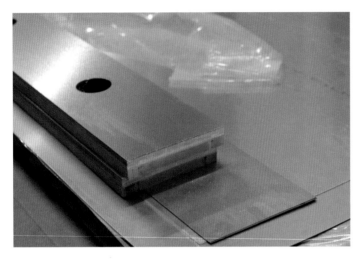

Figure 16-6: These pieces of MDF have a thin sheet of polished aluminum laminated to the surface. When fully assembled, the whole outside will be covered in aluminum with no indication of how thin it actually is. This allowed the artisan to avoid having to construct the entire prop out of aluminum or to come up with a complicated paint treatment to try and simulate it.

Scenic artists in theatre and film traditionally used plaster to coat all the surfaces of the scenery and, while still wet, manipulate it to simulate the texture of wood, metal, marble, and whatever other materials needed to be faked. These artists are known as **plasterers**, and though the materials used today include much more than just plaster, their techniques are useful to the props artisan. **Roping** is a term for dragging a loop of hemp rope through a texture coating that is still wet. The result is a surface that looks like it has been painted over many times, as you would see in an old building. Many other tools and objects can be used for other effects. Combs, for instance, can mimic the heavily grooved surface of old, weathered wood. Brushes, sponges, and rolled-up rags will give you other surfaces. Even just a putty knife or a **screed** (a flat board used to smooth concrete) used without completely smoothing all the wet material can add some depth and texture. Screens and

various fabrics, lumpy fruits and nuts, balls, ridged objects, and many other hard items can be improvised to create an impression with a random or repetitive texture.

Plaster stenciling is a technique that can be modified for other materials such as joint compound. It requires a thicker stencil than the kind used for inks and paints; tape or attach the stencil on top of the smooth surface. Trowel the plaster or other material into the stencil, and scrape it flat with your trowel, or a screed. The thickness of your stencil determines the thickness of your raised design. Keep in mind that many textural materials dry more slowly the thicker they are applied. If you want a thicker design, you can stencil it in layers; for an especially thick design, you may want to reconsider using plaster or dope and think about sculpting or carving it out of a rigid material and applying it to the surface.

The materials listed previously as fillers, such as joint compound, spackle, and putty, can work for texturing as well. Some work less well when spread in thin coats, while others are too fragile and crumbly to be used on a surface. For homemade texturing compounds, it is more useful to mix these fillers with glue and other binders to aid in adhesion and flexibility. Props artisans use the term *scenic dope* to refer to a number of these homemade concoctions mixed from the ingredients common to a props shop.

Scenic dope is a general term for a thick paste that can coat a prop. In the late 19th and early 20th centuries, scenic artists would mix whiting (powdered white chalk) with animal glue and a bit of water. This gave them a very sticky paint that adhered to muslin and canvas flats, giving them a smooth surface that allowed the paint to go on evenly. They found that by adding linseed oil they can make a thicker substance similar to caulk, and adding casein created a predecessor to joint compound. These thicker formulations allowed scenic artists to impart a three-dimensional texture to flat surfaces, even if they were vertical.

With our modern materials, a basic recipe for this scenic dope involves a quart of latex (house) paint, 2 to 5 tubes of latex caulk (*not* silicone caulk), and 1 or 2 cups of joint compound.

Figure 16-7: In this close-up of the torture device worn by the Red Pyramid character, you can see that the appearance of old, weathered wood was simulated by carving a series of overlapping lines of various lengths and depths into the surface. *Silent Hill*, 2006.

You can thin the recipe by increasing the proportion of paint; these formulas are good for self-leveling imperfections in the surface you are coating. Thicker recipes are good for more dimensional textures, or for coating vertical surfaces; very thick formulations are almost as sculptable as clay.

A variation on scenic dope involves mixing joint compound with white glue; start with equal proportions, then vary the amount of joint compound or glue depending on how thick you want your mix. This makes a more flexible dope. Even if your surface is rigid, a flexible dope is sometimes preferred, as straight joint compound can flake and crack off.

You can mix a number of additives and fillers as the basic recipe is fairly chemically inert. Water putty or plaster will make it harder (but more brittle) when dry. Paper pulp can be used to thicken the mix as well, to the point of making a clay. Other materials can help make a rougher or chunkier texture: sand, sawdust, wood chips, or gravel, for example. These can be mixed in or sprinkled on the surface for more of a "crust."

The haunted house industry has developed its own variation on scenic dope known as **monster mud**. Starting with a recipe like one part latex paint to five parts joint compound, you submerge strips of cloth into the mix rather than applying

Figures 16-8 and 16-9: This rusty bollard was coated with Bondo, which was troweled with a putty knife as it dried for a rough and crusty effect. Large grain sand was pushed into the wet Bondo in areas for even more grit. *Andromache*, the Workmen's Circle Theatre, 2009.

it directly. A large weave, like burlap, works the best. The excess mud is squeezed off these strips, and they are laid over the surfaces while still wet. It is similar to cloth-mâché, except that you are using the cloth to create textures rather than trying to make a smooth surface. You can also use large pieces of cloth and drape them over statues so that they will simulate sculpted fabrics, rather than attempting to sculpt the folds and drapes from a solid piece of material.

Depending on the thickness of your dope or mud, it may easily take several days to dry. Though they dry rock hard and are fairly water resistant, they are not entirely waterproof, and will require a further protective coat if used outside or around sources of moisture.

Elastomeric roofing compounds are meant to coat a roof in one application; they are flexible because of the high amounts of expansion and contraction the roof will undergo, and are waterproof and very wear-resistant as well. Prop makers have embraced these products enthusiastically, with one brand; named Jaxsan (Jaxsan 600 to be specific), being the most popular by far. It is essentially a very thick acrylic latex elastomeric paint. It can be tinted with other acrylic paints. They are usually applied in one coat in whatever thickness you need. They can be worked with tools like other textural compounds while wet to shape the surface. They dry to a hard but rubbery surface. One difference from other compounds is their inability to be sanded once dried. You have to get the texture right while it is still wet, and it is virtually impossible to make a smooth coating with it.

A number of polymer emulsions specifically formulated for use in the entertainment industry are used by prop makers. Sculpt or Coat is one; it is meant for applying a thin coat over surfaces, with some dimensional texturing possible. It can also be used as a laminating medium for mâché or as an adhesive. Crystal Gel is useful for similar reasons, though its results are a bit different; it dries clear and has a bit more body.

Acrylic gesso is not the same as traditional gesso. It is a clear acrylic binder mixed with calcium carbonate for body; some brands may include white pigment for extra whiteness.

Figure 16-11: Glitter was applied to this phone headset for Santa Claus.

Figure 16-10: Jaxsan 600 is used as a coating on these sheets of foam to create fake ham slices for a comical sandwich. The Jaxsan imparts a flexible textured surface that will accept paint. Photograph and prop by Anna Warren.

It is meant to coat canvas, so it remains very flexible when dry even though it also seals and protects. Unlike the other materials, which are meant to go on fairly thick, acrylic gesso often needs to go on thinly in several layers. For small props that will be seen up close on camera, it can be a good material for smoothing out a surface without disguising any of the intricate detail.

Texture from Particles

I've already mentioned that particulates such as sawdust, sand, and dirt can be mixed in with some coatings to give it a texture. You may also wish to "paint" these directly on top. Coat your surface with a clear glue or binder, and then sprinkle on your particulates. When the liquid dries, you can brush or blow the excess particulates off.

Glitter is often applied this way. A slightly thinned PVA glue works well, as do decoupage glues and clear polyurethane or acrylic sealers. While this is still wet, you can sprinkle the glitter on from a container with holes in the top (like an oversized salt shaker), or grab a handful and gently blow it onto the wet surface.

Small fiber particles, known as "flock," can be blown or dusted onto a surface coated with adhesive. This process, known as **flocking**, is often done by model builders to simulate grass, dirt, or carpet, but prop makers can find it useful to add texture or tactile effects to numerous types of props, such as adding a faux velvet liner to the inside of a fancy carrying case.

Coating Foam

Foam, particularly extruded polystyrene foam (XPS), is a popular choice for sculpting props, particularly larger items. Left on its own, however, it is difficult to paint and very fragile. You need to coat it with something. Foam coating has so any considerations, it gets its own section here. Many solvents will dissolve foam, so you can't just put anything on it.

Figure 16-12: This map wanted to look like a topographical model. The top was painted with PVA glue, and we sprinkled on model railroad grass, which is a fine, green flock. Here, Jay Duckworth uses the same technique in spots to add individual "trees." *King Lear*, the Public Theater, 2011.

Ask what you need. Is the coating just to let you paint it? Does it need to provide impact resistance to the foam? Do you want to add texture, or perhaps sand it smooth?

If you just want to paint the foam, you only need a thin coating to keep the foam from absorbing the paint; if you want to use spray paint cans, you also need a barrier to keep the solvents from attacking the foam. PVA glue works well, especially if you thin it down a bit and brush it on. Acrylic gesso has more body and dries to more of a "shell," so use it if you need a bit of a thicker coating or if you want to smooth out the surface a bit.

Liquid latex is another option, as are elastomeric paints (the extra thick and rubbery paints used for priming rough surfaces).

For a thicker shell that will protect the foam and allow you to add texture or sand it smooth, try a mix of joint compound and PVA glue. Straight joint compound is usually too fragile, particularly because foam has some "give" that will cause the joint compound to flex and crack. Scenic dope, whose recipes were described earlier, is also useful. Plaster may be used to make a hard and smooth surface, though the final prop will be heavy and, if the plaster is put on thinly, fragile. It is also hard to apply over a three-dimensional surface. Rubberized roofing compounds, such as Jaxsan, can be used, though the resulting surface is not sandable.

A number of ready-made products are available that will give a hard shell to foam. Their advantage is that they are already mixed to the perfect consistency for coating foam, and their properties are superior to just joint compound and glue. Their disadvantage is that they are far more costly than the homemade concoctions.

You can find many custom products specifically made for coating foam. Vanillacryl™ and Sculpt or Coat™ are used like paint, while Rosco Foamcoat™ is more of a paste. Rosco FlexCoat™ gives a more flexible coating, and remains light. StyroSpray™ and Styroplast™ are examples of two-part polyurethane made to be brushed or troweled on XPS or EPS foam. Water-based resins, such as Aqua-Resin™ and Aqua Form™, can also be used as a coating to give a hard shell that can be sanded smooth.

Foam may also be covered in a shell that is laminated on. Papier-mâché and cloth-mâché will provide a strong but lightweight surface for painting. Applying cloth-mâché with cheesecloth rather than muslin will give a very thin coating that will not obscure as much detail as thicker coats.

Fiberglass gives a very strong shell to foam, and foam is often used strictly as the form to give fiberglass its shape. The polyester resin used for fiberglass will dissolve the foam though. You will either need to use epoxy resin (more expensive than polyester) or place a barrier between the foam and the resin. In this case, straight joint compound can be fine, because it is only serving as a chemical barrier rather than an impact barrier. If the loss of detail is acceptable, wrapping aluminum foil or plastic cling wrap around the foam may be the quickest and easiest solution.

Plastic resin without fiberglass may be used as a coating as well. Again, polyester resin will eat the foam; epoxy and polyurethane resins will not. You may need to use laminating versions of these resins, or they may take an especially long time to cure when applied in such thin coats.

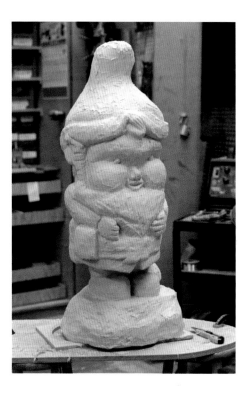

Figure 16-13: This three-foot-tall foam sculpture has been coated in Rosco Foamcoat™. *Broke-ology*, Lincoln Center Theatre, 2009. Scenic design by Donyale Werle.

Distressing and Aging

Weathering, aging, and breaking down a prop is often done with paint and other colorants (covered in Chapter 17), though more severe or textural distressing can be achieved by physically altering the surface itself. For particularly effective results, you will use a combination of physical alteration and paint application. Physically distressing a prop usually works best if you build the prop somewhat nicely and regularly at first, and then do all the distressing at the end. If you build it distressed from the beginning, it might not be sturdy enough, and you will surely end up with a less believable "look" to your distressing.

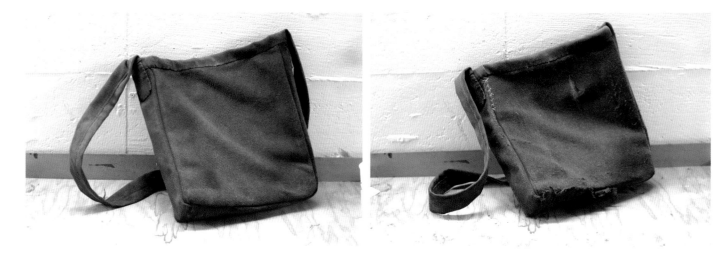

Figures 16-14 and 16-15: To distress this bag, portions were worn with a rasp and even torn. Large hand stitches were added to other parts. Pieces of shredded fabric were sewn on the bottom so it would look as though the bag was torn and coming apart without weakening the structure of the actual bag.

Fabric can be tattered or worn down with a rasp, file, or a surform. If the prop has fabric trim, it can be pulled free and stretched. If you are aging a piece of upholstery, you can layer fabrics so they show through underneath the rips and tears. The cushions can be made saggy or even flattened to show a lot of age and use. You may even unravel the edges so some threads hang down. You can attach other fabric with a loose weave, such as cheesecloth, and then pull the threads so they are hanging free.

Sandpaper, rasps, and files are frequently used to wear down the edges of objects or paint, and areas where other objects would have rubbed against them, such as hands gripping the handle. For more pronounced aging, you can use a jigsaw, reciprocating saw, or other tool to actually cut away chunks and corners. A grinder with a sanding disc or abrasive flap wheel can remove wood quickly, as can a belt sander. For more subtle effects, a palm sander may be all you need, while for smaller props, a rotary tool works great. A rotary tool has a lot of options with different bits depending on whether you want aggressive distressing or subtle aging.

You can run a blowtorch over the wooden board until it is blackened. With a wire-brush in your drill, brush away all the ash. You should reveal a heavily raised grain pattern.

Heat and flame can also be used to scorch the edges of fabric. Always do a test for the degree of flammability on a scrap piece of fabric first, and keep a cup of water and fire extinguisher handy. Many synthetics will melt rather than burn.

Nuts and bolts in a canvas bag or heavy chain can be beaten against surfaces to give them random divots for a "beat-up" look. This works well on wood as well as sheet metal. The effect can often be heightened by darkening the recesses with paint and lightening the raised areas.

Though you may wish to simulate grime with paint, sometimes you just need to rub actual dirt over your prop.

The most important part of aging and distressing is to assemble research and reference pictures and think about what actually happened to your prop: how it was used, where it was stored, and all the other aspects of its life. Do not just pick a technique and start attacking it randomly, or you will end up with those cheap faux vintage objects sold at discount home goods stores.

Protective Coats

Beyond color and appearance, the coatings you apply to your prop also serve as protection. At a minimum, you want to be able to handle your prop without the colors coming off onto your hands. For some products, this can be a nuisance as it stains your skin and possibly your clothes if they come into contact with the prop. For other products, it can actually be a health hazard to touch. If nothing else, you need to seal your prop with a protective coat to keep this from happening. Beyond that, it depends on what your prop will be subjected to. If it will be outside, in a wet environment, or even just in an especially humid place, you may want to think about adding a water-resistant or even waterproof coating to your prop. If your prop will be in a high-heat environment, you need to protect it against that as well. Even display windows at retail stores can be subject to high heat; because of the greenhouse effect, an uninsulated window can raise indoor temperatures up to 300°F. Props that are near automobile engines or other high heat sources need further protection.

These coats can also add or subtract "shininess" to your prop's surface. Some products have an inherent sheen, while others come in a range of choices, from matte to glossy. Many props for both camera and stage benefit from a **satin** finish, which is halfway between matte and glossy. A matte finish often looks dead and sucks up light, while a glossy finish creates a distracting glare. For props in front of the public, such as retail display, trade show props, or convention halls, a glossy finish may be preferred.

The term **varnish** can encompass many materials and substances; it is a generic term for a resin dissolved in a liquid meant to give a hard, clear, and shiny surface over a material when it dries. Resin varnishes are typically dissolved in a solvent, while acrylic varnishes are held in water. Varnishes are also made from polyurethane, epoxy, and oils. It protects the surface it covers, as well as seals in any pigments, dyes, or stains used

and keeps them from rubbing off on skin and clothes. With all the choices in varnish, you can easily find one that will work on your material and give as much, or as little, shine as you desire.

Clear acrylic binder can help seal. Some floor polishes actually deposit a thin coating of acrylic onto a surface, and it is watered down for use in a spray bottle, making it very easy to get even coverage. One extremely popular brand is the cleaning products by Pledge™ containing what they call "Future™ Shine" (formerly known as "Future Floor Wax™"). Acrylic sealers can be quite flexible, and so are good on surfaces that may need to bend or move.

Leather sealer can be any number of different products (modern ones are usually polyurethane or acrylic), but it is meant to be very flexible so that it will not crack or flake off from leather goods. Vegetable-tanned leather needs to be sealed to make it stain and water resistant, and also to keep dyes from rubbing off if you dye it. Most leather sealers will also work well on suede, vinyl, and other flexible plastic sheets.

These and other specially made products can seal fabric as well, but sealing fabric will alter the way it drapes and moves, as well as its appearance. It may be better to start off with a fabric that has a natural water or fire resistance. These days, you can find all sorts of coated fabrics that can repel all manner of stains and particles. Think ahead to what your fabric will be exposed to, and choose accordingly, rather than assuming you can seal it afterward.

Almost all of these sealers mentioned are available in spray versions. When you come across one, check the ingredients to see what type it is; most are some variation of polyurethane or acrylic. Some call themselves "lacquer," but they are not lacquer in the traditional sense; most are either acrylic or polyurethane resins dissolved in a solvent meant to impart a "lacquer-like" finish (meaning a hard and shiny coating). More and more spray coatings are coming out with water-based versions. These help you limit your exposure to solvents, though you should test them out first. The water-based version of a familiar product is not going to act the same as the original solvent-based version.

Wood can be sealed with many of the aforementioned products, and it has some of its own traditional products as well. A number of oils can be used over unsealed and unpainted wood. Sometimes these are necessary because certain water-based sealers are incompatible with certain wood stains (red mahogany stains in particular). Otherwise, they typically contain more solvents than water-based polymer finishes and take far longer to dry (some traditional wood finishes require over a week to apply and dry).

Tung oil is an environmentally friendly and less toxic alternative to more modern wood finishes (be careful, as some synthetic finishes may claim to be "tung oil finishes" despite containing little to no actual tung oil). It is applied over bare or stained wood, imparts a shiny and slightly golden tone to the surface, and is very water resistant. The downside is that it takes

Figure 16-16: Translucent coats can also impart some "texture" to a surface. Here, Rosco's Crystal Gel is painted over this printed portrait to make it look as though it has dimensional brushstrokes. The effect is subtle, but shows up nicely as light hits it from different angles. Photograph by Jay Duckworth.

two to three days for each coat to dry, and the traditional method involves using five to seven coats, with sanding in between each coat; a prop can often get away with one, two, or three coats.

Mineral oil can be used over bare (not stained) wood to create a food-safe finish. As with other oils, it is brushed or rubbed on, left to soak for a few minutes, and then the excess is wiped off.

Flame-Retardant

If your prop is appearing on stage, it most likely needs to be flame retardant to some extent. Fire laws differ wildly between locales, states, and countries, but nearly every nation that allows live theatre has some kind of requirement for the flame-proofing of items appearing in front of an audience. The typical way of testing the materials is by holding a lit match to them. The flame needs to go out after a set amount of time. If the material makes a bigger flame, or if hot molten bits drip off onto other surfaces, then it is probably not a good item to have on stage while several hundred people sit in a closed room with only three exit doors.

In some cases, the finish you are applying is adding some degree of flame-retardancy to your prop. In other cases, you need to add a flame-retardant over your final coat; some flame-retardant chemicals can be mixed in with your paint or coating as well. For many surfaces, the flame-retardant is clear and thus unnoticeable. When you add it to fabrics and other non-rigid materials, you can introduce a level of rigidity to your material that you may not like; if the fabric comes into contact with bare skin, the actor will feel itchy. There are inherently flame-retardant fabrics you can buy; one of the more well known is silk. Theatrical suppliers will also sell inherently flame-retardant versions of common fabrics such as muslin and canvas. If the flame retarding of your prop is going to be an issue, it is better to plan ahead as far as possible. It is far easier to flame-proof a material that is already fairly flame-proof. It is far harder to build something out of gas-soaked matchsticks and then try to make it flame retardant.

seventeen

painting

Figure 17-1: Painting soft polyurethane foam with acrylic paint to resemble French fries.

If you want something to look like brass and you build it out of brass, then your work is done. But in prop making, we are frequently making objects out of one material and want them to look like another. Even when we make it out of a material that it is meant to be made out of, we still may wish to alter and vary the color; for our brass object, we may wish to weather and age it. If we make a wood object, we may wish it to be a bit darker or maybe redder.

We use several methods and materials to change the color of our object: paint, dye, colorants, and ink. We can also modify the color through chemicals, heat, or physical means.

Color Theory

Color has three basic characteristics: hue, saturation, and value.

Hue is the name of the color. Red, green, and blue are hues. **Primary colors** are the three hues that cannot be mixed from other colors, and from which all other colors can be mixed. Artists have traditionally considered red, blue, and yellow to be the primary colors, while modern printers use cyan, magenta, and yellow.

If you make a wheel showing all the colors, the primary colors will be spaced evenly around this wheel. In between each of the primary colors are the **secondary colors**, made by mixing two primary colors together. Using red, yellow, and blue (known as the RYB color model) as our primaries gives us secondary colors of violet, orange, and green. If you mix yellow and blue, you will get green.

Tertiary colors are made by mixing a primary color with its adjacent secondary color. These can have simple hyphenated names, such as red-orange or green-blue, though they also have more traditional names defined by artists.

- red + orange = vermilion
- orange + yellow = amber
- yellow + green = chartreuse
- green + blue = aquamarine
- blue + violet = indigo
- violet + red = violet red

With these 3 primaries, 3 secondaries, and 6 tertiaries, we have 12 hues arranged around our **color wheel**.

Saturation, the second basic characteristic of color, can also be referred to as **intensity** or **chroma**. The saturation is the vividness of the hue. Pure red is very saturated. A grayish red or a pink is less saturated and has a lower chroma. The colors directly across from each other on the color wheel are **complementary colors**. Blue and orange are complementary colors. If you mix complementary colors together in equal amounts, you get a neutral gray. So to decrease the saturation of a particular color, you mix a bit of its complementary color in.

The final characteristic of color is **value**, also called **brightness**. It is the relative lightness or darkness of a color. When you mix white with a color, you raise its value; this is often referred to in scenic painting as a **tint**. If you add black to darken a color, it is called a **shade**.

To further understand the relationships between hue, saturation, and value, we can expand our color wheel into a **color sphere**. The pure hues run around the equator, and neutral

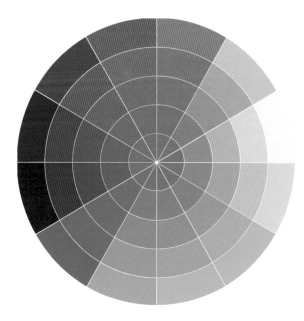

Figure 17-2: One example of a color wheel. The outside has 3 primary colors, 3 secondary colors, and 6 tertiary colors. As the colors approach the center, they lose saturation.

Figure 17-3: This strip shows the hue cyan at different values, with pure white at the top and pure black at the bottom.

gray is in the center. White is the north pole, and black is the south pole. As you fly around the equator, the hue changes. If you dig toward the center, the saturation decreases. If you travel north, the brightness increases, and if you travel south, the darkness increases.

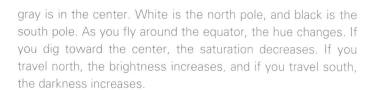

The pure hues (the completely saturated colors) do not have the same brightness as each other; they have different **relative values**. For instance, pure yellow is much brighter than pure purple.

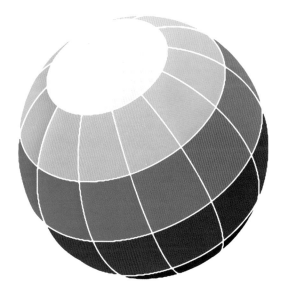

Figure 17-4: The exterior of a color sphere.

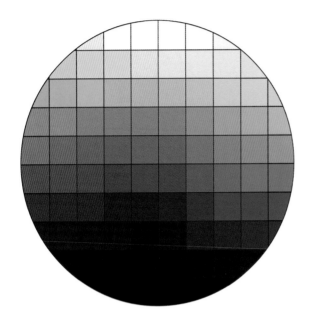

Figure 17-5: An interior section of the color sphere cut in half between cyan and orange. You can see the range of colors possible by moving around the full range of saturation and values.

When mixing your colors, take the most direct route to a color. If you run out in the middle of painting, if you need to repaint your prop, or if you later need the same color for another prop, you want to be able to mix the same color again; if your color involved using a whole lot of paint colors in tiny quantities, it can be impossible to mix the exact same color a second time. It is more expensive to buy separate tubes and cans of every possible color you may use, but it can be worth it. When we look at painting techniques a little later, you will see that you can layer paint on top of each other or add glazes and washes to tone it; it may be easier to paint a pure yellow layer then add a pure raw umber glaze over the top to tone it, than to try to mix the perfect umber-toned yellow in a single coat of paint.

It is also important to note that mixing together different paint colors may not result in exactly what is expected within the color wheel. Paint pigments may not line up exactly with the hues on the color wheel. You also have a whole lot of chemicals working together, and when you mix them, they may react in strange ways. If you mix two different *kinds* of paints together, even more unexpected results may occur. A blue oil paint and a yellow acrylic paint, for instance, will not mix together at all.

Colorant

Colorants can refer to any sort of material that is added to another material to alter the color. It is a general term that includes both pigments and dyes, as well as any other type of substance or chemical that alters the color. All colorants in use today are listed in a database known as the Colour Index International, which began in 1925 and is maintained jointly by the Society of Dyers and Colourists (UK) and the American Association of Textile Chemists and Colorists (US). It currently lists over 13,000 generic color names used in over 27,000 products. Not all of these are used to make paints or dyes.

Good artist paints will identify the pigments used in their paint with a pigment code and/or constitution number. Both the code and the number point to the entry in the database that includes information about the ingredients, origins, and suppliers of that exact pigment. The colorants used in dyes will also be assigned names and numbers in this database. You can use the codes to see how many pigments a paint contains, to compare whether two different brands of paint or dye use the same colorant, and to check their toxicity.

Paint

Paint is really just a colored coating. Coatings can do all sorts of things, such as protect from sunlight, water, impact, etc., and can also change the appearance through color and texture.

Paint is made from three components: pigments, a binder, and a medium (or vehicle). A **pigment** is usually some

An example of the information you can find on a specific colorant in the Colour Index International is shown below.

CI generic name	C.I. constitution number	Common name	Chemical composition	Proprietary, Historic and Marketing Names
PB 16	74100	Heliogen Blue	Metal Free Phthalocyanine CAS 574-93-6	Brilliant Green Blue, Caribbean Blue, Helio Turquoise, Marine Blue, Sapphire blue, etc.

Some pigments have both a CI generic name and a CI constitution number, while some only have one or the other.

The chemical composition lists the name of the chemical used and its CAS number. The CAS number gives you another source to find information about the pigments you are using, including an MSDS from the chemical's supplier. It is vital to know what pigments are in your paint because some of them are toxic and are associated with reproductive and developmental hazards. Lead, for instance, while banned from house paint, can still be found in specialty artist's colors and various paints for industrial use.

When the term *hue* is used in a pigment's name, it indicates an imitation of an expensive or toxic pigment. Chromium Yellow Hue, for example, is meant to be the same color as chromium yellow without containing any actual chromium yellow. Hues do not mix together as well as true pigments, but they are cheaper and less toxic.

kind of substance ground up into a fine powder to act as the colorant.

Most house paint is mixed from as few as 12 to 16 colorants. You will never get the range of colors you can from using pure pigments, particularly with very saturated colors. Also, when you thin paint that contains more than one pigment, the pigments often separate. Black paint you buy at a hardware store can contain 12 different colors that become visible when you thin it down. A black paint containing only one pigment, such as carbon black, will remain black no matter how much you water it down. This is also true when you mix two or more paints; a large number of cheap pigments will result in a muddy mess, where two or three pure pigments will give you the color you were expecting.

The second component of paint is the **medium**, or the fluid that the other ingredients are dissolved or suspended in. Paint becomes dry when the medium fully evaporates away.

The **binder** is the "glue" that adheres the pigment to the surface once dry and keeps it from falling off.

Paintbrushes

A paintbrush has three main parts: the handle, the ferrule, and the bristles. The variations in size, shape, and materials of these three parts lead to an almost endless selection of paintbrushes. With props, you may deal with painting objects that hide in the palm of your hand all the way to items larger than an automobile. The general size of the props you build will determine what kinds of paintbrushes you need, as will the level of visual polish your prop needs.

The bristles are made of either animal hair or from synthetic fibers. Natural hair bristles are usually more expensive and of higher quality than synthetic fibers, though synthetic fibers are becoming more and more refined each year. The ferrule is the piece of metal that is wrapped around both the handle and bristles to hold them together. There is no standard to the naming of the different brushes; they may be differentiated by the shape of the ferrule, the width of the brush, the length of the bristles, the shape of the bristle ends, or even the task the brush is meant for.

A **flat-ferrule** brush is one of the most common shapes and is especially popular in house painting and scenic art. Lay-in brushes and priming brushes are types of flat-ferrule brushes, and their names indicate that one of the advantages of this shape is its ability to quickly apply a lot of paint to a surface. This makes them useful for priming, base coating, dry brushing, glazing, and wet blending as well. A Dutch brush is a particularly wide lay-in brush developed to apply dutchman, which is an early scenic art term for wheat paste or scenic dope.

A sash brush was developed for painting window sashes without getting paint on the surrounding wall. The bristles are

Figure 17-7: A sash brush.

Figure 17-6: A lay-in brush.

Figure 17-8: A fitch.

cut at an angle so that one side is longer than the other. It is actually intended to be held perpendicularly to a regular brush, that is, on edge. This lets you draw a narrow but very sharp line.

Oval-ferrule brushes have elliptically-shaped ferrules. A fitch is one type used by scenic artists for painting organic shapes such as foliage (they are sometimes called "foliage brushes" for this reason). The ferrules are usually tapered so that the bristles fan out a bit. A scenic liner is a type of fitch in which the ferrule is flattened and the bristles are cut in a rounded shape so that the center is longer than the edges; this shape gives them the ability to paint fairly straight lines. An angular liner has the bristles cut at an angle, making them useful for straight lining with a lining stick. A lining stick is simply a straight piece of wood used to guide your paintbrush in a straight line, much as a steel straightedge is used to guide a pencil or knife. The bottom of a lining stick is usually beveled to keep the paintbrush from coming into contact with it.

Round-ferrule brushes include stippling brushes, which are useful on stencils. The paint is dabbed on, rather than brushed.

Lettering brushes can come in a variety of ferrule shapes and are designed for creating all manner of letters for signs. Their bristles are typically squared off so that you can paint

sharp corners with them. They can be useful for a number of precise prop-painting tasks.

If you do a lot of painting, it is good to have a set of nicer brushes for doing higher-quality work as well as having plenty of cheaper brushes around. If you work with interns, students, or less experienced people, you will often find brushes left out with paint still in them, the bristles mashed and spread out, and brushes used for spreading glue and epoxy. Even when you emphasize proper brush care, these things are inevitable, and it is better for them to happen to cheap brushes than to your expensive set.

Remember that true "water-based" paints remain soluble even when dry, while "water-borne" paints made of synthetic polymers actually cure. If your acrylic or household paint dries on your brush, it may not wash off with water. Alkyds, adhesives, and many coatings will also be impossible to remove from the bristles once allowed to dry. If you wish to reuse a brush, but not right away, and do not wish to wash it at that very second, you can keep it from drying out by wrapping it in plastic, such as cling wrap, so that it is not exposed to the air.

Figure 17-10: **Chip brushes** are cheap flat-ferrule brushes sold at most hardware stores meant for applying solvents, stains, glues, and resins; they are also handy for priming and lay-in work. Their cheap price means they can be used as disposable brushes in many shops. They can also have their bristles cut into a variety of shapes and profiles for specialized tasks and faux finishes.

Figure 17-9: Lettering brushes.

Figure 17-11: For more detailed work, **acid brushes** are sold in bulk for economical prices and are meant for the same uses as chip brushes. It is a good idea to have a ready stock of chip and/or acid brushes around for tasks (or people) that may ruin your better-quality brushes.

Paint Rollers

A paint roller consists of a handle, a rotating roller frame, and a removable roller sleeve or cover. The roller cover absorbs the paint, and as you roll it over a surface, it deposits it in an even manner. The paint is typically held in a roller tray, which allows you to coat the roller cover all over. Rollers are useful for covering large surfaces quickly; they also avoid brush strokes (though they can impart their own texture and roller marks if done carelessly).

Like paintbrushes, paint roller covers come in a variety of materials and configurations that have different advantages depending on the surface you are painting. **Nap** refers to the thickness of the material on the cover; shorter naps are great for imparting a smooth coating on a smooth surface, while longer naps will coat rougher and more-textured surfaces better

Figure 17-12: **Foam brushes** are made from a single piece of soft foam rubber rather than bristles, and are useful for pushing paint and other coatings around without creating brush marks.

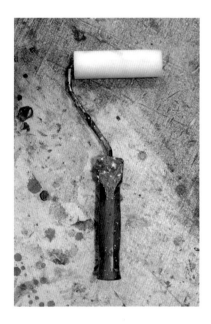

Figure 17-13: While the most common size of paint rollers for house painting is 9", the 4" or 3" kinds are often more useful for the props artisan.

(but may impart its own texture to a very smooth surface). A ½"-¾" nap is typical for "general" use, that is, a smooth surface with some slight texturing, such as wood, plaster, and sheet metal.

For latex paints, you want to stick with rollers made of synthetic materials. Lambskin and other natural materials are useful for alkyds and other solvent-based paints, but they are far too absorbent for latex paint.

Foam roller covers are useful for coating very slick surfaces; the foam absorbs almost none of the paint and imparts barely any texture. Foam roller covers are also indispensable for spreading glue or adhesive.

Specialized roller covers are also available with various textures for imparting effects and faux finishing techniques. **Rag rolling** involves using a fabric-covered roll, which can be purchased or made in the shop by wrapping a rag over a paint roller. Tying string around a roller in random configurations will also allow you to roll out various patterns of paint rather than a solid color.

When using a roller, make sure the surface of the roller cover is fully charged with paint. A roller tray is useful for this. A tray will have a well filled with paint next to an inclined surface. Touch the roller cover to the paint, and then roll it over the

Figure 17-14: Rollers with a 1/4" nap on the left and a 1" nap on the right.

inclined surface. Do this several times to charge all parts of the roller cover; you should never fully submerge the roller cover in a bucket of paint.

Begin rolling out in an unpainted portion. Roll the paint out from there to the edges in long, even rolls. Keep a wet edge. When the roller runs out of paint, recharge it, and then begin working in another unpainted section; work your way back to the previous wet edge. When your surface is completely coated, you can work out paint buildups and roller marks by lightly moving your roller cover over the whole surface to smooth out the paint coverage.

For extremely smooth surfaces, you may need to run your roller over the entire surface after it is painted. Beginning at one end, roll in a straight line from one edge to the other. Move over so that the next roll is slightly overlapping the first one. Hold your roller at a slight angle so you are placing less pressure on the side that is overlapping; in this way, you are feathering the edges as you go along.

Spray Paint

Spray painting can open up a number of effects not achievable through brushing or rolling, such as very smooth and even coats, or subtle transitions from one color to the next.

A **spray can** is an aerosol can of paint filled with its own propellant. These are the easiest to use; you buy the color you want from a paint or hardware store and press the cap to spray the paint. After it becomes empty, the entire can is recycled. You can find a vast array of colors and types of paint, as well as a number of specialty finishes and coatings. These have traditionally been solvent-based alkyds, though you can now find acrylic and latex spray can paints, as well as water-based versions of some of these. "Dusting" with spray cans is a cheap and easy way to add subtle toning without needing to hook up and clean an airbrush.

Spray cans are sometimes called **rattle cans** because of the rattle they make while you shake them. It is vital to shake these extremely well for several minutes before using. The rattle comes from a metal ball inside which helps move the paint around as you shake.

You can also find refillable aerosol cans, which use pressurized air rather than chemical propellants. One of the most common brands is made by Preval and distinguished by its glass jar and long skinny neck; many painters use "Preval" to refer to any hand-pump spray can.

Spray guns come in a wide variety of types and styles, using pressurized air from either an air compressor or from a hand pump.

A **garden sprayer** has a hand pump attached that pressurizes the tank; they were originally intended as a way to spray water or pesticides on home gardens, but they were readily adapted by painters as a cheap and easy way to spritz paint onto a surface. The paint comes out in larger droplets than with other spray guns, so they are often used for spatter effects and other textures rather than for laying down smooth base coats. Popular brand names of smaller garden sprayers include Floretta and the P-50. A larger type of spray gun related to garden sprayers is the **tank sprayer**, so named because it has a detached tank that sits on the ground, with the spray nozzle connected by a hose. One of the most popular brands of tank sprayer is the Hudson™ sprayer, and many painters refer to all tank sprayers as "Hudson sprayers." A quality brass nozzle will help you control the quality of the spray coming out and allow you to achieve almost airbrush-like effects. A cheap plastic nozzle will strip the threads if you try to tighten it down enough to get such a fine spray. Keeping the nozzle clean is also imperative; run warm water through all the parts after every use, and be sure to strain the paint to keep debris and chunks from running through your sprayer.

You can find all sorts of **electric spray guns** meant for the home improver or contractor types. These basically have an air pump built in. They are less adjustable and customizable than those that hook into an air compressor, but they are more portable since you are not limited to use near your air compressor. They are also very loud because the tiny air compressor has to pump constantly. They are better at laying down an even coat of paint than a garden sprayer, though.

An **HPLV** gun stands for "high volume low pressure"; these guns shoot out a lot of paint at a low pressure. This cuts down on overspray and material usage; of course, you will also get the paint too thick if you spray in one location for even a fraction of a second too long. They are one of the best guns for quickly covering a large object with an even coat of paint. Though they require a separate air compressor, they offer more control and better results than an electric spray gun.

An **airbrush** is one of the smaller types of spray guns. This is most popular for model makers and people working on smaller props, as it shoots out far less paint than other guns. The pen-shaped brush is also easier to manipulate. "Airbrushed" often refers to artwork with the subtle and even shading that airbrushes are particularly adept at producing.

There are a couple of techniques that are useful when spray painting regardless of what kind of gun you use. When spraying to get an even coat of paint, do not swing your arm in an arc. Swinging brings the gun or can closer to your material in the center and farther at the sides. Instead, sweep your arm in a parallel line to the surface you are painting so that the gun or can maintains a constant distance while paint is coming out.

When you get to an edge, continue moving and spraying until no more paint is hitting the surface. If you stop moving while paint is still hitting the surface, you will build up a pool of paint in that one spot, which may drip or run. Overlap each subsequent pass of paint.

In most spray guns or cans, as you run out of paint, the paint will sputter and spatter out of the nozzle rather than be emitted in a continuous mist. Always make sure you have enough paint before starting a pass.

Place your object on a turntable to allow you to spray all sides without having to touch any of the surfaces to move it around. If that is impossible, at least ensure that you can reach all the parts you want to paint without having to move the prop. You can suspend an object as well if you need to hit all sides as well as the top and bottom.

Place the object on three pins or spikes so you can paint all the way to the bottom. If you rest a prop on the floor, the paint on the very bottom can adhere the prop to the ground, and when it dries and you pull it up, you can peel a bit of the paint away, leaving a jagged line.

Any kind of reusable spray paint tool demands that you clean and wash it out once you are finished using it. Most spray guns have a network of thin pipes to carry the paint; if even a small amount of paint is allowed to dry inside of these or on the outside of the nozzle, it will slow or completely block the passage of any more paint. For most sprayers, when you are finished using them, you should fill the tank with plain water and spray that out over the sink for a few minutes.

Other Tools

A **sponge** is used to add paint in a random pattern. Natural sponges are preferred by painters because their surfaces are more random and their round shape allows the edges they leave to be feathered.

Figure 17-15: Spraying any kind of paint introduces solvents, hazardous chemicals, and particulates into the air. A spray booth, such as this one at Costume Armour, Inc., is often needed. This helmet is on a turntable, which allows you to rotate while spraying so you can hit all sides without having to touch wet paint.

A **flogger** has strips of muslin or other cloth attached to the end of a stick. It looks like a mop and is used either by slapping it against the prop (called "flogging") or by swishing and twirling it over the surface ("schlepitchka"). Most of the time, it is dipped in paint and wrung out so that it is nearly dry.

Tools such as **feather dusters** and **combs** are useful for various faux finishing techniques, and their use will be discussed in the upcoming sections. **Rags** and other cloths are useful for wiping on coatings, particularly wood stains and clear oil finishes.

While there are certainly hundreds of brushes, rollers, sponges, stamps, and other specialized implements for implementing well-tested painting techniques, do not be afraid of experimenting with nontraditional and offbeat tools. Filling a balloon with paint and squirting it out can give you interesting spray patterns; dropping paint onto a surface that is rapidly spinning can result in very natural-looking burst patterns.

Masking

Not every prop has a uniform color or paint treatment. In many cases, different parts and areas have different colors or even designs. You may try to freehand these different areas, or you

Figure 17-16: A selection of natural sponges.

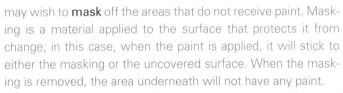

Figure 17-17: The gold and green accents on this park bench were created by sponging on the paint.

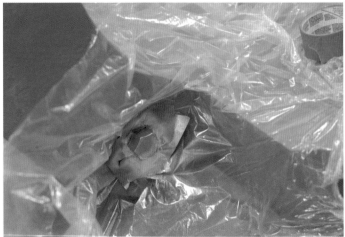

Figure 17-18: When spray painting, you want not just masking tape to give clean edges, but also something to cover the rest of the prop to keep **over-spray** from settling on the surfaces.

may wish to **mask** off the areas that do not receive paint. Masking is a material applied to the surface that protects it from change; in this case, when the paint is applied, it will stick to either the masking or the uncovered surface. When the masking is removed, the area underneath will not have any paint.

Masking tape is one of the most common materials used for masking. It sticks well enough that you can create a sharp line of delineation between paint colors, but it will not stick enough to leave residue or damage the surface underneath. For larger areas, you can lay down any sort of nonabsorbent material as masking and use masking tape along the edges to hold it down and define the edges.

Many different kinds of masking tape exist for different purposes and circumstances. House painter's tape (typically beige) and painter's tape (typically blue) is often rated for staying on a surface anywhere from 1 to 60 days without leaving residue. Auto body masking tape is usually graded to provide extremely clean lines (lesser grades, such as painter's tape, will sometimes allow paint to bleed through underneath resulting in a less than perfect line). Newer tapes (such as the brand

FrogTape™) are coated with polymers to quickly "gel" the paint, preventing it from bleeding underneath.

Masking can also be done with a liquid compound that dries on the surface and can be peeled off after the paint dries. Batik is an effect accomplished by painting a dye-resistant wax to the portions of fabric you wish to remain uncolored. Latex is another example of a material that can be used for masking; just apply it to areas to be masked in a thin layer, and let it dry completely. After painting, lift one corner, and the whole mask should pull right off.

Careful masking does take time and patience; one way to cut down on the need for masking is to paint the different parts before assembling.

Whether you paint with brushes, sprayers, rollers, or other tools, your basic steps in painting remain standard: priming, base coat, overpainting, and breaking down. Painting your prop is more of a concept than a step-by-step process; every prop will require a different method to achieve its final look. Just as you can break down your prop into simpler components, you may wish to break down the coloring of your prop

Figures 17-19 and 17-20: These footlights for the New York City production of *Sleep No More* were painted gloss black with a border of bare metal around each face. I used masking tape to cover these lines; carefully masking off the areas took far longer than the actual application of the paint.

into simpler steps and colors. It may be helpful to develop a painter's elevation (a sample of the paint treatment for your prop) to get approval from a designer first, if one hasn't already been provided to you. It helps to have a research image or reference for the paint treatment needed. I will describe some of the variations for base coats, overpainting, and breaking down that you can apply to your prop; think of these as the tools and ingredients for a paint job. I will describe some examples of how to accomplish the more common faux finishing techniques; think of these as sample "recipes." For the look you are trying to achieve on your own prop, you can use these recipes as is, or alter them slightly with different tools and ingredients. You can also develop your own recipes by combining the tools and ingredients in a new way. As with matching colors, making a paint treatment should be done in the most direct way possible; if you need to match the treatment to another prop, or if you need to touch up areas where the paint has come off, it can be difficult to get an exact match if your treatment has 39 different steps using dozens of different paint colors.

Priming

A prime coat is a coat of paint that completely covers your prop and gives subsequent coats a uniform base to stick to. If your prop is made up of a number of different materials, then your paint will stick differently to each of those materials. Even if it is made of the same material, different areas may react differently with your paint; for example, the end grain of wood is a lot more absorbent than the face. A prime coat seals the underlying material so that any paint added afterward will act consistently regardless of what is underneath.

Some materials require a bit more "oomph" to get primer to stick to them, and so special primers are marketed with extra ingredients. Metal may be primed with "etching" primer, which has an acid in it that etches the surface of the metal a bit to rough it up and remove surface impurities to give the paint good adhesion. Plastic primers often contain solvents that will soften the surface of the plastic a bit to help the paint bond directly into the surface. Primers with these types of solvents require adequate ventilation and a respirator while applying;

they should also be kept in a separate room or a spray booth while drying so that you are not breathing the fumes while working on something else.

Some primers are extra thick, elastomeric, or "spot-filling" primers, which allow them to cover imperfections or fill small spots as they go on.

Shellac can also be used as a primer/sealer. It dries quickly and can even be sanded smooth so that your next coating is smooth as well. Besides straight shellac, you can also buy shellac-based sealers, such as Zinsser B-I-N® Primer/Sealer, which has white pigment added. If you do not like shellac, you can find newer water-based sealers (most based on polyurethane emulsions) for a variety of materials in a hardware or home improvement store.

Liquid latex brushed on flexible or open materials (such as fabric) will give paint something to stick too. Water-based contact cements can be used as well (these are typically latex based as well). A 50/50 mix of PVA and water works well on particularly spongy surfaces such as the ends of MDF.

If you are trying to create an area of flat, smooth color, brush with a figure-eight or infinity sign loop. Even when you cannot see the brush strokes, they may still impart a slight texture that can show up in subsequent coats. If you need an extremely smooth paint finish, you can sand the paint down after it dries. To avoid brush marks, you can also roll or spray your paint on, though these techniques may impart a texture of their own. Stippling the paint on, rather than brushing, is time consuming for larger surfaces, but can create a more abstract and random texture than brush strokes.

It may take two or three coats before the surface is completely sealed; you can tell it needs more primer if the surface looks splotchy after it is dry.

Sometimes, your primer can serve as your base coat. Other times, you can put your base coat directly on without needing a primer. You may even find situations where you do not want to completely cover the underlying material; for example, you may wish to add a glaze over top wood so you can tone the color but still allow the grain to show through.

Figure 17-21: Most primers are a dull or neutral color because they contain much more binder than pigment.

Base Coat

Depending on what kind of finish you're going for, your base coat determines the underlying color. The base coat is flat coat of "average" color you want an area to have. Different areas of your prop may have different base colors. Some treatments demand that you start with a light base coat and build up the darker colors over top, whereas others are better when you start with a dark base and add successively lighter paints.

The base coat is typically applied with a wide flat brush. Thinner paint obscures the brush strokes better. For some paint treatments, you want a directional grain, such as with wood-graining. In these cases, follow the direction of the grain with the brush strokes of your base coat even when you are only using a single color and coating the surface evenly. Again, even though the brush marks are virtually invisible, the slight texture will affect later coats.

Let the base coat dry completely before drybrushing or washing so that the paint won't smear.

"Cutting in" the edges means you paint the edges carefully with a more precise brush or edging tool, and then fill in the rest with your larger brush or roller. Even if the other

Figure 17-22: These book covers have a white primer coat followed by a red base coat. *Cendrillon*, Santa Fe Opera, 2006. Scenic design by Barbara de Limburg. Photograph by Natalie Taylor Hart.

sections are masked off, it can be helpful to cut in the edges when the edge is not a straight line, or when it abuts to another surface that might get hit by paint on the side of your larger brush or roller.

When spraying your base coat, you may reach areas that are easy to spray paint into but will prove difficult to add additional paint to later with a brush. It is helpful to simply paint these areas a dark color or black so that they disappear.

The base coat does not need to be a single color. **Wet blending** is a method for applying two or more colors so that they do not have hard edges separating them. One way to make a wet blend is to use one brush for each color and lay them down in X-strokes, switching colors after every few strokes. You want to leave at least some distinction between colors (otherwise it just becomes a single muddied mess). The wet edges blend the paint for you.

For a little more separation between colors, you can lay in each color with only slight overlapping between them, and then take another brush that is wet but free of paint, and use that to feather and smooth the edges. This technique is helpful too when you wish certain areas to have distinct colors that have a

smooth transition to other areas, such as a **gradient** or an **ombré** blend.

For a more organic and random blending of the colors, you can wet your surface before applying the paint so that the colors "flow" together more naturally. You may also use a single brush for all your colors for an even more subtle blend, but again, you want at least some distinction between colors, otherwise you may as well have just mixed a single color for your base coat.

For more than two colors where one color is meant to be more dominant, you can lay in the two (or more) minor colors, and then use the third color to blend and feather the first two together. The multiple colors can also be applied with a sponge.

If you are planning on adding additional washes and glazes over your base coat, it is important to remember to over-emphasize the contrast and texture you are laying down. It is easier to tone something down, but if you start with a base coat that is already fairly subtle and muddy, it will only get muddier as you add more paint on top. You want the bright and bold colors and patterns hidden under the more subtle tones on top because they will catch the light and change the appearance as the color, intensity, and direction of the lights change, giving your prop more life and character.

Overpainting

Overpainting, as the name implies, involves adding paint over the top of the base coat. Overpainting does not completely obscure the base coat (otherwise, you are simply repainting a new base coat), but it allows some of the base coat to show through, either by using translucent paint, or by being used selectively in certain areas rather than over the full surface. Very few surfaces can be simulated with a single coat or color of paint; a **faux finish** is a combination of overpaint techniques meant to replicate some kind of material through the use of paint.

When attempting a multilayered paint treatment, remember to periodically take steps back and view the prop as a whole. Keep in mind too that it will be viewed in different

Figure 17-23: A mottled wet blend between red and yellow paint.

lighting conditions than those in your shop; theatrical lighting and audience distance often requires more contrast to "read."

A **wash** is where the paint is diluted to the point that individual brush strokes disappear and you achieve a field of uniform color. A **glaze** is when you apply a diluted coat of paint over a dry layer so that the original layer still shows through. This is done usually to alter the original color, either changing its hue or value. It is also used over a number of colors to tone them in a more uniform way. For instance, adding a brown glaze over a painted object will make all the colors slightly warmer. "Wash" and "glaze" are often used interchangeably—they both involve adding a translucent coat of color so that some of the underlying color and detail still show through—but there are some subtle differences. A wash is simply diluted with more of its vehicle (either water or a solvent if using alkyds and solvent-based paints), while a glaze is made transparent by adding more unpigmented medium. For example, if you want to make a glaze with acrylic paint, you can mix it with transparent acrylic medium (often called "matte medium" or "gloss medium" to indicate the sheen it imparts). For most paints, if you dilute it too much with just the vehicle, it will not have enough binder to stick anymore.

Besides toning your whole prop, you can use washes and glazes to deepen the shadows of your recessed areas. Darken your base coat and thin it down. Some artisans may use a mix of half water and half alcohol to thin the paint so that they have more drying time; you can also add a touch of dish soap to let the paint flow off the raised edges better. Push the paint around with a fine tip brush so that it flows into all the recessed areas; you can wipe the paint off the raised areas with an empty and dry paintbrush or just a cloth or rag.

Just as a darker color can add depth to shadows, so can a lighter color be used to add highlights to raised areas. Two techniques useful for this are scumbling and drybrushing.

Scumbling involves taking a dried brush, adding some paint to it, and then wiping or brushing most of the paint off. You then poke or even jab the paint onto the surface little by little. It works best when you are adding an opaque light color to a darker one; you can create subtle highlights that appear to blend together when viewed at a distance. Scumbling can be done with a sponge as well.

Drybrushing begins exactly the same as scumbling; add some paint to a dry paintbrush, and then wipe or brush as much of it off as possible. Where scumbling involves stippling the end of the brush in a manner such as pointillism, drybrushing involves lightly drawing the brush over the surface. This gives more of a "scratchy" result. If the surface has a bit of texture, it is also possible to add paint to only the raised areas. Drybrushing is frequently employed to lighten raised areas. Tint your base coat with white paint, and drybrush this lightly back and forth over the raised areas. You can repeat this with progressively lighter shades to get a smoother transition.

Thin paints can also be poured over surfaces rather than brushed or sprayed on. This can create a natural dripping effect (such as with water stains or rust stains). If the poured paint comes into contact with other wet paints, the ends will blend together in a more random and natural manner than by attempting it manually. You can also make the paint run in multiple directions by tilting your prop back and forth; blowing the paint

Figure 17-24: Look closely at how the recessed areas of this evil clown doll were darkened with paint, giving it more depth and form than if it was just painted with a solid color.

or using a blow dryer can add to your repertoire, or allow you to move paint on a surface that cannot be easily tilted.

Wet-on-wet techniques are used when wet paint is added to layers of paint that are still wet. This allows for a much more organic mixture of colors. Besides the previously described wet blending, techniques include blooms, spattering, and blotting. As with wet blending, some of these techniques may be used on the base coat.

A **bloom** occurs when your paint is still wet and you drop water or thin paint onto it. It will spread out to the edge, pushing the paint with it to create a jagged but random edge. If you are using water-based paint, you can also drop a solvent

Figure 17-25: The yellow was drybrushed over the coat of red.

such as alcohol onto the damp surface; because water and alcohol do not mix, the bloom will push all the pigment away in a random pattern.

As its name implies, **spattering** involves hurling tiny dots of paint onto your surface. A number of techniques exist depending on how big you want your dots, how big you want your spatter pattern, how dense you want it, and other variables. A tiny spatter pattern can be had by dipping an old toothbrush into paint, and then running your thumb along the bristles; the paint shoots out as you do so. You can also spatter with a brush; load it with paint, and then hit it onto your hand or a stick. If your paint is very thin, you can simply wave your brush around and do it all Jackson Pollack style.

You can lay a coat of paint down, let it dry a little, but while it is still wet, blot some of it up. **Blotting** can be done with a sponge or with other absorbent materials. Tissue paper and rags are useful. If you crumple and scrunch these materials, you can impart some random texture as you blot your paint. You can achieve different results depending on how wet your paint is when you blot it up. A similar technique involves covering your still damp surface with a piece of cling wrap plastic that is slightly wrinkled or crumpled. The texture of the plastic wrap allows the paint to collect and pool in a random fashion, but because the paint cannot absorb into the plastic, it leaves harder and more distinct edges and borders. You can leave the cling wrap on until the paint has fully dried for hard borders between the areas of paint, or remove it carefully while the paint is still slightly damp to allow some of the paint to flow back together and soften the edges.

Faux Finishing

Faux finishing techniques are used when you wish one material to mimic another material solely through the use of paint, though a slight bit of texture is added for some techniques. The underlying texture can do a lot to add to a faux finishing technique (while the wrong kind of underlying texture can do a lot to detract from it); be sure to review the texturing techniques in Chapter 16 so that you can develop a texturing and coloring process that works hand in hand.

Good reference material on what you are trying to mimic will reveal all the precise details and qualities in the material that make it recognizable as that material. I will paraphrase the old saying here; "Everyone knows what wood grain looks like until they have to paint wood grain."

Many faux finishing techniques can be achieved by careful application of the techniques I have already discussed. For silver-colored metals, you can start with a black base coat, and then follow that with a drybrush of silver paint. The less drybrush you apply, the older the metal will look. Gold and copper metals can be achieved with a dark brown base coat followed by a drybrush layer of the appropriate shade. Leather can be simulated with a black base coat and brown drybrush. Keep in mind that these techniques, and techniques you may read about elsewhere, are all examples of faux finishing techniques. You may find other ways to achieve the appropriate finish, and in some situations, they may not give you the look you are after.

Graining, or *faux bois* (French for "fake wood") is used in prop making to replicate expensive or hard-to-use woods, to mimic wood on a prop constructed out of another material, and to match woods used in other elements of the production.

Wood graining is aided with special tools such as a rubber grainer (sometimes called a "heel" or a rocker grainer) and combs made from either rubber or steel. The basic idea is to lay down a base coat of one color, and when it is dry, lay on a thinner coat of your second grain color. While this second coat is still wet, you can use a rocker grainer by dragging it in the direction you want the grain to run; slightly rocking the tool back and forth gives you "knots." Combs work similarly, though they will not give you knots. You drag it in the direction you want the grain to run. If you rotate the comb slightly as you drag it, the grain lines will move closer together; you can also slightly track it side to side as you drag it toward you. Many faux woodgrains work better if you create a higher-contrast grain pattern, and then tone it down with a glaze on top. You can again find special brushes for this, such as overgrain brushes, grain brushes, and floggers (not to be confused with the mop-style flogger; a flogger for wood graining is a brush with excessively long bristles). Some grain brushes have individual "tufts" so that they act like a grain comb; props artisans have also been known to use a brush that has dried paint on it, giving it the same action as a comb but in a more random pattern.

Marbling involves using many of the techniques already discussed and adding multiple glaze layers. For instance, a marbling paint treatment might begin with a wet-on-wet layer of two colors, a glaze, a splatter layer, a layer of veins, a sponge layer, and another glaze. Veins are often replicated by using a feather to drag wet paint across the surface. Though every marbling effect is different, most paint treatments rely on wet-on-wet techniques to achieve a natural marble look.

You can achieve some very luminescent effects by adding a lot of translucent glazes on top of your prop. In essence, you are creating a thick coating that holds pigments at different depths, so you can achieve a three-dimensional finish. This is why some surfaces look "real," and others look like a painted object. The surface of many materials change appearance as you turn and rotate them in the light; flat paint will not do this, but several translucent glazes will. Add some **mica powder** to this mix, and you can give a sparkly shine to your surface. Bronze powder, pearlescent pigments, and various other metallic powders and flakes can also be used. Some of these come pre-mixed in liquid form, though they often look flat when applied on their own straight from the bottle.

Breaking Down

Breaking down the prop means using aging, distressing, and weathering techniques to give the prop a bit of history; rarely are the objects in our world perfect and brand-new. Some art directors will claim that every prop needs at least some breaking down before it can go on camera; while this may not be true for retail displays and props for commercial exhibitions, the theatrical, film, and television world require props with some "life" to them.

Aging is the process of mimicking the normal wear and tear that accumulates when an object is used over a long period of time. Many materials develop a patina through extended exposure to air, sunlight, and humidity. **Distressing** may refer to the damage to an object that has become neglected or fallen into disrepair, or that has been exposed to more traumatizing events in its history, such as storms, fires, or wars. **Weathering** can be thought of as what happens to an object when it is left outside for a long period of time. **Antiquing** is meant to make an object look old, but well maintained. Whether you use these terms to denote differences in degree or situation, they all refer to the same premise; objects that are old and have a history look different from newly constructed objects.

Think of an object's age as just one more of its needs; another part broken down from all the complex parts that make up a single prop. It demands as much thought and research as the other parts. How old is this object? How has it been used in its past? Where has it been stored? Have people been taking care of it—maintaining it or even repairing it if necessary? Look at the script or other details of the production for clues; there might be a reference that this prop was left out in the rain one

Figures 17-26 and 17-27: These "before and after" pictures of a gun show how aging and weathering transform a prop from a flat object to an item with a life and a history. Photograph and prop by Harrison Krix.

Figure 17-28: This "metal" table (actually a wooden table covered in hardboard) was meant to look old and rusty. Notice how the rust colors are concentrated along the edges and corners. *The Brothers Size*, the Public Theater, 2009. Scenic design by James Schuette.

Figure 17-29: Colors were drybrushed on top of the base coat to make this oversized garden gnome for Lincoln Center Theatre appear as if it had sat outside in the weather for several decades. *Broke-ology*, Lincoln Center Theatre, 2009. Scenic design by Donyale Werle.

year, or that it has been in the attic for decades. Items that have been through a battle will look very different compared to an item left locked up in a trunk.

Armed with the information about the object's life, now you can look at the materials you have mimicked and research what happens to them over time. Various metals develop a patina over time, or rust if not taken care of. Many surfaces wear away and fade as they are handled by countless hands and bodies. Colors may fade, and paint may crack.

A chair from the 1920s will have around a century's worth of aging and patina. However, if the play or film takes place in the 1920s, that chair should look brand new. Do not age and distress things according to the current year; age and distress them relative to how old they should be in the production.

Distressing can also be done with actual physical manipulation of the prop, not just with paint. See Chapter 16 for these techniques. The line between overpainting and breaking down is not always clear; whether you begin by making a faux antique paint treatment, or begin with a clean paint treatment that is later broken down is up to you and up to the circumstances of the prop.

Watery washes of brown, gray, or black paint can fill cracks and make them seem to be filled with dirt, dust, and mildew. Diluting water-based paint with denatured alcohol will help it flow more evenly and enter all the cracks and crevices, rather than puddling up. Very watery washes can even go over the whole prop to tone it and unify the color a bit more. Some props artisans like to give the prop a **bath** of very translucent glaze, usually with a brown hue. Covering the whole surface of

Figure 17-30: The hotel key found in the janitor's mouth in the film *Silent Hill* was a resin cast, but the detailed paint job made it look like a piece of aged copper. The green spots are known as *verdegris*, and develop when copper oxidizes over time.

the prop with a thin coat of brown glaze gives it an antiqued look and unifies the colors. You may also dust the prop with spray paints, such as black or brown, to dull it down and give it a bit of grime. A spray paint known as Design Master™ Glossy Wood Tone has been prized since at least the mid-1980s by props artisans as a way to quickly age a prop by dusting the surface with it. A hand sprayer (such as a Preval) can be used with a wash, FEV, or watered-down dye for a similar purpose.

Water-Based Paints

The following paints are considered "water-based," but that term can be misleading. It essentially means that water, rather than an oil or solvent, is the vehicle. A water-based paint can be thinned with water and the brushes used to paint it can be washed and cleaned with water. However, since most of these paints "cure" rather than "dry," they become water resistant once all the water has evaporated (watercolors and gouache are the exception).

Though water is the solvent used as the vehicle, there can still be other solvents present in the mix to keep the synthetic polymers soft. While the paint is curing, these solvents are releasing fumes. Some paints advertise themselves as low or no-VOCs, or volatile organic compounds, which are released as solvents dry. Keep in mind that a "water-based" paint can still release VOCs. Also, if a paint advertises itself as no-VOCs, that just means it does not release any of the VOCs officially recognized as VOCs by the EPA; there may be other VOCs or harmful fumes and gases released. A product that advertises itself as "VOC compliant" may have simply switched its solvents to a VOC-exempt chemical. Many chemicals can be listed as low or no-VOCs simply because they have not been tested. However, the fact that they are solvents and that many of them are chemically similar to ones proven or suspected to be hazardous means they are likely to be hazardous as well. Always read the MSDS so that you know exactly what you are working with. Is it better to work with a chemical whose harm is known and so proper safety procedures can be taken, or to work with one whose effects are unknown and so cannot properly be protected against? Understand that any product that "cures" will release chemicals into the air, and it is up to you to determine how harmful they are and in what quantity they are released, so that you know how much ventilation is needed and whether you need PPE such as a respirator. Proper gloves and sleeves may also be needed when there is a chance the paint will get on your skin.

Acrylic paint uses an acrylic polymer emulsion as the binder. An emulsion contains water, so wet acrylic paints can be diluted and washed up with water. As the water evaporates, it begins a process in which the acrylic particles begin fusing together. So acrylic paint isn't simply *drying*, it is also *curing*, which is why it becomes water resistant when dry. You can mix additives into acrylic paint for texture and extra body, such as sand, silicate aggregates, marble dust, sawdust, etc. As long as you mix these in well enough to completely coat them in the paint, they should adhere to the surface you are covering.

Though not as cheap as other kinds of paint, acrylic remains popular for prop making because it is very easy to use, comes in a wide variety of colors, and will stick to many types of materials with very little surface preparation.

"Latex" paint, known as "house" paint, does not actually contain any latex (natural rubber); the term refers to the similarity in appearance between the binder and natural latex. The binders used can be any number of polymers, such as acrylic, vinyl, or PVA, used in any number of combinations. You can find latex paints that are 100% acrylic (also called "acrylic latex"), which is the highest quality but most expensive. Latex paints also tend to use a lot of fillers, so they are not as "pure" as artist's acrylics, which explains why they can be cheaper as well. Their lower price, ease of use, and ready availability make them useful in situations where paint quantity is more important than paint quality.

"Scenic" paint is not a specific type of paint, but refers to any kind of paint formulated for use on scenic elements and used by theatre, film, and television painters. Scenic paint can be acrylic, latex, soy-based, casein, or even oil. While artist's acrylics and paints are good for small hand props, they can get expensive for larger areas and can be fairly thick for quick application. Scenic paint is useful in these cases.

Most scenic paint has much purer pigments in a higher concentration than house paint, as theatrical applications often require more heavy saturation and vivid colors than houses and other buildings. The purer pigments also allow greater control in diluting and color mixing. They often have less binder than house paint since they are not meant to be permanent; this also helps make the colors more vivid. In some cases, painters like to wash the paint off a flat or set piece after a production to reuse it for the next one. Most scenic paint also dries to a flat finish, as gloss can create uncontrollable glare under stage or film lights. Gloss can always be added by putting a gloss coat over top or by mixing the paint with a gloss medium before applying. Scenic paints are useful for the props artisan when you have to match paint treatments and colors of the set, when you have to paint larger pieces, or generally when you wish to have the good pigment quality of artist's paints combined with the ease and convenience of using house paint.

Casein is a protein derived from milk. Because it is a natural protein, casein paint will eventually go bad and turn sour. If you have ever opened old cans of paint found in the back of a scenic paint shop, you are probably very familiar with the smell that bad paint can get.

Soy paints dry inflexible and brittle like egg tempera, so are not useful for fabrics or other flexible surfaces. You can find both oil-based and water-based soy paints. They show promise as a renewable and nontoxic alternative to petrochemical-based paints, but many of the water-based soy paints found in today's stores use so many chemicals and toxins to process it that using soy provides no real environmental benefit.

Watercolor uses water as the medium to hold the pigment and some natural polymer as a binder, with the most common being gum arabic (also known as acacia gum). As watercolors are frequently used on paper or canvas and rely on their translucency over the white of the surface for their effect, we rarely use them for props, which require coating an assortment of materials, such as wood and metal.

Gouache is made of the same stuff as watercolors, but it is opaque, usually because a white pigment, like chalk, is added. Fillers are frequently added to adjust the body or viscosity of the paint, or to affect other properties, such as drying time. Unlike other forms of water-based paint, watercolors remain soluble in water even after dry. Though this means they will wash away if they accidentally get wet, it also allows you to selectively wet sections of previously applied paint to blend them with other colors of paint.

Tempera, or "egg tempera," uses a water-soluble binder material that is traditionally, and most commonly, an egg yolk (called albumen). Egg tempera dries brittle and inflexible, so it is not useful on fabrics or flexible surfaces. Egg tempera is rarely produced commercially, due to its extremely short shelf life. Usually an artist mixes only the paint he or she needs for that day, though with refrigeration, egg tempera paint can keep for almost a week. Tempera paint can only be applied in thin coats. Deep colors or thick coats are achieved by building up dozens or even hundreds of layers. It is time consuming, but tempera is also one of the fastest-drying paints to use.

Commercially available tempera paint, often called **poster paint**, more often uses size or gum arabic as a binder, making it more of a gouache than a tempera. Watercolors, gouache, tempera, and casein paint all operate on the same principle—a pigment and a natural polymer dissolved in water—but they have become differentiated by historical traditions, cultural uses, and marketing lingo. Depending on the pigments used, they can be some of the least toxic and most environmentally friendly paints available.

Oil-Based Paints

Oil paint uses a drying oil as the binder. In some paints, the oil is the medium as well (it hardens as it polymerizes, much like epoxy), though in others, a solvent (usually turpentine) is added to thin it down. The advantage to artists with oil paints is that they take a long time to dry, thus allowing the time necessary to manipulate the colors to perfection. This becomes a disadvantage to the props artisan, who would prefer most paints to dry either instantaneously, or if you need to manipulate it wet for awhile, after a few hours.

Most modern oil paints for home and industrial use are known as **alkyds**. One advantage of alkyds is that they stick to a lot more types of surfaces; because they are solvent-based, most etching primers and plastic primers are typically alkyd paints. The good news is that once the paint is dry, you can use a different type of paint over it. Thus you can take advantage of the sticking power of alkyd paint for use as a primer, and then switch to acrylic paints for subsequent coloring coats. They can also be self-leveling, resulting in less visible brush marks, and give a smoother and glossier surface when dry. Of course, a lot of research and development is devoted to achieving these properties in water-based paint, so oil-based paints become more obsolete with each passing year.

Enameling an object is when you take a powdered glass, like ceramic glaze, and fuse it to the surface of an object, often metal, in a high-heat kiln. **Enamel paint** is meant to refer to paint that mimics this; it is usually an oil-based paint that dries to a hard and glossy coating. It can also be a water-based paint; it can be anything really, because it does not have anything to do with the actual enameling process. It is a marketing term, rather than a distinct substance, to describe any high-sheen and durable paint coating.

Any of the solvent-based finishes discussed in Chapter 16 can also have colorants added to act as solvent-based paints. You can add your own tints to some of these finishes, or find pre-tinted finishes sold as paints. These include urethane (or polyurethane) paints and shellac-based paints. "Lacquer" paints and finishes refer to any coating that dries to a very hard, smooth, and shiny surface. Lacquers have traditionally been oil-based paints, but more and more water-based lacquers are entering the market.

Disposing of Paint

Because of the solvents contained in paint, as well as the heavy metals and other toxic substances used as many colorants, large quantities of paint should never be disposed down a sink. Many shops will have a "slop sink" that allows for the disposal of some waste; these can be used to wash containers and brushes out in, but you should still refrain from emptying any considerable amount of paint into a drain.

Washing water-based paint off your brushes in the sink is alright in small amounts. To use less water and keep too much paint from going down the drain, you can start by wiping as much paint off with a rag. Fill a container with warm (not hot) water, and a little soap if necessary. Clean your brush in this, and then rinse it in another container filled only with water. You can do a final rinse in the sink if needed.

To dispose of large amounts of household and acrylic paint, fill the paint bucket with an absorbent material such as kitty litter or sawdust and let it dry out. Then you can dispose of it with other solid waste. Alternatively, you can spread the paint in thin layers on top of newspapers and let it dry out. If the paint is unneeded but still usable, you can often donate it to community theatres, schools, or other organizations.

Dye

Dyes are the other major way we add color to a prop. A **dye** is different from a paint in that the color soaks into the surface rather than being adhered as a coating over top. While a pigment is insoluble and thus suspended in the vehicle/medium of the paint, a dye is either a liquid color, or a soluble substance that forms a solution with its vehicle/medium. Fabric is often dyed because paint would stiffen the surface. Some wood stains also contain dyes that penetrate the wood's surface and color the wood itself. Any porous material, such as leather, paper, or even some plastics, can be dyed. The colorants for dyes, like the pigments in paint, can be looked up in the Colour Index International.

Most dyeing is done in vats or pots filled with water to allow circulation. Stainless steel pots are the best; many shops repurpose industrial kitchen supplies to use for dying. Copper, iron, and brass react with the chemicals in some dyes and should be avoided. For mixing, glass rods, stainless steel spoons, or plastic spoons are best; wooden stirrers or spoons can be used but will soak in dye over time and need replacing.

Figure 17-31: After dying, these handkerchiefs for the Santa Fe Opera are hung up to dry.

The dye is made soluble in water in the vat. The fabric is then immersed in it, and the dye soaks into the fibers. When the fabric is removed, the dye becomes insoluble again. Most dyes require hot and even boiling water to become fully soluble; silks, wools, and blends are usually dyed in water heated to 190°, while cottons and linens can be boiled.

"Always add wet to dry." If your dye is powdered, mix a small bit of water into it first before adding it to a dye bath. The same is true of any other chemicals or salts you may need to add to the dye bath; dissolve them in their own little bit of water first. Many dyes are also acids, so remember the cardinal rule from chemistry class: add acid to water, not vice versa.

Some shops dye fabrics in a washing machine; though it does not really get hot enough to permanently set the dye, it is far easier to do. Obviously, one washing machine should be set aside for dyeing; do not attempt to wash clothes in a washing machine used for dyeing, and do not dye fabrics in a washing machine meant to clean clothes.

Simmer the fabric in the dye bath for the length of time indicated by the instructions on the dye package (many household dyes average around 45 minutes).

Figure 17-32: A dedicated dye vat like this is hooked up near a water source with either a hose or a moveable faucet that can be maneuvered to fill the top. The PVC pipe at the bottom runs into a drain that is allowed to accept the chemicals in the dyes. It also has a dedicated breaker box. Like others, this one is directly underneath a fume hood to vent as many fumes as possible directly from the source. Many props shops use cooking pots and hot plates or range ovens for their rare dyeing needs, borrowing the costume shop's dye vat for more intense dyeing projects. Remember to pay attention to the requests of whomever you borrow equipment from and to always clean up after yourself when working in someone else's area.

Test your dyes on swatches. The color of the dye in the bottle or in the dye bath is rarely what will end up on your cloth. Also, wet cloth is darker than dry cloth, so you cannot tell what the color will ultimately be just by visual inspection. Dyeing is influenced by countless variables, and even commercial lots vary in color intensity. Overdyeing (dyeing something two or more times) may help, but repeated dyebaths will eventually deteriorate the fibers. After the dyebath, rinse your fabric until water is clear, which can take up to 40 minutes. Many dyes may also require a **fixative**, which is a chemical that prevents a dye from washing out over time.

The success of your dyeing endeavor depends on choosing the correct *dye class* for your fabric. Dyes are a varied group of materials, and the way you prepare one dye is not the same as how you would prepare other dyes. Some require adding additional materials to your dyebath, such as vinegar or washing soda; always read the instructions of the dye you are working with. Dyes also exist for coloring materials other than textiles, such as leather and plastic.

Acid dyes are a large class of synthetic dyes used for wool, silk and nylon. They are typically applied in a bath of nearly boiling water.

Basic Dyes are similar to acid dyes; they work well on silk, wool, and nylon, as well as on acrylic fibers, which are hard to dye with other classes. Acid and basic dyes are frequently diluted with water and used in scenic painting to achieve watercolor-like effects on absorbent materials.

Fiber-reactive dyes were originally developed to dye rayon. As rayon is a cellulosic fiber, they are also the best choice for other cellulosic fibers such as cotton, linen, rayon, raffia, and reed. These dyes only need cool to lukewarm temperatures. Brand names include Procion MX™, Hi-Dye™, Cibacron F™, Dylon™, and Fabdec™.

Disperse dyes were developed specifically for synthetic fibers. Use them to dye acetates, nylon, and polyester to brilliant and intense colors that are very wash-fast. They require extremely high heat in the dye bath. Some disperse dyes require a carrier to assist dye penetration; many of these carriers give off toxic fumes in the bath. Some disperse dyes can cause irritation to the skin when wearing the clothes, and are often only worn over other clothes.

Direct dyes are an inexpensive and simple alternative for cotton, linen, and viscose rayon. You immerse the fiber in the dye solution without any other chemicals. However, a post-dyeing fixative is often needed to improve wash-fastness.

Leather Dye is an alcohol-based dye for coloring leather. Newer leather dyes that use an acrylic base can also be found.

A **Union Dye** is not really a dye class, but a combination of two or more dye classes used to dye fabrics made of a blend of fibers. A **household dye** refers to the kinds of dyes sold in grocery stores, which are most often union dyes. The most common combine a direct dye for cellulose fibers and an acid dye for wool or nylon. Though they do not achieve the brilliance of color as individual dyes, they dye a wide range of fibers and are simple to use. Rit™, Tintex™, Cushings™, and Deka L™ are common brand names.

Another way to dye mixed blend fabrics is by dyeing the fabric in one bath with a dye class for one of the fibers, and then dyeing it in a second bath containing a dye class for the second fiber. Never mix two classes of dye into the same bath.

Union dyes are also useful on plastics that resist conventional paints, such as polyethylene. Like fabric, you want the dye water hot but not boiling. It is helpful to have a second pot of water of ice cold water nearby. As you heat the plastic, it may begin to deform from the temperature; remove it from the hot water, and submerge it in the cold to cool it back down. You may need to do this repeatedly; keep the plastic in the hot water for about 10 seconds or so, douse it in the cold water, and then move it back to the hot water.

Other plastics can be dyed with **solvent dyes**. PVC and ABS, for example, can be dyed by mixing a drop or two of solvent dye into "clear cleaner," a plastic cleaner/primer containing the solvent *tetrahydrofuran*. This solution is simply brushed onto the plastic. When dry, the dye should be an integral part of the plastic as opposed to a coating sitting on top. As with all solvents, it is vital to understand the proper safety precautions to avoid absorbing the solvent through your skin or inhaling the fumes into your lungs.

Figure 17-33: This mop is soaked in a bath of tea to tone the white fibers on its head down to more of a sepia tone. Photograph by Jay Duckworth.

Acid and basic dyes are two types that have been mistakenly called **aniline dyes** by theatre artists for years. Aniline is a substance originally used in making synthetic dyes, but it has practically disappeared from modern fabric dyes. Real aniline dye is still popular for staining wood and leather, though.

Tea and coffee remain popular ingredients for dyeing paper to make it look aged and antique. It can be used on absorbent material to either tone down the whiteness or to give it a fully ancient appearance. As with other dyes, the tea or coffee is brewed in hot or boiling water, and the material to be dyed is left to soak in the bath for several minutes.

Removing Dye

Diluted bleach can take colors out of cellulosic fibers but may ultimately destroy the fiber. Sodium bisulfate may be needed to stop the bleaching action after initial application. Spraying with diluted bleach is very hazardous in terms of inhalation.

Bleach destroys protein fibers and is not recommended for silk, or wool.

Household dye color removers often contain either sodium hydrosulfite (smelly) or thiourea dioxide (stronger). Both are mixed in a high heat bath and require ventilation.

F.E.V.

French Enamel Varnish, or FEV. for short, is shellac tinted with dyes and/or metallic powders, and thinned with denatured alcohol. Because of its ingredients, it is difficult to work with safely, particularly on large-scale projects. Still, it remains popular in some theatres as a finish, and if you can work in a well-ventilated area (or even a spray booth) while wearing a proper respirator and clothing, the results are pretty stunning. It creates a transparent finish that shows off some of the texture and properties of the material below, and it imparts its own light-reflective qualities. So, for example, it can be used to tint and color metal without getting rid of that "metallic" quality. Multiple layers can build up quite a rich and complex surface. The use of alcohol keeps it flexible when dry, so it can be used on leather and fabrics as well.

I've seen recipes that thin the shellac with as much as 16 parts of alcohol, but a good starting recipe is as follows:

- 4 parts denatured alcohol
- 1 part white shellac
- A few drops of dye

The dyes used must be soluble in alcohol, such as leather dyes, aniline dyes, or some acid and basic dyes. Union dyes such as Rit or Tintex are much safer, but they will not work straight out of the bottle. You need to either strain the salts out of the dye before using or rub off with steel wool after applying it.

You can paint, spray, or pour FEV to use it. The shellac is the binder, so once it dries, it is also set. It is not particularly washable or dry-cleanable, however. Remember too that shellac is not entirely waterproof, so further protective coats may be needed if it is an outdoor prop. The randomness and organic flow of FEV, which are part of its appeal, also make it fairly unpredictable. Like any other paint, always test on a sample or hidden portion of your material.

Distressing with Dyes

Aging and breaking-down effects can be achieved with dyes on absorbent materials such as fabric. As mentioned earlier, you can dip your fabric in a bath of tea or coffee to give it an overall dingy effect; any neutral dye, such as warm tan or cool gray, can be used for a similar effect. Dyes and FEV can also be sprayed onto fabric for selective effects. The same safety procedures need to be followed as working with dye baths; dyes and FEV give off harmful fumes that require proper ventilation and a respirator. Spraying them increases the possibility of inhaling toxins. You should also take care to block and mask areas from being hit by the overspray, as well as taking precautions to keep the floor from getting wet and slippery.

You can also apply dye by sponging, dry brushing, or even just pouring it directly over your fabric.

Wood Stain

Wood stain is an oil or dye that penetrates into the pores of wood to color it. Some wood stains are just thinned down pigments that act as a glaze over the wood; you can replicate some wood stains simply by making your own thin glazes from acrylic paint.

Wood stain is useful in making one species of wood appear like another. It is used to match period furniture, which was often stained to darken it or impart a richer color and accentuate the grain pattern of the wood. Wood stain will not obscure the grain pattern of the wood, nor will it show off brush strokes.

Wood stain can be brushed on or wiped on with a soft and clean rag. It is usually left to penetrate into the wood for awhile and then wiped off with another clean and dry rag.

Depending on the intensity of the color you are after, you may wipe the stain off almost immediately after applying it on, after 10–30 minutes, or after several hours. You may also leave it on until it completely dries, which can take 8–12 hours. As with paint and dye, a test on a hidden portion of your prop or scrap material of the same type of wood is very handy. To achieve different colors, you can apply a second stain over one that has already dried.

Wood stain comes in both oil and water-based formulas. The pigments are the same, but the working properties differ between the two kinds. Water-based formulas can be cleaned with soap and water, dry faster, and release far less harmful vapors as they dry. Water-based stains can also be applied over oil stains. Oil-based stains offer better penetration and create more durable finishes. Their slower drying time also helps them create a more even finish. They require better ventilation and even the use of a respirator when being applied; they can "smell" for 8–12 hours after being applied, causing dizziness and headaches, so they need to be left to dry away from workers or actors. Because props need to be built quickly but do not need to last a long time, water-based stains are often the better choice if the correct color can be found.

A stained piece of wood needs to be sealed with a clear protective coating, as the stain can lift off to any skin or costume fabric that comes into contact with it. You can buy stains that are mixed with a polyurethane sealer. These allow you to stain and seal in one step. The disadvantage is that you cannot add more stain if you do not like the color, since the surface is already sealed.

It is also important to note that since stain must penetrate the wood, it will only work on bare wood. (The exception to this is "staining sealers," which are applied before stain in order to even out the application of stain. These can be helpful to apply to the exposed end grain, as the end grain will suck in a lot more stain than the face grain, resulting in a darker color, but otherwise, I have never come across the need to use them on prop furniture.)

Wood stain can be used as a glaze over sealed surfaces to tone them, but the long drying time combined with the fumes released while drying makes them far less desirable than a regular paint glaze. The fumes are a particular problem with wood stain; even after it has been dried off, a piece of stained wood can continue giving off smelly fumes for a day or so. If staining, always plan to do it when you can keep it away from the actors until the smell goes away. Allow it to dry in a well-ventilated area where none of the other props artisans need to work as well. I do a lot of carpentry, and I have become sensitized to the fumes to the point where only a few minutes with an open stain container bring on a headache.

Chemical Coloring

Some materials can be colored by applying chemicals that activate a change in the material itself. Most techniques are geared toward various metals to give them a patina. Many of these techniques use incredibly toxic and caustic chemicals and involve extensive setups (not to mention the need to dispose of these chemicals), so more often than not, the props artisan is better off making a faux finish with paint. There are a few that have proved helpful in props shops that I will mention, though.

Instant gun blue, or "cold" bluing, is a product used on steel to give it a dark black/blue color while also protecting it from rust. It is so called because steel guns are often finished with a bluing process (the "hot" bluing process is tougher and more long-lasting, but involves heating a number of chemicals in a bath. Instant gun blue is popular for mimicking this look on props because of its ease of use). Instant gun blue is wiped on the finished piece of steel or stainless steel with a cloth and immediately wiped off with a second dry cloth.

Writing and Drawing Utensils

Inks can encompass a wide range of colorants, binders, and medium found in both paint and dye; their main difference is their intended use. Inks are generally formulated for use in writing and drawing on paper, or in various printing processes. The pigments and dyes used are usually more finely ground, and they are used in a thinner solution than paint or dye. They also dry to a much thinner film than most paints.

Colored pencils, pens, and markers can also be utilized for various decorating and coloring tasks. Black markers are useful for quickly making a screw head or shiny edge disappear. Brown markers can do the same with scratches and other imperfections on wooden furniture. Markers and pens can also make tasks such as lettering and lining more convenient and consistent.

Metal Leaf

Real gold leaf is actually thin layers of gold that have been hammered out to the thickness of tissue paper. A less costly alternative is imitation gold leaf, sometimes known as Dutch Metal or bronze leaf. These come in a wider variety of colors, allowing you to leaf an object in silver or copper, for example.

The method of applying gold leaf for props is a little less elegant than traditional gilding, both in the materials used and

the amount of time spent, but it gives adequate results for objects on stage.

Porous materials must first be sealed. Latex and acrylic paints work well. Acrylic gesso is preferred if you want to sand the surface smooth before leafing.

Bole (pronounced like "bowl") is applied next. Traditionally, a fine pigmented clay has been used as bole, though today, particularly for props, paint is substituted. The bole gives a base color, and different colors can impart different qualities to the final piece. A black bole gives the gold leaf a cold and hard look you might find in Art Deco pieces, while red bole gives a warm and rich tone to the gold. Because you can use paint both to seal the material and as the bole color, many props artisans simply combine these two steps and use a single coat of paint.

Chrome Plating

Real chrome plating is done by electroplating nickel onto a highly polished surface, and then electroplating chrome onto that. The equipment and chemicals needed (not to mention the permits and regulations to deal with those chemicals) means

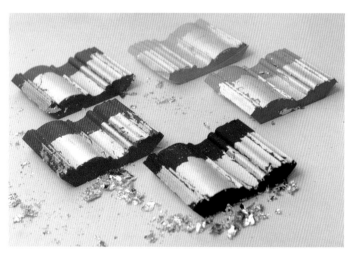

Figure 17-34: These molding samples show what gold leaf look likes over top of different bole colors.

Figure 17-35: To apply gold leaf, first apply gold size (found at craft and art stores) to your sealed and painted surface. Allow it to dry fully.

Figure 17-36: Take a sheet of metal leaf; this is usually very fragile, and is easier to move by using a paintbrush that has been charged with static electricity. Once the leaf touches the size, it will not move, so place it carefully.

even the largest commercial shops will send props off to an outside vendor to be chrome plated.

As an alternative, you can find many "chrome-look" paints, as well as stainless steel and aluminum paints. If your prop is constructed out of aluminum, you can polish it up to look almost like chrome (or, if possible, cover your prop in a skin of thin sheet aluminum). The key to successful results is to start off with as smooth and defect-free a surface as possible, and to do test samples of the paints you wish to try out.

Figure 17-37: When placed, begin feathering the leaf onto the size; a paintbrush works best. Brush the foil over the entire surface. The foil will not get into every crack and crevice. As you brush over it, the loose foil will be brushed away. When you are finished, you may find a lot of missed spots, like in the photograph above. You can pick up smaller flakes of the foil (again, using a statically charged brush is easiest), and place these on the bare spots. The spots may also be bare because no size was applied there; reapply some size to those spots and again wait for it to dry before adding foil. Continue burnishing the surface of the foil until no more flakes or dust come off. Once the whole surface is coated to your satisfaction, you will need to seal it; shellac is a traditional favorite (amber shellac will impart a deep yellow that may help the color of your gold leaf in some situations), while polyurethane and acrylic clear coats may be used for a tougher and more water-resistant sealer.

eighteen

graphics

Graphics are text and illustration on a surface meant to present some kind of information or art. Graphics in the real world are applied by humans; props people can use graphics to replicate these applications, but some of the techniques that follow can also be used for faux finishes and other paint treatments. For example, stencils can help you create a repetitive natural texture, while a complicated marble surface can be printed from a computer and adhered to a hard surface.

A props artisan who enjoys making paper props would do well to learn calligraphy and other handwriting techniques. Many plays, films, and shows require letters and other documents. You can use handwritten fonts on a computer and print them out, but the regularity of the letter spacing and shapes betrays their manufactured origin. In some cases, you can manipulate the individual letters to give them a more natural appearance, but it is often quicker and more visually satisfying to write the text out by hand. You can always photocopy it or scan it in to create a digital file so that you can make multiples as needed.

Figure 18-1: The text and graphics for this newspaper were created on a computer and then printed onto blank newsprint. *All's Well That Ends Well*, the Public Theater, 2011. Scenic design by Scott Pask.

Choosing the text for a paper prop can be a challenge. For film and television, there exists the chance that the text might be seen close up by the camera, so it needs to be "real"; take clues from the script, and make sure any words spoken by the actors are included. Use your research from the period or location to fill in the rest. If you are making a prop for the stage, or you are sure the prop will never be viewed closely, you can use a font or handwriting that is completely illegible so that no words can be made out. Feel free to repeat large blocks of text to fill up space, or to use a "lorem ipsum" generator, which is what graphics designers use to fill a mockup with text that looks like English but is complete gibberish.

The one thing you want to always avoid is the temptation to write something "funny" or "clever." Even the most disciplined actor, on seeing a line of text that looks interesting, will be momentarily distracted or even break character. It is better for the text to be unreadable or so entrenched in the world of the production that the actor will not notice it. These kinds of props often require working closely with the actor; some are very specific about what paper props should have written on them. If they are supposed to be "reading" from the prop, some prefer to have their lines written on the page; others do not want anything resembling their lines written there.

Stencils are shapes and patterns cut from a thicker piece of paper and laid on a surface. Paint or ink is stippled or sprayed over the top. The stencil acts like masking, keeping the color from reaching the surface underneath the parts that are not cut out. They are useful when you need to keep your graphics from looking too "handmade," especially on surfaces that cannot be run through a computer printer; they can also be used to lay

Figures 18-2 and 18-3: This champagne box had a label stenciled on. *Carmen*, the Santa Fe Opera, 2006. Scenic design by Neil Patel.

Figure 18-4: Many materials and objects can be adapted as stencils.

down repetitive images and patterns, by using the stencil on multiple parts of the surface.

Screen printing, also known as **silkscreen**, is like a stencil but uses a design blocked out on a woven mesh. The mesh is fine enough that the ink can pass through it without printing the lines. The mesh is covered with an impermeable material to block areas from receiving ink. This gives it an advantage over stenciling in that it can print designs where blocked areas are unconnected to each other. The disadvantage is that the preparation of the screen is far more complex than simply cutting out a stencil.

Stamps, blocks, and presses are all means to transfer ink or paint from a raised design to a surface. The stamps used by prop makers are often carved from rubber. The design itself has to be in reverse so that when it is touched to the surface you are decorating, it will be oriented the correct way. Rubber stamps of an endless variety can be found in craft and stationery stores

Copying or replicating photographs, illustrations, text, logos, and other graphics often requires permission or clearance from the owner or rights holder. You should never "guess" whether something is alright to use or assume that you won't get in trouble or caught by replicating copyrighted material or trademarked brands and logos. A small regional theatre once replicated the logo of a California high school on giant banners. Though this theatre was hundreds of miles away in another state, the school found out, and a cease-and-desist letter meant they had to reprint the entire banner with a different logo at great expense. Even when something is specified in the script, you may still need separate permission to replicate it. These issues are complicated and span a number of laws and regulations, and you should never accept general advice from someone who is not a lawyer, as every instance has its own unique circumstances; the decisions should be made by someone higher up than you, whether a production manager or a legal department if you are working for a production company that has one.

"Taking a rubbing" means placing a sheet of paper or other thinner material over a textured or carved surface and rubbing graphite (like in a pencil), chalk, or some other material over its top to record the texture. It can be used to record a drawing or engraving, as well as recording random textures (known as frottage). You can use rubbing as another means to transfer the design from a stamp or block. The block is placed right side up, and the paper or fabric is laid over the top. It is then rubbed with a hard piece of wood or other rigid material; the design is burnished onto the surface of the material rather than inked.

Digital Graphics

The types and variations of computer printers are vast, and the technology changes rapidly, so I will not discuss specific makes and models here. Most printers highlight their ability to print photographs, which is less important for the props artisan. We are more concerned with what sizes of paper a printer can

or purchased online. You can also find numerous shops that will custom-make stamps for you from artwork you provide. You may also carve your own stamp from a solid block of material. It need not be rubber; many of us remember making "potato stamps" as a child in school.

A block refers to a rigid material that has been carved with a relief design. Blocks were traditionally cut from wood, though modern blocks are often made from linoleum or composite materials. A block can be stamped, just like stamps, or used in a press. A press is a machine that holds a number of blocks which can be stamped onto paper at the same time.

Figure 18-5: Computer graphics programs such as Adobe Photoshop allow you to assemble and manipulate graphics from a variety of sources. You can see what the document will look like before printing it, and changes can be made quickly and easily—if you know what you are doing.

handle, what types of paper can be used in it (some can even print to fabrics), and what method it uses to print, as some processes require specific ink or toner to be successful. It may be helpful to have several different printers that excel at specific common tasks rather than one printer that does everything only marginally well.

The two major types of printers on the market (other kinds exist as well) are ink-jet and laser. An **ink-jet** printer shoots tiny drops of ink through jets to transfer a graphic to the paper. These printers are the most common, and often the most affordable. Most are built to deliver finely detailed photographs. The colors are mixed from a set of different colored inks; printers can use anywhere from a single black cartridge up to 12 different cartridges, and most use 4 to 6. Some even allow you to use different sets of specialty ink cartridges, such as white ink or metallic colors. Most inks used by ink-jet printers are water-soluble, so the image can be smeared if the paper gets wet.

Laser printers use lasers to melt black or colored toner onto paper. This is the same technology used by most photocopiers. Though often more expensive to print than ink-jet, they can, in some circumstances, be faster and cheaper, particularly when printing black and white text. Their printing process results in waterproof prints; it also gives it the ability to print onto acetate and other transparent plastic sheets, which are far too slick for ink-jet ink to stick to. While color laser printers have certainly come down in price over the past several years, a color laser printer that can print anything larger than a standard sheet of paper is far more expensive than an ink-jet printer that can print gigantic photo-quality prints.

A **plotter** is a large-format printer used for printing out CAD and other line drawings. Most "plotters" today are actually regular wide-format printers that can print any kind of graphic or photograph. The most common can use paper up to 40" wide; with paper on rolls, they can print almost any length. A few props shops have their own. Plotters are very often found in scene shops for printing out draftings of the scenery, and they may allow the props shop to use them for

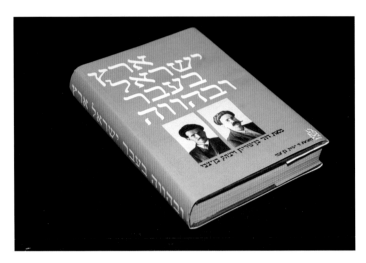

Figure 18-6: Printing out a book cover and placing it over a book is a quick and easy way to make a fake book. If the actor is supposed to flip through the pages, make sure they match up with what the book is supposed to be. It should not have color photographs inside if it is meant to be a period text. A book of poems will also look different from a book of prose.

the occasional newspaper or large oil painting that needs to be printed from a computer.

It is also helpful to explore local print shops to find out their capabilities and pricing. When you have to print especially large pieces or use particularly unusual paper, it can be advantageous to get it printed rather than investing in a brand-new type of printer for that one job. For copies of prints in exceptionally large quantities, it can also be more cost-effective to have a shop duplicate them rather than printing them all from your computer.

A **scanner** is useful for creating digital versions of printed material. While you can also get pictures on a computer through a digital camera, it is difficult to make an exact replica of a printed sheet of paper in terms of even lighting, flat positioning, and maintenance of proportion. Besides using it to scan found images, a scanner also allows you to create paper props by

Figure 18-7: These tickets to the Ark in the film *2012* were printed on clear plastic with metallic ink used as highlights. They were then encased in a rigid plastic case.

hand and then turn it into a digital file for multiple copies or backups.

Besides creating paper props, computer programs and printers can be used to create graphics that are applied to other surfaces as part of their decoration. Some means for achieving this include decals, stickers, and découpage. The advantage of decals, stickers, and découpage is to get a design or graphic onto the surface of a three-dimensional object. Usually, the design is either printed from a computer or received from a professional print shop (pictures clipped from magazines, books, and other found sources can also be used); this gives your prop a more mass-produced look where hand painting would not look slick enough. They can also allow you to save time and labor in adding more intricate, precise, or repetitive designs to your prop.

A **decal** (short for *decalcomania*) is a special kind of paper, often clear, that can be printed on. The back has an adhesive that is activated when the decal soaks in water for a few minutes. It is then applied to a smooth surface while wet. Some decals can be activated by heat as well. Most decals can only be printed with laser printers, as the ink from ink-jet printers will wash off when soaked in water.

A **sticker** is a more general term for a piece of paper or film with a design on one side and an adhesive on the other. Stickers may also be printed on transparent paper, though the kind of adhesive used may be visible. You can turn any paper or film into a sticker by coating the back with an adhesive; typical adhesives used for this purpose include spray adhesives or contact cement.

Découpage is the art of gluing paper over a surface until it is completely covered; in many cases, multiple pieces of colored, printed, and patterned papers are used to create a layered or collage effect. In traditional découpage, the idea is to make the surface look painted or like inlay work. For props, the idea is similar to making your own stickers.

Remember earlier how photocopiers and laser printers create images by melting toner onto paper or acetate? This toner can be remelted and transferred onto other surfaces such as fabric. Soak the print in a solvent (acetone works well), and then lay it face down on your material. The toner should transfer to your material in reverse.

Aging Paper Props

Paper props, such as pages in a book, letters, posters, and the like, can be aged and distressed like other props. The same thought and consideration goes into how and why they will be distressed as well. There are also some aging techniques specific to paper that props artisans should know. The most common is soaking a sheet of paper in a bath of coffee or tea. Brew the tea or coffee as you would normally, and let it cool. It is helpful to use a baking sheet or cookie sheet large enough to fit the paper laying down flat with a lip to hold in a small amount of liquid. You can also "paint" the paper with the tea bag or a rag soaked in coffee. Remove the paper from the liquid, and let it dry. Alternatively, you can put it in an oven for a

Figure 18-8: Decals applied to the surface of this AER9 Laser Rifle from *Fallout 3* give it a mass-produced look. Photograph and prop by Harrison Krix.

few minutes to dry it. The oven should be preheated to 200°F (paper burns at 451°F, and will smolder before that). If you used a baking sheet, you can get rid of the excess liquid, and place the paper in that when it goes in the oven. Besides an oven, you can also put it in a microwave for a few minutes, or use a hair dryer or heat gun to dry it.

For more dramatic effects, you can rub used coffee grounds or used tea leaves removed from the tea bag directly onto the surface of the paper. Sprinkling individual instant coffee crystals on top and allowing them to soak will create "blooms" on the surface of your paper. These techniques can be combined for more control over the effect; soaking creates a uniform color, painting gives a more varied look, while the grounds, leaves, and crystals can be added for more selective coloring.

For a different kind of texture, cover the paper loosely with wax paper or plastic as it dries—as with the cling wrap plastic texturing technique discussed earlier, this will cause different concentrations of dye to collect randomly over the surface to create variable coloring over the surface.

Figure 18-9: This vintage rubber cement jar was created by scanning in a modern label, altering it with computer graphics software, printing it out, and adhering it to a regular rubber cement jar. *Sherlock Holmes: The Final Adventure*, Actors Theatre of Louisville, 2006. Scenic design by Neil Patel.

Figure 18-10: Paper can be cut with a razor knife (such as an X-acto blade) along a straight edge, or with a paper cutter as seen here.

Crumpling the paper beforehand and then flattening it by hand or with an iron adds an additional layer of texture.

Another handy technique involves lemon juice and heat. The paper will brown wherever the lemon juice is, so specific parts of the paper can be colored, or the lemon juice can be spattered randomly all over. Bake it in the oven, or use a hot air gun to dry the lemon juice and brown the paper. Other useful dyes are walnut ink crystals and soy sauce.

Some inks will run when you soak them in these solutions, so you may need to age your paper first, and add the graphics after it dries. The downside to this is that your writing may look like new writing on old paper, as opposed to writing that has aged along with the paper. If your paper is wrinkled and curled, it may also jam in some computer printers.

Finally, I implore you not to burn the edges of your paper. This is a common practice for crafters and scrapbookers, but unless your document was literally in a fire, there is no reason for the edges to be burnt. For rough edges, tear the edges (a deckled straight edge can help) or rub them with your finger while wet.

nineteen

budget estimates

The final step in determining which materials and methods to construct your prop with is determining what makes the most sense economically and practically. You have a budget in the things you are limited in: time, money, and expertise. For every prop, or for all the props in a production, you need to figure out how much of each you have and how best to allocate them so you stay within your limits.

The Project Triangle

Theatre technicians frequently point to the project triangle for help with deciding on the materials and methods for accomplishing something. I've seen a number of variations, but the most common has a triangle with the three points labeled "fast," "cheap," and "good."

You can pick two of these points, but you can never have all three. In other words, if you want something fast and cheap, it will not be good (in terms of quality). If you want something good and fast, it won't be cheap. Hollywood is a place where they do not ask "how much," just "how soon." Most productions require more of a juggling act though, as a single prop can vary drastically between "expensive, fast, and good" or "cheap, slow, and good." (I find it hard justifying making a "bad" prop just because time or money is scarce. Of course, these are not

Figure 19-1: The Project Triangle. Fast, cheap, and good. you can have any two.

discrete points, but a spectrum. You can have a lower-quality, but still acceptable, prop if you need to save time or money.)

When you start dealing with several materials or methods, the comparisons become more of a gradation than a hard choice. For instance, solution A and solution B may result in the same quality; solution A is a lot faster but just a little more expensive than solution B. Depending on the specifics of your budget, it is often worth it to spend a little money to save a lot of time. If solution A cost over twice as much and only saved an hour, then it probably would not be worth choosing it.

In most cases, your prop does not exist independently, but has to fit within the budget of an entire production. Every change in the cost and labor of one prop can have ripple effects for all the other props. For instance, if you save enough money on one prop, it may make possible a more expensive, but preferable, solution for another prop.

You will see that the results you can achieve with the Project Triangle (fast, cheap, and good) correspond with the resources you are limited in (time, money, and expertise).

These three resources are a balancing act. Say you need a smooth, flat surface. You may choose CDX plywood, which is very cheap but has a rough surface. It will take a lot longer to sand and coat it to make a smooth surface. Nicer plywood or

> Do not neglect to consider the safety infrastructure needed for working with certain materials. A product such as expanding spray foam may seem quick and easy for a number of props, but it requires adequate ventilation, a respirator with forced or supplied air, and the appropriate chemical gloves and sleeves. You should never think safety is an optional expense. You only get one life, and you want to spend as much of it as possible building props.

MDF will be more expensive, but you need far less labor to make it smooth. When you factor in the cost of labor, a labor-intensive process with cheaper materials may actually cost more than more expensive, but nicer, materials. If you decide to go with the cheap material and do not spend the time on sanding and coating it, you will end up with a bad prop. As you can see, when it comes to fast, cheap, and good, you can only have two at a time. Now let us look at each of the three resources in turn.

Money

When estimating the price of materials and supplies, it is helpful to be as precise as possible. Include every little bit and piece, even if you already have the materials in stock; after all, you will want to replenish your supply. For some materials, you can check catalogs, websites, or even call vendors for quotes to get exact prices. For other goods, such as lumber or steel, prices fluctuate, so you should develop a list of what the usual price is just for estimation purposes. Include everything, no matter how minor it may seem. I once had to estimate a chandelier for the Broadway version of *Merchant of Venice*. I knew I needed electrical cords to connect all the bulb sockets to the main plug, and I figured it would only be a couple of bucks. When I actually calculated how much I would need, it turned out to be a grand total of 700 feet, which would cost $350 to buy. You certainly don't want to miss something like that in your estimate. So count everything, even the screws, nuts, and bolts. Do not forget about taxes, delivery charges, or other fees. You do not want to spend all your budget on a prop only to face an $85 shipping fee to deliver it to the theatre or filming location.

Where can you buy supplies? Lumber stores, and timber and builder's merchants are obvious places to purchase lumber products as well as the tools and accessories needed to work with them. Hardware stores will have some of these tools and accessories as well. You can find metal and metal-working tools at these stores too, though you can find a bigger selection

at specialized steel suppliers. For metal pipes, plumber's suppliers are a great bet; they will also have selections of PVC pipes and fittings. Smaller metal pieces and tools can be found at jewelers' suppliers. Artists' suppliers and craft shops are a great source for all sorts of materials and tools when you can find them. These stores stock not only paints and brushes, but everything from sculpting materials and tools, printing supplies, ceramics, small wood and metal pieces, plastic sheets, rods and tubes, various foams, casting supplies, etc. Some resins and reinforcing materials such as fiberglass can be found at car accessory shops and boat suppliers. For fabrics and soft goods, search for fabric stores, upholstery suppliers, leather stores, haberdashery shops, and cane suppliers. Department stores often have small selections of craft supplies, fabrics, and tools among other items. Hobby stores can be helpful, whether for general hobbies, or specific ones such as model railroad shops. Antique restorers will carry a number of cleaners and finishes for wood, leather, metal, and fabrics, as well as some tools. If you are interested in leather or vinyl, you may have luck at small shoe repair shops; they often carry polishes, spray paints, and other supplies you can't find at more general stores. Pharmacists and drug stores carry useful materials, some of which are hard to find elsewhere: mineral oil and glycerin (both sold in the "laxative" section), plaster bandages, shoe polish, acetone (nail polish remover), alcohol, etc. Grocery stores will also carry some needed supplies, such as aluminum foil, gelatin, and various containers, cups, and mixing implements.

These are just the general sorts of stores that most people can find nearby. There are many specialized shops too; it is not always readily apparent what they can supply you with until you check them out. For example, sign-maker shops may have corrugated plastics and cutting tools for you to purchase, while fishing shops carry hot-melt vinyl for making fishing lures. Finally, theatrical suppliers carry all sorts of specialized materials and tools for prop makers, though these are rarely found outside the larger cities. Companies that make the products you want will often provide the names and addresses of retailers who sell their products either on their website or when you call them up. You can discover all sorts of alternative sources for your supplies in this way, such as school supply stores for clays.

When all else fails, you can have nearly anything shipped to you. You certainly have to watch out for shipping charges and delivery times (though picking things up yourself costs gas and time). In some cases though, the cheaper prices you find online, or the discounts you get for buying larger quantities, when combined with the time you save driving around, can make up for the extra costs in shipping. A good prop maker is always developing his or her vendor list to find the most economical source for tools, supplies, and materials depending on the situation.

The Internet is the prop maker's friend. You can find suppliers—including local suppliers—for almost anything. If you do not know what kind of store sells the material you want to find, you can research that as well. You can even compare prices and see if local stores currently have your materials in stock. With further searching, you can find MSDS sheets on potential materials as well as tutorials and videos on how to use them (which will also inform you about whatever tools and additional materials or supplies you might need).

Even after adding everything together, factor in a **contingency**. Typically, props people add 20–25% to the final estimate. So if you estimate a prop will cost $100 in materials and supplies, and you want a 20% contingency, that would be $20, so the total estimate would be $120. This is to cover all the things that cannot be accounted for, or for emergencies and unseen events.

If a properties director or lead artisan is doing the budgeting for all the props in the show, he or she may begin to take shortcuts with the simpler props, based on past experience. If they have upholstered a wingback chair in a previous show, they can check the records to see how much it cost in time and materials, and use that as the estimate to upholster another wingback chair.

Often there is not enough time to accurately calculate the cost of everything, and designs and needs change and evolve during the preproduction process after the budget has

Figure 19-2: When making multiples of an object, you may want to create a separate budget for prototypes and one for copies. The first one will cost more and take longer because you are figuring it out, building models and jigs, experimenting with the finishing process, and generally coming up with the best materials and process for the job. Additional copies will be cheaper and quicker both because you solved all the problems and because you have patterns and templates for the new pieces.

already been set. This may mean the budgeting may happen in reverse; a maximum cost is determined for a prop, and then a method to achieve that prop within that cost limit needs to be found.

Time

It can be helpful to keep a daily journal of what you work on and how long it takes. After several months, you have a good set of data for how long certain tasks take to accomplish. A properties director or shop foreman who maintains records of how long different items took to build in the past will be able to anticipate the build schedule for future productions. For example, I used to ignore the time it took to put casters on the bottom of a piece of furniture when estimating how long it would take to build. When I finally timed myself, I realized my mistake. Gathering the materials, drilling sixteen holes (four per caster, four casters per piece of furniture), and attaching and tightening 16 nuts and bolts ended up taking between 30 minutes and an hour—not a length of time you want to ignore.

We are usually lousy at predicting how long a task will take; many of us are overly optimistic, especially when trying to impress the boss. It will make your life simpler to break the estimate down into smaller tasks. You may not know how long you need to construct a dead goose, but you can probably make an accurate guess to how long it takes to glue on twelve hackle pads, or paint two goose feet.

As with materials, you want to add a contingency to your labor time. This covers all those unforeseen circumstances. Sometimes you start a project and realize you left your hammer in another building. Or you open up the can of paint you want to use and realize it has completely dried up.

Labor is not the only thing that adds time to a process. Some products, particularly paints and adhesives, require time to dry, while others, such as resins and plaster, need time to cure. Again, this is a balancing act. Products that take longer to dry or cure tend to have better properties than those that are ready faster. Alternatively, the products that dry or cure faster are frequently more toxic than the slower ones.

Turnaround time means the sum total of hours, days, or weeks it will take before your prop is ready. With labor, you are only figuring out the hours you actually work on a prop so that you can estimate the labor cost. You are not counting the time it takes to wait for paint to dry or the hours you spend at home sleeping. You need to factor in the time it takes for materials to be shipped to you, the time it takes to go out shopping for materials, setup time, drying and curing time, cleanup time, and delivery time. You also have to estimate how much time you or the other artisans can work on the project each day. If you only have two hours a day to work on an eight-hour project, it will take at least four days to complete.

Turnaround time should be built into any schedule you make. Figuring out how long it will be before a prop is ready is important to the stage managers, the director, the designers, the other departments if the prop needs to be integrated in some way, and the actors. When you calculate the turnaround time for all the props in a production, you can also see whether it is possible to meet all your deadlines or if you will need to hire more help (or simplify the props list).

It is better to focus on the most critical deadlines and backtrack from there. You may know, for instance, if you do not order certain materials by Friday, you will not get them until Monday, and then you lose a whole weekend's worth of work. Or you may know that the final coat of paint will take three hours to dry, so you must be finished painting at least three hours before the curtain rises. If you can backtrack enough, then you may get to a point where you can tell your designer that he or she needs to submit the final drawing for a certain prop by a certain date if he or she wants it to be ready by the first day of technical rehearsals.

When managing several artisans, it is helpful to assign a few tasks of varying scale to each person. This way, if one of the artisans is waiting for paint to dry on her major project, she can cut out paper props in the meantime. Otherwise, she will be asking you for another project while you are trying to work on something else. Many props shop managers will write out a master "to-do" list with all projects and notes written down. This is hung up where all the artisans can see. If one of them needs a project, they check the list and pick one that fits their skill level and the amount of time they have to devote to it. Have the artisans write their name next to a project when they start it, otherwise another artisan may check the list and start working on the same project.

It is especially helpful for this list to include both major and minor projects. If it is 15 minutes before lunch and a prop maker cannot proceed on his project, he will want a quick and easy project, such as "shorten the magic wand by one inch." If he is waiting for materials to be shipped before continuing on a project, he may want a bigger project that will keep him busy for a few days.

Expertise

Your labor time depends on your skill and experience. Someone more skilled than you may be able to perform some tasks quicker; you do not want to estimate how long it will take you to do something based on their speed.

If you are a good carpenter and have a lot of woodworking tools and machines, it makes sense to build props out of wood (if wood is one of the materials that will fulfill a prop's needs). Fiberglass may have great properties, but if I do not know how to work with it properly, I would be better off using Styrofoam with a hard coating, particularly if time is short and the schedule leaves no room for experimentation and learning.

Conclusion

The ability to make accurate budget and schedule estimates for a project is a skill that is often underestimated. Don't worry when your estimates do not remain accurate over the course of a production. You have a lot of variables to deal with. Every prop can be built with a number of materials, every step of the process can take an indeterminate amount of time, and little setbacks and problems crop up to throw you off. Over the course of the whole production, the designs may change, and the needs for each prop may evolve. Your tools may break, your materials may exhibit unexpected properties, and your employees may call in sick. You may experience unexpected bottlenecks, such as when everyone simultaneously needs to use the table saw, or when you run out of room in your shop because projects are set up in various stages of completion throughout. Someone may want to paint while someone else wants to sand, but you cannot do both at the same time as you will get dust in the wet paint.

special note

In the image descriptions, this book takes steps to identify and provide provenance for the prop shown. In many cases, the props shown were used in or in conjunction with motion pictures or other programs. This book in no way claims any connection to or relationship with the producers of the motion picture or other program. In all cases, the use of the titles or other elements of a motion picture or other program is for informational purposes only.

Throughout the text, I make reference to brand names and specific companies that manufacture certain products. This is done to clarify; in many cases, the brand names are used generically, while in others, a brand name may be the only type of its product on the market. I do not mean to endorse these products or imply that they are superior to other products. Likewise, many of the photographs throughout the book show artisans brandishing brand name tools and using brand name machines. For the most part, the photograph was taken to illustrate a technique or a method, and the brand of the tool being used is what was available in the shop at the time. This book in no way claims any connection to or relationship with the manufacturers or distributors of any tools or products shown and discussed in this book.

Bibliography

The following is a list of books I find helpful as a props artisan and which I have found useful in researching this book. Some of the books are listed under the chapter of my book they best correspond to, though in some cases the information they contain may bridge several chapters.

Theatrical Props

Carnaby, Ann J. *A Guidebook for Creating Three-Dimensional Theatre Art*. Portsmouth, NH: Heinemann, 1997.

Conway, Heather. *Stage Properties*. London: H. Jenkins, 1959.

Govier, Jacquie. *Create Your Own Stage Props*. Englewood Cliffs, NJ: Prentice-Hall, 1984.

James, Thurston. *The Theater Props Handbook: A Comprehensive Guide to Theater Properties, Materials, and Construction*. White Hall, VA: Betterway Publications, 1987.

Kenton, Warren. *Stage Properties and How to Make Them*. London: Sir Isaac Pitman & Sons, 1964.

Motley. *Theatre Props*. New York: Drama Book Specialists-Publishers, 1975.

Mussman, Amy. *The Prop Master: A Guidebook for Successful Theatrical Prop Management*. Colorado Springs, CO: Meriwether Pub., 2008.

Nesfield-Cookson, Mary (Jones-Parry). *Small Stage Properties and Furniture*. London: G. Allen & Unwin, 1934.

Strawn, Sandra. *The Properties Directors Handbook: Props for the Theatre*. Accessed January 28, 2009. http://www.prophandbook.com/PROPS/HOME.html.

Wilson, Andy. *Making Stage Props*. Ramsbury, Marlborough, Wiltshire: Crowood, 2003.

Technical Theatre

Carter, Paul, and Sally Friedman. *Backstage Handbook: An Illustrated Almanac of Technical Information*. Shelter Island, NY: Broadway, 1994.

Gillette, J. Michael. *Theatrical Design and Production: An Introduction to Scenic Design and Construction, Lighting, Sound, Costume, and Makeup*. Boston: McGraw-Hill Higher Education, 2008.

Moss, Sylvia. *Costumes & Chemistry: A Comprehensive Guide to Materials and Applications*. New York: Costume & Fashion Press, 2001.

- Don't let the title fool you; this book is vital to the props artisan. It covers topics such as plastics, adhesives, foams, coatings, paints, and the full range of materials we have at our disposal. This is the reference book you use to see what brands of acrylic paint work best with ABS sheets, what glues work best on polycarbonate, or what temperature to heat styrene to for vacuum forming.

Art Direction for Film and Television

Preston, Ward. *What an Art Director Does: An Introduction to Motion Picture Production Design*. Los Angeles: Silman-James, 1994.

Safety

Rossol, Monona. *The Health and Safety Guide for Film, TV, and Theater*. 2nd ed. Allworth Press, 2011.

- This book should be part of every prop builder's library and should be required reading for every student in a technical theatre, film, or TV program. No one has worked so tirelessly for the past several decades to protect workers in our industry, nor researched both the science of the hazards and the legalities of safety in the workplace as Monona Rossol.

Anderson, James, and Earl E. Tatro. *Shop Theory*. New York: McGraw-Hill, 1968.

Michel, Karen. *Green Guide for Artists: Nontoxic Recipes, Green Art Ideas, & Resources for the Eco-conscious Artist*. Beverly, MA: Quarry, 2009.

Drafting

Woodbridge, Patricia, and Hal Tiné. *Designer Drafting and Visualizing for the Entertainment World*. Burlington, MA: Focal Press, 2012.

Carpentry

Ehrlich, Jeffrey, and Marc Mannheimer. *The Carpenter's Manifesto*. New York: Henry Holt, 1990.

Lapidus, Saul. *Wood, Metal, and Plastic*. New York: D. McKay, 1978.

Rogowski, Gary. *The Complete Illustrated Guide to Joinery*. Newtown, CT: Taunton, 2002.

Metalworking

Taylor, Douglas C. *Metalworking for the Designer and Technician*. New York: Drama Book Specialists, 1979.

Plastics

Harper, Charles A., and Edward M. Petrie. *Plastics Materials and Processes: A Concise Encyclopedia*. Hoboken, NJ: Wiley-Interscience, 2003.

Hollander, Harry B. *Plastics for Artists and Craftsmen*. New York: Watson-Guptill, 1972.

Leinwoll, Stanley. *Plasticrafts*. New York: Simon and Schuster, 1973.

Newman, Thelma R. *Plastics as an Art Form: Rev. Ed*. Philadelphia, NY: Chilton, 1972.

Sculpture

Rich, Jack C. *The Materials and Methods of Sculpture*. 10th ed. New York: Dover Publications, 1988.

Fabric

Ingham, Rosemary, and Liz Covey. *The Costume Technician's Handbook*. Portsmouth, NH: Heinemann, 2003.

Singer Upholstery Basics. Chanhassen, MN: Creative International, 1997.

Patterning

Adams, Charles Francis, and Deborah B. Adams. *Model Design & Blueprinting Handbook*. Seattle, WA: ModelersNotebook.com, 2007.

Allison, Drew, and Donald Devet. *The Foam Book*. Charlotte, NC: Grey Seal, 1997.

Molding and Casting

Cementex Mold-Making Manual and Catalog. New York, NY: Cementex Latex, 1993.

James, Thurston. *The Prop Builder's Molding & Casting Handbook*. White Hall, VA: Betterway, 1989.

Savini, Tom. *Grande Illusions: A Learn-by Example Guide to the Art and Technique of Special Make-Up Effects from the Films of Tom Savini*. Pittsburgh, PA: Imagine, 1983.

- The followup, *Grande Illusions, Book II*, is equally useful.

Smooth-On promotional materials and videos (http:/www.smooth-on.com/)

Painting

Crabtree, Susan, and Peter Beudert. *Scenic Art for the Theatre*. Waltham, Mass: Focal Press, 2012.

Pecktal, Lynn. *Designing and Painting for the Theatre*. New York: Holt, Rinehart and Winston, 1975.

Jobs

Lawler, Mike. *Careers in Technical Theater*. New York: Allworth, 2007.

Moody, James L. *The Business of Theatrical Design*. New York: Allworth, 2002.

Portfolios

Jaen, Rafael. *Show Case: Developing, Maintaining, and Presenting a Design-tech Portfolio for Theatre and Allied Fields*. Waltham, MA: Focal Press, 2012.

- Some may recognize this book by its older title, Developing and Maintaining a Design-Tech Portfolio: A Guide for Theatre, Film, & TV.

Internet Forums

Control Booth (http://www.controlbooth.com/)

The Replica Prop Forum (http://www.therpf.com/)

index

website

Your prop building adventures continue at www.propbuildingguidebook.com! There you'll find:
- A bonus chapter covering formal training and finding work
- A second bonus chapter covering photographing your work and building your portfolio
- Videos detailing tools and techniques described in this book
- A link to the author's blog, Eric Hart's "Prop Agenda", where he documents his ongoing prop building projects

The book and website give you a complete cache of construction advice for all your prop building needs. Have fun, be safe, and happy building!